The Cambridge Companion to Milton provides an accessible and helpful guide for any student of Milton, whether undergraduate or graduate, introducing readers to the scope of Milton's work, the richness of its historical relations, and the range of current approaches to it. This second edition contains several new and revised essays, reflecting increasing emphasis on Milton's politics, the social conditions of his authorship and the climate in which his works were published and received, a fresh sense of the importance of his early poems and *Samson Agonistes*, and the changes wrought by gender studies on the criticism of the previous decade. By contrast with other introductions to Milton, this *Companion* gathers an international team of scholars, whose informative, stimulating, and often argumentative essays will provoke thought and discussion in and out of the classroom. The *Companion*'s reading lists and extended bibliography offer readers the necessary tools for further informed exploration of Milton studies.

Dennis Danielson is Professor of English at the University of British Columbia in Vancouver. He has taught and lectured in Germany, China, and South Africa. His publications include *Milton's Good God* (1982) and articles in a wide range of scholarly journals in literary studies, religious studies, and intellectual history.

CAMBRIDGE COMPANIONS TO LITERATURE

The Cambridge Companion to Greek Tragedy
edited by P. E. Easterling

The Cambridge Companion to Virgil
edited by Charles Martindale

The Cambridge Companion to Old English Literature
edited by Malcolm Godden and Michael Lapidge

The Cambridge Companion to Dante
edited by Rachel Jacoff

The Cambridge Chaucer Companion
edited by Piero Boitani and Jill Mann

The Cambridge Companion to Medieval English Theatre
edited by Richard Beadle

The Cambridge Companion to Shakespeare Studies
edited by Stanley Wells

The Cambridge Companion to English Renaissance Drama
edited by A. R. Braunmuller and Michael Hattaway

The Cambridge Companion to English Poetry, Donne to Marvell
edited by Thomas N. Corns

The Cambridge Companion to Milton
edited by Dennis Danielson

The Cambridge Companion to British Romanticism
edited by Stuart Curran

The Cambridge Companion to James Joyce
edited by Derek Attridge

The Cambridge Companion to Ibsen
edited by James McFarlane

The Cambridge Companion to Brecht
edited by Peter Thomason and Glendyr Sacks

The Cambridge Companion to Beckett
edited by John Pilling

The Cambridge Companion to T. S. Eliot
edited by A. David Moody

The Cambridge Companion to Renaissance Humanism
edited by Jill Kraye

The Cambridge Companion to Joseph Conrad
edited by J. H. Stape

The Cambridge Companion to William Faulkner
edited by Philip M. Weinstein

The Cambridge Companion to Henry David Thoreau
edited by Joel Myerson

The Cambridge Companion to Edith Wharton
edited by Millicent Bell

The Cambridge Companion to American Realism and Naturalism
edited by Donald Pizer

The Cambridge Companion to Mark Twain
edited by Forrest G. Robinson

The Cambridge Companion to Walt Whitman
edited by Ezra Greenspan

The Cambridge Companion to Ernest Hemingway
edited by Scott Donaldson

The Cambridge Companion to the Eighteenth-Century Novel
edited by John Richetti

The Cambridge Companion to Jane Austen
edited by Edward Copeland and Juliet McMaster

The Cambridge Companion to Samuel Johnson
edited by Gregory Clingham

The Cambridge Companion to Oscar Wilde
edited by Peter Raby

The Cambridge Companion to Tennessee Williams
edited by Matthew C. Roudané

The Cambridge Companion to Arthur Miller
edited by Christopher Bigsby

The Cambridge Companion to the French Novel: from 1800 to the Present
edited by Timothy Unwin

The Cambridge Companion to the Classic Russian Novel
edited by Malcolm V. Jones and Robin Feuer Miller

See continuation at the back of the book

frontispiece William Faithorne's engraved portrait of Milton for the frontispiece of *The History of Britain* (1670)

THE CAMBRIDGE COMPANION TO MILTON

second edition

EDITED BY

DENNIS DANIELSON

PUBLISHED BY THE PRESS SYNDICATE OF THE UNIVERSITY OF CAMBRIDGE
The Pitt Building, Trumpington Street, Cambridge, United Kingdom

CAMBRIDGE UNIVERSITY PRESS
The Edinburgh Building, Cambridge CB2 2RU, UK
40 West 20th Street, New York, NY 10011–4211, USA
477 Williamstown Road, Port Melbourne, VIC 3207, Australia
Ruiz de Alarcón 13, 28014 Madrid, Spain
Dock House, The Waterfront, Cape Town 8001, South Africa

http://www.cambridge.org

First published 1989, second edition 1999, reprinted 2001, 2002, 2003

Printed in the United Kingdom at the University Press, Cambridge

Typeset in Sabon 10/13 pt. [CE]

A catalogue record for this book is available from the British Library

Library of Congress cataloging in publication data

The Cambridge companion to Milton / edited by Dennis Danielson. – 2nd ed.
p. cm. – (Cambridge companions to culture)
Includes index.
ISBN 0 521 65226 X (hb)
1. Milton, John, 1608–1674 – Criticism and interpretation.
I. Danielson, Dennis Richard, 1949– . II. Series.
PR3588.C27 1999
821′.4–dc21 99-10915 CIP

ISBN 0 521 65226 X hardback
ISBN 0 521 65543 9 paperback

CONTENTS

CONTRIBUTORS

JOAN S. BENNETT, University of Delaware
CEDRIC BROWN, University of Reading
COLIN BURROW, Gonville and Caius College, Cambridge
JOHN CAREY, Merton College, Oxford
GEORGIA CHRISTOPHER, late of Emory University, Atlanta
THOMAS N. CORNS, University of Wales, Bangor
DENNIS DANIELSON, University of British Columbia
STEPHEN B. DOBRANSKI, Georgia State University
MARTIN DZELZAINIS, Royal Holloway and Bedford New College, University of London
J. MARTIN EVANS, Stanford University
R. F. HALL, Rhodes University
WILLIAM KERRIGAN, University of Massachusetts
JOHN LEONARD, University of Western Ontario
BARBARA KIEFER LEWALSKI, Harvard University
DIANE K. MCCOLLEY, Rutgers University, Camden, New Jersey
MARY ANN RADZINOWICZ, (emerita) Cornell University
R. G. SIEMENS, University of Alberta
NICHOLAS VON MALTZAHN, University of Ottawa

ILLUSTRATIONS

PREFACE

This book, as its title suggests, is intended to provide friendly and helpful company for any student of Milton; and this second edition aims to build on the apparent success of the first in performing that mission. In the late 1980s Cambridge University Press began by asking me to plan a book – and a team of contributors – which would introduce readers of Milton to both the scope of his work and the range of current approaches to it. In response I put forward a list of chapters that I hoped might most nearly accomplish this task, and then recruited a range of outstanding academics whose contributions made the *Cambridge Companion to Milton* a reality. At that time, ours was only the third volume – preceded by Chaucer and Shakespeare – in what has since become a prominent series of (at this writing) thirty-odd Cambridge Companions to literature. Then in the late 1990s, after roughly a decade in print, with continued lively interest in the book from students and other academics, this *Companion* seemed ripe for revision; and the present volume is the fruit of our collective response.

Seven of the eighteen essays that follow – those by Dobranski, Brown, Burrow, Dzelzainis, Hall, von Maltzahn, and Siemens – I had the pleasure of commissioning for this second edition, and five more have been revised in varying degrees from what they were. All eighteen chapters embody critical thought, serious study, and a process of understanding, and all encourage more of the same in both our and Milton's readers. Moreover, I have invited each author to speak in his or her own voice, and without condescension. The resulting eighteen original essays are thus by eighteen conspicuously different human beings, who would (and do) disagree with each other about innumerable issues, but who are here united by their desire to say in an informative, responsible, sometimes argumentative way something important about a subject they love.

Although readers may consult the contents list and pick chapters to read according to their specific needs or interests, I have tried to arrange the book so that it has some rough logical or chronological continuity. Stephen

Dobranski's fresh chapter on Milton's 'social life' is followed by Cedric Brown's historically (and likewise socially) informative chapter on Milton's Ludlow Masque, sometimes known as '*Comus*'. Martin Evans's stimulating essay on *Lycidas* is similarly of biographical as well as literary interest. The theme of historically embedded biography is pursued further in Colin Burrow's perceptive chapter on the 1645 *Poems of Mr John Milton*. The focus of the two following pieces is Milton's prose: Martin Dzelzainis providing a lively primer on Milton's politics, and Thomas Corns tracing the development of Milton's prose style. After these introductions to Milton's prose and early poetic career comes Ron Hall's chapter examining Milton's sonnets as history and as poetry; followed by three further essays, by Barbara Lewalski, John Leonard, and myself, on the forms and purposes of Milton's great heroic poem: the genres, language, and theodicy of *Paradise Lost*. Two of the most perennially controversial topics related to *Paradise Lost* – Milton's Satan and Milton's treatment of the sexes – are introduced in lively essays by John Carey and Diane McColley respectively. The chapter by the late Georgia Christopher provides valuable insight into the relationship between Milton's work and the spirit and hermeneutics of the Reformation. Mary Ann Radzinowicz and Joan Bennett lead us next into readings of the other two 'great poems', *Paradise Regained* and *Samson Agonistes*, exploring Milton's rich, complex relationship (respectively) to the Bible and to the timeless issue of human freedom. Our historical perspectives on Milton are then lengthened and deepened by Nicholas von Maltzahn's discussion of the reception and subsequent 'institution' of Milton, and by William Kerrigan's essay on the place of Milton in intellectual history. Each of these seventeen chapters is accompanied by a reading list. Finally comes Ray Siemens's veritable tool kit of helps – including Internet resources – for all who wish to pursue their Miltonic studies beyond Milton and this *Companion*. The same bibliography's availability on the Internet, we hope, will doubly enhance its utility.

Assembling this book has taught me afresh both to recognize and to enjoy the social, economic, historical, and spiritual complexity of an artifact that appears, deceptively, as a single material object between two covers. Its eighteen contributors do not constitute the full *Companion* team, although my gratitude to and respect for each of them is immense. In addition I would like to thank those valued colleagues either whose essays were not carried over into this second edition or who agreed to contribute to it and then, through a combination of circumstances, were not included. I am also grateful for the enormous amount of advice (written and oral) I received from many scholars from around the world during this edition's gestation. They are too many to name, but I do want to offer special thanks to John Leonard, who is himself a true Milton companion. Finally, I am deeply thankful to Josie Dixon, senior editor at Cambridge University Press, who with great humanity and professionalism has shepherded me and this edition from its inception.

If I were the sole author of this book I could here conclude, as authors often inaccurately do, by claiming responsibility for all its errors and shortcomings. But I am only its editor; and however much blame I do genuinely and undoubtedly deserve, responsibility for this *Companion*'s failures as well as successes – like the pleasure of reading Milton – is happily something I may share with others.

DENNIS DANIELSON

JOHN MILTON: SIGNIFICANT DATES

1608 Milton born in Cheapside, London (9 December)
1620 Enters St Paul's School, London
1625 Admitted to Christ's College, Cambridge
King Charles I crowned
1628 First poem printed (probably *De Idea Platonica*)
1629 Takes BA degree (January)
1632 Takes MA degree, *cum laude* (July)
'An Epitaph on the admirable Dramaticke Poet W. Shakespeare' published in Shakespeare's Second Folio
Takes up residence with family in Hammersmith
1634 *A Masque Presented at Ludlow Castle* performed (29 September)
1635 Takes up residence with family at Horton
1637 His mother dies (April)
A Masque Presented at Ludlow Castle published
1638 *Lycidas* published in *Justa Edouardo King*
Travels to France and Italy
Charles Diodati dies
1639 Returns to England (July)
1640 *Epitaphium Damonis* published
Moves to his own house in Aldersgate and begins teaching two students, John and Edward Phillips
1641 *Of Reformation Touching Church-Discipline in England* (May) published
Of Prelatical Episcopacy (June or July) published
Animadversions upon the Remonstrants Defence (July) published
1642 *The Reason of Church-Government Urg'd against Prelaty* (January or February) published
An Apology Against a Pamphlet Called A Modest Confutation (April) published

	Marries Mary Powell, who returns home to her family about one month later
	The Civil War begins
1643	*The Doctrine and Discipline of Divorce* (August) published
1644	Revised second edition of *The Doctrine and Discipline of Divorce* (February) published
	Of Education (June) published
	The Judgement of Martin Bucer (August) published
	Areopagitica (November) published
1645	*Tetrachordon* and *Colasterion* (March) published
	Poems of Mr. John Milton, both English and Latin, Compos'd at Several Times registered (published January 1646)
	Marry Powell Milton returns to her husband
1646	Daughter Anne born (July)
1647	His father dies (March)
1648	Daughter Mary born (October)
1649	King Charles I executed (January)
	The Tenure of Kings and Magistrates (February) published
	Appointed Secretary for Foreign Languages (March)
	Articles of Peace (May) published
	Eikonoklastes (October) published
1651	*Pro Populo Anglicano Defensio* (February) published
	Son John born (March)
1652	Becomes completely blind
	Daughter Deborah born (May)
	Mary Powell Milton dies (May)
	Son John dies (June)
1653	Oliver Cromwell established as Lord Protector (December)
1654	*Pro Populo Anglicano Defensio Secunda* (May) published
1655	*Pro Se Defensio* (August) published
1656	Marries second wife, Katherine Woodcock (November)
1657	Daughter Katherine born (October)
1658	Katherine Woodcock Milton dies (February)
	Daughter Katherine dies (March)
	Oliver Cromwell dies; his son Richard installed as successor (September)
	Revised second edition of *Pro Populo Anglicano Defensio* (October) published
1659	*A Treatise of Civil Power* (February) published
	Considerations Touching the Likeliest Means to Remove Hirelings (August) published

Letter to a Friend Concerning the Ruptures of the Commonwealth (October) written (first published in 1698)
Proposalls of Certaine Expedients (November) written (first published in 1938)

1660 *The Readie and Easie Way to Establish a Free Commonwealth* (February) published (the revised second edition appeared in April)
The Present Means . . . of a Free Commonwealth (March) written (first published 1698)
Brief Notes upon a Late Sermon (April) published
Charles II returns and monarchy restored in England (May)
Milton briefly imprisoned and fined

1663 Marries third wife, Elizabeth Minshull (February)

1667 *Paradise Lost. A Poem in Ten Books* (October) published

1669 *Accedence Commenc't Grammar* (June) published

1670 *The History of Britain* (November) published

1671 *Paradise Regain'd . . . Samson Agonistes* published

1672 *Artis Logicæ* published

1673 *Of True Religion, Hæresie, Schism, and Toleration* published
Poems, &c. upon Several Occasions with *Of Education* published

1674 *Paradise Lost. A Poem in Twelve Books* (second edition) published
Milton's translation of *A Declaration or Letters Patent* (July) published
Epistolarum Familiarium published
Milton dies at age 65 (8 or 9 November); and is buried on 12 November in St Giles Church in Cripplegate

1676 *Literae Pseudo-Senatus Anglicani* (Letters of State) published

1681 *Character of the Long Parliament* published

1682 *A Brief History of Moscovia* published

1694 *Letters of State* (English translation) published, including Milton's sonnets to Cromwell, Fairfax, Vane, and Cyriack Skinner

1823 Manuscript of *De doctrina Christiana* discovered (published 1825)

1874 Milton's Commonplace Book discovered (published 1876)

NOTE ON THE TEXT AND LIST OF ABBREVIATIONS

References to works quoted or mentioned are given in the text, usually in an abbreviated form that cites the author's name, the date (where necessary), and the page. Fuller details of works thus cited may be found in the reading list that follows each chapter but the last. All biblical quotations, except as otherwise indicated, are from the Authorized (King James) Version.

Poems	*The Poems of John Milton*, ed. John Carey and Alastair Fowler (London, 1968). All quotations of Milton's poetry are from this edition.
YP	*Complete Prose Works of John Milton*, 8 vols., ed. Don M. Wolfe *et al.* (New Haven, 1953–82)
CM	*The Works of John Milton*, 18 vols., ed. Frank Allen Patterson *et al.* (New York, 1931–8)
CD	*Christian Doctrine* (original Latin title: *De doctrina christiana)*
PL	*Paradise Lost*
PR	*Paradise Regained*
SA	*Samson Agonistes*

I

STEPHEN B. DOBRANSKI

Milton's social life

That eight biographies of John Milton were written within sixty years of his death in 1674 not only demonstrates the popularity of his works during the first half of the eighteenth century, but also suggests the enduring strength of Milton's personality. Because most of these accounts were published with editions of Milton's works, readers became accustomed to interpreting his writings biographically. Milton still had his detractors – William Winstanley in his 1687 dictionary of English poets, for example, dismissed Milton as 'a notorious Traytor' who had 'most impiously and villanously bely'd that blessed Martyr, King *Charles* the First' (195) – but such attacks only encouraged readers to approach Milton's works as a function of his identity. As Samuel Johnson complained in his *Lives of the English Poets*, the 'blaze' of Milton's reputation was preventing people from examining his poetry objectively (1: 163, 165).

Much of the information in Milton's early biographies came from Milton himself, a useful but not entirely reliable source. Whereas we know relatively little about other contemporary writers, Milton includes provocative autobiographical digressions in some of his poems and pamphlets, as if inviting readers to organize his works according to his sense of them. He describes his aspirations and experiences in *The Reason of Church-Government* (1642), *An Apology Against a Pamphlet* (1642), and *Pro Populo Anglicano Defensio Secunda* (1654), and continues to construct a narrative of his poetic progress in other publications such as his collected *Poems* (1645, 1673) and *Paradise Lost* (1667, 1674). If scholars in discussing his works have overemphasized Milton's agency, the blame lies at least in part with Milton: his strong authorial voice has virtually drowned out the social conditions of his writing and publishing.

In its most recent and extreme form, this image of Milton as an independent author has mutated into the caricature of an isolated pedant. We imagine an aloof and avid scholar, cut off from seventeenth-century culture and holding conversation exclusively with Homer, Virgil, and God.

Rumours about Milton's domestic life also conjure the dubious but compelling image of a brilliant blind man bullying his frightened daughters for the sake of his art. And how can modern readers not feel daunted by Milton? Introducing a selection of his works, the editors of *The Norton Anthology* coolly observe that 'in his time' he 'likely' 'read just about everything of importance written in English, Latin, Greek, and Italian', adding parenthetically that 'of course, he had the Bible by heart' (1: 1434).

To remedy the misapprehension of Milton's autonomy, we need to approach him as a working writer and acknowledge the various social sites of his authorship. As epic poet and political pamphleteer; defender of divorce and supporter of regicide; teacher, businessman, and government employee – Milton was necessarily influenced by his changing historical circumstances. Reading beyond the persona of the independent poet that Milton implies in many of his texts, we discover a complex, sometimes inconsistent writer, predisposed to socializing and dependent on his friends and acquaintances as part of the creative process.

From an entry in Milton's handwriting in his family's Bible we learn that he was born on Friday, 9 December 1608, at 6.30 am; he was baptized eleven days later in the parish church of All Hallows, Bread Street. Milton's boyhood home in the heart of London afforded the young poet little opportunity for quiet and seclusion. Growing up amid merchants and drinking houses and not far from London's busiest business district in Old Cheap, Milton must have become accustomed at an early age to the noise and activity of the city. The family's six-storey tenement was in a building, the White Bear, occupied by at least seven other residents. Milton's family consisted of his parents, older sister Anne, and younger brother Christopher; his father, the elder John Milton, was a Scrivener (a trade involving money-lending and deed-writing) and may also have invited his apprentices to live with the family, as was common practice. In addition to servants, nurses, and tutors, the home saw the visits of various composers seeking the elder Milton's company: the poet's father had become well known as a musician, and the White Bear may have been the scene of musical performances for select audiences. Although we know considerably less about Sara Milton, the poet's mother, she too was active in the surrounding parish. In one of the few references that Milton makes about her in print, he notes her reputation throughout the neighbourhood for her acts of charity.

That Milton's parents arranged for a formal portrait of him to be painted at age ten suggests, as William Riley Parker has observed, both the family's pride and prosperity (8). The painter, commonly thought to be Cornelius

Janssen, has captured a serious-looking boy, not completely comfortable in his genteel doublet and starched collar. Milton's close-cropped haircut was probably given him by Thomas Young, his first preceptor. Again Milton's parents were indulging in behaviour more typical of the gentry than the middle class: before beginning formal schooling, Milton was taught at home, first by his father, then by the Scottish minister Young. Although Young may have occupied this position for only a few years, he later played an important role in the antiprelatical controversy of the 1640s and probably influenced Milton's early Presbyterian sympathies.

According to Milton's widow, it was around age ten that the author composed his first poetry, now lost. The earliest surviving works by Milton that we can confidently identify are his English translations of Psalms 114 and 136, which he wrote at age fifteen, perhaps as an assignment during his last year at St Paul's School. The language of these poems reflects Milton's early interest in Ovid and Propertius; the fact that he chose to translate songs from the Old Testament suggests his religious conviction and his father's musical influence. Although few records exist about Milton's time at St Paul's, we know that he learned to read and write Latin fluently, and eventually studied Greek and Hebrew. There he befriended the under-usher, Alexander Gil, Jr, with whom he would continue to exchange poetry and correspondence after graduating. Also at St Paul's, Milton formed a special friendship with one of his schoolmates, Charles Diodati. From their surviving correspondence (Diodati's written in Greek, Milton's in Latin) we sense that this relationship was important for both young men; Milton wrote at least four of his early verses to or about Diodati.

Finishing at St Paul's in 1624, Milton began attending Christ's College, Cambridge, where he would ultimately earn his BA in 1629 and graduate *cum laude* with his MA three years later. At Cambridge, Milton claimed to have received 'more then ordinary favour and respect . . . above any of my equals' (*YP* 1: 884). Milton's nephew, Edward Phillips, also reports that the author 'was lov'd and admir'd by the whole University, particularly by the Fellows and most Ingenious Persons of his House'. When Milton left Cambridge, Phillips claims, it caused 'no small trouble' to his 'Fellow-Collegiates, who in general regretted his Absence' (Darbishire, 54, 55). Even if we suspect Milton and Phillips of overstating Milton's reputation, his peers liked him well enough to invite him to speak at various university functions. The sly allusions and coarse puns in Milton's surviving Latin orations imply that he had a good rapport with members of the college. Thus, as the biographer Christopher Hill suggests, Milton's university nickname 'the Lady of Christ's' need not have been pejorative (35). In his vacation exercise, Milton seems to appreciate such humour as he playfully derides his classmates' poor grammar and devises a list of bawdy explanations for the epithet.

During this time, Milton stayed in contact with Thomas Young, and probably formed lasting relationships with some of his acquaintances from Cambridge, such as Henry More, an undergraduate with Milton; Joseph Meade, a Fellow of Christ's College; Thomas Bainbrigge, the Master of Christ's; and the Reverend Nathaniel Tovey, Milton's second tutor at Christ's. In *An Apology Against a Pamphlet*, Milton refers to the 'many Letters full of kindness and loving respect' that he received from his friends at Cambridge both before and after his graduation (*YP* 1: 884). Surely Milton would have stayed in contact with his 'learned Friend' Edward King, whose tragic death in 1637 inspired *Lycidas* and with whom, Edward Phillips claims, Milton had 'contracted a particular Friendship and Intimacy' (Darbishire, 54).

In Milton's familiar letters we glimpse not a reclusive scholar but an author who so enjoyed companionship that, hearing on one occasion of Charles Diodati's visit to London, he dashed 'straightway and as if by storm' ('*confestim & quasi* autoboei *proripui me ad cellam tuam*') to meet his boyhood friend (*CM* 12: 20–1). While not all Milton's friendships were as intimate as his relationship with Diodati, Milton's enthusiasm for his former schoolfellow contributes to our sense of the social author. 'Why do you complain that poetry is a fugitive from wine and feasting?' ('*Quid quereris refugam vino dapibusque poesin*?' line 13), Milton asks his friend in Elegy 6, referring to the classical tradition that associates inspiration and pleasure. In one of Milton's oratorical exercises from Cambridge, he admits that those who immerse themselves in study 'find it much easier to converse with gods than with men' (*YP* 1: 295). On the other hand, Milton claims, no one cultivates a friendship more diligently than a man who has devoted himself to learning. For Milton, 'the chief part of human happiness is derived from the society of one's fellows and the formation of friendships' (*CM* 12: 262).

Not all of Milton's memories of Cambridge would have been pleasant, however. In 1626 he was suspended and briefly returned to his parents' home in London. Although the exact reason for Milton's suspension remains unknown, it may have involved his first tutor, William Chappell, reputedly a strict disciplinarian. The seventeenth-century biographer John Aubrey recorded that Milton received 'some unkindnesse' from Chappell and has added in the margin, 'whip't him' (Darbishire, 10).

It is the six years after Milton left Cambridge that modern critics have especially characterized as a period of intense study and isolation. From 1632 to 1635, Milton lived with his parents in Hammersmith, a suburban town about six or seven miles west of St Paul's Cathedral, and from 1635 to 1638 the family resided at Horton, a town even further west, approximately seventeen miles outside of London. Living with his family outside of London, away from the distractions that the city offered, Milton no doubt had ample opportunity to concentrate on his studies. In a letter to Charles Diodati from London in 1637, Milton compares his friend's reading habits with his own:

> I know your method of studying to be so arranged that you frequently take breath in the middle, visit your friends, write much, sometimes make a journey, whereas my genius is such that no delay, no rest, no care or thought almost of anything, holds me aside until I reach the end I am making for, and round off, as it were, some great period of my studies. (*CM* 12: 18–19)

The entries in Milton's Commonplace Book also attest to the extensive reading that he accomplished after graduating from Cambridge, and in *Defensio Secunda* Milton specifically recalls his time in the country as a period of intense study: 'At my father's country place, wither he had retired to spend his declining years, I devoted myself entirely to the study of Greek and Latin writers, completely at leisure' (*YP* 4: 613–14).

Although such claims suggest Milton's passion for learning, we ought not to mistake his avidity for reclusiveness. Milton says not that he but that his father had retired to the country. When he does refer to his own retirement in Elegy 1 to Charles Diodati, he is most likely writing euphemistically about his suspension from Cambridge in 1626. In this poem Milton at first claims that his books are his life and that he devotes his time to them and the Muses ('*Tempora nam licet hic placidis dare libera Musis, / Et totum rapiunt me mea vita libri*', lines 25–6) – but here, too, he admits to his friend that he frequents the theatre and often enjoys leaving the city to watch young women.

Milton's letters and publications suggest that even while living in Hammersmith and Horton he travelled frequently and socialized often. In *Defensio Secunda* he fondly remembers travelling to London, 'exchanging the country for the city, either to purchase books or to become acquainted with some new discovery in mathematics or music' (*YP* 4: 614). Living with his family in the country posed little difficulty for such journeys: he needed only two hours to travel from Horton to London, and travelling from the suburb of Hammersmith to London required considerably less time. Rather than secluding himself at his parents' home to pursue his studies, Milton may have chosen to live with his family out of convenience. Just out of college, he had not yet chosen a vocation and had no ostensible means of supporting himself while formulating his plans. Milton writes in

The Reason of Church-Government that he had been preparing from his earliest youth for a career in the ministry 'by the intentions of my parents and friends . . . and in mine own resolutions' (*YP* 1: 822). He became disillusioned, however, by the clergy's corrupt practices. In his own words, he was 'Church-outed by the Prelats' (*YP* 1: 823), that is, he grew so disgusted with the Episcopal form of church-government that he could not in good conscience be ordained.

This decision must have come as a disappointment to Milton's parents, in particular his father, whom Milton credits with providing his education. In the poem *Ad Patrem* Milton thanks his father for not forcing him into business or law, and tries to convince him that his own musical abilities resemble his son's poetic skills. We may detect a similarly defensive tone in a letter Milton penned to an unknown friend shortly after graduating from Cambridge. Milton denies that he has chosen a life of seclusion. Although he admits that 'I am something suspicious of my selfe, & doe take notice of a certaine belatednesse in me' (*CM* 12: 325), he insists that he is not indulging in 'the endlesse delight of speculation'; on the contrary, he is preparing himself for his career, 'not taking thought of beeing late so it give advantage to be more fit' (*CM* 12: 324).

As part of this preparation, Milton found his acquaintances and friends especially useful. In 1633 Milton received an invitation from the Countess-Dowager of Derby to contribute to an entertainment called *Arcades*, which her family had planned in her honour; and his decision one year later to write *A Masque Presented at Ludlow Castle* again grew out of an association with the Egerton family, specifically the Earl of Bridgewater, the step-son to the Countess-Dowager. Although Milton may have agreed to compose these courtly entertainments because he was considering the Egertons as potential patrons, we do not know why the family chose to have Milton write for them. One of the most highly regarded families in England, the Egertons could have presumably called upon a writer with a more established reputation, someone like Ben Jonson, rather than selecting a relatively inexperienced young poet from Hammersmith.

If Milton had indeed led a secluded life, he would not have earned such prestigious, aristocratic commissions. Nor would he have written two affectionately humorous poems to the University Mail Carrier, Hobson, on his death in January 1631; versions of these poems circulated in manuscript and were printed in three separate verse collections. It also seems unlikely that a shy, bookish young man would have published *Lycidas* or 'An Epitaph on the admirable Dramaticke Poet W. Shakespeare'. In the former case, Milton's reputation at the university surely recommended him as a contributor to *Justa Edouardo King*, the 1638 anthology of poems commemorating his late friend; and the inclusion of Milton's 'Epitaph' in the Second Folio of Shakespeare's plays raises the possibility that members of the book trade – perhaps through his father's intervention? – were also familiar with Milton as early as the 1630s.

'An Epitaph on . . . Shakespeare' was probably not, however, Milton's first published poem: he may have had published an earlier work while still at Cambridge. In a letter to Alexander Gil, Jr, dated 2 July 1628, Milton refers to the customary commencement verses that a fellow of his college asked him to write. He enclosed a printed copy of the verses with his letter as a gift for Gil to judge, but because Gil's copy is now lost, we cannot determine which poem Milton composed and had printed for this event – perhaps *Naturam non pati senium*, or, more likely, *De Idea Platonica*.

In all these instances – *Arcades*, *A Masque*, the Hobson poems, *Lycidas*, 'An Epitaph on . . . Shakespeare', and the commencement verses – Milton was writing for or about someone else. Collectively, these texts suggest the social nature of even his earliest authorship; he was familiar with both the courtly world of the Egertons and the culture of printing. In both contexts, what Milton wrote and where his writing appeared depended on the interaction and collaboration of a number of agents – even if we do not know for certain who those agents were. As E. M. W. Tillyard has observed, Milton 'first broke silence concerning his poetic ambitions' in 1628 at age nineteen when he delivered the annual vacation exercise at Cambridge, a public occasion, which 'argues something very different from the instinct of isolation' (170).

The success of Milton's subsequent trip to the continent exemplifies his sociability. Following the death of his mother in April 1637, the author undertook a fifteen-month Italian journey that brought him in contact with people who continued to influence his writing throughout his life. Accompanied by a servant and armed with letters of introduction from friends such as senior diplomat Sir Henry Wotton and court musician Henry Lawes, Milton was able to put aside his anti-Catholicism and 'at once became the friend of many gentlemen eminent in rank and learning, whose private academies I frequented' (*YP* 4: 614–15). In Italy he was befriended by, among others, the scholar Carlo Dati, the nobleman Giovanni Battista Manso, the theologian Giovanni Diodati (Charles Diodati's uncle), and the poet Antonio Malatesti; he also visited Hugo Grotius in Paris and, very likely, Galileo in Florence. In *Defensio Secunda* Milton describes his Italian trip not in terms of the places or things he saw but in terms of the people he met. In order to establish his credibility and illustrate that 'I have always led a pure and honourable life' (*YP* 4: 611), Milton would naturally have emphasized his distinguished foreign acquaintances. But his praise for

Italian academies exceeds the requirements of the rhetorical occasion; from among his many experiences abroad, he celebrates this one institution, 'which deserves great praise not only for promoting humane studies but also for encouraging friendly intercourse' (*YP* 4: 615–16).

Milton's Italian journey was a manifestation of his social nature complementary to, not in conflict with, the behaviour he exhibited while with his family. In Italian academies he found a public model for what he had already pursued with Diodati, Gil, and his other Cambridge and London acquaintances. Instead of closeting himself away to compose his works, Milton was inspired by and wrote about social occasions; instead of trying to control all aspects of his publications, he developed a method of authorship that was similarly 'social' – that is, he solicited friends' advice while writing his works, shared printed and scribal copies with friends, and depended on members of the book trade in publishing his texts. He even needed his acquaintances to help him distribute his poems. As J. W. Saunders has observed, Milton would later ask friends, such as Andrew Marvell and Henry Oldenburg, to act as his 'postmen' and circulate complimentary copies of his works in England and on the continent (89).

To understand why so many critics have overlooked this social dimension of Milton's works, we need to examine the authorial persona he helped to create during the antiprelatical controversy of the 1640s. In late January 1639 Charles I had declared war against Scotland over its rejection of the Episcopal policies that he wanted to enforce on the Presbyterian Church. Scottish success in defying the King's authority encouraged a resistance of national proportions. Although Milton had already criticized the Episcopal clergy in *Lycidas* – there he describes bishops as worldly-minded shepherds who 'for their bellies sake, / Creep and intrude, and climb into the fold' (lines 114–15) – he now focused his energies more fully on the debate against Episcopacy and wrote five prose tracts during a period of twelve months. Returning from Italy prematurely in 1639, he joined forces with 'Smectymnuus', a group of Presbyterian clerics who defined their collective identity by combining their initials – Stephen Marshall, Edmund Calamy, Thomas Young, Matthew Newcomen, and William Spurstowe. These five men collaborated on a pair of treatises and probably invited Milton to assist them. Young had tutored Milton in Bread Street, and Newcomen and Spurstowe, Milton's contemporaries at Cambridge, would have heard the young author delivering his speech in 1627 at the college's annual vacation exercise.

Ironically, Milton's church-government pamphlets, though produced through a social process, first established the perception of the author as a solitary figure; Milton emerged from the debate against Episcopacy with a discrete, authorial identity. His first three pamphlets appeared anonymously – *Of Reformation Touching Church-Discipline in England* (May 1641), *Of Prelatical Episcopacy* (June or July 1641), and *Animadversions upon the Remonstrants Defence* (July 1641). However, with the fourth tract, *The Reason of Church-Government Urg'd against Prelaty* (January or February 1642), not only does the title page read 'By Mr. *John Milton*', but the preface to Book 2 addresses Milton's career as a poet. In the middle of the pamphlet, Milton turns away from his argument about the bishops to talk about himself.

The specific author we encounter in *The Reason of Church-Government* is the aloof and avid scholar who has mesmerized modern critics. This persona serves in part as an ethical proof: Milton portrays himself as a bookish young man who has chosen to endure the 'unlearned drudgery' of his Episcopal opponents and is magnanimously sacrificing 'a calme and pleasing solitarynes' (*YP* 1: 821–2). Milton contrasts the dishonest prelates' self-interested motives with his own desire 'to impart and bestow without any gain to himselfe . . . sharp, but saving words' (*YP* 1: 804). He characterizes his opponents as pseudo-intellectuals, 'men whose learning and beleif [*sic*] lies in marginal stuffings' (*YP* 1: 822). He, on the other hand, has been training to become a national poet, 'to be an interpreter & relater of the best and sagest things among mine own Citizens throughout this Iland in the mother dialect' (*YP* 1: 811–12). Whereas he has the use 'but of my left hand' in this present prose controversy, he claims to be 'led by the genial power of nature' to a higher, poetic task (*YP* 1: 808). He announces audaciously – and with uncanny accuracy – 'I might perhaps leave something so written to aftertimes, as they should not willingly let it die' (*YP* 1: 810).

In his next prose tract, Milton continued to construct this authorial persona in the process of refuting an ad hominem attack on his character. In January 1642, around the same time that *The Reason of Church-Government* was published, an anonymous author lashed out at the 'grim, lowring, bitter fool' who had written *Animadversions*. Three months later, Milton responded with *An Apology Against a Pamphlet Called A Modest Confutation* (April 1642), again emphasizing his virtue and learning. Here he offers his famous prescription that 'he who would not be frustrate of his hope to write well hereafter in laudable things, ought him selfe to bee a true Poem' (*YP* 1: 890). Whether Milton actually lived up to this high standard, we do not know. But in describing his studies and forecasting his accomplishments, he had already begun to draft for us the 'Poem' of his life – and it remains one of the things he left 'written to aftertimes' that critics have refused to let die.

Rather than distracting Milton from his future poetic endeavours, his prose-writing thus complemented them. Milton relied on his participation in the debate against Episcopacy both to forge his individual identity and assist his development as a writer. The experience he gained as a pamphleteer – first during the antiprelatical debate, later during the divorce controversy and as a defender of Commonwealth and regicide – helped him to mature as an author; it enabled him to fulfil the role he casts for himself in *The Reason of Church-Government*.

During the 1640s Milton was also establishing his career as a teacher and at the encouragement of Samuel Hartlib would eventually commit his pedagogical philosophy to print in a small treatise entitled *Of Education* (June 1644). Taking up residence in London after his journey to Italy, Milton began a school with two pupils, his sister's sons, John and Edward Phillips, aged eight and nine. It was also at this time that Milton composed and had published separately *Epitaphium Damonis* (1640), his elegy to his recently deceased friend, Charles Diodati: in the guise of a shepherd, the poet mourns his lost companion and wonders who will now inspire him with conversation and song.

In *Epitaphium Damonis* and *Mansus*, another Latin poem probably composed around 1638–9, Milton continues to discuss his poetic aspirations, specifically raising the possibility of writing a longer work about various British and biblical subjects. Milton was turning his thoughts away from the pastoral mode to a more ambitious genre. From seven pages of his surviving manuscript notes, we know that he was considering an epic about King Arthur or King Alfred, as well as a play about such topics as Abraham, John the Baptist, 'Sodom Burning', 'Moabitides or Phineas', or 'Christus Patiens'. Perhaps most notably, he began outlining ideas for a tragedy to be called 'Adam unparadiz'd' or 'Paradise Lost' (French, 2: 3–4).

Financially, though, even Milton's greatest poetic achievements would never be especially rewarding. During the seventeenth century writers were sometimes paid a small sum for their work, but only when publishers were confident of books selling well. More often authors turned over their manuscripts to printers and received a few complimentary copies; or they subsidized the publication themselves, sometimes with the help of a patron. Milton's contract with Samuel Simmons for the publication of *Paradise Lost* in 1667 remains the earliest surviving formal agreement of its kind in England: Milton received £5 up front and £5 (along with perhaps 200 copies) at the end of the first three impressions. Although these terms were fair by seventeenth-century standards, Milton could hardly support his family on this income. For much of his life he instead lived off the interest from his father's, and subsequently his own, loans and investments.

Sometime around 1627, for example, Milton's father had lent Richard Powell of Oxfordshire £300 with a £500 bond. In June 1642 Milton travelled to Oxfordshire – according to Edward Phillips, 'no body about him certainly knowing the Reason' (Darbishire, 63). We do know, however, that one month later Milton returned to London with a seventeen-year-old bride, Powell's eldest daughter Mary, and the promise of a £1000 dowry which he would never receive. When Mary Powell went to visit her family in Oxfordshire about a month after the marriage, she refused to come back to London. Milton's letters to her were unanswered, and an emissary sent to inquire after her was, according to Milton's nephew, turned away 'with some sort of Contempt' (Darbishire, 65).

Had Milton originally travelled to Oxfordshire for the express purpose of collecting his father's debt, of securing a bride, or of visiting friends and relatives in the area? Did Mary Powell refuse to return to her husband because she was unhappy with him, because her family needed her assistance, or because she was homesick? One seventeenth-century biographer suggests that Milton's bride 'had bin bred in a family of plenty and freedom' and did not like her new husband's 'reserv'd manner of life' (Darbishire, 22). Surely Powell's reluctance to return to Milton was exacerbated by the mounting hostility between the King and Parliament. As the controversy over church-government escalated from a religious to political conflict, Charles I had set up headquarters in Oxford, making travel between Oxford and London dangerous and complicating efforts for the estranged couple to communicate and thus reconcile. Also politics may have played a role in keeping the couple apart: Milton sided with Parliament; the Powell family were staunch Royalists.

While we may be tempted to interpret Milton's ensuing pamphlets defending divorce as merely personal, an entry in his Commonplace Book indicates that he had begun thinking about the institution of divorce prior to his own marriage. Of course, his experience with Mary Powell must have prompted his sudden enthusiasm to pursue the subject in print. But nowhere in his four divorce tracts – *The Doctrine and Discipline of Divorce* (August 1643; February 1644), *The Judgement of Martin Bucer* (July 1644), *Tetrachordon* (March 1645), and *Colasterion* (March 1645) – does Milton address his own situation with Mary Powell, nor, more generally, does he discuss desertion as grounds for divorce. Instead he appeals to his readers' reason and focuses attention on the references to divorce in the Old and New Testaments. For Milton, marriage represents 'the apt and cheerfull conversation of man with woman, to comfort and refresh him against the evill of solitary life' (*YP* 2: 235). Writing at a time when divorce was permitted only in cases of adultery, he took the radical position of emphasizing spiritual compatibility. If a man and woman did not get along, Milton argued, then their relationship undermined God's reason for creating matrimony. A marriage between two incompatible people was not, according to Milton, a marriage at all.

Milton and Mary Powell were ultimately reconciled in 1645, and they stayed together until she died in 1652, a few days after giving birth to their third daughter, Deborah. Although early biographers may be overstating the case in praising the poet's 'Gentleness and Humanity' for agreeing to take back his wife 'after she had so obstinately absented from him' (Darbishire, 31), Milton at least deserves credit for the generosity he showed the Powell family. In addition to waiving some of the money that the Powells owed him, he agreed shortly after his wife's return to have her mother, father, and an unknown number of her brothers and sisters temporarily share his new house in Barbican. Along with the poet's father, and soon afterwards, the couple's first daughter, Anne, Milton once again found himself living in a crowded, hectic household.

Perhaps to help put the controversy of his divorce pamphlets behind him, Milton decided in 1645 to have his collected *Poems* published; by then, at least five writers had criticized his position on marriage in print. In the same year Milton published his last two divorce tracts, *Tetrachordon* (meaning 'four-stringed'), which discusses four passages in scripture that deal with marriage; and *Colasterion* (meaning 'instrument of punishment'), in which he refutes one of his anonymous detractors. If *Tetrachordon*'s scholarly method and tone contribute to the perception Milton cultivated elsewhere of the withdrawn poet-scholar, *Colasterion* reveals the author at his most vehemently human. Angry at being misunderstood, he lashes out, sometimes cruelly, dismissing his opponent as a 'fleamy clodd' (*YP* 2: 740), an 'Idiot by breeding' (*YP* 2: 741), and 'a presumptuous lozel' (*YP* 2: 756). Years later in *Defensio Secunda* Milton would regret that he had ever written his divorce tracts in English, wishing instead that he had used Latin to target his ideas to a more select audience.

Milton's 1645 *Poems*, by comparison, sidesteps or soft-pedals his early radicalism, avoiding almost all references to the Civil War and the prose controversies in which he had participated. Entitled *Poems of Mr. John Milton, both English and Latin, Compos'd at Several Times*, the collection comprises fifty-four poems, including all of those, such as *A Mask*, *Epitaphium Damonis*, and 'An Epitaph on . . . Shakespeare', that had previously been published anonymously. Here the book's publisher Humphrey Moseley presents these verses as the work of a learned gentleman: the Milton whom we encounter in 1645 has written for clergy and aristocrats; has composed poems in English, Latin, Greek, and Italian; and has received, as the book again and again avers, '*the highest Commendations and Applause of the learnedst* Academicks, *both domestick and forrein*' (*CM* 1: 414). Once again, Milton emerges as a social author, depending on the assistance of various people to produce his collected works. In addition to collaborating with material agents of production, he has addressed individual poems to friends, and his various acquaintances have contributed laudatory verses and letters.

A year before the first edition of the *Poems* was published, Milton wrote *Areopagitica* (November 1644), a landmark argument against censorship and a defence of the type of collaborative production that his collected verses manifest. This tract represents another of Milton's more personal treatises, written on behalf of his friends in the book trade as well as in response to critics like the preacher Herbert Palmer, who had favoured censorship in his attack on Milton's divorce pamphlets. Three months before the publication of *Areopagitica*, a petition of the Stationers' Company to the House of Commons (24 August 1644) had also objected to the unlicensed publication of Milton's divorce tracts. By not having a license to print his works, Milton and the pamphlet's publisher were disregarding the Long Parliament's Order for Printing (14 June 1643), which stipulated that all printed matter be first approved and licensed by a government agent, then officially entered in the *Register* of the Stationers' Company.

In *Areopagitica* Milton suggests that book-writing and book-making require a more involved practice than such licensing acts allowed. Rather than sanctioning a select group of agents – whether licensers or monopolists – to regulate the book trade, Milton advocates a social process by which knowledge is shared. He wants to remove pre-publication censorship so as to transfer the control of knowledge from a few, ignorant men, whom Parliament had empowered, to the trade's many agents, whose dynamic interaction would lead to the increase of truth. Whereas Parliament's policy of pre-publication licensing represented an attempt to master a potentially threatening force, Milton foresaw the central role that the printing press would come to play and aligned its unfettered operation 'with truth, with learning, and the Commonwealth' (*YP* 2: 488).

It was around this time that Milton probably started work on both a theological treatise and a chronicle of British history up to the Norman Conquest. Although he did not publish another prose work until the end of the Civil War – when he had printed a defence of regicide, *The Tenure of Kings and Magistrates* – he remained active, sociable, and involved during the intervening four years. Milton continued with his teaching and perhaps began composing his *Artis Logicæ* and another pamphlet, *A Brief History of Moscovia*. He also continued to be inspired by specific people and events: in addition to writing two sonnets about the divorce controversy, he composed a sonnet to the musician Henry Lawes, who had collaborated with him on the songs for his court entertainments; he wrote a sonnet to his friend Catharine Thomason, the wife of the bookseller and collector George Thomason; and when the copy of his 1645 *Poems* was lost or pilfered from the library at Oxford University, Milton composed an elaborate Latin ode to the librarian John Rouse.

Politically, Milton now allied himself with the Independents. While he had found it convenient to work with Presbyterians during the antiprelatical controversy, he came to suspect that they had opposed the king for their own personal gain. In 'On the New Forcers of Conscience under the Long Parliament' Milton criticizes Presbyterians for committing some of the same mistakes as the Prelates they ousted. 'New *Presbyter* is but old *Priest* writ large' (line 20), he complains in this poem. He specifically opposed the Presbyterian policies of tithes and pluralities, and, as a tolerationist, objected to their using political power to impose religious doctrines.

Milton developed his attack on Presbyterians in his twelfth prose work, *The Tenure of Kings and Magistrates* (February 1649). In contrast to those 'Malignant backsliders' who 'are onely verbal against the pulling down or punishing of Tyrants' (*YP* 3: 222, 255), Milton insists on the need to punish the king and carry the Civil War through to its logical conclusion. Published days after Charles I's execution, the tract does not explicitly identify the king as a tyrant; instead, Milton argues theoretically that people have the right and obligation to hold all kings and magistrates accountable. He emphasizes that 'Justice is the onely true sovran and supreme Majesty upon earth' and that 'justice don upon a Tyrant is no more but the necessary self-defence of a whole Common wealth' (*YP* 3: 237, 254).

Despite taking such a decisive stand against monarchy, Milton claimed to be surprised one month later when Oliver Cromwell and the newly formed government approached him about working for the republic. Recollecting the offer, in *Defensio Secunda* he again cast himself as a withdrawn and isolated poet, dragged reluctantly into the public arena, just as he had alleged during the antiprelatical controversy. He had completed four books of *The History of Britain*, 'when lo! . . . the council of state, as it is called, now first constituted by authority of parliament, invited me to lend them my services in the department more particularly of foreign affairs – an event which had never entered my thoughts!' (*CM* 8: 137–9).

For the next eleven years as secretary under the Commonwealth, Milton served primarily as a translator. He translated into Latin the Council of

State's foreign correspondence, worked as an interpreter at conferences between Council members and visiting ambassadors, and translated into English letters that the Council received from the continent. He also prepared four original pamphlets – the *Articles of Peace* (May 1649), *Eikonoklastes* (October 1649; 1650), *Pro Populo Anglicano Defensio* (February 1651), and *Pro Populo Anglicano Defensio Secunda* (May 1654). Commissioned by the Council, these tracts alternately defended the new government and attacked its adversaries.

When, for example, *Eikon Basilike* was published in 1649 shortly after the king's execution, Milton was called upon to compose the government's official answer. Also known as the King's Book and allegedly containing Charles I's private meditations, *Eikon Basilike* ('Image of the King') was an almost immediate bestseller, prompting London printers to produce thirty-five editions in a single year. Milton's thankless task: to try to stem the tide of Royalist nostalgia. In his appropriately entitled *Eikonoklastes* ('image-breaker'), Milton attempted to shatter the image of the king as martyr. He literally broke *Eikon Basilike* into small quotations so that he could then, one by one, systematically refute its Royalist arguments.

Although such a methodical approach could not compete with the popular appeal of *Eikon Basilike*'s sentimentalism, Milton later had more success responding to the esteemed classical scholar Salmasius. At the request of the exiled Charles II, Salmasius had written *Defensio Regia pro Carolo I* (November 1649), an indictment of regicide and England's new government. In this case, Milton had the somewhat easier assignment of defending his country's actions against the censure of a foreigner; he no longer had to worry about the decorum of directly criticizing a deceased monarch.

The resulting pamphlet, *Pro Populo Anglicano Defensio*, did more for Milton's reputation than any of his other writings during his lifetime. The relatively unknown Englishman challenged an international celebrity – and won. Appearing throughout Europe as his country's official spokesperson, Milton became famous, both at home and on the continent. People started coming to London expressly to meet the man who had defeated Salmasius, and some, according to seventeenth-century biographers, walked 'out of pure devotion' down Bread Street 'to see the house and chamber where he was born' (Darbishire, 48, 7). As during the antiprelatical and divorce controversies, Milton was relying on scripture as his ultimate authority; kingship is based on merit, he argued, and a people, even a minority of them, have the moral right to depose a tyrant. He once again attacked his opponent on every conceivable front, both his ideas and character. He insults Salmasius as a 'busybody', a 'grammerian', and a 'hireling pimp of slavery' (*YP* 4: 457, 476, 461); he ridicules Salmasius's intelligence, motives – even his marriage. Milton asks contemptuously, 'What lad fresh from school, or what fat friar from any cloister, would not have declaimed on this ruin with greater skill and even in better Latin than this royal advocate?' (*YP* 4: 313).

Presumably, Milton cared more about the republic's principles than he did his annual salary of £288 13*s*. 6½*d*. As testimony to his conviction, he wrote nothing during his secretaryship that contradicts his other works, and, based on a cancelled entry in the Council's Order Books, he may have refused a monetary reward for his rebuttal of Salmasius. Nevertheless, in practical terms, which his detractors were quick to emphasize, Milton was working as a hired pen: a writer who earned his reputation and livelihood by attending to the wishes and, as a translator, the very words of others.

While Milton's writings are consistent with his earlier publications, some of his official duties seem to contradict his argument against pre-publication licensing in *Areopagitica*. During Milton's first years as secretary he worked more as a censor than translator. For over ten months, between 17 March 1651 and 22 January 1652, for example, the name 'Master Milton' is entered regularly in the Stationers' *Register* as licenser of one of the government's newsbooks, *Mercurius Politicus*. According to the Council's Order Books, Milton prepared only seven letters and wrote two translations during his first year as a government employee. If these records are complete, he found himself mostly policing the papers of people the government thought suspicious.

Modern critics have wondered how such an eloquent critic of censorship could serve as licenser and assist the republic in silencing opponents by seizing incriminating evidence. Had Milton's argument in *Areopagitica* been sincere, or merely politically expedient? From a manuscript report by the Dutch ambassador Leo ab Aitzema, we learn that Milton also may have licensed a heretical, Socinian manifesto known as *The Racovian Catechism*. This report would allow us to infer that he remained true to his tolerationalist principles and did not take seriously his duties as licenser: in approving a pamphlet that the government later deemed blasphemous and dangerous, he was disregarding the government's interests in favour of his own beliefs.

But because there is so little evidence corroborating Aitzema's second-hand account, we ought to hesitate before using it to judge Milton as licenser. Rather than trying to make Milton into an autonomous, completely consistent author, we need to respect the effect of his changing historical circumstances. Milton had never ruled out the need to adapt his behaviour and modify his beliefs. In *Areopagitica* he argues that the process of truth requires an openness to change – that we will arrive at virtue through 'triall, and triall is by what is contrary' (*YP* 2: 515). Milton vehemently attacked Episcopacy, yet wrote poems honouring the Bishops of Ely and Winchester; he criticized 'the troublesome and modern bondage of Riming' in a preface to *Paradise Lost*, but experimented with rhyme in many of his early verses; and he initially accepted a dualistic conception of the body and soul, but would become a materialist by the late 1650s. In like manner, Milton suddenly had the chance to help establish a republican form of government in 1649 by serving as licenser. Five years earlier when he predicted that all future licensers would be 'either ignorant, imperious, and remisse, or basely pecuniary' (*YP* 2: 530) he could not have foreseen this opportunity, nor the drastic political changes that had occurred during the interim.

Of all Milton's government writings, modern readers typically turn to *Defensio Secunda* for its information about the author. In *Regii Sanguinis Clamor* (1652) an anonymous writer had come to Salmasius's defence in maligning Milton and denouncing the English republic. *Defensio Secunda* consequently includes a long autobiographical digression, establishing both his lack of worldly ambition and his experience as a polemicist; here we learn about Milton's formal schooling, European travels, and his father's wishes. Because this tract devotes so much attention to Milton's life, we may be tempted to read it as the work of a single individual. But we need to remember that Milton was writing about himself in the middle of an international document, commissioned by the republic. As opposed to the autonomous authorial persona that Milton implies in many of his texts, he was again depending on a public occasion to compose his writings and define himself.

Milton's secretaryship represents another social site of authorship that he claims has distracted him from his poetic ambitions (*YP* 4: 627–8), but which in fact helped him to achieve his goals by enhancing his reputation, expanding his connections, and, in practical terms, providing him with an income. More importantly, working for the Commonwealth gave Milton the kind of firsthand experience that complemented his studies and enabled him to produce his later masterpieces, *Paradise Lost*, *Paradise Regain'd*, and *Samson Agonistes*. These publications are not the work of an independent, reclusive poet and pedant; rather, they benefit from a combination of scholarship, inspiration, and the experiences of an author who knew both failure and compromise, and who would witness the censure and execution of many of his collaborators.

A series of personal tragedies while Milton still worked as secretary also contributed to the tone and manner of his later writings. As far as we can tell, he became completely blind in 1652; in the same year his wife died, and the couple's only son, named after his father, died six weeks afterwards at fifteen months. In a letter to a friend, the diplomat and scholar Leonard Philaras, Milton recalled that his sight had worsened over roughly a ten-year period. He describes 'the darkness which is perpetually before me' as 'always nearer to a whitish than a blackish' and explains that his eyes, which still looked healthy, could sometimes glimpse 'a certain little trifle of light' (*CM* 12: 69).

Blind, widowed, and suffering from painful fits of gout, Milton probably found it difficult to raise his three daughters, Anne, Mary, and Deborah. The few surviving anecdotal accounts suggest that the author and his children did not get along well. A maid-servant remembered that Milton's daughters stole some of their father's books and had encouraged her to cheat him. On another occasion, when the maid-servant told Anne Milton of her father's intention to remarry, the young girl had allegedly replied that she would prefer to receive news of his death. We do not know whether Milton's second marriage improved or worsened the situation. Scant information survives about his second wife, Katherine Woodcock: twenty years her husband's junior, she married him on 12 November 1656. She died fifteen months later, having fallen ill after giving birth to their only child, who also died within a month.

Despite these personal losses and hardships, Milton remained active, both immediately before and for many years after the Restoration. Although his blindness and poor health probably reduced his official government duties, he had enough energy to revise *Pro Populo Anglicano Defensio* (October 1658) and to compose *Pro Se Defensio* (August 1655), in which he violently upheld his claim from *Defensio Secunda* that Alexander More had authored *Regii Sanguinis Clamor.* Milton argues that all of a book's collaborators, regardless of their particular involvement, can be held responsible for a finished text.

During the final year of Milton's secretaryship, in the months leading up to the Restoration, he hastily composed five additional prose tracts, all of them addressing England's political and religious crisis. Within a year of Oliver Cromwell's death the country was on the verge of returning to monarchy, and Milton was scrambling to present remedies that would preserve a republican government. Events were occurring so rapidly, however, that by the time he had published the first edition of *The Readie and Easie Way to Establish a Free Commonwealth* (February 1660), his proposal for a perpetual Long Parliament had become defunct. In the revised and much enlarged second edition (April 1660) he continued to endorse a permanent Grand Council, but here he already sounds unconfident about England's political prospects.

When Charles II returned to England the following month, on 25 May, the country once again became a monarchy. Milton was forced into hiding for three months, his books were publicly burnt, and, narrowly escaping execution, he was briefly imprisoned and fined. The former Secretary for Foreign Languages under the Commonwealth, Milton witnessed the disinterment, hanging, and mutilation of many of his friends and collaborators – 'thir carkasses / To dogs and fowls a prey, or else captiv'd', as he would allude in *Samson Agonistes* (693–4). In addition to exacting revenge on Commonwealth leaders and Cromwell's supporters, the government under Charles II enacted a series of laws by which England resumed a general policy of absolutism. The government restricted individual liberty, resurrected universal censorship, and, despite an initial declaration to the contrary, re-established a rigid Episcopal church-government.

We might expect the author and former secretary to have responded to the country's lost revolution by retreating from society; all the policies that he had worked for so passionately had suddenly been abrogated. But instead of withdrawing from society, as some critics have suggested, Milton remained social, no longer participating directly in politics, but continuing to host foreign visitors and to work closely with friends and acquaintances as he produced some of his greatest writings. Awakening at four in the morning, having someone read to him, and devoting some time to quiet contemplation, Milton was then ready to compose. The poet would sit 'leaning Backward Obliquely in an Easy Chair, with his Leg flung over the Elbow of it', and ask (as he sometimes called it) 'to bee milkd' – that is, he would dictate to an amanuensis the 'good Stock of Verses' that he had formulated during the previous night (Darbishire 6, 291, 33). In addition to soliciting his daughters' aid, Milton asked his students to serve as his amanuenses. The seventeenth-century biographer Jonathan Richardson reports that Milton was 'perpetually Asking One Friend or Another who Visited him to Write a Quantity of Verses he had ready in his Mind, or what should Then occur' (Darbishire, 289).

Milton also continued to share manuscript copies of his works with students and visitors. Edward Phillips claims that he 'had the perusal' of *Paradise Lost* 'from the very beginning' and helped his uncle proof the poem, 'which being Written by whatever hand came next, might possibly want Correction as to the Orthography and Pointing' (Darbishire, 73). Another former pupil, Thomas Ellwood, was given a manuscript of *Paradise Lost* while calling on the author at his home in Chalfont in 1665. Ellwood's account of the visit suggests that Milton actively sought the young man's advice and willingly acted on his critical opinion. When months later Ellwood visited the author again, Milton showed him

Paradise Regain'd and 'in a pleasant Tone said to me, *This is owing to you: for you put it into my Head, by the Question you put to me at* Chalfont; *which before I had not thought of*' (199–200).

Around the same time that Milton was composing *Paradise Lost* he was probably doing most of the work on his theological treatise, *de doctrina Christiana*. John Aubrey lists a manuscript called 'Idea Theologiae' as one of Milton's last compositions; an anonymous seventeenth-century biographer also refers to the author 'framing a *Body of Divinity* out of the Bible'; and Edward Phillips similarly recalls his uncle collecting 'from the ablest of Divines . . . A perfect System of Divinity' (Darbishire, 9, 29, 61). Within the community of Milton scholars a debate has recently arisen whether the manuscript of *de doctrina Christiana*, discovered in the State Papers Office in 1823, represents the work that these early biographers are describing. At stake is Milton's theology, for although we can glean various heretical opinions from some of Milton's other works, most notably *Paradise Lost*, this treatise offers an explicit, systematic description of his heterodox beliefs.

Most of the historical and bibliographical data on this topic were assembled by Maurice Kelley in 1941 and remains unchallenged. We know that Milton possessed the manuscript of *de doctrina* by 1658, from which time he reworked and revised it with the aid of several amanuenses. We also know that Daniel Skinner, one of Milton's amanuenses who copied much of the manuscript's first half, attempted after the author's death to publish it as one of Milton's works along with his state papers. If Milton did not author the treatise, we must seek another mid-century Englishman, likely visually impaired – also an Arminian, monist-materialist, mortalist, divorcer, who was opposed to tithing, mandatory sabbath observance, and civil interference in religious affairs.

Although a full discussion of Milton's relationship to the treatise exceeds the scope of this essay, the debate over *de doctrina* helps to illustrate the problem of ignoring the social conditions of his authorship. The 1996 report, 'The Provenance of *De Doctrina Christiana*', by the committee that was formed to investigate the matter, for example, acknowledges that 'much of the manuscript probably constitutes a Miltonic appropriation and transformation' and identifies the prefatory epistle as Miltonic in style. But because Milton may not have produced every word of *de doctrina* – because its 'authorial genesis' seems 'much more complex' than his other works (108) – the report concludes that the treatise's 'relationship . . . to the Milton oeuvre must remain uncertain' (110).

We need not hedge on the question of Milton's authorship, however. Of course Milton did not produce *de doctrina* alone – but to hold any of his writings to such a standard is to misunderstand seventeenth-century practices of authorship in general and Milton's method of writing in particular. In *Areopagitica* Milton describes writing as a social process that requires an author 'to be inform'd in what he writes, as well as any that writ before him' (*YP* 2: 532). Part of this process included the customary method of culling *loci communes* or commonplaces: during the Middle Ages and Renaissance, as Walter Ong has observed, 'no one hesitated to use lines of thought or even quite specific wordings from another person without crediting the other person, for these were all taken to be – and most often were – part of the common tradition' (Introduction, *The Art of Logic*, *YP* 8: 187). In Milton's prefatory epistle, he explains that he has intentionally limited his commentary: 'I . . . have striven to cram my pages even to overflowing, with quotations drawn from all parts of the Bible and to leave as little space as possible for my own words, even when they arise from the putting together of actual scriptural texts' (*YP* 6: 122). If the author were someone besides Milton, we would also have to account for Milton's dishonesty in the prefatory epistle where he claims the treatise as his own, his 'dearest and best possession' (*YP* 6: 590).

Because *de doctrina* is incomplete and was not published during Milton's lifetime, as the committee further reasons, we do not know whether he would have made additional revisions, perhaps even deleting specific heretical doctrines. However, Milton rarely considered any of his works complete and instead continued revising many of them, sometimes substantially, even after they appeared in print. If Milton had published the treatise, we would also have to account for a new set of participants (printers, compositors, correctors) who could have influenced its meaning. Would we attribute the deletion of some heresies to Milton or to the exigencies of licensing and publishing? Distracted by the persona of the autonomous author that many of Milton's texts conjure, we fail to realize that all of his works – including *de doctrina Christiana* – emerged from what the committee calls a 'complex authorial genesis' (108).

In a reissue of the first edition of *Paradise Lost*, for example, Milton added a defence of the verse and the arguments that summarize each book, but he did so at the request of his lifelong friend, the printer/publisher Samuel Simmons. We also know that the Episcopal licenser Thomas Tomkins almost ordered – 'among other frivolous Exceptions' – that six lines (594–9) be excised from Book 1 of *Paradise Lost* because of the possible allusion to deposing Charles II (Darbishire, 180). Ultimately Tomkins did not have the passage removed, but the incident again reminds us of the many people besides Milton who had authority over his texts.

Sometime between 8 and 10 November 1674, the same year that the revised, second edition of *Paradise Lost* was published, John Milton died. According to an anonymous seventeenth-century biographer, he passed away 'with so little pain that the time of his expiring was not perceived by those in the room' (Darbishire, 33). When Milton was buried four days later on 12 November 1674, 'all his learned and great Friends in *London*, not without a friendly concourse of the Vulgar', accompanied his body from the author's home in Artillery Walk to St Giles Church in Cripplegate (Darbishire, 193). Milton was survived by his third wife, the then thirty-five-year-old Elizabeth Minshull, whom he had married on 24 February 1663, and to whom we remain indebted for information about Milton's habits and character.

The diversity of Milton's publications during his later life has prompted some biographers to imagine the elderly author ridding himself of half-forgotten manuscripts as a way of tidying his closet. But Milton may have had a more specific purpose in bringing out so many texts in his final years, for these books aptly encapsulate his career as both a poet and prose-writer. After 1669 he published not only the second edition of *Paradise Lost*, but also *Paradise Regain'd* together with *Samson Agonistes* (1671), as well as *Of True Religion* (1673), which reiterates the principles of toleration that inform *Areopagitica* and his antiprelatical pamphlets. As Milton continued to polish *de doctrina Christiana*, he was preparing for the press a collection of his familiar letters and college orations, *Epistolarum Familiarium* (1674). *Accedence Commenc't Grammar* (1669), *Artis Logicæ* (1672), and the reprinted *Of Education* (1673) demonstrate Milton's enduring interest in pedagogy, and both *The History of Britain* (1670) and *A Declaration or Letters Patent* (1674) suggest the author's vast scholarship. Only Milton's argument in favour of divorce did not reoccur during his later years, but he does allude to the controversy it provoked in two sonnets, first published in the second edition of his *Poems* (1673).

Perhaps Milton was publishing so many works in his last years, as William Riley Parker suggests, because he had become increasingly aware of his own mortality (608–9). In contradiction to the warning on the title page of the 1645 *Poems* ('*ne vati noceat mala lingua futuro*'), more than one ill tongue had harmed the bard-to-be. Throughout the intervening years, Milton had come under repeated attack for his writings and had seen the burning of his books in England and on the continent. Such personal concerns may have found expression in the sense of loss that pervades the works added to the second edition of his *Poems* and may also have influenced the persona of the professional writer that Milton seems to have cultivated during his later years. In response to his failing health and a lost revolution, Milton took solace in print.

We may be reminded of *Areopagitica*'s image of 'the sad friends of Truth' who must work together to re-assemble her body 'into an immortall feature of lovelines and perfection' (*YP* 2: 549). During the final years of his life, Milton was working with amanuenses and members of the book trade to assemble his own body of work so that it, too, could live immortal. Through an analysis of these final publications, we glimpse Milton repeatedly participating in a process of social authorship, struggling to make sense of a lost revolution, and trying tirelessly to reinvent himself.

FURTHER READING

Abrams, M. H., gen. ed., *The Norton Anthology of English Literature*, 6th edn, 2 vols. (New York, 1993)

Campbell, Gordon, *A Milton Chronology* (London and New York, 1997)

Campbell, Gordon, and Thomas N. Corns, John K. Hale, David I. Holmes, and Fiona J. Tweedie, 'The Provenance of *De Doctrina Christiana*', *Milton Quarterly* 31 (1997), 67–117

Darbishire, Helen, ed., *The Early Lives of Milton* (London, 1932)

Dobranski, Stephen B., *Milton, Authorship, and the Book Trade* (Cambridge, 1999)

Dobranski, Stephen B., and John P. Rumrich, 'Introduction: Heretical Milton', in *Milton and Heresy*, ed. Stephen B. Dobranski and John P. Rumrich (Cambridge, 1998), 1–17

Ellwood, Thomas, *The History of the Life of Thomas Ellwood*, ed. S. Graveson, with an intro. by W. H. Summers (London, 1906)

French, J. Milton, ed., *The Life Records of John Milton*, 5 vols. (New Brunswick, NJ, 1956)

Grose, Christopher, *Milton and the Sense of Tradition* (New Haven, 1988)

Hill, Christopher, *Milton and the English Revolution* (London, 1977)

'Professor William B. Hunter, Bishop Burgess, and John Milton', *SEL* 34 (1994), 165–93

Hunter, William B., 'The Provenance of the *Christian Doctrine*', *SEL* 32 (1992), 129–42. Responses by Barbara K. Lewalski and John T. Shawcross, as well as a rebuttal by Hunter, follow Hunter's essay under the title, 'Forum: Milton's *Christian Doctrine*', 143–66

Johnson, Samuel, *Lives of the English Poets*, ed. George Birkbeck Hill, 3 vols. (Oxford, 1905; New York, 1967)

Kelley, Maurice, *This Great Argument: A Study of Milton's 'De Doctrina Christiana' as a Gloss upon 'Paradise Lost'* (1941; Gloucester, MA, 1962)

'The Provenance of John Milton's *Christian Doctrine*: A Reply to William B. Hunter', *SEL* 34 (1994), 153–63

Masson, David, *The Life of John Milton*, 7 vols. (1877–96; New York, 1946)

Parker, William Riley, *Milton: A Biography*, 2nd edn, ed. Gordon Campbell, 2 vols. (1968; Oxford, 1996)

Patrick, J. Max, 'The Influence of Thomas Ellwood Upon Milton's Epics', in *Essays in History and Literature (Presented by Fellows of The Newberry Library to Stanley Pargellis)*, ed. Heinz Bluhm (Chicago, 1965), 119–32

Saunders, J. W., *The Profession of English Letters* (London, 1964)
Tillyard, E. M. W., *The Miltonic Setting* (London, 1947)
Winstanley, William, *The Lives of the Most Famous English Poets*, ed. William Riley Parker (London, 1687; Gainesville, FL, 1963)

2

CEDRIC BROWN

Milton's Ludlow Masque

Matters of occasion

On first encountering Milton's Ludlow Masque – often referred to as '*Comus*' – one might begin by considering what kind of text it is. A masque is a special kind of commissioned work, spectacular and 'multi-media' in presentation, and inevitably collaborative. It cannot be treated simply as its writer's 'poem' or a play. This kind of entertainment developed at the Jacobean and Caroline courts up to the time of the English Civil War. Ben Jonson (as poet until the early 1630s) and Inigo Jones (as designer) were the genre's most innovative exponents, though there were others. It was for masques that proscenium arch stages and movable scenery were first introduced in England. Masques were usually performed during the winter festive season after Christmas, or occasionally at other times, and they often represented the spectacular highpoint, involving huge expense. They featured younger courtiers as the 'masquers', who personated symbolic figures – often chaste goddesses, if it was a ladies' masque, or martial heroes, if it was a lords' masque – and whose function, apart from representing virtue, was to dance. They did not, at least until the arrival of Queen Henrietta Maria, usually speak, or sing: that was left to the servants.

The action was usually structured by the supplanting of anti-masques (comic-grotesque dance representations of disorder) with masque dances (symbolizing harmony). Masques mythologized the court itself, sometimes offering loyalty, engaging in political defence, or promoting some royal philosophy to the imagined good of the nation. At the end of the dramatic performance, the masquers descended from a raised stage at one end of the hall, danced in the central area of floor (probably several times), and then presented themselves to the monarch who sat in a 'state', a ceremonial chair, at the other end of the hall. All perspective was directed at him, the monarch, as chief beholder, and he was surrounded on both sides and down the hall by tiers of seated courtiers arranged in strict diplomatic order. Then masque dances turned to revels: that is, the masquers eventually took partners from those sitting round, signalling the beginning of a wider social display, which continued for hours. They had a ball. Events began in the evening after supper, which was early, and continued into the night, when a banquet (a light meal) and drink were produced, to keep people going. The costume was always exotic, creating an atmosphere of fantasy; and, over years of development, stage sets became elaborate, with wings and sliding flats introduced, and more and more complicated machinery used that allowed whole groups to descend by wire, or rise from the understage area. Often, many musicians were also involved, symbolically dressed too, either at stage level or up in the 'heavens' of the set. Masques thus presented court ritual of a notoriously expensive kind, and they were prepared usually for one performance only.

What Milton wrote, of course, was a text not for a fully fledged court masque but for a more modest provincial one, to be performed in the 60′ x 30′ great hall of Ludlow Castle. Nor did he have king or queen in chairs of state, but the king's deputy in Wales and the Marches, John Egerton, Earl of Bridgewater, with his wife, the Countess. Nor did he have a large group of masquers, the ten to sixteen who might be expected at court, but instead just three children, a uniquely small, young dancing group, and rather awkward, because there was one girl of fifteen and two boys of eleven and nine. These were the three youngest and only unmarried children of Lord and Lady Bridgewater and had come with their parents for a first residential stay at Ludlow: Lady Alice Egerton; John, Lord Brackley (the eldest surviving son); and Thomas. Nor, it seems, did Milton have the machinery and technical resources for a very elaborate masque: there were three 'scenes', and the river-goddess Sabrina rose through the stage, with her chariot; but the Attendant Spirit, who begins and ends the action, seems simply to have walked on and off, though originally intended to descend and ascend. The children played themselves, not splendidly costumed gods or goddesses. This provincial downscaling seems of the essence of the masque, because the text points to the luxurious (i.e. sensual) dangers customarily attendant on too much rich festivity in princely halls. Yet even here Comus, the false enchanter, the spirit of degenerate revelling, infects the festivity, and so joins in the general assembling of forces at the beginning of the action.

In all this, Milton had restricted power of choice. He had to accept the three masquers, their young ages, and their mixed sex; he had no choice over the nature of the occasion, or the location, or probably over the various people to be employed, some coming undoubtedly from the vicinity of Ludlow as well as from the circle of the Egerton family. These factors might look compromising, but we can sketch enough of the circumstances leading into the performance on Michaelmas night, 29 September 1634, to see how the masque takes definition from the special conjunction of resources drawn from different places.

The Earl of Bridgewater, a Privy Councillor, had been nominated as the next President of Wales and the Marches back in 1631. The appointment involved his heading the prerogative court at Ludlow: the President was the direct representative of the king overseeing the judicial administration of the principality of Wales and the border counties (Marches). In practice, Lords President were also Lords Lieutenant in the region, and therefore had wider responsibilities on behalf of the crown, including arranging musters of the militia. But the day-to-day administration at Ludlow was done by deputies, and Bridgewater did not put in an appearance nor reside with his family at Ludlow until the summer of 1634. The arrival had been long expected. A basic function of the Ludlow Masque was to mark the auspicious coming together, at last, of the President's family and the region.

The Egertons actually arrived in July, but then spent much of the summer in further travelling up the borders and through Denbighshire. They were on a kind of 'progress', a ceremonial journey showing the President to the region and entertaining him in houses of the greater gentry. (We have another dramatic text for his visit to Chirk Castle.) Then they had a spell, which looks like vacation, with relatives at Lyme Park, Cheshire, back in England, before travelling south again via Market Drayton, more privately, to re-enter Ludlow only a day or two before the performance. We know that Henry Lawes, the court musician, was with the family party at Lyme Park. He wrote the music that survives for the masque, and was in any case Lady Alice's singing teacher. Lawes also knew other children of the family through their minor supporting roles in court masques, and he played the part of the Attendant Spirit. Some parts of the masque were already in preparation at Lyme, chiefly those concerning the children and the Spirit, whilst other parts, other music, and other practical things were being readied at Ludlow, using local resources. The resources of family and place were coming together. As far as the children were concerned, the rehearsals and performance must have loomed as a huge vacation project.

So far we can already see that the Ludlow Masque celebrates a state occasion, marking the presence of a new magistrate and governor in the region, whilst the idea of travel is embedded in the action and in the roles of the three children. They, the 'fair offspring nursed in princely lore', come through trials in treacherous country 'to attend their father's state, / And new-entrusted sceptre' (34–5). Michaelmas is a traditional season for marking new governance, and the ecclesiastical festival celebrates angels, thus supporting Lawes' part as Attendant Spirit, a kind of guardian angel. At the same time, the masque's focus is on the people and region to which the family has come, 'An old, and haughty nation proud in arms', says Milton's text (33) in neo-Virgilian fashion. So we are dealing with matters of good governance and heroic spirit in a place of heroic associations. The masque is to define ideals of personal and national governance. Yet as well as embodying these themes of state, it also dealt in a special way with youth and education, and the resources were kept much more within a familial context than was usual. When reading the text, we must not forget the ages of the Lady and the two brothers. Some of the masque's effects, especially for the boys, depend upon a calculated celebratory/comic tone in the writing: that they can display so much moral sense and book-learning, not to mention their memorizing such long parts, is to be admired; that they can nevertheless appear naive in some things creates both some indulgent humour and an opportunity for sterner didactic reminders of the problems of the real world, as the text presents it. Built around young masquers, this is, for them and for everyone in the hall, a very educational masque.

These specific conditions add interest to Milton's text, for several reasons. We have to recognize that a high proportion of poetry especially in the early modern period is occasional, and we will never appreciate the skill of many writers without understanding such diplomatic arts. The paradox is that Milton's Ludlow Masque is also in some ways a very 'personal' document: many themes articulated at Ludlow were also preoccupations of Milton's other, mainly later, writing, particularly as they concern patterns of education and models of governance in the reformed Protestant state. What is more, as we shall see, there is a wonderful survival of records showing a tension between what Milton first wrote and the demands of the organizers on the ground, which resulted in many changes in the text for purposes of performance. For subsequent publication, Milton generally restored, and augmented, his own ideas.

Quests, journeys, and gender roles

To see how the dramatic invention is built upon its occasion, we can compare *A Masque* with an earlier entertainment text Milton wrote for the same aristocratic family group about two years earlier. In a short sequence, merely the opening part of an evening's festivities, that he later called *Arcades* (the Arcadians), Milton made it possible for young members of the family of the Countess Dowager of Derby, at Harefield in Middlesex, to pay tribute to her and thank her for her good offices. (She had housed two granddaughters of one of her daughters, who was impoverished, and taken over the care of three children of another daughter who had become victims of the infamous sexual malpractices of the Earl of Castlehaven; there may be a purgatory function in the ritual.) Here, as in a hall set out for a masque, the Countess sits in a chair of state at one end of the room. In the playing space at the other end the group of young family members enters, dressed as Arcadians (with some supporting servants) and pretend that they are on a quest to find a new 'rural queen' of whom Fame has spoken. They are guided by Genius, a musical servant-spirit who helps care for the estate, to the light at the other end of the room, where the Countess sits. They move towards her, to 'kiss her sacred vesture's hem' (83), and are invited to give up their stony homeland for a better Arcadia in Harefield. Thus they signal their thanks for actually being housed there.

Here the movement of the Arcadians to the state is fictionalized as a quest. At Ludlow, the chief action is likewise provided by the movement of the three children to be presented to their parents in their chairs, but this journey is imagined to cross not a park but a dark wood of trial and temptation which exercises their virtue. Thus, when they finally arrive, they have proved themselves in the very qualities that reflect the ones their parents need in order to guide 'with tempered awe' (32):

Here behold so goodly grown
Three fair branches of your own,
Heaven hath timely tried their youth,
Their faith, their patience, and their truth,
And sent them here through hard assays
With a crown of deathless praise,
To triumph in victorious dance
O'er sensual folly and intemperance. (967–74)

Both *Arcades* and the masque share pastoral modes, but the masque also incorporates a little epic achievement, for the journey through trial is partly modelled on the homecoming of Odysseus past the dangers of the witch Circe, and thus has a heroic dimension.

Both journeys define virtues. The Arcadians learn that the qualities of the rural queen create, as it were, a better regime, whilst the children at Ludlow encounter a specific danger, the spirit of degenerate revelry, so that they may be educated in the dangers of princely festive halls before being allowed to be masque dancers. The action of Milton's masque is therefore self-reflexive: it identifies, resists, and finally banishes those things of luxury which can spoil the very ritual in which they partake. The name Comus is the usual Latin version of *komos*, which means revelry, though in the New Testament the word is used in the negative sense of 'riot, and ill-managed merriment', which is what the Lady thinks she heard in the wood (171). Comus's opening speech, written in wonderfully flexible short lines –

> Meanwhile, welcome joy, and feast,
> Midnight shout and revelry,
> Tipsy dance, and jollity

– dramatizes the slide from a mood of festive joy into dangerous provocation, into boastfulness, into nocturnal venery, and finally into rites of false religion and witchcraft, in guilty 'concealed solemnity'. When things go wrong in princely halls, they evidently go the whole way.

This pastoral-epic action is also like chivalric romance: the boys, as little knights errant, free the Lady from the house of a false enchanter. This event highlights the fact that the organizers of the masque divided the action into two gendered parts. It is the fifteen-year-old Lady, accidentally separated from her brothers in the wood, who faces the specific temptations of Comus. He tries to entice her to take the inebriating cup with the aim of predisposing her to sport, and he has tricked her into sitting at his luxurious feast, in his palace deceptively hidden in the wood. He seeks her, the daughter of the President, as his 'queen' (264), so as to infect the Ludlow regime from the very top. It is a seduction which threatens to turn into rape. But the Lady has chastity uppermost in her mind, constantly threatens to see through Comus's deceptions, and, when she finally realizes the trap, resists all his arguments for luxury with well schooled, godly principles of temperance. It is a remarkable moment in masque, the ways of which are usually rich and splendid, when Lady Alice Egerton argues for a temperate use of nature in all things. The boys, however, must have a quite different action defined for them, and in their care for their sister and their attempts at rescue they present a nicely differentiated study in fortitude and the control of fear, in which there are little ironies. The Younger Brother, whilst having too much fear, is nevertheless nearer a sense of acute moral danger than the Elder Brother, who is nonetheless splendid in his brave attempts to control the fears of the little one.

As already emphasized, Milton could not choose the gender of his three masquers. However, critics have long been interested in the cultural assumptions about women that come through in Milton's texts, and it is of course tempting to compare the depiction of female agency in these aristocratic entertainments with those more notorious cases of Eve in *Paradise Lost* and Dalila in *Samson Agonistes*. Some continuities are worth noting: the Lady is by no means demonized *as* the root agency of evil; rather

Circe's son sees her as the potential vessel through whom he can work, just as Satan works through Eve, and as the pagan priests of Philistia work through Dalila. In this pattern, woman is potentially the weak vessel, but the result is that splendid exceptions stand out all the more brightly. Analogies between the literary and the historical are plain to see and correspond with prejudices widely held in Milton's day: many feared evil influences coming through Catholicism and worldly excess at court, especially as these played upon women courtiers. Something like paranoia seized zealous reforming spirits when they looked at queens and courtiers of false religion at Whitehall, in the reigns both of James I and of Charles I. But, even allowing for the special celebratory circumstances at Harefield and Ludlow, *Arcades* and *A Masque* are also remarkable for offering positive roles for women through the active exercise of piety: the Countess of Derby rules through pious virtue; the godly Lady, in addition to being well mannered and carefully trained in music, resists Comus's arguments as he has never been resisted before; and the virgin goddess Sabrina displays her capacity to 'unlock' 'the clasping spell' (851–2). Eve too, by the end of *Paradise Lost*, will learn to play her godly part. But there is something notable about the early poems' celebratory roles, almost as if Milton needed to build positive models which he could set against examples of less virtuous court custom. Likewise in other aspects of the masque we shall see how a sense of the ideal plays off against an assumption of customary degeneracy.

The promise of the land

Arcades claims that the virtue of old Lady Derby has created a land about her, a new Arcadia. Thus the newly discovered 'rural queen' is compared implicitly to the queen of England (Henrietta Maria), whose own court culture featured pastoral-Arcadian self-definitions; and the formation of an ideal regime is seen to depend upon the conduct of those who rule. The Ludlow Masque also presents a vision of an ideal land with a symbol of good personal governance, Sabrina, at its centre. Like the President, she 'sways' (824) over her area, her river, and its adjoining lands. The Severn, the traditional boundary between England and Wales in its lower reaches, rises in the heart of Wales, and so could be said to preside over the Principality and the Marches, representing Wales but also joining it to England. When the President's children find themselves unable completely to undo the residual effects of luxurious custom still binding the Lady to the chair, the Spirit calls up another 'means' to resolve the crisis (820), a mythical goddess whose chaste presence counters mundane evil so as to create a special environment:

still she retains
Her maiden gentleness, and oft at eve
Visits the herds along the twilight meadows,
Helping all urchin blasts, and ill-luck signs
That the shrewd meddling elf delights to make,
Which she with precious vialed liquors heals. (841–6)

For these 'divine' offices the local inhabitants render tributes of thanks:

For which the shepherds at their festivals
Carol her goodness loud in rustic lays,
And throw sweet garland wreaths into her stream
Of pansies, pinks, and gaudy daffodils. (847–50)

Sabrina's saving rites touch the site of potential participation in the luxurious feast – the chair – and purify heart ('breast'; 910), touch ('finger's tip'), and sensual pleasure, or perhaps speech ('rubied lip'). The Spirit then wishes her lands even greater prosperity, that they may show 'many a tower and terrace round, / And here and there thy banks upon / With groves of myrrh, and cinnamon' (933–6). Though focussed on the river, the speech is an augury for virtuous and prosperous rule.

The vision of Sabrina's lands sets up a model for governance which even the President, the royal representative, must consider as deriving from the mythology of the region rather than the court. At the beginning of the masque there is a general acknowledgement of patterns of authority – 'blue-haired deities' being 'tributary gods' in the 'imperial' rule of Neptune and Jove for island Britain (18–29). Sabrina could equally be said to have been summoned by the President's servant. But the mythology built around the region depends chiefly upon the memory supposedly preserved there of chaste personal virtue. As in *Arcades*, one suspects that a comparison is being invited (though not stated) with the royal court, where Comus's luxury might not be so easily countered. What is more, if we stretched a point and measured the description of royal authority over an outlying region by the more extravagant model of colonial rule, we would see that Milton's configuration in *A Masque* offers an interesting difference. Modern scholars have noticed that colonial discourses often depict the distant land in gendered terms, as a woman to be mastered and possessed. Like those discourses, Milton's text uses the idea of virginity, but here it is not a virgin land which requires the mastery of outside rule. Rather, the region itself produces its own ruling spirit, and the discipline of virginity is a principle that defines an exemplary spirit of place which the court visitors are asked to note.

The general tendency to present visions of lands can be seen as a conventional poetic figure. It may also connect with a widespread concern in early modern Europe to model forms of state and nationhood. But given Milton's later socio-political writings, an arrangement such as we observe in *Arcades* and *A Masque* can also be understood as agreeing with his subsequent interest in devolved structures and responsibilities within the domains of church, state, and education. More specifically, when Milton was working on the masque and thinking of the Ludlow occasion, he probably remembered the sort of literary-historical-cartographical representation of the regions of England and Wales given in Drayton's *Poly-Olbion* (1613 and 1622), where rivers figuratively preside over their areas and where love of nationhood, according to the scholar Richard Helgerson, represents a pattern of greatness which breaks away from reference to a centralized monarchy. In the kind of surprise that masques are suited to create, the Earl and Countess of Bridgewater see their children saved by something implicit in the region over which they have come to exercise governance.

That the dramatic moment held some potential for embarrassment is shown by the evidence of textual variants. The early manuscript text and the printed texts show that Milton intended all the verses summoning Sabrina, from line 866 to line 886, to be spoken by the Attendant Spirit, whilst everyone watched and listened in silence. But the Bridgewater Manuscript, a copy presented to the President and assumed to record what was actually performed, distributes the couplets from line 870 ('By hoary Nereus' wrinkled look') down to line 886 ('Sleeking her soft alluring looks') between the two boys, in alternate fashion. Someone probably thought that it was undignified before the President for the two little heroes to be reduced to helpless silence whilst a musician-servant spoke. Milton's idea, however, seems to have been for everyone to attend to what the musical spirit-presenter had to teach.

Sabrina is constructed from patriotic Trojan/British legend and conveys the idea of a nation founded upon religious and educational discipline. Ultimately, although she is figured in a 'literary' way, she probably also reflected Protestant-nationalist discourses of the kind occurring in sermons that Milton would have heard as a boy in Jacobean London. The assumption is that the nation, like Israel and Judah in the Old Testament, must constantly strive to live up to expectations. Later, in *The History of Britain* and in *Paradise Lost* Milton discerned a see-saw progress through history for England and Israel, in which there are constant fallings away from great opportunities or from divine covenants. Sabrina does not show what the nation has already achieved and possesses in perpetuity; she does show that there have been tokens of great discipline and prosperity and that such thoughts may still be aroused by those who struggle with a cultural inheritance of laxness. As in Spenser's *The Faerie Queene*, the disciplined greatness of the Protestant English state is a matter of constant striving and becoming.

But the vision of future possibility was peculiarly fitting to the Ludlow situation, which again we can measure against that of Harefield. In *Arcades* the regime, though freshly discovered, is presented as fully established and existing. That suits the celebration of an elderly woman who had shown good Protestant patronage over a lifetime. In the Ludlow Masque, the occasion is about the beginning of a period of governance, and the masquers are children who have most of their lives still ahead of them. The achievement sits naturally in the future.

The office of the poet

Such an emphasis also reveals the vocational drive of the poet. Young John Milton carried little authority, was probably not present in Ludlow, and lost control of his text once it came into the hands of the organizers. Yet the case of the Ludlow Masque presents posterity with an unrivalled amount of evidence about a masque's textual development before, during, and after performance, as the piece was prepared for the press. Broadly speaking, the Trinity Manuscript shows authorial revisions in several layers before and after performance, the Bridgewater Manuscript probably records what actually happened in performance, and the added evidence of the carefully prepared, separately printed text of 1637 (closely followed by its appearance in the *Poems* of 1645) provides evidence of how Milton adapted his text for a general readership – and therefore for a somewhat different set of functions – after the event. Nevertheless, in all these transactions over several years, amid competing interests and new occasions, one thing remains constant and marks out the Ludlow Masque as a special case amongst masques: the poet's strongly advertised vocational idealism embedded in the action.

There are two moments in the action when the Attendant Spirit reminds masquers and audience of the importance of special sources of teaching and strength. The first involves the two boys, after the Elder Brother has determined to storm off with his sword and fix the foul enchanter holding his sister (598–608). This half comic, half celebratory moment offers a gentle but firm reminder to all present that the roots of the problem of the *komos* are in ungodliness: 'Far other arms, and other weapons must / Be those that quell the might of hellish charms.' In other words, the struggle is really against principalities and powers, against deceptions embedded in culture; and the victory requires recollection of religious teachings which guide one towards the Truth – 'for by this means / I knew the foul enchanter though disguised' (643–4). This resource is then playfully (and notoriously) wrapped up in a biblical-pastoral fable (617–47) which reworks the Odysseus and Circe story: the Homeric talismanic herb moly becomes the prickly herb Haemony, which figures the importance of godly teaching of the Word. Godly discipline involves humility ('small, unsightly'), not the temptations of princely riches; and the discipline entails tribulation ('prickles on it'), but its rewards are eternal ('in another country . . . / Bore a bright golden flower'). This must be the foundation of all resistance to false, ungodly ideas, and is always to be remembered ('bade me keep it'), though most ('the dull swain') do not heed or remember. The provider of this invaluable strength is likewise figured in playful pastoral:

> Brought to my mind a certain shepherd lad
> Of small regard to see to, yet well skilled
> In every virtuous plant and healing herb . . . (618–20)

Here the audience glimpses the type of the true pastor, the unworldly teacher.

All this expresses religious reform. The usual ideological markers are there, separating true teaching from false, and true religion from false (usually Catholic, and associated with some kind of witchcraft or enchantment). Moreover, because most do not heed ('Unknown, and like esteemed'), some evangelical push seems to be necessary. Such expressions of godly fervour, however wrapped up in pastoral, are unusual in masque. Perhaps the elaborateness of the pastoral function inevitably takes the edge off the fervour. And perhaps things did come unstuck in performance, for a vital section of the Haemony allegory (631–6) was removed, again probably for diplomatic reasons. The rude remarks about 'the dull swain' are associated in the text with 'this soil', meaning, of course, on earth; but the gesture might be dreadfully and undiplomatically misconstrued, with 'this soil' taken as referring not to earth but to Wales, with the Welsh thus emerging as godless boors. Everything we know about Henry Lawes, who was probably central to the event's organization, suggests that he was a consummate diplomat. Yet the religious allegory was vital to the meaning of Milton's text, as he had written it, and he restored it in subsequent printed versions.

A note of godly ardour is perhaps not so surprising in the context of Milton's relationship to an aristocratic group. When he was employed for *Arcades* at Harefield, it was almost certainly as a promising, learned new minister who had just finished his studies at Cambridge in 1632 and was beginning to look for patronage. Oxford and Cambridge primarily produced ministers for the church (about 80 percent of their graduate employment), this family had a long history of supporting Protestant pastors, and Milton's biographical record indicates an early expectation that he would train for the church. Idealistically, then, the young poet was demonstrating the vocation which might be expected of him. But we should also notice the second special resource which the Attendant Spirit summons in the fight against customary luxury in the princely hall: the river goddess Sabrina.

In both cases the Spirit speaks a pastoral fiction, and defers to typical authorities; but whereas it is a humble pastor who enjoined the strength of godliness, it is an exemplary Virgilian poet, Meliboeus, who conveyed the story of Sabrina:

> Some other means I have which may be used,
> Which once of Meliboeus old I learnt
> The soothest shepherd that e'er piped on plains. (820–2)

The Spirit points, then, to the authority of two kinds of vocational 'shepherd': pastor and poet (a pairing that will reappear in *Lycidas*). Again, we understand such figures best in context, and the fiction of Sabrina as much as that of Comus reflects the present occasion: bad customary magic is countered by a mind that aspires to ideal models afforded by national, heroic myths of the land, forged from the materials of post-Virgilian Trojan/British story. The whole last phase of the masque's action is to be, in effect, a spectacular display of all the persuasive powers of 'true' poetry. It is, apparently, the special role of poetry (and, here, masque-drama) to instruct and inspire minds with visions of the ideal, even at that point in the action at which mundane custom has proved so hard to break. The persuasive mixture of dark, resistant worlds and ideal fictional worlds is once more reminiscent of the methods of Spenser's *Faerie Queene*.

Milton's idealistic claim for his vocation as poet – that he could, as much as the priest, furnish things which were 'doctrinal to a nation' – is well known. It is less often recognized that this claim for the reforming power of poetry was actually built into the scheme of the Ludlow Masque and enacted on the poet's behalf by the Attendant Spirit and others in the President's hall. We do not know exactly when Milton abandoned his intention of entering the church. The decision may be visible in *Lycidas*, written at the end of 1637, a crisis year for the consciences of many of the godly trying to remain within the pales of the Laudian church. But the option of serving the Protestant nation as learned poet as well as learned priest is posted already in the masque of 1634, and we could even call the final part of the action at Ludlow a gloriously staged apology for poetry.

From this point of view, it is also understandable that Milton would wish to see the text of the masque in print. The Egerton family itself had a scribally produced memorial manuscript, but what was produced in print in 1637 was really something different. The preliminaries of the volume use various disguising diplomacies, feigning that Lawes himself has suggested publication, having tired his pen with the demand for copies. However, what Milton actually does with his text indicates that he took the opportunity of publication extremely seriously. He not only undid the various cuts and changes that had been made for Ludlow in 1634, but also reinforced the text in the spirit of addressing the nation at large as shepherd-teacher. The epilogue, for example, is enlarged in late changes to the Trinity Manuscript and in print in 1637 to include further gestures about the general inadequacy of mundane youthful festivities, the Adonia, when compared to the heavenly festivities at the end of time, Psyche's reception and marriage. Also, a powerful last section (782–812) is added to the debate between the Lady and Comus, demonstrating the power of religious truth as well as Comus's acknowledgement of that power. The poet thus used the voices of the masque to be more preacherly, through poetry, thereby constructing his own vocational role as poet to the nation. So in 1637 and 1638, in the printed masque and in *Lycidas*, as his social and moral commentary achieved increasing definition and visibility, Milton was actually showing the nation, though not from the pulpit, what he regarded as the right offices of a poet serving the causes of the Protestant state.

FURTHER READING

Breasted, Barbara, 'Comus and the Castlehaven Scandal', *Milton Studies* 3 (1971), 201–24

Brown, Cedric C., 'Milton's *Arcades*: Context, Form, and Function', *Renaissance Drama* 8 (1977), 245–74

John Milton's Aristocratic Entertainments (Cambridge, 1985)

'Occasions, Impulses, and the Sense of Vocation: From "Arcades" to "Lycidas"', in *John Milton: A Literary Life* (Basingstoke, 1995)

Christopher, Georgia, 'The Virginity of Faith: *Comus* as a Reformation Conceit', *ELH* 44 (1976), 479–99

Cox, J. D., 'Poetry and History: Milton's Country Masque', *ELH* 44 (1977), 622–40

Creaser, John, '"The present aid of this occasion": The Setting of *Comus*', in Lindley, ed., *The Court Masque*

Demaray, John G., *Milton and the Masque Tradition* (Cambridge, MA, 1968)

Diekhoff, John S., ed., *A Maske at Ludlow: Essays on Milton's Comus* (Cleveland, 1968)

Flannagan, Roy, ed., *'Comus': Contexts*, special number of *Milton Quarterly* 21 (1977)

Halley, Janet E., 'Female Autonomy in Milton's Sexual Poetics', in *Milton and the Idea of Woman*, ed. Julia M. Walker (Urbana, 1988), 230–53

Helgerson, Richard, *Forms of Nationhood: The Elizabethan Writing of England* (Chicago, 1992)

Jenkins, Hugh, 'Milton's *Comus* and the Country-House Poem', *Milton Studies* 32 (1995), 169–86

Kendrick, Christopher, 'Milton and Sexuality: A Symptomatic Reading of *Comus*', in *Re-Membering Milton: Essays on the Texts and Traditions*, ed. Mary Nyquist and Margaret W. Ferguson (London and New York, 1987), 43–73

Lindley, David, ed., *The Court Masque* (Manchester, 1984)

Loewenstein, David, '"Fair Offspring Nurs't in Princely Lore": On the Question of Milton's Early Radicalism', *Milton Studies* 28 (1992), 37–48

Marcus, Leah S., 'Milton's Anti-Laudian Masque', in *The Politics of Mirth: Jonson, Herrick, Milton, Marvell and the Defense of Old Holiday Pastimes* (Chicago, 1986)

'Justice for Margery Evans: A "Local" Reading of *Comus*', in Walker, ed., *Milton and the Idea of Woman*, 66–85

McGuire, Maryann, *Milton's Puritan Masque* (Athens, GA, 1983)

Norbrook, David, 'The Politics of Milton's Early Poetry', in *John Milton*, ed. Annabel Patterson (Harlow, 1992), 46–64

'The Reformation of the Masque', in Lindley, ed., *The Court Masque*, 94–110

Orgel, Stephen and Roy Strong, *Inigo Jones: The Theatre of the Stuart Court*, 2 vols. (London, 1973)

Sprott, S. E., *John Milton, 'A Maske': The Earlier Versions* (Toronto, 1973)

Tuve, Rosemund, *Images and Themes in Five Poems by Milton* (Cambridge, MA, 1957)

Walker, Julia, ed., *Milton and the Idea of Woman* (Urbana, 1988)

3

J. MARTIN EVANS

Lycidas

On 10 August 1637 a pious young Cambridge graduate called Edward King was drowned in the Irish Sea when the ship carrying him to Ireland to visit his family struck a rock off the Welsh coast and sank. The author of some rather undistinguished Latin verses, King had intended to take Holy Orders and pursue a career in the church, but in 1637 he was still a fellow at Milton's old college, Christ's, which he had entered when Milton was in his second year. He was evidently a well respected and popular figure in the University community, so much so that when the news of his death reached Cambridge a group of his friends and colleagues decided to organize a volume of memorial verses in his honour. Although Milton does not appear to have been a particularly close friend of King's, he was nevertheless invited to contribute to the collection. Published in 1638 under the title *Justa Edouardo King naufrago*, the volume contained thirty-six poems in all, twenty-three in Greek or Latin followed by thirteen in English. Milton's contribution, the last in the collection, was *Lycidas*.

Unlike the other verse memorials in *Justa Edouardo King naufrago*, *Lycidas* is a pastoral elegy. It belongs, that is to say, to a long-established generic tradition characterized by a number of stylistic and structural conventions which enable the reader to recognize it as an heir to such works as Spenser's 'Astrophel', Moschus's 'Lament for Bion', Virgil's 'Eclogue X' and Theocritus's 'Idyl I' (see Hanford; Harrison; Kirkconnell). In poems written within this tradition the poet typically represents himself as a shepherd mourning the death of a beloved companion whose departure has afflicted the entire natural world with grief. After consigning his sheep to the care of another shepherd and invoking the assistance of the muses of pastoral poetry, he proceeds to sing a dirge to his deceased friend in which he recalls the idyllic days they spent together in the countryside.

According to the great eighteenth-century critic Dr Samuel Johnson, Milton's choice of the pastoral elegy as the vehicle for his tribute to Edward King was distinctly unfortunate. In a famous passage in his 'Life of Milton' he declared that *Lycidas* 'is not to be considered as the effusion of real passion; for passion runs not after remote allusions and obscure opinions. Passion plucks no berries from the myrtle and ivy, nor calls upon Arethuse and Mincius, nor tells of rough satyrs and fauns with cloven heel. Where there is leisure for fiction, there is little grief.' What possible point could there be in representing King and Milton as shepherds tending their flocks in the English countryside, Johnson asks, when we know perfectly well that they were both students pursuing their studies at Cambridge University? 'Nothing', he concludes, 'can less display knowledge or less exercise invention than to tell how a shepherd has lost his companion and must now feed his flocks alone, without any judge of his skill in piping; and how one god asks another god what is become of Lycidas, and how neither god can tell. He who thus grieves will excite no sympathy; and he who thus praises will confer no honour' (quoted in Patrides, 60–1). What Johnson is objecting to, in short, is what he takes to be the essential artificiality of Milton's elegy and the consequent absence of natural human feeling. The author of *Lycidas*, he insists, simply does not sound like a man deeply afflicted with grief. The poem is insincere.

There are two main lines of defence against this charge. The first was most persuasively stated by the Cambridge critic E. M. W. Tillyard. When Milton wrote *Lycidas*, he begins by noting, the poet was still a young man himself. Like King he had intended to pursue a career in the church, like King he nurtured literary ambitions, and like King he would shortly be undertaking a sea voyage. How then, asks Tillyard, could Milton have missed the analogy between King and himself? In considering King's premature death, how could he have failed to confront the possibility that he might complete the analogy by getting drowned as well? 'Most criticism of "Lycidas" is off the mark', Tillyard therefore concludes, 'because it fails to distinguish between the nominal and the real subject, what the poem professes to be about and what it is about. It assumes that Edward King is the real whereas he is but the nominal subject. Fundamentally, *Lycidas* concerns Milton himself; King is but the excuse for one of Milton's most personal poems' (Tillyard, 79–80). At its deepest level, then, *Lycidas* is about Milton's anxieties concerning the possibility of his own premature death, akin perhaps to those expressed by John Keats in his sonnet 'When I have fears that I may cease to be / Before my pen has gleaned my teeming brain.'

The second line of defence against Johnson's charges takes exactly the opposite tack. Instead of arguing that the poem does express sincere human feeling (albeit about the author rather than about his ostensible subject), it insists that in real life grief is usually inarticulate, or at best monosyllabic like Lear's 'Howl, howl, howl, howl'. Faced with an actual bereavement, we are simply incapable of translating our feelings into words with any great eloquence. Any completely articulate expression of grief, then, is bound to be 'artificial' simply by virtue of the fact that it is articulate. Traditional forms such as the pastoral elegy thus fulfil a deep human need. Like the ritual of the funeral service itself, they provide us with a way of giving shape and order to what otherwise might have been chaotic, fragmented, and unspoken. The artifice of the pastoral convention with its shepherds, nymphs, and pastoral deities can serve as a machine for feeling with, an apparatus of lament which, if used to contain any private sorrow, at once absorbs it into the timeless.

Lycidas, according to this view, is deliberately impersonal in nature. To accept Johnson's assumption that a poem must express 'real passion' in naturalistic terms is to misunderstand the kind of poem Milton was trying to write. For, like most of Milton's early works, *Lycidas* is an occasional poem. As such, it is public, ceremonial, and formal rather than private, personal, and spontaneous. As C. S. Lewis once observed in a lecture, to complain because Milton sounds unmoved by grief in *Lycidas* is like complaining because the organist playing the funeral march does not break down in tears during the burial service.

Both lines of argument seem to me inadequate in one way or another. The first ignores the essentially conventional nature of the form in which Milton chose to cast his tribute to Edward King, while the second takes no account of the reservoir of deep feeling at the centre of the poem. I would like to propose, therefore, a reading of *Lycidas* which recognizes the poem's relationship to the generic traditions lying behind it but also admits the presence of intense personal emotion lying just beneath the marmoreal formality of the surface. It was precisely through his dialogue with the tradition of the pastoral elegy, I shall argue, that Milton first came face to face with some of his most profound and personal anxieties about the future direction of his own life.

Of all Milton's poems, we may begin by noting, *Lycidas* is the most specifically imitative. It is closely modelled on Virgil's Tenth Eclogue commemorating the death of the famous soldier, statesman, and poet Cornelius Gallus. Set in Arcadia, the legendary landscape of pastoral, this poem depicts Gallus as a lover whose mistress, Lycoris, has deserted him for another man. After a short prologue setting the scene, the formal lament begins with the following question: 'What groves, what glades were your abode, ye virgin Naiads, when Gallus was pining with a love unrequited? For no heights of Parnassus or of Pindus, no Aonian Aganippe made you tarry.' Virgil then proceeds to describe a series of visitors who arrive to comfort or to admonish Gallus as he lies at the brink of death. Apollo, the god of poetry, urges him to forget his mistress: 'Gallus, what madness is this? Thy sweetheart Lycoris hath followed another amid snows and amid rugged camps.' A rustic deity called Silvanus arrives waving fennel flowers and tall lilies. And Pan, the god of shepherds, advises Gallus to stop grieving: 'Will there be no end? Love recks naught of this: neither is cruel Love sated with tears, nor the grass with the rills, nor bees with the clover, nor goats with leaves.' But despite these admonishments, Gallus continues to love the unfaithful Lycoris, and with his last words affirms the sovereignty of Eros: 'Love conquers all; let us, too, yield to Love.'

Together with Virgil's other Eclogues this poem was a standard fixture in the curriculum of seventeenth-century grammar schools, and most, if not all, of Milton's readers would have been intimately familiar with it. Virgil, they would have learned from their school texts, wrote the poem not to celebrate the value of love but to warn us against its insidious power. 'In this Eclogue', declared one contemporary authority, 'is set forth the picture of a foolish lover, so that by looking at this picture we may learn to avoid all the occasions and enticements by which this fire is wont to be aroused' (Philip Melanchthon, *Argumenta . . . in Eclogas Virgili*, 1568, sig. G8). According to the Renaissance schoolmaster, John Brinsley, Gallus could have cured himself 'by giving his mind to the studie of Poetrie' (*Virgil's Eclogues* (1620), 98). So when Virgil asked the nymphs where they were while Gallus was dying he was really rebuking the Muses 'that they were so careless of Gallus to let him so leave his studies and to perish in such unbeseeming love'.

Other commentators, noting Gallus's career as a statesman, found in him 'a memorable example of the kind of fortune one gets at court' (Melanchthon, sig. G6r) and interpreted Virgil's questions to the nymphs in political terms. Parnassus and Pindus, wrote William Lisle, 'were the places of Gallus his retrait amongst the Muses, and the study of sweete Poesie: wherein if hee had still retir'd himselfe . . . and had not aspired to the great Imployments, and Business of state, which caus'd his ruin, hee had still liv'd' (*Virgil's Eclogues* (1628), 184). According to this view of the poem, then, Virgil's lament for Gallus was a warning against the perils of politics.

Now the resemblances between 'Eclogue X' and *Lycidas* are striking and numerous. Phoebus Apollo appears at a crucial juncture in both poems. Silvanus, wearing 'rustic glories on his brow, waving his fennel flowers and tall lilies', is clearly the prototype of Camus with his 'mantle hairy, and his bonnet sedge, / Inwrought with figures dim' (104–5). Pan, the god of shepherds, has his counterpart in Peter, the founder of the church. Both poems ask the same question: 'Who would refuse verses to Gallus?' 'Who would not sing for Lycidas?' (10). Both poems appeal to Arethusa for aid. Both poems interrogate the nymphs, though Milton substitutes British for Arcadian landmarks in his adaptation of Virgil's lines:

> Where were ye nymphs when the remorseless deep
> Closed o'er the head of your loved Lycidas?
> For neither were ye playing on the steep,
> Where your old bards, the famous Druids, lie,
> Nor on the shaggy top of Mona high,
> Nor yet where Deva spreads her wizard stream. (50–5)

And both poems conclude with the image of a shepherd rising to his feet at evening and setting off home with his flock.

But striking as they are, these formal resemblances pale beside the fundamental substantive difference between the two elegies. Virgil is mourning a lover who died of unrequited passion. Milton is celebrating the memory of a studious young virgin *who died by accident*. In accordance with the advice of commentators like Brinsley and Lisle, Edward King had abstained from the allurements of love and politics, yet he had still been cut off 'ere his prime' (8). His death simply could not be attributed, as Gallus's could, to some fatal error on his part. It was morally meaningless. Small wonder, then, that after paraphrasing Virgil's questions to the Naiads, Milton comments so bitterly:

> Ay me, I fondly dream
> Had ye been there – for what could that have done? (56–7)

If chastity, retirement, and the study of poetry were no protection against the blind Fury and her shears, what was the point of sexual and political self-denial?

The primary allusive context within which Milton chose to lament the death of his fellow student, I would therefore suggest, may have served to trigger his anxieties not about the possibility of his own premature death, as Tillyard suggested, but rather about the validity of the 'fugitive and cloistered virtue' exemplified by Edward King, and still more to the point, about the validity of the kind of life Milton himself had been leading for the past five years.

When he composed the poem in November 1637, we should remember, Milton himself was almost twenty-nine years old. Since coming down from Cambridge in 1632 he had been living with his parents, first in Hammersmith and later in the rural village of Horton, where he had immersed himself in an intensive reading programme in theology, church history, and classical literature. Thanks to the ever-increasing pressure on Puritan clergy to conform to the rites and doctrines of the Anglican church, he had probably abandoned by now his earlier intention of making a career in the church. 'Church-outed by the prelates', unmarried, unemployed, and relatively unknown, he was preparing himself to be a great poet.

A Latin poem Milton wrote to his father (*Ad Patrem*) offers a convenient window into his state of mind during this period. Rejecting 'the golden hope of making piles of money' or a career dedicated to the study of 'our nation's ill-preserved statutes' (70–1), Milton declares that he has taken refuge from 'the din of the city' in 'this deep seclusion . . . amidst the leisurely delights of the Aonian spring' where he can walk 'by Phoebus's side' (74–6). In the Arcadian security of his studies at Horton, he assures his father, he will be invulnerable to the ills which afflict those who have chosen to pursue wealth or public office: 'Away with you, sleep-destroying worries, away with you, complaints, and the squinting eye of envy with its crooked goatish look. Do not stretch your snaky jaws at me, cruel calumny. Your whole filthy gang can do me no harm: I am not within your power. I shall stride on in safety with an unwounded heart, lifted high above your viperous sting' (105–10).

This boundless confidence in the Muse's capacity to protect her followers from the ills of the world must have been severely shaken by the death of Edward King. Hence, perhaps, the particular pastoral name which Milton chose to give his dead friend. For Lycidas is the protagonist of the bleakest of Virgil's Eclogues, the ninth, in which the power of poetry to shape events is called into serious question. At the beginning of the poem Virgil's Lycidas believes that poetry can preserve pastoral life from destruction, but he soon learns that 'amid the weapons of war . . . our songs avail as much as, they say, the doves of Chaonia when the eagle comes'. As he ponders the meaningless death of another Lycidas, Milton is brought face to face with the same question as Virgil: if the Muse is not only thankless but powerless as well, then what is the point of serving her so strictly? Perhaps there was something to be said, after all, for the active life of sexual and political engagement. Far from recording Milton's discovery of his role as a divinely inspired epic poet, as some critics have recently argued (see, for example, Friedman, Wittreich), *Lycidas* calls into question the worth of the poetic vocation itself.

All three of the issues I have mentioned, chastity, retirement, and poetry, come into even sharper focus in Milton's treatment of Edward King's mythical surrogate within the poem: Orpheus. After chastising the nymphs for their absence from the scene of King's death, Milton goes on:

> What could the muse herself that Orpheus bore,
> The muse herself for her enchanting son
> Whom universal nature did lament,

When by the rout that made the hideous roar,
His gory visage down the stream was sent,
Down the swift Hebrus to the Lesbian shore. (58–63)

The allusion here is to an episode which haunted Milton's imagination for the rest of his life, the legend of Orpheus's death, as recounted, for example, by Ovid in the *Metamorphoses*. Saddened by the death of Eurydice, Ovid relates, Orpheus shunned the company of women and devoted himself to singing songs of such beauty that all nature was moved to respond. Enraged by his rejection of their amorous advances, the female followers of Bacchus drowned out Orpheus's music with their howls, and tore him limb from limb.

In the Renaissance, Orpheus's power to move the natural world with his song was interpreted as a symbol of the power of poetry to control both physical and psychological reality (see, for instance, the song which opens Act III of Shakespeare's *Henry VIII*). Like the angelic choir in the 'Nativity Ode', the Muse's son had the power to restore the age of gold with his redemptive song. In *Ad Patrem*, for example, Milton had assured his father that there was virtually nothing that human eloquence could not accomplish when divinely inspired. Poets, he claimed, were the acknowledged legislators of the world, and their original prototype was Orpheus, 'who with his singing . . . held streams spellbound and gave ears to the oak-trees and moved lifeless phantoms to tears' (52–5).

It is a far cry from this majestic figure to the helpless victim of the 'rout that made the hideous roar'. Even though they both derive from the same original myth, the Orpheus whose song could make rivers stand still in *Ad Patrem* and the Orpheus whose 'gory visage down the stream was sent' in *Lycidas* are scarcely recognizable as the same character. We could hardly have been given a more precise or vivid way of measuring the impact which the death of Edward King must have had upon Milton's conception of the poetic vocation. The youthful optimism which had animated the verse epistle to his father has collapsed in a nightmare of senseless destruction which even the Muse was powerless to prevent.

The bitter questions which immediately follow the Orpheus episode have often been called digressive, as though they had little or nothing to do with the rest of the poem (see French). But once the point of the Orpheus allusion has been recognized, it should be readily apparent that Milton's misgivings about the worth of 'the homely slighted shepherd's trade' are anything but a sudden or unexpected interruption. After the allusions to Virgil's 'Eclogue X' and the Orpheus story, the questions Milton asks are not merely relevant; they are inescapable:

Alas! What boots it with uncessant care
To tend the homely slighted shepherd's trade,
And strictly meditate the thankless muse?
Were it not better done as others use,
To sport with Amaryllis in the shade,
Or with the tangles of Neaera's hair? (64–9)

The sense of release in these lines is almost as powerful as the sense of angry bafflement they simultaneously express. The undercurrent of anxiety which has slowly been gathering strength beneath the allusions to Lycidas, Gallus, and Orpheus has finally broken through to the surface.

That it should prove to be such intensely sexual anxiety – Amaryllis and Neaera were the traditional names of the nymphs who alternately torment and gratify the shepherds in pastoral poetry – should come as no surprise after all the doubts that the Orpheus allusion in particular has tacitly directed at the ideal of chastity. For in the eyes of Milton and his contemporaries, Orpheus was an exemplar not only of poetic eloquence but also of the sexual abstinence necessary to achieve it. As Milton wrote in his *Elegia sexta*, the poet must live a life 'chaste and free from crime . . . In this way, so it is said . . . old Orpheus lived, when he tamed the wild beasts among lonely caves' (63–70). But the brutal scene on the banks of the Hebrus totally subverts this simple-minded faith in the efficacy of pastoral virtue. Despite their determination to scorn delights and live laborious days, both Orpheus and Lycidas have gone to a watery death anyway.

Small wonder, then, that Milton is led to question the fundamental principle upon which his whole conception of the poetic vocation had been based: the denial of the flesh. Perhaps, after all, the suppression of the sexual impulse was too high a price to pay for an art he might never survive to practise. In light of Orpheus's fate, would it not be more sensible to follow Volpone's advice and prove 'while we can, the sports of love' (Ben Jonson, *Volpone*, 3.7.167)? Better, surely, to risk gathering rosebuds too soon than to suffer the fate of the 'rathe primrose' (142) which, in an earlier draft of *Lycidas*, died 'unwedded', 'colouring the pale cheek of uninjoyed love'.

Milton's treatment of this issue owes a great deal of its power, I suspect, to the intimate connection that existed in his own mind between poetic productivity on the one hand and sexual abstinence on the other. For when the pursuit of one activity is made dependent upon the avoidance of some other, the first often turns out to be a sublimated version of the second. Alternatives, in other words, have a way of becoming substitutes. So by insisting that the poetic impulse could not be fulfilled unless the sexual impulse was repressed, Milton was in effect creating an equivalence between them. The Muse, Calliope, displaces Venus, and her followers make poems instead of love. It was only natural, then, that Milton should have equated the frustration of literary potentiality with the denial of sexual fulfilment. To cut off the possibility of great literary works was analogous to destroying the opportunity to beget children. As a result, the assault of the abhorred shears feels like nothing so much as a castration:

> Fame is the spur that the clear spirit doth raise
> (That last infirmity of noble mind)
> To scorn delights, and live laborious days;
> But the fair guerdon when we hope to find,
> And think to burst out into sudden blaze,
> Comes the blind Fury with th'abhorred shears,
> And slits the thin-spun life. (70–6)

In response to this crisis, the poem initially offers two provisional solutions, neither of which, I shall argue, is entirely satisfying. The first of them is provided by the god of poetry, Phoebus Apollo, who intervenes to remind his disciple that true fame is to be found not on earth but in heaven. Dramatic as it is, the god's revelation completely misses Milton's point, which had to do not so much with losing fame as with losing the chance to earn it. Confronted with the possibility that he may never be allowed to run the race for which he has spent most of his adult life training himself, what possible consolation can Milton be expected to find in the announcement that the prize-giving will take place in heaven? Divine approval of the rigour of his preparations would no doubt be gratifying, but it would hardly compensate for the utter futility of undertaking them. The solution simply does not address the problem, and one is left with a sense of incompleteness, of answers yet to be given.

The same is true of the second solution, offered by St Peter shortly afterwards. The saint's enigmatic promise that corrupt ministers will be punished by 'that two-handed engine at the door' (130) postpones the reform of the church until the day of judgement. To a sensibility as passionately concerned as Milton's certainly was with the social and political realities of his immediate situation, an eschatological solution to a contemporary problem could scarcely have been satisfying. For Milton the most important question was always: what should be done *now*? Even granted that St Michael's sword will smite the faithless herdsmen on the last day, how is the flock to be protected in the meantime? Shouldn't some attempt be made to remedy the current condition of the church, to banish false shepherds from the fold and hunt down the wolf in his lair?

That Milton was troubled by such questions appears all the more likely when we consider one of his most significant departures from the pastoral tradition: his violation of the long-standing convention whereby the sheep are delegated to the care of a companion while the shepherd himself is performing the song. For the duration of *Lycidas* no one is tending the flock. Milton is warbling his Doric lay and Edward King is dead. In the meantime, the sheepfold has been left to the mercies of ignorant and greedy hirelings. Like the lambs in the *Epitaphium Damonis* who 'go home unfed' (18) because their master is too busy singing his song to attend to them, the 'hungry sheep' (125) are starving for want of adequate nourishment. The absence of the shepherd's traditional companion thus poses a further set of questions: instead of playing on his 'oaten flute' (33), shouldn't the uncouth swain be feeding the flock himself? Were it not better done, if not to sport with Amaryllis in the shade, at least to labour for St Peter in the sheepfold? Instead of writing poems, shouldn't John Milton be ministering to the religious needs of his fellow countrymen?

For many years, of course, that is exactly what he had planned to do. According to the autobiographical preface to Book II of *Reason of Church-Government*, Milton was destined for the ministry both 'by the intentions of my parents and friends' and 'in mine own resolutions' (*YP* 1: 822). As he goes on to explain, however, 'perceaving what tyranny had invaded the Church' he had subsequently abandoned his plans to enter Holy Orders and had decided to devote himself wholly to poetry, an activity which he believed to be an alternative priesthood (see *Elegia sexta*, 65 ff.). The situation he describes in St Peter's speech must, surely, have given him some qualms about his decision. For as we have seen, the death of Edward King has brought Milton face to face with the possibility that he has been over-estimating the power of poetry. Suppose, after all, that the poet's voice was not capable of replacing the preacher's? If Orpheus's song could not allay the perturbations of the Bacchantes, what hope could Milton have of charming their seventeenth-century counterparts? Won't the lean and flashy songs of false shepherds drown out his music just as surely as the hideous roar of the Maenads overwhelmed the song of Orpheus? Perhaps Milton's mouth, too, is blind. The headnote added to the 1645 edition of *Lycidas* may affirm the prophetic efficacy of Milton's words, but in 1637 when the corrupted clergy was 'in their height' there was no reason to suppose that the Laudian church was destined to collapse so soon. St Peter's speech thus serves to intensify, not assuage, the anxieties which we saw earlier were implicit in the poem's title, and in the allusion to Orpheus. Far from being a digression, as it is still sometimes called, it touches on the central issue of Milton's entire career. In a land threatened by wolves, who will listen to the shepherd's piping?

All three issues that we have examined (chastity, retirement, and poetry) are finally resolved at two levels. So far as Edward King is concerned, the scene in heaven offers the answer:

> So Lycidas sunk low, but mounted high,
> Through the dear might of him that walked the waves;
> Where other groves, and other streams along,
> With nectar pure his oozy locks he laves,
> And hears the unexpressive nuptial song,
> In the blest kingdoms meek of joy and love.
> There entertain him all the saints above,
> In solemn troops, and sweet societies
> That sing, and singing in their glory move,
> And wipe the tears for ever from his eyes. (172–81)

Whereas Phoebus's speech failed to offer any genuine solace for the frustration of the homely slighted shepherd's sexual and poetic aspirations, this second account of divine reward restores the dead swain to an idealized landscape in which both impulses can be satisfied, albeit vicariously. For the 'blest kingdoms meek' are characterized by two qualities that were conspicuous by their absence in Jove's bleak court: 'joy and love'; joy expressed in the singing of the 'sweet societies', love in the 'nuptial' union they are celebrating. As the poem's original readers would have needed no reminding, Lycidas is attending the marriage of the lamb:

> And I heard the voice of harpers harping with their harps: And they sung as it were a new song before the throne . . . and no man could learn that song but the hundred and forty and four thousand, which were redeemed from the earth. These are they which were not defiled with women; for they are virgins . . .
>
> And I heard as it were the voice of a great multitude, and as the voice of the mighty thunderings, saying Alleluia! for the Lord God omnipotent reigneth. Let us be glad and rejoice, and give honour to him; for the marriage of the Lamb is come, and his wife hath made herself ready. (Rev. 14: 2–4; 19: 6–7)

But Milton's description of Lycidas among the saints is not only a Christian fulfilment of the scene originally adumbrated by Phoebus Apollo. It is also a celestial re-enactment of the events which took place still earlier in the poem on the banks of the Hebrus. The apotheosis of Lycidas, that is to say, bears a striking resemblance to the death of Orpheus. Orpheus's gory visage 'down the stream was sent'; Lycidas washes his oozy locks 'other streams along'. Orpheus's head was carried to 'the Lesbian shore';

Lycidas will henceforth serve as 'the Genius of the shore'. Orpheus was killed by 'the rout that made the hideous roar' because he resisted marriage; Lycidas is entertained by 'solemn troops, and sweet societies' singing a 'nuptial song'. The scene in heaven thus transfigures the scene in Thrace, harmonizing its dissonance, sublimating its violence, reviving its protagonist. In the final analysis it is the resurrection of Lycidas rather than the intervention of Phoebus that dispels the horror of Orpheus's and Edward King's deaths.

Yet for Milton himself the question remains: how is he to live out the rest of his life? At this terrestrial level, the solution comes in the final eight lines of the poem:

> Thus sang the uncouth swain to the oaks and rills.
> While the still morn went out with sandals grey,
> He touched the tender stops of various quills,
> With eager thought warbling his Doric lay:
> And now the sun had stretched out all the hills,
> And now was dropped into the western bay;
> At last he rose, and twitched his mantle blue:
> Tomorrow to fresh woods, and pastures new. (186–93)

This is one of the most extraordinary moments in English poetry. For Milton's unexpected introduction of a third-person narrator at the end of a first-person poem violates one of the oldest and most fundamental covenants governing a writer's relationship with his reader: the implicit understanding that the genre of the work will remain constant, that a play will not turn into an epic half-way through, or vice versa.

Now *Lycidas*, the headnote informs us, is a 'Monody'. The term derives, as Milton certainly knew, from Greek tragedy, where it means an ode sung by a single character. The ensuing tribute to Edward King, we are thus led to expect, will be dramatic in nature. And indeed it reads very much like a soliloquy. Up to line 185, that is to say, we seem to be in the presence of a single speaker who is addressing us in the dramatic present. But in line 186 a second, unidentified speaker suddenly emerges from the wings and with a single preterite verb thrusts the original speaker (and his speech) back into the narrative past: 'Thus sang the uncouth swain . . .' A work that began as drama has ended as narrative.

The immediate effect of this startling shift in the poem's modality is readily apparent. It establishes a clear distinction between the fictional *persona* who speaks the first 185 lines and the living poet who speaks the last eight. The question is: why does Milton suppress this distinction until the poem is almost over? Or, to put it another way, why is there no matching narrative introduction to warn us in advance that the 'uncouth swain' is a character in, rather than the author of, the elegy? Because, I would suggest, the distinction between the swain and the poet simply did not obtain at the beginning of *Lycidas*, because, initially at least, the two figures were identical. 'In this Monody', the headnote declares, 'the author bewails a learned friend', and there is nothing in the opening paragraphs of the poem to prevent us from taking this announcement quite literally. The voice we hear at the beginning of *Lycidas* is, unmistakably, the voice of John Milton himself, agonizing over his poetic immaturity, showing off his classical learning, recalling with evident nostalgia his days as a student in Cambridge.

As the poem proceeds, however, the owner of that voice gradually sheds his historical identity, and finally turns into a fictional character whose values and attitudes Milton no longer necessarily shares. The first major fissure in the speaker's identity comes with Phoebus Apollo's dramatic intervention in line 76: 'But not the praise, / Phoebus replied, and touched my trembling ears.' The tense here suddenly lapses from the dramatic present to the narrative past, and as the experience of lines 1–75 is thrust back into an earlier time-plane a gulf opens up between the speaker who remembers Phoebus's advice and the speaker who received it. The two figures are still recognizably the same person – the ears that Phoebus touches are 'my ears' not 'his' – but the second figure, enlightened by the revelations of the god of poetry, speaks from a perspective considerably broader than that of his earlier manifestation.

After St Peter's speech, the speaker's identity undergoes another transformation: it expands to include an undefined chorus of fellow mourners who share the speaker's 'false surmise' (153) and his subsequent disillusion as he remembers the true fate of Lycidas's body. The 'frail thoughts' and 'moist vows' (153, 159) belong now to a multiple consciousness – they are 'ours' rather than 'mine'. And a still more violent change occurs shortly afterwards when at line 165 the speaker dissociates himself from his fellow mourners in a change of viewpoint so extreme that more than one critic has attributed the lines that follow to a completely different character, St Michael (see Madsen). As we have seen, a yet more radical disjunction awaits us in line 186: what we took for fact turns into fiction, and the swain is transformed into a figment of Milton's poetic imagination. The entire poem, one might say, records Milton's emergence from the *persona* of the uncouth swain. *Lycidas* is one long act of disengagement.

The conclusion of *Lycidas* thus enacts in an extraordinarily vivid way an experience analogous to, though not, I think, identical with, the Christian conversion experience. As the old speaker fades away, a new speaker is born. Like a snake sloughing its skin, the singer withdraws from his song and in the final lines begins what is essentially a new song which contains the old one. It is as if the self of a dream had suddenly awakened into the self of everyday reality. The elegy and the swain who sang it recede into the distance, and we are left with the sense that we have witnessed a rebirth. In Pauline terms, Milton has cast off the old man.

But who is this new man, and what does he represent? As is so often the case with Milton's poetry, the verse form itself holds the key. Whereas the first 185 lines have been written in irregular stanzas modelled (as F. T. Prince has shown) on the Italian *canzone*, the concluding eight lines are in *ottava rima*, the major vehicle of the sixteenth-century romantic epic, the stanza not only of Tasso's *Gerusalemme Liberata* and Ariosto's *Orlando Furioso* but also of their English translations by Fairfax and Harington. As the verse form in which the amorous and military conquests of Roland and Godfrey had been celebrated, the *ottava rima* naturally invokes the turbulent world of heroic action and romantic love. The concluding stanza of *Lycidas* thus carries with it a set of values diametrically opposed to those associated with the pastoral as a genre or with Edward King as a character. After the meditative, loosely organized *canzoni* preceding it, it acts like a sudden burst of adrenalin, rousing the singer from his reverie and propelling him towards the wars of truth in which 'the true warfaring Christian' could show his mettle. The new verse form thus opens up the possibility of living an entirely different kind of life, animated no longer by the ideals of the pastoral eclogue but rather by those of the Christian epic. The course of Milton's life, it suggests, is about to undergo a drastic change.

And so, of course, it did. Rather than remaining in the cloistered calm of Horton, Milton travelled extensively in France and Italy and shortly afterwards plunged into public life in London. Rather than remaining chaste, he soon married Mary Powell. And rather than fulfilling his poetic ambitions, he devoted the next twenty years of his life to establishing himself as one of the principal public champions of the Puritan and Parliamentarian cause. *Lycidas* is thus a pivotal work in Milton's career. Like Marvell's 'Horatian Ode', it is about an epiphany. No longer content to sing his numbers languishing in the shades of Horton, Milton is about to abandon that part of himself represented by the swain, with his devotion to retirement, chastity, and poetry, in order to pursue an open-ended future of heroic and sexual engagement. For the fact is that, with the exception of a few sonnets, *Lycidas* is the last poem Milton wrote in English for the next twenty years. Not until the dying days of the Commonwealth when he was almost sixty would Milton reassume that part of his identity which he had discarded at the end of *Lycidas* and take up the mantle of the shepherd–poet 'yet once more'.

FURTHER READING

Alpers, Paul, 'The Eclogue Tradition and the Nature of Pastoral', *College English* 34 (1972), 352–71

Baker, S. A., 'Milton's Uncouth Swain', *Milton Studies* 3 (1971), 35–53

Berkeley, D. S., *Inwrought With Figures Dim* (The Hague, 1974)

Elledge, Scott, *Milton's Lycidas* (New York, 1966)

Evans, J. Martin, *The Road From Horton: Looking Backwards in 'Lycidas'* (Victoria, 1983)

Fairclough, H. R., *Virgil: Eclogues, Georgics, Aeneid 1–6* (London, 1967)

Fish, S. E., '*Lycidas:* A Poem Finally Anonymous', *Glyph* 8 (1981), 1–18 (and in Patrides, *Milton's 'Lycidas'*)

French, J. M., 'The Digressions in Milton's *Lycidas*', *Studies in Philology* 50 (1953), 485–90

Friedman, D. M., '*Lycidas:* the Swain's Paideia', *Milton Studies* 3 (1971), 3–34 (and in Patrides, *Milton's 'Lycidas'*)

Hanford, J. H., 'The Pastoral Elegy and Milton's *Lycidas*', *PMLA* 25 (1910), 403–47 (and in Patrides, *Milton's 'Lycidas'*)

Harrison, T. P., *The Pastoral Elegy* (Austin, 1939)

Hunt, Clay, *Lycidas and the Italian Critics* (New Haven, 1979)

Kirkconnell, W., *Awake the Courteous Echo* (Toronto, 1973)

Lambert, E. Z., *Placing Sorrow: A Study of the Pastoral Elegy Tradition from Theocritus to Milton* (Chapel Hill, NC, 1976)

Madsen, W. B., 'The Voice of Michael in *Lycidas*', *Studies in English Literature* 3 (1963), 1–7

Martz, L., 'Who is Lycidas?', *Yale French Studies* 47 (1972), 170–88

Mayerson, C. W., 'The Orpheus Image in *Lycidas*', *PMLA* 64 (1949), 189–207 (and in Patrides, *Milton's 'Lycidas'*)

Patrides, C. A., *Milton's 'Lycidas': The Tradition and the Poem*, rev. edn (Columbia, MS, 1983)

Pigman, G. W., *Grief and English Renaissance Elegy* (Cambridge, 1985)

Prince, F. T., *The Italian Element in Milton's Verse* (Oxford, 1954)

Ransom, J. C., 'A Poem Nearly Anonymous', in Patrides, *Milton's 'Lycidas'*

Smith, Eric, *By Mourning Tongues: Studies in English Elegy* (Ipswich, 1977)

Tillyard, E. M. W., *Milton* (London, 1930)

Tuve, Rosemund, *Images and Themes in Five Poems by Milton* (Cambridge, MA, 1957)

Wittreich, J. A., *Visionary Poetics: Milton's Tradition and his Legacy* (San Marino, CA, 1979)

Woodhouse, A. S. P. and D. Bush, *A Variorum Commentary on the Poems of John Milton*, vol. 2 (New York, 1972)

4

COLIN BURROW

Poems 1645: the future poet

On 2 January 1646, at the age of thirty-eight, John Milton printed his first collection of verse: *Poems of Mr John Milton, both English and Latin, Compos'd at Several Times. Printed by his true Copies. Poems 1645*, as it is usually known, is a carefully structured volume of extraordinarily rangy and rich poems. It begins with a section of English verse, which modulates through the opening *On the Morning of Christ's Nativity* – how better to begin? – to the sombre elegiac mode of *Lycidas*. En route from Christian beginnings to mortal endings readers are treated to some rather wobbly undergraduate jokes in the poems *On the Death of the University Carrier*, some flighty musings in *L'Allegro* and *Il Penseroso*, and an odd youthful stub, *The Passion*, which breaks off before it actually musters enough energy to describe the crucifixion, its purported subject, with a prose note: 'This subject the author finding to be above the years he had when he wrote it, and nothing satisfied with what was begun, left it unfinished.' There is a separate mini-sequence of Sonnets, English and Italian. A central section contains *A Masque Presented at Ludlow Castle* ('*Comus*'), which is followed by a separate collection of Latin poems introduced by its own separate title page.

Scattered throughout the volume are signs that the poems belong to an earlier stage of Milton's life: the translations of the Psalms are billed as having been 'done by the author at fifteen years old'; the poem *On the Morning of Christ's Nativity* gives 1629 as its date of composition; Sonnet 7 opens 'How soon hath time the subtle thief of youth, / Stol'n on his wing my three and twentieth year!' Young though he apparently was, Milton had a vast vocabulary: a run of distinctively Miltonic words – 'sheen', 'ooze', 'shining', 'glister', 'weltering' – blend with Spenserian archaisms – 'wight', 'y-pointing', 'ychained' – to compose the most idiosyncratic lexis presented in any seventeenth-century collection of lyrics, a lexis at once sparklingly fresh and decorously rooted in earlier English poetic traditions. The poems draw moods and words freely from the Shakespeare of the comedies and romances, and create a range of atmospheres which came to permeate English poetry by the mid-eighteenth century: fadings of twilight or glimmerings of dawn, numinous creatures tripping lightly on the grass, music heard in the distance, a persona who blends into a magical landscape full of echoes of the fay side of Spenser and Shakespeare. A glistering freshness emanates from even the slightest pieces, such as the 'Song on May Morning':

> Now the bright morning Star, Day's harbinger,
> Comes dancing from the east, and leads with her
> The flowery May, who from her green lap throws
> The yellow Cowslip, and the pale Primrose.
> Hail bounteous May that dost inspire
> Mirth and youth, and warm desire,
> Woods and groves, are of thy dressing,
> Hill and dale doth boast thy blessing.
> Thus we salute thee with our early song,
> And welcome thee, and wish thee long.

The flowerscape is woven into a naturally ornamented festivity. The poem has a willing mirthfulness which runs through the whole volume, through the lavish fifth Latin Elegy on the coming of spring to the sad catalogue of mourning flowers in *Lycidas*. It conveys both the freshness (it is an 'early song') and the love of song which animate many poems in the collection, and which, in 'At a Solemn Music', can forge a union between God and man: 'till God ere long / To his celestial consort us unite'. Although their vocabulary and idiom have been familiarized by generations of imitators, these poems still feel among the freshest and most musical in English; or, as Humphrey Moseley, the publisher of the volume, put it in his epistle to the reader, 'as true a Birth, as the Muses have brought forth since our famous Spenser wrote'.

Uniquely among printed volumes by seventeenth-century lyric poets, *Poems 1645* includes a separate section of equally achieved Latin verse (as Hale shows). Other poets mingled Latin poems in amongst their English verse, and several, such as Crashaw, printed separate volumes of Latin works, but Milton's collections of vernacular and Latin poems are uniquely equal in bulk and quality. The Latin poems have a separate title page and may well have been circulated separately by Milton to his continental friends and admirers. They include a book of Elegies, portentously billed as the *First* Book of Elegies (*Elegiarum liber primus*), and a separate section of miscellaneous poems *Silvarum Liber* ('Silvae' were occasional and spontaneous pieces, but might hint at greater things to come: Statius had presented his 'Silvae' as preludes to his epic *Thebaid*). Youthful poems on the gunpowder plot co-exist with anxious meditations on how best to use learning in a poetic career. Spry elegiac accounts of failed pursuits of damsels in the suburbs are followed by a severe renunciation of such Ovidian excesses. The ending of the Latin volume matches the sombre close of the English, concluding the whole twin volume with the *Epitaphium Damonis*, an elegy for the death of Milton's friend Charles Diodati, to whom the first of the sprightly Elegies was addressed. The *Epitaphium* ends the volume with a reminder that friends are ageing and dying as we read, but it also offers a more clearly focussed hope for its author's future than anything envisioned in the English poems: 'O, if I have any time left to live, you, my pastoral pipe, will hang far away on the branch of some old pine tree, utterly forgotten by me, or else, transformed by my native muses, you will rasp out a British tune' (trans. Carey, 168–71). The collection frequently reaches out to the future, promising in *On the Morning of Christ's Nativity* that 'Time will run back, and fetch the age of gold', and looking forward with the uncouth swain at the end of *Lycidas*, 'Tomorrow to fresh woods, and pastures new'; but the Latin poems at the end of the volume sketch out Milton's own poetic future. Milton's promise at the end of the volume to write a British epic resonates with the epigraph from Virgil's eclogues which appears on the title page: 'gird my brows with ivy, lest slanderous tongues should harm the future poet' (*vates futurus*). The whole volume might grandly in retrospect be seen as a prophecy of future poetic greatness: friends die, but this poet struggles forward, through pastoral, through the tangles of elegy and 'Silvae', into an unknown future, determined to make an epic.

Critics have often stressed the purposiveness of the volume. C. W. R. D. Moseley has presented it as a 'manifesto for the "New Poet"' (Moseley, 203), and Louis Martz has presented the poet of 1645 as one who all but knew he was going to write *Paradise Lost* twenty years later: 'The poems themselves have been arranged to convey a sense of the predestined bard's rising powers' (Martz, 38). The certainty which Martz's 'predestined' implies about the destiny of this relatively little-known poet (as he was in 1646) is quite misleading. Readers who picked up the volume of poems early in 1646 might have thought of Milton, if they thought of him at all, as someone who had argued in his divorce tracts for the voluntary dissolution of marriage (as Corns has argued). By this date Milton was, if a poet at all, only a future poet in the minds of the London book-buying public. He had set only his initials to *Lycidas* in 1638, and anonymous editions of *A Masque* had appeared in 1637 and of *Epitaphium Damonis* in about 1640. The year 1632 had seen the anonymous printing of his elegy on Shakespeare in the second folio. In 1645 Milton did not know he was going to write the greatest long poem in the language, and nor did his readers. The volume is haunted by the death of the vates (poet-prophet) Orpheus, who failed to revive Eurydice from death and was then torn apart by maenads. The pieces which close *Poems 1645* hint at early deaths and poetic unfulfillment. Both *Lycidas* and *Epitaphium Damonis* link the subjects of their elegies so closely with Milton – he and Lycidas (Edward King) were 'nursed upon the self-same hill' (23) – that the poems seem to be exorcizing by surrogate the death of the poet himself. *Epitaphium Damonis*, before it states Milton's intention to write a British Epic, twice echoes the word 'futurus' (about to be) from the title page of the volume, and does so in contexts which shut down futurity in the face of end-stopped grief: 'Nothing moves me, whatever it might be, nor do I have any hope for the future' ('Nil me, si quid adest, movet, aut spes ulla futuri' (92; my translation); 'Forgetting your death, I grasped too readily at future things which I had hoped for and imagined them to be present realities' ('Et quae tum facili sperabam mente futura / Arripui voto levis, et praesentia finxi'; 145–6). *Mansus*, the last poem but one in the volume, also outlines Milton's ambition to compose a British epic, but puts those ambitions only hypothetically ('*if* I ever will recall in my poems the kings of my native land'; 80), and follows them immediately with an anticipation of the poet's death. The poems are oppressed with the burden of having an unknown future, and with the contingencies and frailties which circumscribe a poet's growth. They are not simply triumphal.

Much in the volume encourages us to see Milton's poetic identity as far less centred and goal-directed, and far less readily graspable, than it is often supposed to be. First-person or implicitly autobiographical passages often intrude with an audible grate into the poems: as *Lycidas* pulls back at its end to reveal the 'uncouth swain' readying himself for fresh woods and pastures new, most readers do a double-take: who is he? A figure of the poet? When *L'Allegro* and *Il Penseroso* conclude with statements of intent ('Mirth with thee, I mean to live', or 'And I with thee will choose to live'), their readers are left wondering whether this is a direct piece of autobiography, or merely an extension of the musing exploration of varying temperaments which have run through the poems. Even the physical image of the poet presented in the 1645 volume offers only an uncertain guide to Milton's appearance: the portrait of Milton which faces the title page was engraved by one of the foremost engravers of literary figures in the period, William Marshall, whose works included portraits of Herrick, Suckling, Shirley, Donne, and Shakespeare.

It is said to represent the poet at the age of twenty. The portrait shows a poet who looks a crumpled forty, sitting by a window with a pastoral scene

1. Engraved portrait of Milton, from *Poems* 1645

in the background. Engraved below it is a jokey Greek epigram which says: 'Since you do not recognize the man portrayed, my friends, laugh at this inaccurate picture by a sorry artist.'

A reader who tried to tease out a biography of the poet from the collection would encounter similar false leads. Several poems give dates of composition, several give the age of the author when he composed them, but none gives both the year of composition and their author's age: only Milton's friends would know what he looked like, and only his friends would know how old he was in 1645. The latest age given for Milton in the volume is twenty-three; the latest date for a poem is 1638. If one put these together and did some maths it would appear that Milton was only twenty-eight (ten years younger than he actually was) when the volume appeared, and that the volume might belong to a small class of seventeenth-century collections of verse which could be called 'prodigy volumes'. These begin with Abraham Cowley's *Poetical Blossomes* of 1632, which were printed (with a portrait of the boy genius) when the poet was only sixteen. The tradition continues with the volume printed (with a portrait of the nineteen-year-old prodigy by William Marshall) by Milton's great admirer John Hall almost exactly a year after *Poems 1645*, in January 1646: Hall's volume, like Milton's, contains poems with a distinctly Cambridgey feel (he writes one Ode to his Tutor), as well as 'A Hymne' which, like *The Passion*, breaks off from its divine subject with a prose apology for the youthful incapacity of the poet. Milton's *Poems 1645* is a belated prodigy volume, in which it is never quite clear how old its author is or what precise calibrations between date of composition and the age of the poet one should make in reading the poems it includes.

Contemporary readers might also have been unsure about the political position implicit in the collection. It ostentatiously fails to match the royal opening of Edmund Waller's *Poems* 1645 ('Of the Danger of his Majesty (being Prince) Escaped at the Road at St Andere') or of Cowley's *Silvae* ('On his Majesties Return out of Scotland'). The volume also audibly lacks poems of the kind beloved by the Cavalier poets Suckling, Lovelace, and Waller, which urge on a mistress immediate sensual enjoyment in the *carpe diem* tradition (the only such appeal in the volume is uttered by the wicked enchanter Comus: 'List Lady be not coy, and be not cozened / With that same vaunted name virginity'; 736–7). But there are poems which give off rather different signals. The elegies on the death of the Bishop of Winchester, Lancelot Andrewes, and on the death of the Marchioness of Winchester, seem to tally with the note on the title page that the songs 'were set in music by Mr. Henry Lawes Gentleman of the King's Chapel and one of his Majesties Private Musick' in giving a royal and aristocratic slant to the collection. That association of the poems with royal music may, however, not be Milton's: it may derive from the publisher Humphrey Moseley, who made the same claim on the title page to his volumes of poems by Carew (1651) and Suckling (1648). Moseley is often said to be a 'royalist' printer, who was attempting through the 1640s to build up a canon of English and predominantly royalist writers (Reed). But this picture is not quite accurate: by 1645 Moseley had published only a handful of literary works, and had specialized in texts which presented the political outlooks of their authors as multi-faceted to the point of self-contradiction. The volume of poems by Edmund Waller, for instance, which Moseley printed in 1645, contained poems of unequivocal praise for the King, but also included at its end a set of Parliamentary speeches in which Waller spoke vehemently against arbitrary extensions of the royal prerogative and in favour of the authority of Parliament. One of Moseley's most prolific authors, James Howell, also published a volume in 1645 in which he defended himself against the charge, levelled against him by the militant Puritan William Prynne, that he was 'No friend to Parliaments, and a malignant'. Howell (in prison at the time, so he may have had his fingers crossed as he wrote) professed that Parliament was 'the bulwark of our liberties, the main boundary and bank which keeps us from slavery'. What makes Milton's *Poems 1645* characteristic of a Moseley volume in this period is not its crypto-royalism but its political multi-facetedness. Milton in *Poems 1645* is a plural and a shifting subject, who invites his readers to drift through the past twenty years as they read.

In reading the 1645 collection we should try to see the poems it includes in a double perspective: as the Milton who compiled the volume in 1645 would have wanted them to appear, with a retrospective purpose to them; but also as the more vulnerable, transient things which they might have appeared to be when they were composed. The collection generates a continual stress – sometimes a counterpoint, and sometimes outright discord – between the time of the poems' composition and the time of their printing, between the Milton who wrote them, and the Milton who put them together into a collection in 1645. What the collection offers, that is, is not a manifesto or a self-portrait of a rising bard but a group of poems which explore the many past impulses, half-formed ideas, personal connections and ties which make up the life of a poet, and on which he attempts to impose a retrospective structure. And, as we shall see, they do not simply present the personal history and development of John Milton: they also offer windows onto the processes of history over which Milton had little or no control.

The first poem in the volume, *On the Morning of Christ's Nativity.*

Composed 1629, illustrates the artful interplay of time-schemes which runs through the volume. The poem is continually and carefully confusing about tenses. The first lines of the poem take us back to the morning of the nativity with 'This is the month, and this the happy morn / Wherein the Son of heaven's eternal King, / Of wedded maid and virgin mother born, / Our great redemption from above did bring.' It does, that is, until one thinks about it: the events of the Christian ritual year have the unique quality of being at once single historical actions (Christ was born on one day) and repeated ritual events (Christ is born on every day on which Christmas is celebrated). The opening of the poem inconspicuously exploits this temporal uncertainty: on *this* (present) morning Christ *did* (in the past) bring us our redemption. Its tenses evoke a ritual occasion, in which a present moment is a memorial re-enactment of the past. Oscillations of tense are an ingrained feature of the poem: 'But peaceful was [past] the night / . . . While birds of calm sit [present] brooding on the charmed wave' (61–8). Across those shifting tenses intrudes the ambition of the poet, who directly intervenes in the drama, in order to 'prevent' (that is 'precede') the arrival of the Wise Men with the gift of a poem to Christ. This gesture is the first of the many moments in the volume when a representation of the poet in the first person seems intrusive, as he barges in to disrupt the nativity scene with a precocious zeal to get in first. It is an early sign of the kind of genius which wrote *Paradise Lost*, in which getting in first, going back to the origins of the human world before any other epic poet, is a vital indicator of poetic originality. But to a reader who read the volume early in January 1646, at a time when it was traditional to exchange New Year's gifts with friends and patrons (Suckling's collection of poems from 1648 begins with such a gift: 'On New Year's day 1640: To the King'), the poet's eagerness to present his redeemer with a gift before anyone else does would have an immediate timeliness: this poem, and perhaps this volume, are a New Year's gift to his God. As that reader proceeded through the volume, the time of the poem's composition would take on a new particularity: the sixth Latin Elegy to Diodati describes how the poet is writing a poem on the birth of his saviour (79–90), which is presumably *On the Morning of Christ's Nativity*. The simple phrase 'This is the month, and this the happy morn' has layer upon layer of temporal referents: it at once evokes a universal series of Christmas mornings, and the particular morning in 1629 when John Milton huddled over his desk in order to write both a vernacular poem to his saviour and a Latin poem to his best friend.

Readers of the collection in early 1646 also might feel that *On the Morning of Christ's Nativity* had a particular relevance to the year in which they read the poem. In June 1645 Charles I had been defeated by

Parliamentarian forces at the battle of Naseby. In January 1645 the Westminster Assembly had issued their *Directory for Public Prayer*, which was designed to replace the *Book of Common Prayer* (described as 'no better than an idol'). The *Directory* austerely stated that 'Festival days, vulgarly called Holy days, having no warrant in the Word of God, are not to be continued.' Christmas festivities theoretically came to an end with those words. The banishment of the pagan gods with which 'On the Morning' concludes ('And sullen Moloch fled, / Hath left in shadows dread, / His burning idol all of blackest hue'; 205–7) might to some readers in 1645–6 have echoed the sober words of the *Directory*: old feasts, old forms of worship, are no more, leaving only pure hymns to Christ composed by a holy poet who seeks to imagine the unsullied origins of Christian history. The headnote's reminder of 1629, the year in which Charles I forcibly dissolved Parliament and began his period of personal rule, might also set up disturbing resonances for many readers. Time had come full circle: the old gods were finally banished.

This takes us to the critical and more or less unanswerable question about the 1645 volume: are the politics and attitudes of Milton in the 1620s and 30s the same as, or continuous with, those of Milton in the 1640s? Many critics have felt that there is a clear line of continuity between the godly poet of the 1620s and the anti-episcopal pamphleteer of the 1640s (among these are Norbrook, Wilding, and Revard; Loewenstein has presented a more flexible and sceptical view of the politics of Milton's early verse). This is probably how Milton, the editor of the collection, wished it to appear: the volume invites us to see the shadowy outlines of Milton the anti-episcopal poet in his earlier self. So the Psalm paraphrases 'done by the author at fifteen years old' might take on new, prophetic resonances in light of the defeat of Charles I at the Battle of Naseby. In 1646 Psalm 114 might seem pointedly topical: 'When the blest seed of Terah's faithful son [The Israelites, children of Abraham], / After long toil their liberty had won'; 1–2). Psalm 136 might become a hymn of triumph for those zealous Protestants who believed that the elect nation had triumphed at Naseby: 'His chosen people he did bless / In the wasteful wilderness. / . . . In bloody battle he brought down / Kings of prowess and renown' (56–62). Even the end of *At a Solemn Music* could be whirled into the excited and uncertain mood of 1646:

> O may we soon again renew that song,
> And keep in tune with heaven, till God ere long
> To his celestial consort us unite,
> To live with him, and sing in endless morn of light.
>
> (*At a Solemn Music*, 25–8)

That phrase 'ere long' is re-echoed at the end of 'Upon the Circumcision', when Christ 'seals obedience first with wounding smart / This day, but O ere long / Huge pangs and strong / Will pierce more near his heart' (25–8). That surge forwards from the present ('this day') to the future ('ere long') is part of the early Miltonic style, always urging us to see the future in the instant. Some of Milton's readers might have put down the volume with a sense that the 'vates futurus' referred to on the title page was not just an 'up and coming poet' but a 'poet-prophet of the future', whose early verse foreshadows the apocalyptic excitements of their age and of the end of time to come. The headnote appended to *Lycidas* in *Poems 1645* would play to the same expectations: 'In this monody the author bewails a learned friend, unfortunately drowned on his passage from Chester on the Irish Seas, 1637. And by occasion foretells the ruin of our corrupted clergy then in their height.' Readers are invited to recall the hey-day of Archbishop Laud's persecution of those like the Puritans William Prynne, John Bastwick, and Henry Burton, who sought to resist his imposition of ceremonial forms of worship on the English Church (Leonard), and to see young Milton as a poet who prophetically foresaw the ultimate destruction of Laudian modes of worship. The Latin Elegy to Thomas Young, which boasts it was written when Milton was eighteen, would confirm this impression of early reforming zeal, as Milton attacks the English Church for forcing Young into exile. Reforming readers might find 'something like prophetic strain' (*Il Penseroso*, 174) sounding through much of the volume.

But Reforming readers were only some readers. The volume also acknowledges an absolutely vital principle of Miltonic poetics, outlined in *Areopagitica* only a year or so before, that the various dispositions of readers shape what they read. *Poems 1645*, like many texts from the early to-mid-1640s, is keenly aware that works written while a country is at war should accommodate a variety of readerly attitudes. Its strategy of giving poems dates early in Milton's career has a double effect which accommodates this divided readership. On the one hand it makes the poems seem precociously and perhaps even prophetically aware of problems in the Church and State; on the other it might for some readers detach the poems from the present and invite a less zealous form of reading, a reading in which the many anticipations of the future in the volume intersect with the anxieties of a young poet trying to form a poetic oeuvre, who is never quite sure of where he is going or of what lies ahead of him. *Poems 1645* continually plays off these two forms of 'future poet' against each other: the one is nervy, musing, tentative, aware that the world is all before him but unsure what it contains; the other is sturdily founded on hindsight, a visionary of the future state of the nation. The first group of poems on

religious themes, time, and the music of the future allows the poet-prophet to dominate, but they are followed by a brief group of vernacular elegies on the Marchioness of Winchester and on the University Carrier. These have a leisurely destinylessness, as Milton quips, quips, and quips again about the busyness of Hobson, the University messenger, and muses on the early death of the Marchioness. The volume includes the voice of Milton the chirpily nervous undergraduate as well as that of Milton the rising prophet, the voice of Milton the lover of May mornings (traditionally occasions for rural merry-making of the kind attacked by many reforming Puritans), as well as that of Milton the prophet of the ruin of our corrupted clergy.

The companion poems *L'Allegro* and *Il Penseroso* also sit uneasily beside firmly teleological or prophetic readings of the volume. *Il Penseroso*, the longer and later poem, is sometimes seen as the victor in an internal debate within Milton as to whether to sport with Amaryllis in the shade or get on with the serious business of becoming famous. But the poems function both as a dialectical forward-looking structure and also as simple companion mood pieces, musing undirectedly, and perhaps impersonally, on different modes and moods of living. Their fluidly associative syntax invites readers to entertain options which do not crystallize into firm choices, tricking one along into moving through a landscape before one even knows one is in motion. *L'Allegro* in particular does not push a reader even into determining the grammatical subject of many of its clauses, as Milton enjoys the loosely associative forms of articulating sentences which are available in the vernacular. In Latin one has to decide on the noun with which any given participle will agree in gender and number; in English one can devolve that choice onto a reader. The syntax of *Il Penseroso* has slightly less of the drifting parataxis of its companion poem, and so can be read as evoking a greater sense of resolve (as Greene has argued). Even here, though, those slippery participles still give a delightsome freedom to its persona and its reader alike:

> And missing thee [the nightingale], I walk unseen
> On the dry smooth-shaven green,
> To behold the wandering moon,
> Riding near her highest noon,
> Like one that had been led astray
> Through the heaven's wide pathless way.
>
> (*Il Penseroso*, 65–70)

It takes an effort of whimsy to take 'Riding' as referring back to 'I' rather than its more obvious consort the moon, but it can be done. And 'Like one'? Is that the moon or the melancholy man? Whimsically free reading, in which persons absorb themselves into landscapes and resolved syntactic formations dissolve, is what these two poems encourage, as mazy syntax evokes meandering thoughts (as Fish has argued). *Il Penseroso* prepares for the sequence of Sonnets which follow it: the apostrophe to the nightingale as 'Sweet bird that shunn'st the noise of folly, / Most musical, most melancholy! / Thee chantress oft the woods among, / I woo to hear thy even-song' (61–4) anticipates Sonnet I, 'O nightingale, that on yon bloomy spray / Warblest at eve, when all the woods are still'. This creates a continuity of mood, but it does not necessarily mean that Milton has grown up, or that *Il Penseroso* has emerged as the victor in its dialogue with *L'Allegro*. The voice of *Il Penseroso* runs on through the sequence, but it does not drown the sprightly bustle of the lovers in Milton's Italian sonnets, which follow it, nor does it dominate the erotic visions of delight evoked in the early Latin Elegies.

Indeed, when one arrives at the Ovidian elegies and sees them presented as 'The First Book of Elegies', one could imagine a whole new start for the poet, as someone who plans a multi-volume collection which engages with the achievements of Ovid and Propertius as erotic poets (a case put forward by Revard). The Elegies are followed by a retractation ('Haec ego mente') which says they are the product of youthful folly; but while they are being read their most striking feature is their tendency to modulate from the mournful tones of Ovid's elegiac poems of exile, the *Tristia*, to the cheerier mode of his *Amores* (see, for example, Elegy 1, 17–24; Elegy 3, 2; Elegy 4, 1–4). *L'Allegro* is not banished by *Il Penseroso* and his unconvivial final retreat into his hermitage to work away at developing 'something like prophetic strain' does not terminate the sociability of the volume. The voice of the poet-prophet does not exclusively dominate this fitfully moody collection of poems.

Poems 1645 encourages its readers to respond to its poems historically, but it offers a multiplicity of histories – of Milton himself, of the Church, of the State – against which to read them. The ten Sonnets, for example, are given neither dates nor titles. Their readers have to assume responsibility for assigning dates to them. This is clearly deliberate: the Trinity Manuscript (Milton's own heavily revised manuscript volume of works in progress) gives several sonnets headings which associate them with particular periods or events, but none of these appears with the printed versions (see Patterson's account of this aspect of the Sonnets). The flow of the mini-sequence of Sonnets in 1645, from the initial poem on the Nightingale to the final sonnet addressed to 'Daughter to that good Earl, once president / Of England's Council', moves the genre towards political themes and topical allusions. Political references could be unpicked, but only by very astute readers: the allusion in the final sonnet to 'the sad breaking of that Parliament' refers back to 1629, when Charles I dissolved Parliament. That year is also the date of the very first poem in the collection. But the suggestion that the political events of 1629 played a formative role in Milton's poetic development is left implicit: history is for readers to supply. Sonnet 8 begins 'Captain or colonel, or knight in arms, / Whose chance on these defenceless doors may seize, / If deed of honour did thee ever please, / Guard them, and him within protect from harms.' In the Trinity Manuscript this poem is entitled 'When the assault was intended to the city. 1642', making the poem a record of the fears of a Parliamentarian poet in the face of Royalist advances on London in 1642. Even in the Trinity Manuscript, though, Milton fought shy of dating the poem precisely: he scored through the date, as though determined to widen the temporal reference of the poem, leaving it to stand as a general witness to the vulnerability of poetry rather than as a record of a precise personal event. The volume allows and encourages a variety of readers to trace from it a variety of stories about Milton's life, about the role of poetry within a polity, and about the times through which the poet lived and wrote.

One of the many mini-narratives which run through the volume is a narrative of change in Milton's attitudes to his native land. *Epitaphium Damonis*, as we have seen, ends the volume with a promise of a British epic. Milton's conception of Britain, however, changed profoundly in the poems written between 1626 and 1638. In the earlier poems nationhood is a relatively simple matter: Milton is the poet of London, who occasionally ventures into the suburbs to see British beauties airing their charms (Elegy 7), and who casually uses 'British' as a synonym for 'English'. The poems from the 1620s present Britain as a sceptred isle girded off from contact with Catholic Europe by impregnably sheer white cliffs, and united in its opposition to the plots of a satanically inspired Pope. These poems evoke, in rather Anglo-centric form, the united kingdom of 'Great Britain' into which James VI and I attempted to fashion England and Scotland at his accession to the English throne (*In Quintum Novembris*, 1–6, 25–6; Elegy 4, 87–8). The later poems register a slight but very significant change in this outlook. Milton's Britain becomes much larger and much more varied in its texture and local flavour. There is room in the *Epitaphium Damonis* for the Orkneys, the Tamar, the Thames, the Humber, and the Trent (175–8); in *Lycidas* the eye of the poet stretches out into the Irish Sea to the West, up to the Hebrides in the North, and down to St Michael's Mount at the tip of Cornwall in the South, as though pacing the boundaries of the multiple kingdom of Britain. There is also a growing sense of the importance of place: *L'Allegro* and *Il Penseroso* do not simply muse on different lifestyles, but move through a complex mingling of urban and pastoral landscapes, watching different kinds of labour and sampling the atmosphere of halls, theatres, and fields. Each place, too, in the poems from the 1630s, is quite likely to have its own local genius or tutelary deity: this might be the hermit sunk in his cell who ends *Il Penseroso*, the spirit of Sabrina, goddess of the Severn, who finally releases the lady in *A Masque*, the Genius of the Wood in *Arcades*, or the 'genius of the shore' into which Lycidas is transformed (von Maltzahn, 100–3). This interest in the spirits of particular regions has its roots in the Spenserianism of the volume: Michael Drayton's Spenserian epic *Poly-Olbion* had toured the country relating the many local myths and spirits which hide in the contours of the British landscape.

Increasingly, however, Milton's landscape gods are gods not just of places but of boundaries: *A Masque* was composed for the inauguration of the Earl of Bridgewater as President of the Council of Wales, the most administratively integrated region of Stuart Britain. Bridgewater began his jurisdiction over the Marches between England and Wales in a period when there were debates as to whether the Church Courts, under the auspices of Archbishop Laud, or the Council of Wales should have jurisdiction over sexual offences such as rape or marital infidelity (Marcus (1986), 203–7). The figure of Sabrina, the chaste goddess of the river which spans the boundary between England and Wales, is a symbol not only of the contested boundaries of the Earl's authority, but also of the edgy margins of Englishness. Emerging from the collection's later poems is an imaginative regionalism that is a profound element both of their literary effect and of their political mood. (*Lycidas* would simply not be the same poem if it were not set looking outwards on the most awkward British boundary of all, the sea between Chester, perched on the edges of England, and Ireland.) Through the early decades of the seventeenth century there was a widespread shift of imaginative focus from the King to the country, its local habits and its local landowners (as Helgerson has argued). There was also increasing stress within the extremely disunified tripartite kingdom which made up Great Britain – so much so that many historians regard Charles I's mismanagement of the needs of the four kingdoms over which he ruled (England, Ireland, Scotland, and Wales) as the principal cause of the English Civil War (as Russell attempts to show). Milton is only dimly aware of these stress-points in the nation: by 1649 he would have seen the war as the consequence of the tyrannical attempts of Charles I to over-ride Parliament and to impose alien forms of worship on the consciences of English people, rather than as the consequence of tactical mishandling of a multiple kingdom. But in the poems of the 1630s he is intimately sensitized to the growing significance of location and of locality, and of the stressful margins of his none too unified kingdom. When he claims in *Epitaphium Damonis* and in *Mansus* to be about to write a British epic, therefore, we should be sceptical: *Poems 1645* leaves traces of evidence that he was becoming increasingly aware that Britain was too multiple an entity, containing too many regions and too many distinctive habitats, to have one unifying epic poem written about it. One can read *Poems 1645* as trumpeting the plans of a rising poet for a British epic, in *Mansus* and *Epitaphium Damonis*; but one can also see it as a volume which testifies to the growing difficulty of uniting the nation around a single British theme.

So what sort of Milton emerges from the volume? Is he an author who presents a majestic over-view of his past work and a masterful prospect of his future work as a *vates* (poet/prophet)? Is he presenting himself as an apocalyptically minded radical Protestant from the very start of his career? I have suggested that these retrospective refashionings of Milton's career are a part, but only a part, of what we should find in the volume. We should treat them with just as much scepticism as we do Milton's efforts to present himself as a programmatic defender of liberty in *The Second Defence* (1654) or as a man of unqualified chastity and industry in *An Apology for Smectymnuus* (1642): his autobiographical images are always fashioned by the demands of occasion. We should also find in the volume multiple lesser narratives about Milton: Milton the would-be Ovidian elegist, Milton the Cambridge poet, dutifully composing elegies to order, Milton the Italian *petrarchista*, Milton the lover of music, Milton the young poet anxiously uncertain about what he will do next. The volume presents a tangle of those multiple filaments which make up someone's identity: there are the past projects which came unstuck (a shot at being an elegiac poet, a very brief sonnet sequence); the poems in which a young poet confronted the overbearing magnitude of his task (*The Passion*); the threads of gratitude and friendship which extend a person's life into the aspect of community (*Ad Patrem*, *Ad Carolum Diodatum*). Many points in the collection evoke less personal histories that interact with the development of Milton the poet: the collapse of consensus within the English Church; the growing stress between London and the localities of the scarcely united kingdom. All of these histories press down on, and many of them conflict with, the shaping intelligence of the editor of *Poems 1645*. No one can honestly look backwards at their life and see it as singly pointing to the present, and Milton was no exception. Milton encourages his godly readers to hear 'something like prophetic strain' emerging from his early works. But his complex readership was as diverse as his early opinions were complex. He allows his readers to hear a multiplicity of voices and political concerns in this volume of poems belatedly presented by this middle-aged prodigy.

FURTHER READING

Corns, Thomas N., 'Milton's Quest for Respectability', *Modern Language Review* 77 (1982), 769–79

Fish, Stanley E., 'What It's Like to Read *L'Allegro* and *Il Penseroso*', *Milton Studies* 7 (1975), 77–99

Greene, Thomas M., 'The Meeting Soul in Milton's Companion Poems', *ELR* 14 (1984), 159–74

Hale, John K., 'Milton's Self-Presentation in Poems . . . 1645', *Milton Quarterly* 25 (1991), 37–48

Helgerson, Richard, *Forms of Nationhood: The Elizabethan Writing of England* (Chicago, 1992)

Leonard, John, '"Trembling Ears": The Historical Moment of *Lycidas*', *Journal of Medieval and Renaissance Studies* 21 (1991), 59–81

Loewenstein, '"Fair offspring Nurs't in Princely Lore": On the Question of Milton's Early Radicalism', *Milton Studies* 28 (1992), 37–48

Maltzahn, Nicholas von, *Milton's History of Britain: Republican Historiography in the English Revolution* (Oxford, 1991)

Marcus, Leah S., *The Politics of Mirth: Jonson, Herrick, Milton, Marvell and the Defense of Old Holiday Pastimes* (Chicago and London, 1986)

Unediting the Renaissance: Shakespeare, Marlowe, Milton (London and New York, 1996), ch. 6

Martz, Louis, *Milton: Poet of Exile*, 2nd edn (New Haven and London, 1986), ch. 2

Moseley, C. W. R. D., *The Poetic Birth: Milton's Poems of 1645* (Aldershot, 1991)

Norbrook, David, *Poetry and Politics in the English Renaissance* (London, 1984)

Patterson, Annabel, 'That Old Man Eloquent', in *Literary Milton*, ed. Diana Treviño Benet and Michael Lieb (Pittsburgh, 1994), 22–44

Postlethwaite, Norman, and Gordon Campbell, eds., 'Edward King, Milton's "Lycidas": Poems and Documents', *Milton Quarterly* 28 (1994), 77–111

Reed, John Curtis, 'Humphrey Moseley, Publisher', *Oxford Bibliographical Society Proceedings and Papers* 2 (1927–30), 57–142

Revard, Stella, *Milton and the Tangles of Neaera's Hair: The Making of the 1645 Poems* (Columbia and London, 1997)

Russell, Conrad, *The Causes of the English Civil War* (Oxford, 1990)

Wilding, Michael, *Dragon's Teeth: Literature in the English Revolution* (Oxford, 1987), 7–27

5

MARTIN DZELZAINIS

Milton's politics

In 1740 the Whig scholar Francis Peck announced that *Tyrannicall-Government Anatomized*, published (according to its title page) on 30 January 1642 by order of a committee of the House of Commons, was in fact the work of John Milton. Peck argued, plausibly enough, that the publication of this work (which he identified as a translation of *Baptistes* (*The Baptist*), a Latin tragedy by the sixteenth-century humanist George Buchanan) was a riposte to Charles I's notorious attempt to arrest five members of the Commons in January 1642. For the leading figures in Buchanan's dramatization of the conspiracy against John the Baptist 'might be understood to answer to the characters of divers great persons then living'. The seventeenth-century counterparts of King Herod, his wife Herodias, and the High Priest Malchus, were King Charles I, Queen Henrietta Maria, and Archbishop Laud; and the play thus formed a stinging commentary on the 'league between LAUD & HENRIETTA MARIA, to extirpate the protestant religion in the three nations'. Peck's case for declaring Milton the translator rested on Milton's 'utter aversion for the clergy of every sort', on the fact that 'LIBERTY was MILTON'S darling subject', and on 'the republican turn of his principles' (Peck, 271, 274, 276, 279).

Although Milton admired Buchanan (like all true poets, he was 'bitterly hostile to tyrants'), denounced the king's attempt to arrest the five MPs for opposing 'his tyrannous proceedings', and rehearsed the allegation that the queen 'had quite perverted him' in religion, he was not the translator of *Baptistes* (*YP* 3: 379, 422; 4: 592). Moreover, Peck's Milton – anticlerical, libertarian, republican – was obviously fashioned in the mould of the eighteenth-century commonwealthsmen. However, before we simply dismiss Peck as misled by his Whig convictions into seeing what he wanted to see, it is worth reflecting how similar our own assumptions and procedures are to his. After all, Milton was until relatively recently credited with a string of prose works from the early 1640s, none of which is actually by him (these include works listed in Wing, *Short-Title Catalogue*, M2107, M2130, M2131, M2176, M2179; see also *CM* 18: 634–9). The driving force behind these mis-attributions was the sense that someone as committed as Milton was to the parliamentary cause *ought* to have been more visibly active on its behalf from the start.

Something similar is going on when Milton's earlier writings – *On the Morning of Christ's Nativity*, *A Masque* ('*Comus*'), *Lycidas*, even *L'Allegro* – are combed for their 'latent radicalism'. Although there are 'undoubtedly discontinuities and inconsistencies in Milton's canon', such that we cannot speak of 'a simple, steadfast march towards the Puritan revolution', it remains the case that these radical 'ideas', while 'not yet fully articulated', are nevertheless 'implicit in the major works of the 1630s' (Norbrook, 17, 238–9; see also Hill, 41–52, 80–92; Wilding, 7–27). We are also urged to scrutinize Milton's 'unpublished writings, where he could express himself more freely', a procedure which reveals that his 'radicalism developed remarkably early'. One example of these 'precocious' tendencies is the Commonplace Book entry made between 1640 and 1642, where Milton's reading of Machiavelli's *Arte della guerra* yields the subversive conclusion that a 'commonwealth is to be preferred to a monarchy' (Worden, 1990, 231–2; *YP* 1: 421; see also Patterson, 226–32). Milton went much further here than he was prepared to in print. In *Of Reformation* (May 1641), he confined himself to praising the classical ideal of a mixed constitution, 'where under a free, and untutor'd *Monarch*, the noblest, worthiest, and most prudent men, with full approbation, and suffrage of the People have in their power the supreame, and finall determination of highest Affaires' (*YP* 1: 599). As Thomas Hobbes later pointed out, however, even Charles I's closest advisers 'thought the government of England was not an absolute, but a mixed monarchy' (Hobbes, 114).

It is also likely that the 'latent radicalism' we are supposed to bring to the surface will turn out on inspection to involve one or other of Peck's trio of Whig principles: anticlericalism, devotion to liberty, republicanism. Indeed, it would be a strange account of Milton's politics that contrived to leave them out of the picture. This essay will accordingly examine how they informed some of Milton's prose writings of the 1640s, the decade which, it is agreed on all sides, was crucial to his development. But it is also important to remember that, as J. G. A. Pocock puts it, a text can and must be seen as both an action and an event (23), and that in these writings Milton was usually *doing* something.

The first thing we should note, however, is that Milton, notwithstanding this alleged radicalism, in fact never published anything directly supporting the Long Parliament's war effort. It is true that he addressed several of his works to the two Houses, and even eulogized the parliamentary leadership. In *An Apology against a Pamphlet* (April 1642), for example, he hailed them as 'reformers of the Church and the restorers of the Commonwealth', who deserved to be 'saluted the Fathers of their countrey; and sit as gods among daily Petitions and publick thanks' (*YP* 1: 924, 926). But such commendation was part of a campaign on the issue of the episcopacy that had run its course by the time hostilities commenced. Indeed, for the first year of the war, when Parliament came perilously close to defeat, Milton published nothing at all – hence the string of mis-attributions showing him in a posture of commitment that he himself failed to assume. And when he finally did break silence, in August 1643, it was not to offer ideological support or to issue a call to arms, but to set out *The Doctrine and Discipline of Divorce*.

One reason for this marked reticence is that Milton's faith in the parliamentary leadership was eroded during the first two years of the conflict, and had collapsed altogether by the later 1640s. The first signs of this erosion are inscribed in the differences between the two editions of *The Doctrine and Discipline of Divorce*. The 1643 version is an austere, forbidding exercise in scriptural exegesis, which Milton later claimed to have composed in self-imposed intellectual isolation:

> *For that I ow no light, or leading receav'd from any man in the discovery of this truth, what time I first undertook it in* the doctrine and discipline of divorce, *and had only the infallible grounds of Scripture to be my guide, he who tries the inmost heart, and saw with what severe industry and examination of my self, I set down every period, will be my witnes.* (*YP* 2: 433)

Several features of the text bear out this claim. Not only does Milton cite a mere handful of modern authorities, but he also observes a self-denying ordinance in relation to classical learning (for the exceptions, see *YP* 2: 240, 252, 327, 340, 348). In short, there is nothing to suggest that the work was written by a formidable classicist, or that he wrote while a civil war was raging, still less that his side was sliding towards defeat. By contrast, the 'revis'd and much augmented' version published in February 1644 is a far more accessible and outward-looking text. Here Milton draws on a full range of modern writers, deploys his classical learning with real ostentation, and equips the work with a signed prefatory address, 'TO THE PARLAMENT OF ENGLAND, with the ASSEMBLY', in which he politicizes the case for divorce.

In the address, as Ernest Sirluck observes, Milton floated 'a remarkable and pregnant analogy between divorce and political reformation' (*YP* 2: 152):

> He who marries, intends as little to conspire his own ruine, as he that swears Allegiance: and as a whole people is in proportion to an ill Government, so is one man to an ill mariage. If they against any authority, Covnant, or Statute, may by the soveraign edict of charity, save not only their lives, but honest liberties from unworthy bondage, as well may he against any private Covnant, which hee never enter'd to his mischief, redeem himself from unsupportable disturbances to honest peace, and just contentment: And much the rather, for that to resist the Magistrat though tyrannizing, God never gave us expresse allowance, only he gave us reason, charity, nature and good example to bear us out. (*YP* 2: 229)

The case for divorce was thus stronger than that for resistance to tyranny, for which there was no express scriptural warrant. But Sirluck's claim that it is 'excellent rhetoric for Milton to relate his own case to that of Parliament' is debatable (*YP* 2: 152). After all, the analogy could easily be reversed to suggest the opposite conclusion: that resistance was just as *un*acceptable as divorce. In John M. Perlette's view, Milton had unwittingly produced an argument which, because 'of the strength of contemporary opinion against divorce', had the 'potential for a severely debilitating embarrassment of the very Parliament to which Milton was appealing' (209).

Nevertheless, it is unlikely that the politicization of divorce was a naïve miscalculation on Milton's part. His awareness of the weight of received opinion explains why the 1644 address takes the form of an attack on customary ways of thinking. Only a Parliament freed from custom and error could be expected to embrace an enlightened measure in the teeth of popular opposition. The strategy of the preface is accordingly to project a vision of statesmanship upon the two Houses which Milton hopes they will exhibit in adopting his proposal. Hence his praise of their 'eminence and fortitude', 'steddy hands', 'magnanimous example', and 'couragious and heroick resolutions' (*YP* 2: 226, 230, 231, 233).

Of course, these standards might prove too exacting, as Milton conceded when pouring scorn on the argument that Moses permitted but did not approve of divorce:

> But for a Judge, but for a Magistrate the Shepheard of his people to surrender up his approbation against law & his own judgment to the obstinacie of his heard, what more un-Judge-like, more un-Magistrate-like, and in warre more un-commander-like? Twice in a short time it was the undoing of the Roman State, first when *Pompey*, next when *Marcus Brutus* had not magnanimity anough but to make so poore a resignation of what they approv'd, to what the boisterous Tribunes and Souldiers bawl'd for. Twice it was the saving of two the greatest Common-wealths in the world, of *Athens* by *Themistocles* at

> the Sea fight of *Salamis*; of *Rome* by *Fabius Maximus* in the *Punick* warre, for that these two matchlesse Generalls had the fortitude at home against the rashnes and the clamours of their own Captains and confederates to withstand the doing or permitting of what they could not approve in the duty of their great command. Thus farre of civill prudence. (*YP* 2: 314–15)

This is a remarkable excursion: unthinkable in the 1643 *Doctrine*, still striking in the thoroughly classicized 1644 version. Its account of how the 'saving' or 'undoing' of commonwealths hinged upon the moral qualities of their generals suggests that Milton had been pondering the fortunes of the parliamentary war effort. In terms of 'civill prudence', however, it encapsulates his views on political leadership as such.

Milton derives his analysis of these examples from perhaps the most influential classical work of moral philosophy: *De Officiis* (*On Duties*) by the Roman statesman and orator Cicero. In Book I of *De Officiis*, Cicero considers the four cardinal virtues in turn. Of these, fortitude, which is made up of courage and greatness of spirit or magnanimity (*magnitudo animi*), is the one he deems indispensable for those holding public office, since they will never be able to discharge their military or civic duties satisfactorily if they lack it (see Cicero 1975, 72–9 (I.22.72–23.77)). As Milton puts it, whereas the lack of 'magnanimity anough' proved ruinous in the case of Pompey and Brutus, Themistocles and Fabius 'had the fortitude' required to triumph (for Cicero on Themistocles and Fabius, see Cicero 1975, 76–7, 84–7, 110–11 (I.22.75, I.24.85, I.30.108)).

The acid test of fortitude is the capacity to withstand moral and political pressure; that is, to do something or to forebear doing it, as the case may be, in the face of popular opposition. It was the test Pompey and Brutus failed when they yielded 'to what the boisterous Tribunes and Souldiers bawled for'. And it was the test passed by Themistocles and Fabius when they withstood 'the rashnes and the clamours of their own Captains and confederates'. The application to the 1644 *Doctrine* itself is clear: if Parliament wishes to demonstrate that it is truly possessed of fortitude, it can do so most conspicuously by withstanding the clamours and bawlings of those who oppose the reform of divorce.

This was the Ciceronian template against which Milton henceforth measured the performance of the Long Parliament, and, in *Of Education* (June 1644), it was found sadly wanting (see Dzelzainis 1995b). The tract appeared a month before Parliament secured its first important victory, at Marston Moor, so the sense of malaise afflicting the parliamentary cause had not yet lifted (and would descend again by the autumn, when the advantage was surrendered). Accordingly, one of the timely features of the system Milton outlines is to teach students

> To know the beginning, end, and reasons of politicall societies; that they may not in a dangerous fit of the common-wealth be such poor, shaken, uncertain reeds, of such a tottering conscience, as many of our great counsellers have lately shewn themselves. (*YP* 2: 398)

Preventing any such collective failure of nerve would require a programme of instruction laced with 'seasonable lectures and precepts' on 'true fortitude', for only if the students' resolve were stiffened in this way would they prove 'renowned and perfect Commanders in the service of their country' and 'stedfast pillars of the State' (*YP* 2: 398, 409, 412).

In some ways, *Areopagitica* (November 1644) embodies an even sharper rebuke. As the full title reveals, it is cast in the form of *A Speech of Mr. John Milton for the Liberty of Unlicenc'd Printing, To the Parlament* – rather as if a prefatory address (the genre employed by Milton again in the preliminaries to *The Judgement of Martin Bucer*, August 1644) had subsumed the text it would otherwise have introduced. Milton's aim was to persuade the two Houses to rescind their Licensing Order, which they had passed in June 1643, imposing pre-publication censorship. As part of his deliberative strategy, he once more praised their 'undaunted Wisdome', 'indefatigable vertues', and 'magnanimity' (*YP* 2: 487–8). The hope was that a consciousness of their greatness of spirit would lead them to embrace a role larger than that of enforcing the small-minded regulations of pre-publication censorship.

When Milton comes to explain how and why he wrote the tract in the first place, however, he strikes a note of disenchantment. Reflecting on his Italian journey, he says the intellectuals he met envied his being 'born in such a place of *Philosophic* freedom, as they suppos'd England was, while themselvs did nothing but bemoan the servil condition into which lerning amongst them was brought' – a depressing state of affairs symbolized by the figure of Galileo, 'grown old, a prisner to the Inquisition' (*YP* 2: 537–8). But any complacency induced in Milton (or the reader) is shattered upon his discovering

> that what words of complaint I heard among lerned men of other parts utter'd against the Inquisition, the same I should hear by as lerned men at home utterd in time of Parlament against an order of licencing; and that so generally, that when I had disclos'd my self a companion of their discontent, I might say, if without envy, that he whom an honest *quaestorship* had indear'd to the *Sicilians*, was not more by them importun'd against Verres, then the favourable opinion which I had among many who honour ye, and are known and respected by ye, loaded me with entreaties and perswasions; that I would not despair to lay together that which just reason should bring into my mind, toward the removal of an undeserved thraldom upon learning. (*YP* 2: 539)

Milton identifies himself with, but modestly does not name, Cicero, who served as quaestor (treasury official) in Sicily in 75 BC, and who five years later appeared (for the only time) as prosecutor, presenting the case against Gaius Verres, the Sicilians' former governor. This suggests that the usual classification of *Areopagitica* as a deliberative oration (one urging or dissuading from some course of action) is incomplete: it is also a forensic performance in which Milton is the prosecutor and the Licensing Order the accused. After all, in the opening sentence Milton reminds the two Houses that they constitute the 'High Court of Parlament' (*YP* 2: 486). This being the case, the allusion to Cicero's *Verrine Orations* also embodies a political threat. When prosecuting Verres in the Extortion Court, Cicero reminded the court that it was itself on trial; unless it found Verres guilty, it would succumb to the pressure for reform from outside. So that when Milton tells the two Houses that 'they who counsell ye to such a suppressing, doe as good as bid ye suppresse your selves', he is not only alerting them to the self-contradiction involved in professing to uphold freedom of speech while actually promoting censorship, but also warning them about its potentially catastrophic political consequences (*YP* 2: 559).

Milton's argument is also informed by at least two of the traits highlighted by Peck: his anticlericalism and his devotion to liberty. Although he professes in *Areopagitica* to value 'the liberty to know, to utter, and to argue freely according to conscience, above all liberties', what he says about the freedom of speech also applies to other civil liberties. It should be noted, however, that Milton accepts that these freedoms are to be defined negatively; that is to say, that citizens are free only to the extent that they are not constrained by the state into conducting themselves otherwise than they would have done if left to their own devices. He further accepts that the state can legitimately 'take notice of' books which are 'either blasphemous and Atheisticall, or Libellous'. Anyone who publishes a work does so subject 'to the hazard of law and penalty', and the appropriate 'remedy' for books which are 'found mischievous and libellous' is the 'fire and the executioner'. In short, Milton has no quarrel with the proposition that the state should 'have a vigilant eye how Bookes demeane themselves, as well as men; and thereafter to confine, imprison, and do sharpest justice on them as malefactors' (*YP* 2: 492, 494, 531, 560, 569).

Milton, however, posits an exchange in which a stationer is asked 'who shall warrant' the 'judgement' of the licenser: 'The State Sir, replies the Stationer, but has a quick return, The State shall be my governours, but not my criticks' (*YP* 2: 534). This presupposes that one can differentiate between objectionable and unobjectionable actions by the state, without specifying how this is to be done. But it is likely that Milton, in common with the other neo-Roman writers recently discussed by Quentin Skinner, drew a clear line between due process and discretionary power. For these writers,

> the difference between the rule of law and government by personal prerogative is not that the former leaves you in full possession of your liberty while the latter does not; it is rather that the former only coerces you while the latter additionally leaves you in a state of dependence. (Skinner 1998, 83n)

While coercion may circumscribe your freedom, being in a state of dependency means that your freedom may at any moment be taken away altogether, in which case you are no better off than a slave; indeed, to be dependent in this way *is* to be a slave (see Skinner 1998, 39–53, 82–9). And since licensing, which required books to be approved prior to publication, necessarily involved the exercise of discretionary power, it follows that its effect was to nullify freedom of speech and erect a 'tyranny over learning'. Henceforth, Milton protests, authors would be 'captivat under a perpetuall childhood of prescription'; licensers would 'let passe nothing but what is vulgarly receiv'd already'; and 'every acute reader' would reject such approved matter (*YP* 2: 514, 533, 534, 539). Even a text that emerged physically unchanged in every last detail from the process of licensing would still be compromised. Nor would it make any difference if the system were to be administered with all possible efficiency by the most enlightened and indulgent officials. For what Milton opposes is not the way the system is managed, but the fact that it is in place at all.

Another reason for Milton's intransigence is that the Licensing Order was identified with the Presbyterians' attempts to enforce religious orthodoxy. Although Milton supported their attack on the bishops in the early 1640s, their hostile response to his writings on divorce proved a turning point. The 'Post-script' to Martin Bucer hints darkly at attempts to silence him issuing from 'this working mystery of ignorance and ecclesiastical thraldom, which under new shapes and disguises begins afresh to grow upon us', while in *Areopagitica* he bluntly concludes 'that Bishops and Presbyters are the same to us both name and thing' (*YP* 2: 479, 539).

But this parting of the ways also had a political dimension. As Richard Tuck argues, 'what Calvinists all over Europe in the late sixteenth and early seventeenth centuries wished to do was to *capture* their monarchs and use their power to establish a Presbyterian system of Church government' (203). The intervention of the Scots in the Civil War followed precisely this trajectory. Their terms for fighting on the parliamentary side were set out in the Solemn League and Covenant (September 1643). The first article anticipated 'the reformation of religion' on Presbyterian lines; the second the 'extirpation' of popery and prelacy; and the third the 'endeavour . . . to preserve and defend the King's person and authority' (Gardiner, 268–9). This determination to uphold a monarchical element in the constitution explains why Charles I himself was able to sign the Covenant in December 1647, with the Scots agreeing to re-enter the conflict on his side (see Gardiner, 347–52). For many in the New Model Army (the force created when Parliament reorganized its armies in 1645), this renewed resort to arms sealed the king's reputation as a 'man of blood' (for the scriptural and emotional resonances of this phrase, see Crawford). When it appeared that Charles, despite another defeat, was close to being restored to the throne on Presbyterian terms, the Army purged Parliament on 6 December 1648, so clearing the way for the so-called Rump to stage his trial and execution in January 1649.

Although Milton had taken the Covenant, and still spoke in March 1645 of his '*addicted fidelity*' to the Long Parliament, '*that supreme and majestick Tribunal*', when the parliamentary coalition disintegrated in 1648 he at once sided publicly with the Army and the Rump (*YP*: 578, 582). The first of his purely political writings, *The Tenure of Kings and Magistrates* (February 1649), was thus occasioned by the downfall of those whom he had once addressed as '*so grave a Magistracy sitting in Parlament*' (*YP* 2: 584). Now Milton hailed the new 'Parlament and Military Councel' as the joint repository of 'wisdom, vertue, and magnanimity', and as an example to 'future ages' of 'a better fortitude, to dare execute highest Justice' (*YP* 3: 237–8).

While *The Tenure* is often assumed to be just a regicide tract, this is not quite how it identifies itself on the title page:

> PROVING, *That it is Lawfull, and hath been held so through all Ages, for any, who have the Power, to call to account a Tyrant, or wicked* KING, *and after due conviction, to depose, and put him to death; if the ordinary* MAGISTRATE *have neglected, or deny'd to doe it. And that they, who of late so much blame Deposing, are the Men that did it themselves.* (*YP* 3: 189)

The issue is not whether a tyrant may be brought to justice, but *who* is to execute justice when the 'ordinary MAGISTRATE' (the Long Parliament) has failed to act. In such a case, Milton undertakes to prove, it is open to 'any' to take the initiative. But why did Milton frame his thesis in just these terms? The answer lies in the nature of the arguments brought to bear by the Presbyterians ('they, who of late so much blame Deposing').

Naturally, the Presbyterians invoked the Covenant, and much of *The Tenure* is given over to deriding their interpretation of it; not only had the king violated it, but so too had they in waging war upon him (see *YP* 3:

194, 229–33, cf. 324–5, 493–7, 593–6; for Milton's attack on Presbyterian hypocrisy, see Dzelzainis 1989). But they also relied on what for three quarters of a century had been one of the most powerful ideologies in Europe: the Calvinist theory of resistance (see Skinner 1978, 2: 189–348). One of the chief concerns of this theory was to spell out who was and was not qualified to resist a tyrant. No one denied that, in the case of a foreign usurper, even a private person could take up arms. But when a legitimate ruler descended into tyranny, resistance was confined to inferior magistrates. These distinctions were usually illustrated by reference to Old Testament examples of those who overthrew oppressors of Israel. Some of these were uncontroversial – either private persons resisting a foreign usurper, or magistrates resisting domestic tyrants. But others, such as Moses, Ehud, and Jehu, were problematic, since they could be taken as instances of private resistance even to domestic tyranny. These cases were typically disposed of in two stages. The first was to suggest that they were not actually private persons at all. As the Huguenot author of the *Vindiciae contra tyrannos* (*A Defence of Liberty against Tyrants*, 1579) argued, since we know that they received an extraordinary calling from God, 'not only do we not consider them private individuals, but we deem them to be more powerful than any ordinary magistrate'. The second stage was to warn that, while God 'may raise up a few extraordinary liberators from time to time', this was a matter about which 'we should be especially sober and circumspect'. Anyone claiming to be 'inspired by the holy spirit . . . should certainly make sure that he is not puffed up with pride, that he is not God to himself, that he does not derive that great spirit for himself from within himself' (62).

Drawing on their Calvinist heritage, the Presbyterians now argued that since the Army had originally been raised by the Long Parliament (the inferior magistrate) it was merely a collection of private persons, and hence incapable of any political initiative. The king was also manifestly not a foreign usurper liable to individual resistance. Nor could any of the scriptural examples of individual resistance to domestic tyranny be invoked without opening up the issue of extraordinary callings. Those who claimed that their actions were sanctioned by these examples would in effect identify themselves as antinomians (that is, not bound by the law), as gods to themselves, and so place themselves politically beyond the pale.

Milton simply erases these distinctions. There is no difference between foreign usurpers and domestic tyrants, and, even supposing that there were, Ehud slew the legitimate but tyrannous Eglon without any 'speciall warrant' from God, acting solely 'on just principles'. Whereas Jehu did have a 'speciall command to slay *Jehoram*', this did not make his action 'less imitable', since it was 'grounded so much on natural reason' that God's command served but to 'establish' its 'lawfulness' (*YP* 3: 213–16). Milton had already announced in the preface to the 1644 *Doctrine* 'that to resist the highest Magistrat though tyrannizing, God never gave us expresse allowance' (*YP* 2: 229). He now spells out the implications of this remark: in seeking 'what the people lawfully may doe' in dealing with a tyrant, 'I suppose no man of cleare judgement need goe furder to be guided then by the very principles of nature in him' (*YP* 3: 212).

Milton thus sought to legitimize exactly what the Calvinist theory was designed to preclude: intervention by the individual in the sphere of politics. He then moves on to demolish another Calvinist orthodoxy concerning the sword of justice, or power to punish. The standard view was that this power ultimately came from God, and was exercised only by those in public authority. As the author of the *Vindiciae* puts it, 'private individuals have no power, fill no magistracy, hold no command nor any right of the sword' (60). Milton, by contrast, treats this power as human in origin, since it belonged to each individual in the state of nature. But although this power had been entrusted to 'thir Deputies and Commissioners', it was still open to anyone to punish those who degraded themselves – as tyrants did – to the subhuman level of 'a savage Beast' or 'common pest' (*YP* 3: 199, 206, 212). Before Milton, the only writers to advance claims comparable to these were Buchanan, in *De Iure regni apud Scotos* (*The Right of the Kingdom in Scotland*, 1579), and the anonymous author of the *Discours politiques* (1574), works which Milton may well not have known (see Skinner 1978, 2: 305–6, 342–4). Underlying all three accounts, however, is the analysis of tyrannicide in Cicero's *De Officiis*, where he asserts, in anti-Caesarist vein, that all such 'fierce and savage monsters in human form should be cut off from what may be called the common body of humanity' (Cicero 1969, 298–9 (III.6.32); see II.7.23–8.28, III.4.19, III.21.82–5).

There is a point, however, when Milton begins to leave the Calvinist agenda behind altogether. He of course remains adamant that kings 'turning to Tyranny . . . may be . . . lawfully depos'd and punish'd'. But he also suggests that this is merely an obvious and incontestable exertion of the people's 'power, which is the root and sourse of all liberty, to dispose and *oeconomize* in the Land which God hath giv'n them, as Maisters of Family'. It is, for Milton, beyond question that the people may 'reassume' their power 'if by kings or Magistrates it be abus'd', but he immediately adds the rider that they may also 'dispose of it by any alteration, as they shall judge most conducing to the public good'. Since 'the King or Magistrate holds his autoritie of the people', it follows that they should be able to 'retaine him or depose him though no Tyrant, meerly by the liberty and right of free born men, to be govern'd as seems to them best'. Should they lack this 'natural and essential power of a free Nation', however, then they are 'no better then slaves and vassals born, in the tenure and occupation of another inheriting Lord. Whose government, though not illegal or intolerable, hangs over them as a Lordly scourge, not as a free government; and therfore to be abrogated' (*YP* 3: 198, 206, 212, 237). In passages such as these, the topic of resistance is being overtaken by a preoccupation with the right of self-determination.

Part of the explanation is that Milton was addressing not just one revolutionary act, the regicide, but a whole sequence, which began in December and which was still in progress in February when *The Tenure* appeared. The exact shape of the new regime was far from being established (the act declaring 'a Commonwealth and Free State', for example, was not passed until 19 May 1649; see Gardiner, 388). But Milton's engagement with the topics of freedom and slavery does point towards (in Peck's resonant phrase) 'the republican turn of his principles'. Milton's most striking claim is that even a government which conducts itself neither illegally nor intolerably may be removed in that this innocuousness alone does not save the government from being despotic. For, conversely, it is only when you are in no way subject to the discretionary power of another that you can be said to be free. This was a point on which Milton continued to insist with great vehemence. As he later remarked, merely being unmolested in enjoying the fruits of one's labours was no more than 'what the Turks, Jewes, and Mores enjoy under the Turkish Monarchy'. It was an absolutely minimal condition, without which 'no kind of Government, no Societie, just or unjust, could stand'. Accordingly, there was 'somthing more, that must distinguish free Government from slavish' – this 'somthing more' being simply the rule of law in the absence of any discretionary powers whatsoever (*YP* 3: 574). The shape of the argument is familiar because it is what underpinned Milton's attack on the Licensing Order in 1644. In 1649, however, it is more a matter of Milton's starting to lay down the guidelines to which the Commonwealth would have to conform if it was also to prove a Free State.

Arguably, Milton never again published a work quite as radical as *The Tenure*. Indeed, he himself seemed to retreat from some of its anarchic implications in the second edition (what Sirluck regards as a difficulty 'inherent' in Milton's thought is actually a shift between the two editions (212, 214)). The works which followed were notable in different ways: *Eikonoklastes* (October 1649), for the unmatched ferocity of its assault on Stuart kingship; or *Pro Populo Anglicano Defensio* (February 1651), which established Milton's European reputation, for the brilliance with which it defended the Commonwealth; or *The Readie and Easie Way to Establish a Free Commonwealth* (February and April 1660), published on the eve of the Restoration, for the fullness and coherence with which he expounded his republican beliefs. But in many ways the decade he spent serving successive regimes in his capacity as Secretary for Foreign Tongues recapitulated his experience as an outsider during the 1640s: an initial period of enthusiasm followed by a grim slide towards disenchantment. The turning point this time was Cromwell's installation as Lord Protector in December 1653. As Blair Worden has shown, Milton's panegyric on Cromwell in *Pro Populo Anglicano Defensio Secunda* (May 1654) is a 'two-edged instrument' which, as we saw with the addresses of the 1640s, praises in order to advise and caution (Worden 1998, 258). Like many other republicans – James Harrington, Marchamont Nedham, and Sir Henry Vane – Milton was driven into opposition by the increasingly pronounced monarchical tendencies of the later Protectorate (on which see Woolrych, and the essays by Worden, Dzelzainis, and Armitage in part 3 of *Milton and Republicanism*). In fact, he may never in his life have lived under a political regime of which he could wholeheartedly approve.

FURTHER READING

Armitage, David, 'John Milton: Poet against Empire', in *Milton and Republicanism*, ed. David Armitage, Armand Himy, and Quentin Skinner (Cambridge, 1995)

Cicero, *De Officiis*, translated by Walter Miller (Cambridge, MA, and London, 1969)

Philippics, translated by Walter C. A. Ker (Cambridge, MA, and London, 1975)

Crawford, Patricia, '"Charles Stuart, That Man of Blood"', *Journal of British Studies* 16 (1977), 41–61

Dzelzainis, Martin, 'Milton, Macbeth, and Buchanan', *The Seventeenth Century* 4 (1989), 53–66

'Milton and the Protectorate in 1658', in *Milton and Republicanism*, ed. Armitage et al.

'Milton's Classical Republicanism', in *Milton and Republicanism*, ed. Armitage et al.

Gardiner, S. R., ed., *The Constitutional Documents of the Puritan Revolution 1625–1660*, 3rd edn (Oxford, 1979)

Hill, Christopher, *Milton and the English Revolution* (London, 1977)

Norbrook, David, *Poetry and Politics in the English Renaissance* (London, 1984)

Patterson, Annabel, *Reading Between the Lines* (London, 1993)

Peck, Francis, *New Memoirs of the Life and Poetical Works of Mr. John Milton* (London, 1740)

Perlette, John M., 'Milton, Ascham, and the Rhetoric of the Divorce Controversy', *Milton Studies* 10 (1977), 195–215

Pocock, J. G. A., 'Texts as Events: Reflections on the History of Political Thought', in *Politics of Discourse: The Literature and History of Seventeenth-Century England*, ed. Kevin Sharpe and Steven N. Zwicker (Berkeley, 1987)

Sirluck, Ernest, 'Milton's Political Thought: The First Cycle', *Modern Philology* 61 (1964), 209–24

Skinner, Quentin, *The Foundations of Modern Political Thought*, 2 vols. (Cambridge, 1978)

Liberty before Liberalism (Cambridge, 1998)

Tuck, Richard, *Philosophy and Government 1572–1651* (Cambridge, 1993)

Vindiciae contra tyrannos, ed. and translated George Garnett (Cambridge, 1994)

Wilding, Michael, *Dragon's Teeth: Literature in the English Revolution* (Oxford, 1987)

Woolrych, Austin, 'Milton and Cromwell: "A Short But Scandalous Night of Interruption"?', in *Achievements of the Left Hand: Essays on the Prose of John Milton*, ed. Michael Lieb and John T. Shawcross (Amherst, MA, 1974)

Worden, Blair, 'Milton's Republicanism and the Tyranny of Heaven', in *Machiavelli and Republicanism*, ed. Gisela Bock, Quentin Skinner, and Maurizio Viroli (Cambridge, 1990)

'Milton and Marchamont Nedham', in *Milton and Republicanism*, ed. Armitage *et al.*

'John Milton and Oliver Cromwell', in *Soldiers, Writers and Statesmen of the English Revolution*, ed. Ian Gentles, John Morrill, and Blair Worden (Cambridge, 1998)

6

THOMAS N. CORNS

Milton's prose

Milton's prose is probably most often approached from the perspective of its political content or its polemical skill. Much of it was written during the period 1641–60, when Milton contributed to the attack on episcopacy, opposed more conservative Puritans by redefining the relationship between church and state and by proposing changes to the law relating to the right to publish, and defended the English republic while justifying the execution of Charles I. Milton's mastery of the arts of persuasion makes a rewarding study in itself, and demonstrably the political values explicitly developed in the prose suffuse his major poems in pervasive and complex ways. Martin Dzelzainis offers an account of Milton's politics in chapter five; my principal concern is with Milton's style, though, as we shall see, issues of style cannot be separated from politics.

All of Milton's earliest vernacular prose, that is, his five antiprelatical tracts of 1641–2, and some of his pamphlets of 1643–5, including what is currently his most popular, *Areopagitica* (1644), are characterized by a flamboyant style, rich in imagery and lexically innovative to the point of playfulness. In it, metaphors and similes abound, often in great elaboration. Thus, near the start of his first pamphlet, *Of Reformation* (1641), we encounter this wholly typical paragraph, in which Milton is talking about how the Reformation revitalized Christianity after the error and torpor of Catholicism:

> But to dwell no longer in characterizing the *Depravities* of the Church, and how they sprung, and how they tooke increase; when I recall to mind at last, after so many darke Ages, wherein the huge overshadowing traine of *Error* had almost swept all the Starres out of the Firmament of the *Church*; how the bright and blissful *Reformation* (by Divine Power) strook through the black and settled Night of *Ignorance* and *Antichristian Tyranny*, me thinks a soveraigne and reviving joy must needs rush into the bosome of him that reads or heares; and the sweet Odour of the returning *Gospell* imbath his Soule with the fragrancy of Heaven. Then was the Sacred BIBLE sought out of

> the dusty corners where prophane Falshood and Neglect had throwne it, the *Schooles* opened, *Divine* and *Humane Learning* rak't out of the *embers* of *forgotten Tongues*, the *Princes* and *Cities* trooping apace to the new erected Banner of *Salvation*; the *Martyrs*, with the unresistable *might* of *Weaknesse*, shaking the *Powers* of *Darknesse*, and scorning the *fiery rage* of the old *red Dragon*. (*YP* 1: 524–5)

With every sentence and almost every clause interwoven with simile or metaphor, the passage seems a riotous profusion. And the passage is profuse, though there is also in it something of an organizing principle that we can identify. The central image – of the darkness of ignorance and the light of truth – is familiar, perhaps to the point of triteness. But note how Milton revitalizes it, invoking, brilliantly reworked, an image from the Book of Revelation: the 'traine' of Error plainly invites identification with the 'great red dragon' whose 'tail drew the third part of the stars of heaven, and did cast them to the earth' (Rev. 12:3–4). Milton, however, strengthens and makes more concrete the image he adopts. The 'tail' or 'traine' (the words are synonymous in seventeenth-century English) is rendered 'huge' and 'overshadowing'; the rather flaccid 'drew' (the translation favoured also by the Geneva Bible) gives way to the vigorously precise 'almost swept'. Such embellishment is wholly characteristic of the way in which biblical imagery is transformed into a livelier Miltonic idiom in the early prose. As we shall see, Milton later becomes more restrained, and more deferential to the minutiae of biblical phraseology.

The polarity of light and darkness is jostled before and after by diverse images, of the organic growth of '*Error*' and of 'the sweet Odour of the . . . *Gospell*'. However, the clash of allusion here is perhaps more apparent than real. Once more, the biblical intertext is at work, and again the imagery is millenarian or chiliastic. The image, '*Depravities* [which] . . . sprung, and . . . tooke increase', has its remote origins in the parable of the tares (Matt. 13), with its promise of the 'furnace of fire' for the nefarious. Again, the perfume metaphor evokes another image from Revelation, of the 'four and twenty elders' who fall down before the Lamb with 'golden vials full of odours, which are the prayers of saints' (Rev. 5:8).

Thereafter the schema peters out, overwhelmed by the fertility of the Miltonic imagination. Milton, especially in his early prose, develops a way of speaking about abstract notions as if they were concrete and even living things. Here, 'Falshood' and 'Neglect', which are abstract nouns, have 'throwne' (a verb usually used only with concrete agents) the Bible into 'dusty corners'. Similarly, '*Learning*', also abstract, is conceptualized as a still-glowing coal, to be 'rak't' from the remains of ancient languages.

Milton, especially in the early 1640s, seems reluctant to argue his case at levels of high abstraction. Instead, his imagination clothes the concepts and sets them in action. Good and evil, learning and ignorance, appear as mighty forces in physical conflict.

The next image is biblical, but not apocalyptic. '*Princes* and *Cities* trooping apace to the new erected Banner of *Salvation*' is a vigorous reworking of the psalmist's 'We will rejoice in thy salvation, and in the name of our God we will set up our banners' (Ps. 20:5), once more with a characteristic refinement of detail. The paradox – a less common figure of speech and habit of thought in Milton than, for instance, in Sir Thomas Browne – of 'the unresistable *might* of *Weaknesse*' is Pauline (2 Cor. 12:7–10), as is the phrase '*Powers of Darknesse*' (Col. 1:13). The paragraph then ends with a further reference to the apocalyptic image with which we started, the 'old *red Dragon*' of Revelation (12:3).

The function of the biblical allusion is complex. Obviously, Milton's imagination is shot through with the language and images of the Bible, and his perception of recent history and current affairs is shaped by its models and archetypes. Among Protestants in an age of faith this is not surprising, though such an insistent iteration of biblical reference is probably commoner among those of Puritan leanings. Milton's imagination functions in a fertile dialectic with the Scriptures. As biblical images and expressions shape and inform his perception of the present world, so too his creative genius transforms them into material appropriate to the brilliant texture of his early prose. Moreover, the crises of mid-century England, rendered in terms of the abiding struggles between the godly and the impious, and of the final struggle of the apocalypse, present one phase of the larger conflict – one phase, and yet, perhaps, the final phase: the millenarian perspective, so common among his revolutionary contemporaries, is central to much of Milton's excited thinking of the early 1640s.

Modern readers are often staggered by the length and complexity of the sentences in Milton's prose. However, we must beware of over-reacting to an element of style which is fairly commonplace in serious, erudite prose of the middle of the seventeenth century. The first sentence of the quoted paragraph from *Of Reformation*, from 'But to dwell no longer' to 'the fragrancy of Heaven', is well over a hundred words long. Such sentences are quite frequent in Milton's vernacular prose. In most of his pamphlets, roughly 20 or 25 per cent of the sentences have over a hundred words each, a remarkably large proportion by modern standards. However, many learned prose writers contemporary with Milton show a similar predilection for length. And their style, of course, is sometimes labelled 'Latinate' or 'periodic' or 'Ciceronian'.

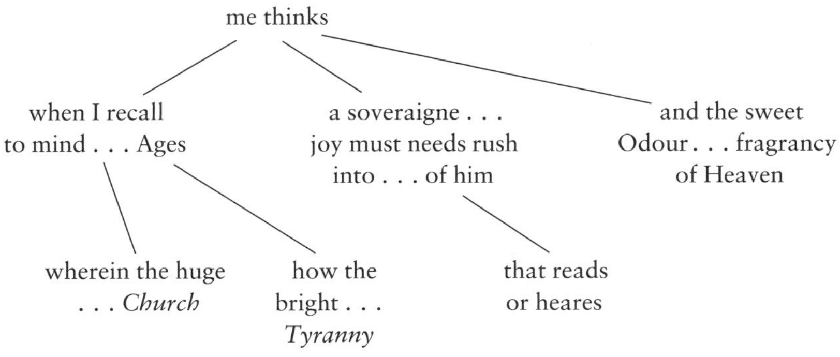

Diagram 1

A consciousness of Ciceronian stylistic practices may in some way have seemed to legitimize such syntactical copiousness. Cicero's political prose no doubt constitutes an active intertext to Milton's writing in a complex way, and Milton's fashioning of himself as an orator merits consideration (Dzelzainis, 1997). Stylistically, though, 'Ciceronian' remains a misleading term that disguises the community of Milton's practice with that of other educated English writers. Long sentences are so much the norm for serious English prose of the time, and are so pervasive among such a diversity of authors, that a specific, foreign, literary influence or model seems improbable.

Nor can the actual structure of such sentences composed by Milton accurately be termed 'Ciceronian' or 'periodic' in the sense of following a Latin rather than early-modern English word-order or clausal organization. For, in complex sentences, Milton rarely postpones completion of his main clause to the end; nor does he in the example here being considered. Rather, in a wholly English way, the sentence grows through the accretion of phrases and subordinate clauses, which are appended to the material on which they depend either in front (sometimes termed 'left-branching'), behind (right-branching), or in the middle (embedded). And subordinate material often supports further subordinate clauses or phrases.

Thus, the sentence we are considering, though it contains some minor elements of syntactical ambiguity, can probably best be conceptualized as in diagram 1. The main clause, the impersonal verb 'me thinks', supports, to its left, one immediately dependent clause, and to its right a further two. (The complex syntactical structure 'But to dwell . . . increase' can probably best be regarded as ancillary to 'me thinks'.) Two of the subordinate clauses in turn support yet further subordinate material, the effect being a sort of pyramid of syntactical subordination. Such constructions are by no means uniquely Miltonic, but statistics show that he is likelier than his contemporaries to produce main clauses which support a multiplicity of directly subordinate clauses and that these clauses in their turn are likelier to support further subordination. However, the distinctiveness of these features, as characteristics of Miltonic prose, should not be overstated. Syntactical complexity is widespread among prose writers contemporary with Milton, and I would suggest that much of our pleasure in reading many of them comes as we appreciate their muscular syntactical control – the ways in which they achieve expressions of causality and purpose, temporal precision, and refined definition by means of such subordinate structures. I add parenthetically that Milton's commitment to such syntactical complexity extends to his mature poetry, and that the sort of structures analyzed here are frequently found in his epics. In this respect, however, he differs quite sharply from the preferences and practices of contemporary *poets*; paradoxically, the most distinctive feature of his late poetic style is the common ground it shares with syntactical aspects of his prose, though of course its stylistic merits extend far wider than that (Corns 1990, 10–49).

Milton's prose vocabulary, like his syntax, has sometimes been regarded as Latinate, that is, characterized either by frequent use of Latin loanwords, or else by the use of 'naturalised' but etymologically Latinate words in non-English senses redolent of their Latin significations. But neither aspect of this view about his vocabulary can be substantiated. Milton himself is openly critical of what he considers to be the redundant or affected coinage of words from classical languages (Corns 1982, 69–70). For example, when, in *Eikon Basilike* (a pamphlet offered to the public as the executed Charles I's apologia) Milton finds the newly coined 'Demagogues', he indignantly objects to 'the affrightment of this Goblin word; for the King by his leave cannot coine English as he could Money, to be current' (*Eikonoklastes*; *YP* 3: 393). In this instance, of course, the word proved a useful addition to the English wordstock.

Milton himself neologizes fairly freely, and he readily extends the signification of established vocabulary, but displays no affected classicism or inkhorn enthusiasm for learned ostentation. Most of his coinings come through the usual processes of word-formation in English, through prefixation and suffixation and through compounding. Much of it is quite unremarkable. In *Of Reformation* we find, for example, 'griffonlike', 'Africanisms', and 'unmonopolizing' (*YP* 1: 543, 568, 613). But sometimes the neologizing is to brilliant stylistic effect, as in the following ironic flourish against the appetitiveness of the prelates, in which Milton wonders how a bishop's lifestyle in the primitive church would be perceived by a Caroline bishop: 'what a rich bootie it would be, what a plump endowment to the many-benefice-gaping mouth of a Prelate, what a relish it would give to his canary-sucking, and swan-eating palat' (549). There is something strikingly absurd, grotesque, overblown in Milton's compounds here, but it is appropriate to his decorum of abuse. Moreover, by coining words for the bishops' conduct, Milton cleverly suggests the habituation of their actions: sybaritic feasting and mawing down pluralities are what they persistently do; so there ought to be words for their practices.

When Milton does borrow directly from classical tongues, it is usually either a technical term or else a word that he coins to connote the outlandish fustiness of a concept. In the first category, in *Of Reformation*, we find the phrase 'coming to the Bishop with *Supplication* into the *Salutatory*' (607). 'Salutatory' is coined directly from medieval Latin *salutatorium*, an audience chamber attached to a church or monastery. Even here, there may be something of a hostile flavour to the word, perhaps suggestive of the obscurantism of monasticism; Milton makes the contrast by appending his own gloss in plain English: 'some out Porch of the Church'. Elsewhere in *Of Reformation*, Milton is concerned to dismiss the efforts of those seeking to validate episcopalian government by reference to the records of the early Christian church, and he does so by postulating a choice between the opaque writings of the church fathers and plain Scripture truth. He asks which is better,

> to dote upon immeasurable, innumerable, and therfore unnecessary, and unmerciful volumes, choosing rather to erre with the specious name of the Fathers, or to take a sound Truth at the hand of a plain upright man that all his dayes hath bin diligently reading the holy Scriptures, and thereto imploring *Gods* grace, while the admirers of Antiquity have bin beating their brains about their *Ambones*, their *Diptychs*, and *Meniaia's*? (568)

The unfamiliarity of the concluding vocabulary contributes considerably to our response to this passage. 'Ambones', the plural of 'Ambo', the special name for the pulpit or reading desk of the early Christian church, is Milton's coining from late Latin. The 'meniaia' (unrecorded in the *OED*) are the books containing offices for the immoveable feasts of the Byzantine rite. As the Yale editor observes, we should note Milton's contemptuous use of the double plural, Greek and English. 'Diptychs', a word borrowed from Greek in the 1620s, had only recently been used in the technical sense of the tablets of wax on which, in the early church, the names of the orthodox, both living and dead, were recorded. Brilliantly, through his choices of vocabulary, Milton points up the distinction between the sterility, obscurity, and alienness of antiquarianism, and the forthrightness of the approach, described in simple English, of the 'plain upright man'.

Milton, as already noted, has sometimes been thought of as using words with Greek or Latin etymologies in senses not current in English. We must beware, however, of ignoring the dynamics of semantic change. When words become English, it is often in senses close to the original. Later, other meanings may develop and the original ones fall into disuse. It is easy, if we do not consult a historical dictionary (such as the *OED*), to attribute to Milton's prose a Latinism and a semantic atavism which, in the context of seventeenth-century linguistic practice, it does not truly possess. For example, in *The Reason of Church-Government*, a slightly later antiprelatical pamphlet, Milton observes that churchmen 'should be to us a pattern of temperance and frugal mediocrity' (*YP* 1: 856). The Yale editor notes that 'mediocrity' has the Latin sense of moderation or temperance. Quite so, but we must not be misled. That was also a normal *English* signification of the word from the early sixteenth century to the later eighteenth century. It is quite rare for Milton – and quite rare generally for mid-seventeenth-century writers of serious prose – to use words with classical etymologies in genuinely un-English significations. Milton's Latin prose, written to a European audience, manifests a complete mastery of neo-Latin artistry that was much appreciated, in its own terms, in its own age even by those who shared few of his ideological premises (see Hale 82–102).

The kind of writing I have been analyzing, characterized by a high incidence of simile and metaphor, a vigorous assimilation of biblical material, and considerable lexical creativity, is uniformly present in Milton's antiprelatical pamphlets of 1641–2. In the next two or three years, however, while retaining this style for the elevated oratory of *Areopagitica* and the heated vituperation of *Colasterion* (1645), Milton develops another voice, one that uses imagery much more sparingly, for other kinds of writing, such as *Tetrachordon* (the careful exegetical justification of his thesis on divorce, 1645) or *Of Education* (1644), which is scarcely more than a list of proposals about how education ought to be organized. Then, after being silent in print from 1646 through to 1648, Milton in 1649 produces three pamphlets in defence of revolutionary independency, *The Tenure of Kings and Magistrates*, *Observations upon the late Articles of Peace*, and *Eikonoklastes*; and these works are yet further subdued in their imagery, though they retain some of Milton's earlier lexical vigour.

For the next ten years Milton writes no more vernacular prose pamphlets. But when, in 1659, he breaks his silence to consider issues concerning

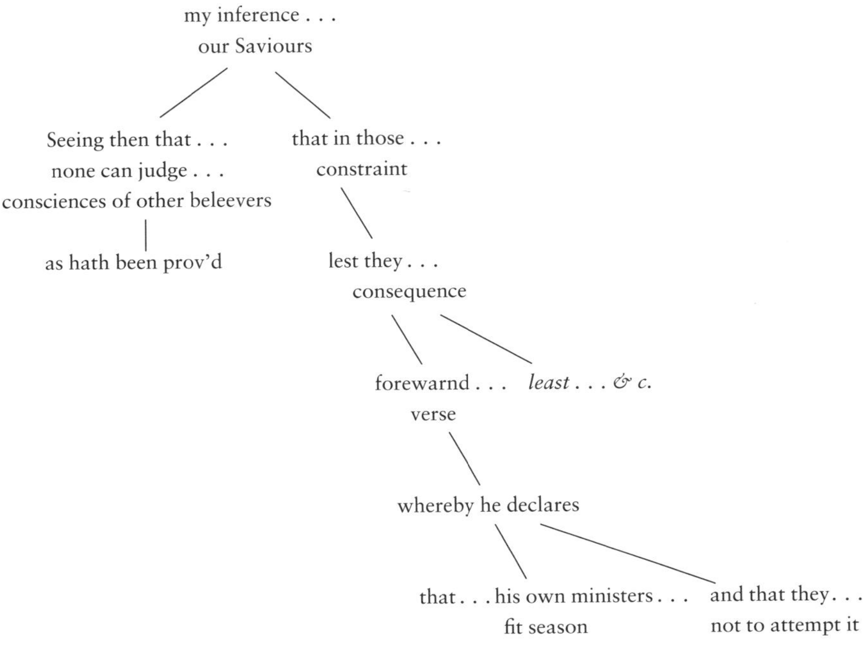

Diagram 2

church funding and the relationship between church and state – in *A Treatise of Civil Power* and *The Likeliest Means to Remove Hirelings out of the Church* – it is a still different voice we hear. Consider the following:

> Seeing then that in matters of religion, as hath been prov'd, none can judge or determin here on earth, no not church-governors themselves against the consciences of other beleevers, my inference is, or rather not mine but our Saviours own, that in those matters they neither can command nor use constraint; lest they run rashly on a pernicious consequence, forewarnd in that parable *Mat.* 13. from the 26 to the 31 verse: *least while ye gather up the tares, ye root up also the wheat with them. Let both grow together until the harvest: and in the time of harvest I will say to the reapers, Gather ye together first the tares &c.* whereby he declares that this work neither his own ministers nor any els can discerningly anough or judgingly perform without his own immediat direction, in his own fit season; and that they ought till then not to attempt it. (*A Treatise of Civil Power*; *YP* 7 (rev. edn): 244–5)

Syntactically, we are on familiar ground – a sentence of well over a hundred words, organized in a hierarchy of subordination which can be schematically represented by diagram 2.

The main clause, 'my inference . . . our Saviours own', supports, to the left, a clause of circumstance, in which another clause is embedded. To the right of the main clause, subordinate clause supports subordinate clause, which supports subordinate clause, through a long chain of dependency. Milton's predilection for such structures remains constant throughout the prose oeuvre, save for his last tract, *Of True Religion*, written, after a long intermission, in 1673, by which time the norms of the genre may well have changed in favour of a greater syntactical simplicity.

But our example shows how other characteristics of Milton's earlier style have been expunged. Note the use of the biblical material. Previously, Milton had freely reworked it into his own idiom. Now the biblical allusion – once more, to the parable of the tares – stands adjacent to his own discourse in the status of a proof text. He follows the Authorized Version verbatim, and even gives (albeit a little inaccurately) reference to chapter and verse. In the purely Miltonic part, there is neither simile nor metaphor, nor any creative deviation from the customary lexical usages of seventeenth-century English. What had been flamboyant, even pyrotechnic, prose has given way to a sober functionalism.

Inevitably, we must wonder why Milton changed. There is little external evidence. Although, as we shall see, Milton makes some useful observations on style, he gives no explicit account of his own development. Yet he is not simply following stylistic trends. Certainly, the prose style of the Restoration tended to be less figurative and its artistry was less obtrusive. Thus, in 1673, Samuel Parker, no lover of Milton's politics, takes exception also to his prose style, citing a passage from *Areopagitica* very similar to the one quoted earlier and remarking with heavy irony, 'Such fustian bumbast [*sic*] as this past for stately wit and sence in that Age of politeness and reformation' (French, 5: 51). But in the period 1641–60 no general trend towards a plainer style is evident. The developments in Milton's prose must therefore be seen as resulting from changes in his own stylistic preferences rather than from any mere conformity with the practices of his contemporaries.

Why, then, should brilliance have given way to an (albeit elegant) functionalism? We may only hypothesize. Certainly, though, arguments about failing literary creativity must be discounted. As Milton produces his least exciting prose, he is simultaneously writing his greatest poetry. Perhaps those who favour a psychological explanation may see a connection. Maybe in the 1640s, when the polemical responsibilities he assumed precluded writing major poetry, the creative impulse found deflected expression in his prose works. Milton's early prose style may thus be perceived as the rechannelling of that creative mental energy which later found a proper discharge in *Paradise Lost*. Such an argument has its attractions, though I am not sure how by itself it could explain, for example, the variations in the pamphlets of 1643–5. The changes in Milton's prose style should probably be seen instead as part of his complex response to the polemical context in which he wrote and to his own perceptions of his role within it.

In his earlier prose, Milton constructs an image of himself as a poet who has turned to the prose genre both temporarily and a little reluctantly, out of a love for his country and an enthusiasm for its thoroughgoing reformation, and he seems troubled by the decorum of elevated, creative writing in this medium. In his fifth and final antiprelatical tract, *An Apology Against a Pamphlet* (1642), he interrupts an elaborate, apocalyptic image about the 'fiery Chariot' of 'Zeale' with a defensive parenthesis: '(that I may have leave to soare a while as the Poets use)' (*YP* 1: 900), thus suggesting that his is a poetic impulse, ill confined in the medium of prose. Once more on the defensive, in *The Reason of Church-Government*, he counters the charge that he writes controversial prose only to win notoriety, and he does so by asserting his own sense of poetic calling. He is 'led by the genial power of nature to another task' (that is, to poetry), and he glances with apparent envy at the 'Poet soaring . . . with his garland and singing robes about him'. By contrast, prose, that 'cool element', is something Milton writes with his 'left hand' (*YP* 1: 808). And yet the prose of 1641–2 is not really that much 'cooler' than poetry. Rather, it represents the efforts of a writer who still thinks of himself as a poet who happens to be writing, though only temporarily, in prose.

The *variety* of styles Milton develops over the next three years obviously does not reflect major changes in personality or a restriction of ability, since the variety subsists in closely contemporary works. Instead, Milton seems to be looking ever more closely at the nuances of genre and at how various styles of writing are appropriate to various rhetorical situations. The close exegesis of biblical texts invites a kind of exposition quite different from the lofty or impassioned enunciation of high principle or the vehement assailing of one's opponents. At the same time, Milton during these years offers us a more idealized image of the prose writer. Now, he tells us, 'When a man writes to the world, he summons up all his reason and deliberation to assist him; he searches, meditats, is industrious, and likely consults and conferrs with his judicious friends.' His writing – and it is plain from the context that Milton is speaking here of non-fictional prose – is 'the most consummat act of his fidelity and ripenesse', the product of 'his midnight watchings' (*Areopagitica*; *YP* 2: 532). And so he accommodates himself to his role as . . . prose polemicist.

Milton in 1641–2 was somewhat on the fringes of political controversy, writing to second the arguments of others and, perhaps, to nudge them a little further down the path to root-and-branch extirpation of episcopalian church government. But in 1643–5, with a new notoriety, he stands at the centre of heated argument, both about the heterodox divorce reforms he advocated and about the rights of radicals to express such opinions. Yet still generally on the defensive, and excluded from circles of power and influence, he speaks with a challenging, oppositional voice. By 1649, however, Milton has become the spokesperson of the new ascendancy. Revolutionary independency, the political faction with which he identified himself, had, by the late 1640s, captured the most important institutions of the state. It predominated among the officer cadre of the victorious New Model Army; since Pride's Purge, it had controlled Parliament; and now it was bringing the King to the scaffold and republican government to England. Milton, after several years of silence, thus re-emerges in 1649 as ideologue of a now successful political faction.

His first tract of 1649, *The Tenure of Kings and Magistrates*, is a theoretical justification for Parliament's treatment of the King. Thereafter, he became a paid civil servant of the new regime, as Secretary for Foreign Tongues to the Council of State. Milton's holding this position indicates the *official* and rather corporate nature of the publications for which he was responsible during this period. *Observations upon the Late Articles of Peace* is a response ordered by the Council of State to the Royalists' attempted settlement of Ireland on terms that would permit it to be used as a base for the restoration of Charles II. *Eikonoklastes*, the refutation of the Royalist apologia *Eikon Basilike* (1649), was similarly commissioned by Milton's political masters. In his pamphlet Milton himself stresses that it was a task undertaken, perhaps reluctantly, on behalf of the state: 'I take it on me as a work assign'd rather, then by me chos'n or affected' (*YP* 3: 339).

Defending the regicide government imposed on Milton a different set of imperatives and obligations from those he felt when, poet by calling, polemicist but for the moment, he lent his talents in support of the antiprelatical movement. Of course, his earliest tracts were serious contributions to a debate close to the heart of the developing crisis between King and Parliament. But Milton, for all the *élan* of his early writings, functioned in the early 1640s essentially on the fringes of that debate. However, in 1649, particularly in *Eikonoklastes*, Milton achieves a position of preeminence as chief adversary of the Royalists' most important propaganda initiative, namely *Eikon Basilike*, which, despite the fact that the republicans had in their hands the whole apparatus of state control of the press, appeared in no less than forty clandestine editions in 1649 alone.

The high seriousness of Milton's tasks in 1649 may well account for the new sobriety of his style. In *Eikonoklastes*, Milton bases his attack on *Eikon Basilike* in part on its 'literary', artful, poetic style, which he adduces as evidence of its remoteness from plain truth. Thus, when King Charles (or his ghost writer, John Gauden) produces an elaborate image, likening the King's withdrawal from Westminster to a man's putting to sea without proper provisioning, Milton responds with questions about literary decorum. The image, he complains, is 'somwhat more Poetical' than the genre permits, and shows that the King thinks more about poetry than about statesmanship. Indeed, 'the whole Book might perhaps be intended a peece of Poetrie' (*YP* 3: 406). This is quite a shift from Milton's earlier posture, when he would arrest his oratory to beg permission to 'soare' like a poet! Yet his avowed suspicion of 'poetic' prose, while it serves his immediate purpose of blackening the image of the King, also accords well with the austerity of his own practice in 1649.

The final phase in the development of Milton's prose, that further levelling down of lexical creativity which we have already considered, was perhaps no more than the logical extension of the restrained stylistic decorum that informed the pamphlets of 1649. Of course, for the modern reader, the changes must be disappointing. Milton's early prose matches that of any of the great prose writers of his age in the pleasure it can still give. It rivals the best of Donne and probably transcends all but the best of Browne. To the end of his career, Milton retains his power of syntactical control, and he likewise maintains a tone of savage indignation which anticipates, perhaps, the voice of Dr Johnson at his most incisive. He can still scythe through nonsense and pretension. For example, *Eikon Basilike* claims that the King, when he attempted to arrest Pym and his four colleagues, was 'attended with some Gentlemen'. Milton responds: 'Gentlemen indeed; the ragged Infantrie of Stewes and Brothels' (*YP* 3: 380). Again, of Charles's well known cry, 'the birds have flown', Milton asks, 'If som Vultur in the Mountains could have op'nd his beak intelligibly and spoke, what fitter words could he have utter'd at the loss of his prey?' (439). Thus Milton's is a powerful voice still, but the zest of *Of Reformation* is not to be recovered.

For the modern reader, then, the progression of Milton's prose towards ordinariness can be disappointing, though alternatively it can be seen as not so much a falling off as a growing up (see Corns 1982, 102). Milton's early prose seems to presuppose the power of creative writing to fashion opinion and precipitate reform. The sober discourses of 1649 and later seem, by contrast, to recognize the irrelevance of fine writing to the shaping of political events. Yet they are, in several senses, more professional, the work of an increasingly experienced – and, of course, publicly employed –

political activist. The earlier brilliance came, perhaps, from the friction of genius and genre, as Milton the poet redirected his energies in the limiting medium of prose. The later work comes from a maturer Milton, securely embedded in the milieu of prose controversy.

FURTHER READING

Achinstein, Sharon, *Milton and the Revolutionary Reader* (Princeton, 1994), especially chs. 1, 3, and 4

Armitage, David, Armand Himy, and Quentin Skinner, eds., *Milton and Republicanism* (Cambridge, 1995), especially chs. 1, 2, 4, and 5

Corns, Thomas N., *The Development of Milton's Prose Style* (Oxford, 1982)

Uncloistered Virtue: English Political Literature 1640–1660 (Oxford, 1992)

John Milton: The Prose Works (New York, 1998)

Dzelzainis, Martin, 'Milton and the Limits of Ciceronian Rhetoric', in *English Renaissance Prose: History, Language, and Politics*, ed. Neil Rhodes (Tempe, AZ, 1997)

Egan, James, *The Inward Teacher: Milton's Rhetoric of Christian Liberty* (University Park, PA, 1980)

'Milton and the Marprelate Tradition', *Milton Studies* 8 (1975)

Fish, Stanley E., *Self-Consuming Artifacts* (Berkeley, Los Angeles, and London, 1972)

French, J. Milton, ed., *The Life Records of John Milton*, 5 vols. (New Brunswick, NJ, 1956)

Hale, John K., *Milton's Languages:The Impact of Multilingualism on Style* (Cambridge, 1997), especially ch. 5

Hamilton, K. G., 'The Structure of Milton's Prose', in *Language and Style in Milton*, ed. R. D . Emma and J. T. Shawcross (New York, 1967)

Hill, Christopher, *Milton and the English Revolution* (London, 1977)

Kranidas, Thomas, '"Decorum" and the Style of Milton's Antiprelatical Tracts', *Studies in Philology* 62 (1965)

'Milton's *Of Reformation*: The Politics of Vision', *ELH* 49 (1982)

'Words, Words, Words, and the Word: Milton's *Of Prelaticall Episcopacy*', *Milton Studies* 16 (1982)

'Style and Rectitude in Seventeenth-Century Prose: Hall, Smectynmuus, and Milton', *Huntington Library Quarterly* 46 (1983)

'Polarity and Structure in Milton's *Areopagitica*', *ELR* 14 (1984)

Lieb, Michael and J. T. Shawcross, eds., *Achievements of the Left Hand: Essays on the Prose of John Milton* (Amherst, MA, 1974)

Loewenstein, David, *Milton and the Drama of History* (Cambridge, 1990), especially chs. 1, 2, 3, and 4

Loewenstein, David and James Grantham Turner, eds., *Politics, Poetics, and Hermeneutics in Milton's Prose* (Cambridge, 1990)

Milner, Andrew, *John Milton and the English Revolution* (London, 1981)

Nyquist, Mary and Margaret W. Ferguson, eds., *Re-membering Milton: Essays on the Texts and Traditions* (New York and London, 1987), especially chs. 4 and 11

Skerpan, Elizabeth, *The Rhetoric of Politics in the English Revolution, 1642–1660* (Columbia and London, 1992)
Smith, Nigel, *Literature and Revolution in England 1640–1660* (New Haven and London, 1994)
Stavely, Keith W., *The Politics of Milton's Prose Style* (New Haven, 1975)
Webber, Joan, *The Eloquent 'I': Style and Self in Seventeenth-Century Prose* (Madison, Wisconsin, and London, 1968)
Wilding, Michael, 'Milton's *Areopagitica*: Freedom for the Sects', *Prose Studies* 9 (1986); rpt. in *The Literature of Controversy: Polemical Strategy from Milton to Junius*, ed. Thomas N. Corns (London, 1987)

7

R. F. HALL

Milton's sonnets and his contemporaries

The body of work known as Milton's sonnets comprises twenty-five poems: twenty-three fourteen-line sonnets (five in Italian, eighteen in English); one fifteen-line *canzone* in Italian; and one English 'tailed' sonnet (the twenty-line 'On the New Forcers of Conscience'). The first ten sonnets, including the five Italian ones plus the *canzone*, were published in Milton's *Poems* of 1645. These and the rest, save for those addressed to Fairfax, Cromwell, Vane, and the second one to Cyriack Skinner – apparently omitted for political reasons but included in the Trinity Manuscript – appeared in the *Poems* of 1673. Setting aside debates concerning the sonnets' dating and sequence, we shall focus here on some eleven of Milton's English sonnets, and on specific individuals or groups addressed or mentioned in them.

The public, topical, even heroic sonnet; the sonnet praising or counselling a friend, threatening or mocking an enemy; the sonnet marking a point or problem in the poet's own career – all these were recognized and accepted variations of the genre in sixteenth-century Italy, but were most unusual in mid-seventeenth-century England when Milton turned to them in conscious imitation of such models as the Italian poets Della Casa and Tasso. For English readers, the sonnet was concerned with human love and sometimes, as in Donne and Herbert and one or two memorable occasions in Spenser, with divine love.

Therefore it may seem ironic that Milton deliberately chose the Italian language to attempt the love sonnet then so familiar to English ears, but chose the English language to write sonnets of a kind far more familiar to Italian ears: those on civic, political, topical and controversial, social, and ethical matters. It is less surprising, however, when we remember Milton's familiarity with Italian and perhaps too his eagerness, like Spenser's, to expand and enrich the generic possibilities of English poetry. Whatever his motivations, his extension of the range of the English sonnet was both fortunate and, in the long run, highly influential: for despite the sonnet's virtual eclipse in the eighteenth century, with the coming of Wordsworth and the nineteenth century the Miltonic model of the occasional and political sonnet came very much into its own.

About half of Milton's English sonnets explicitly address individual men or women whom he knew personally, and with several of whom he had worked in the spheres of poetry or politics or education. Where such individuals are not addressed, most of the remaining sonnets focus on some aspect of the poet's own career: his slow beginnings, his status as poet, apparent hindrances to his creativity, or hostile receptions of his prose works. What this amounts to is that almost all these sonnets are concerned either directly or indirectly with the poet's career and the convictions and loyalties informing it. If a single unifying theme may be detected, it is *affirmation of values*, be it through praise or challenge or blame. Nor is it surprising that a poetic genre used for praise is also used for a wide range of its opposites. Condemnation, invective, menace, satire, reproach (including occasionally self-reproach or self-questioning) appear along with the concomitant range of wish, exhortation, counsel, reassurance, and sometimes prophecy.

We turn now to a few sonnets, not necessarily in traditional sequence, to see these features emerging. Several major twentieth-century editions (such as those of Leonard, Honigmann, and Carey) order and number the sonnets differently. The commonest numbering – that found in the editions of Merritt Hughes, Helen Darbishire, and Gordon Campbell – is used in what follows.

The sonnet to Sir Thomas Fairfax (XV; 'Fairfax, whose name in arms through Europe rings') addresses one of the greatest Parliamentary generals near the close of the Civil War, in 1648. The focus of this sonnet moves significantly from Fairfax's more obviously heroic and classical attributes, his 'name' and 'virtue', to the humbler but 'nobler task' awaiting him; that is, from his renown abroad (first quatrain) and his courage and leadership in the field (second quatrain), to the statesmanlike task now enjoined upon him, of dealing with corruption and greed in administration – a task arguably not only nobler but also more difficult than those on the field of battle. (Milton's internalizing of heroic values is not by any means confined to *Paradise Lost*.)

This appeal was made, as it happens, at the peak of Fairfax's military success, but also at the very point when his public importance and influence were nearly over. The unintentional irony of this, perceived only in historical hindsight, lends a certain poignancy to the poet's fervour. Fairfax, after his capture of Colchester from the Royalists, soon withdrew from military leadership, had hesitations about the execution of Charles I, and in 1650 retired to his estate at Nun Appleton in Yorkshire, where he engaged as his daughter's tutor the poet Andrew Marvell – who subsequently became Milton's colleague (as well as his good friend) in the Latin Secretariat, the foreign affairs office of Cromwell's Commonwealth government.

Milton's 1652 sonnet to Cromwell (XVI; 'Cromwell, our chief of men') resembles the Fairfax one in structure, but this time the Parliamentary leader's military prowess, moral fortitude, and religious faith are all praised together in the first quatrain. Then the military triumphs are more firmly and exclusively resounded in the place-names – Darwen, Dunbar, Worcester – of the second quatrain (with the trophies of victory appearing as splendid replacement for the severed head of King Charles: 'on the neck of crowned fortune proud'). As with Fairfax, however, the immediate and pressing task, the real occasion of the sonnet, is reserved for mention in the sestet: this task is to protect freedom of conscience against those erstwhile allies who now threaten it, namely certain Independents whose rigidly doctrinaire proposals to the Parliamentary Committee for the Propagation of the Gospel made them as dangerous in Milton's eyes as those other 'hireling wolves' he had attacked for quite different reasons fifteen years earlier in *Lycidas*.

In each sonnet the deeds of war and the deeds of peace are contrasted, and the urgent task becomes that of restoring or protecting liberty. The Fairfax and Cromwell sestets tend to reinforce each other: 'O yet a nobler task awaits thy hand' (but not Fairfax's military hand) reads the one; and the other, 'yet much remains / To conquer still' (but not in Cromwell's military conquest). The poet approves military conquest, yet knows it is futile unless the power gained is used to good effect in civic life: war can only 'endless war still breed, / Till Truth and Right from Violence be freed', and 'peace hath her victories / No less renown'd than war, new foes arise'. Military metaphor tends to lead on to miniature allegory peopled by figures called Peace, War, Truth, Right, Violence, and Valour. In the Fairfax sestet, the threat is from fraud and corruption; in the Cromwell one, from ex-allies and a still more galling source, religious intolerance. The appeal to Fairfax, first couched in fervent but courteous statement, ends in poised generality ('In vain doth Valour bleed'), whereas the appeal to Cromwell acquires added urgency from the direct imperative of the final couplet ('Help us to save') as well as from the far greater violence of the imagery throughout the sonnet: 'plough'd', 'on the neck', 'with blood imbru'd', and of course the 'paw' and 'maw' of the 'hireling wolves' and the chains with which they threaten to bind.

A basic belief of Milton's is that Christ came to set consciences free, not to bind them; and we again find him attacking religious intolerance in sardonic sonnets on current affairs such as 'I did but prompt the age' (XII, on hostility to his own divorce-law proposals) and the unnumbered 'On the New Forcers of Conscience' (on conflict over a new religious establishment). Despite an array of personal names appearing in the latter, they focus not so much on individual contemporaries as on religious bigots who, in Milton's view, were menacing the very liberty of conscience that so much of the civil conflict of the 1640s was waged to achieve.

Perhaps Milton's finest compliment to a contemporary is his sonnet addressed to Sir Henry Vane (XVII).

Vane, young in years, but in sage counsel old,
  Than whom a better senator ne'er held
  The helm of Rome, when gowns not arms repelled
  The fierce Epirot and the African bold.
Whether to settle peace or to unfold
  The drift of hollow states, hard to be spelled,
  Then to advise how war may best, upheld,
  Move by her two main nerves, Iron and Gold
In all her equipage: besides to know
  Both spiritual power and civil, what each means,
  What severs each, thou hast learnt, which few have done.
The bounds of either sword to thee we owe;
  Therefore on thy firm hand Religion leans
  In peace, and reck'ns thee her eldest son.

This time no task is urged in the sestet: we hear that Vane has already been successfully completing profoundly important tasks – and this was indeed, by all accounts, the case. An excellent Parliamentarian and diplomat, and a sharer of Milton's views on religious toleration, Vane apparently combined shrewd negotiating powers with sturdy independence of judgement and 'plain heroic magnitude of mind' (*Samson Agonistes* 1279). We possess also in hindsight the knowledge that he died for his convictions, executed by the Restoration government of Charles II in 1662 when he was forty-nine years old.

This poem is arguably the most poised, monumentally Roman and heroic in spirit of the sonnets. It was probably inspired by Vane's successful penetration of the motives of a group of Dutch ambassadors in June 1652, when England and Holland were beginning that maritime rivalry which led to the naval war of the next decade.

The Vane sonnet warrants some syntactical analysis. In many apostrophic sonnets, those explicitly addressed to a person, the initial address by name ushers in a series of qualifying clauses governed by *who/whose/whom*, and syntactic closure in the form of a main verb may be suspended for a considerable time, as the poem builds towards a climax as do some prayer-book collects (in the formula 'Lord who . . . ', followed by attributes of praise and mighty acts, followed by specific petition). In the Fairfax sonnet examined above, the *whose* clause lasts four lines; and in the Cromwell sonnet the *who* clause lasts eight-and-a-half lines, thus reflecting the fluidity of the octave-sestet transition that Milton adopted from some Italian poets. But in the Vane sonnet, the *who* section, syntactically introduced by 'Than whom', carries us all the way to the end of line eleven, finding resolution in the climactic main verb 'hast learnt'. Vane's discernment, thus celebrated, becomes in turn the basis for the remarkable assertion that religion 'leans' on him and 'reck'ns' him her eldest son.

There reappears here a distinction we have already met in the Fairfax and Cromwell sonnets: that between the necessary roles of peace and of war. Sometimes 'gowns' and not arms must repel enemies – which is appropriate to Vane's recent diplomatic exercise with the Dutch visitors suspected of espionage. The Roman comparison confers a statuesque dignity on Milton's subject in the first quatrain, and this is carried through by other means to the end. One of the works of peace was to 'unfold / The drift' of potential enemies (the 'hollow states' here probably hinting at Holland); but sometimes the result of this would entail advising on how to conduct war. However, the chief compliment has not yet been reached. As we might expect by now, it is reserved for the sestet – and this time it is a culminating compliment unaccompanied by a culminating new task. Meanwhile the air of balanced and careful discrimination characterizing the man is also a strong stylistic feature of the sonnet itself: 'young . . . but old', 'gowns not arms', 'to settle peace or to unfold / The drift', 'Iron and Gold'. And now comes the most important distinction for Milton, that between the necessary civil authority and those spiritual authorities and freedoms which the civil power is meant to uphold, not attack: thus, 'to know / Both spiritual power and civil, what each means, / What severs each' is the culminating statement of what Vane has learnt – whereas, in contrast, 'few have done' so. This crucial claim is more firmly set in our minds by the syntactically complete and independent line twelve, 'The bounds of either sword to thee we owe', where the swords represent the different brands of authority. Vane, presented at the start as 'young in years' (he was, for that age, a ripe thirty-nine), develops through the image of the Roman Senator, the settling, unfolding and advising, learning and knowing, to appear by the end as a seasoned sage on whose 'firm hand' religion itself could lean.

In an essay of this scope, little can be said about Milton's artistry in sound; but a little should indeed be said. Rhyming syllables, and even their final consonants, often influence the prevailing mood of a poem. In the Fairfax sonnet, much is achieved by the warm buzz of *z* (that is to say, voiced *s*) consonants at all the line-ends of the octave, giving way to the quiet but more insistent *d* at the sestet line-ends. In the Cromwell sonnet, a darker energy fills the *d*-dominated octave endings, while this time the voiced *s* briefly appears in the sestet before yielding to the indignant *paw/ maw* rhyme. In the Vane sonnet, a marble-like poise is afforded to the octave by the consistently firm and quiet *-ld* endings to every one of the eight lines, softening then to the variety of the sestet endings. And when we turn to the sonnet on the Vaudois massacre (XVIII), no fewer than eleven of the fourteen lines through their long *o* vowels create a supporting impression of lament modulating to menace:

Avenge O Lord thy slaughtered Saints, whose bones
  Lie scattered on the Alpine mountains cold,
  Even them who kept thy truth so pure of old
  When all our fathers worshipped stocks and stones,
Forget not: in thy book record their groans
  Who were thy sheep and in their ancient fold
  Slain by the bloody Piedmontese that rolled
  Mother with infant down the rocks. Their moans
The vales redoubled to the hills, and they
  To heaven. Their martyred blood and ashes sow
  O'er all the Italian fields where still doth sway
The triple Tyrant: that from these may grow
  A hundredfold, who having learnt thy way
  Early may fly the Babylonian woe.

One of the great poems of outrage in the language, this sonnet was a direct response to the deliberate slaughter in Piedmont of many Vaudois (or Waldensian) Protestants by the army of the Catholic Duke of Savoy in April 1655. Waves of protest followed throughout Europe, and Cromwell threatened military intervention. As Latin Secretary to the English Commonwealth government, Milton had to compose and/or translate letters for dispatch to foreign powers and would have been responsible for much of the correspondence that immediately followed this incident. The remaining Vaudois eventually rallied against Savoy and had their ancient residence rights restored to them. Meanwhile the atrocity had called forth the only sonnet of Milton's to take the form of direct prayer and petition addressed throughout to God. Accordingly, narrative details of the massacre are governed and contained by the imperatives beseeching the Lord to 'Avenge

. . . Forget not . . . record their groans' and 'sow' their blood and ashes over the papal fields of Italy.

The image of sowing compacts three allusions: first, the blood of the martyrs is the seed of the Church (in Milton's view, the true Protestant church); second, the 'hundredfold' arising from the sowing will increase the kingdom of God, as in Christ's parable of the sower (e.g., Matt. 13); and third, in the myth of Cadmus, the sowing of the dragon's teeth made a host of armed warriors spring up out of the earth, and by implication such a consequence will likewise follow this event. (In *Areopagitica*, Milton's great work on press liberty, images of sowing and springing crops had exerted a comparable force.) The last of these images suggests an army ready for revenge, especially in view of the sonnet's opening; yet the hundredfold harvest is imagined as fleeing from the Babylonian 'woe' (that is, the woe reserved for the Roman church and papacy). So it appears that the revenge contemplated is ultimately no more violent than the increase of Protestants and perhaps the conversion of misguided Catholics. 'Avenge' at the beginning certainly sounds strong and potentially violent; 'Forget not' is a little less so; 'in thy book record their groans' less so still; and by the time we come to a hundredfold harvest of a Cadmian army, most of the anticipated violence has melted into a sense of the pity and pathos of the event, even while the anti-Catholic and anti-papal anger ('triple Tyrant') remains. This is not to claim that the poem peters out from its initial force, but to say that the sense of outrage, proper as it is, must rightly modulate into pity as we contemplate the details, confirmed in contemporary accounts, of 'Mother with infant' rolled 'down the rocks'. Here, more than in any other of his sonnets, Milton achieves much of his effect by insistent enjambment, which despite its rhymes approaches the craggy majesty of the rolling enjambed periods of *Paradise Lost* or some of the speeches of Samson in *Samson Agonistes*.

Only one of Milton's sonnets addresses a contemporary who was also a notable creative artist: Henry Lawes, musician and composer, who in 1634 had been Milton's musical collaborator in *A Masque* (*'Comus'*) for the Earl of Bridgewater, whose family employed Lawes as a music tutor. Between poet and musician a very warm friendship continued in the next decade, even though Lawes was a prominent Royalist. He set to music many contemporary poems and was associated with the new recitative style in which the music adapted itself to the words rather than vice versa.

The tone of this sonnet (XIII) is intimate and gently humorous – in the deliberate use of the nickname Harry, the allusion to the ass's ears of Midas, and the closing hint that Lawes is destined straight for Heaven and is therefore by implication too good for Purgatory. If Lawes here corresponds to Casella, Milton presumably corresponds to Dante in these closing lines: a high but also, one assumes, a whimsical compliment to himself. (He is similarly high-spirited in the 'Captain or Colonel' sonnet (VIII) when he compares himself by implication to the poet Pindar and to Euripides.) The very phrase 'the milder shades' allows us to hear a tribute to Dante's imagination along with a light dismissal of any literal belief in the Catholic doctrine of Purgatory.

A few of Milton's sonnets are tributes both to contemporary friends and to their parents or forebears. The one (X) addressed to the Lady Margaret Ley – wife to Captain John Hobson and, with her husband, a close friend of the poet – constitutes a tribute simultaneously to a dead father and a living daughter. The father, James Ley, had been Lord Treasurer and President of the Council under Charles I, and earlier Lord Chief Justice when he had to impose sentence on Francis Bacon after his trial for corruption. This event lurks in the subtext of the phrase 'unstain'd with gold or fee', that is, with bribery. More important, perhaps, is the assertion that retirement from high office left this man of integrity 'more in himself content': Milton repeatedly affirms inner spiritual values as a reminder of not merely the transience but also the relativity and potential vanity of the more worldly ones. Charles I's forcible dissolution of Parliament in 1629 becomes (in the second quatrain) the inglorious equivalent of Philip of Macedon's victory at Chaeronea, which destroyed the long-cherished liberties of democratic Greece. The dissolution also becomes, allegedly, the last straw that broke the old man's health and hastened his death. This allusion aligns Ley with the Athenian orator Isocrates and with his passion for reform and political integrity. These tributes to a man of public principle and private virtue are in the sestet turned, as on a smooth pivot, into tribute to the daughter of his old age. 'Daughter' and 'Margaret', the first and last words, elegantly frame the praise of both, and they domesticate without downgrading the tribute to an eminent public man.

The first of Milton's sonnets to his friend Cyriack Skinner (XXI) is essentially an Horatian invitation piece. Beginning with a tribute to Skinner's renowned grandfather, the former Chief Justice Sir Edward Coke, one of the greatest of British jurists, it soon moves on to cheerful considerations of leisure. Writing in conscious imitation of Horace's capacious manner, Milton embraces an almost intractable mixture of commemoration and compliment, classical allusion, topical political references, and slightly jocular courtesy. (The rhyme leading from 'bench' through 'wrench' and 'drench' to 'French' just manages to be acceptable if we decline to take it seriously.) It is a scholarly mirth that the poet enjoins; and the measured elegance of the sestet does much to redeem a poem imperilled by the ponderous cheer of its octave. This elegance arises from a fine balance of direct counsel and moral adage about not refusing to accept heaven-sent leisure and solace. Milton never appears as an *anti-festive* Puritan, and it is too seldom remarked that ever since *L'Allegro*, *Il Penseroso*, and *A Masque*, as a poet Milton was much concerned with the range and variety of happiness, whether as profound spiritual joy, family affection, simply civilized sociability, or festive jollity. Not surprisingly, therefore, his sonnets include festive invitation as well as public tribute, civic outrage, and personal grief.

To the more personal sonnets we now turn.

Deservedly one of the most celebrated of Milton's short poems is Sonnet XXIII, on his dead wife:

Methought I saw my late espoused saint
  Brought to me like Alcestis from the grave,
  Whom Jove's great son to her glad husband gave,
  Rescued from death by force though pale and faint.
Mine as whom washed from spot of childbed taint,
  Purification in the Old Law did save,
  And such, as yet once more I trust to have
  Full sight of her in heaven without restraint,
Came vested all in white, pure as her mind:
  Her face was veiled, yet to my fancied sight,
  Love, sweetness, goodness in her person shined
So clear, as in no face with more delight.
  But O as to embrace me she enclined,
  I waked, she fled, and day brought back my night.

This poem has elicited considerable debate, both about its relation to the Alcestis story, and about which wife is being commemorated: Mary Powell, the first (d. 1652), or the second, Katherine Woodcock (d. 1658). That in the dream her face was veiled and yet the poet recognized her, better supports the claim of the second wife. The earlier allusion to Heracles' rescue of Alcestis from the grave cannot alter this, since in Euripides' play Alcestis' veil made her initially unrecognizable even by her husband Admetus. To see one's wife veiled and *yet* to know her seems more appropriate to the husband who has never seen his wife's face at all, as was the case in Milton's second marriage. The poet's hope of seeing her in Heaven 'without restraint' further supports this reading.

The dream and the blindness are poignantly combined from the opening phrase 'Methought I saw'. Unlike Alcestis in the play who was 'pale and faint' at her restoration, the dream wife appears as if both ritually purified from childbirth and perfected as in her resurrection body in Heaven. Reference to purification should not distract us into debates over which wife did or did not have time for liturgical purification; the purification is after all an 'as if' in a dream-sequence, and in any case the allusion is to the 'Old Law' of the Hebrew rites, not to Christian ritual such as the Churching of Women.

The musical movement of this sonnet defies brief analysis; yet it is worth noticing that, as in some others we have met, the power of rhyme is not confined to rhyming syllables as wholes. Quiet insistence on a particular vowel or consonant may well exert its own influence apart from the rest of the syllable, as we saw in the *o* vowels of the Vaudois sonnet as a whole. Here, in the sonnet on his dead wife, we find octave rhymes pervaded by the long *a* vowel while the consonantal endings in *-v* and *-nt* in either case sustain a lingering effect; and when we come to the sestet, a similar dominance is assumed by the long *i* vowel amid an alternation of lingering *-nd* with *-t*.

The long *a* vowel sets up its own plangency through its frequent use in key words quite outside the rhyming ones, continuing from the octave into the sestet: 'late', 'great', 'pale', 'Came', 'face', 'embrace', 'waked', 'day'. And a richly assonantal interplay of vowels, especially the two key ones, is most evident in the last two lines: 'But O as to embrace me she inclined, I waked, she fled, and day brought back my night.' The final paradox makes more moving the 'empty arms' image, a virtual archetype hallowed by the classical poets, notably Virgil in the scene of Aeneas's vain attempt to embrace the shade of his wife Creusa. This, together with allusion to Alcestis and the Old Law's purification rites, confers on the dead dream-woman a powerfully mythic stature at the same time as it speaks of the poet's own affection, grief, and longing.

The sonnet about his dead wife is also very much about the consciousness of the blind dreamer, firmly framed as it is by 'Methought I saw' and 'day brought back my night'. 'My night' in the sense of Milton's blindness dominates two other sonnets. In them Milton is as conscious of presenting or commemorating stages of his life and career as he is elsewhere of paying tribute to contemporaries. Ignoring chronology, we begin with the later and lesser of these; then, after looking at an important early one, we will return to the subject of his blindness in his best-known sonnet of all.

'Cyriack, this three years' day' (XXII) is somewhat strange in being addressed to a person of whom it otherwise takes no notice while the poet focuses on Milton himself. Cyriack Skinner (also the addressee of XXI, examined earlier) was a lawyer and probably at this stage also a faithful friend, neighbour, and amanuensis of the poet. He was an ex-pupil too, and in all these respects might be seen as an apt addressee (if any can be apt) of the poem's self-reassuring sentiments. In it Milton accepts his blindness and takes pride in having spent his eyesight in the service of liberty (and in the fact that his blindness did not disfigure his appearance). Shortly before his total blindness in 1652 he had written the first of his two Latin defences of the execution of Charles I (intended for readers throughout Europe); and soon afterwards came the second, *Defensio Secunda* – these works in response to anti-regicide tracts by Pierre Saumaise (known as Salmasius) and Alexander More. Rumour hostile to Milton claimed that his blindness was God's visitation upon him for his wickedness in defending regicides. Never at a loss for a defence, Milton turns this around and elevates the blindness into an accepted affliction inseparable from the supreme satisfaction of having served the cause of liberty.

It is a poem little commented upon except for debates about its date centring on the phrase 'this three years' day' (which simply signifies 'for about three years now'). One wonders whether embarrassment keeps Miltonists comparatively silent on it; one wonders, too, whether it is not perhaps Milton's worst sonnet. The private sentiments may be legitimate, but the rhetorically uttered combination of self-pity and self-praise is bothering, there is no audible tone of pain or conflict to balance it, and the poem as a whole tends to sound facile and smug where it should be a moving declaration of heroic faith.

Stylistic features contributing to this response are visible in the too-glib balances of 'blemish' and 'spot', 'sun', 'moon' and 'star', 'Heaven's hand' and 'will', 'heart' and 'hope'; also in the bland abruptness of the *-ot* rhymes in the octave; in the strangely unmotivated nautical metaphor of lines 8–9; and in the ventriloquial question-and-answer mode of the sestet's opening. Did Skinner really ask him what supported him, we wonder? And would it make a difference if we knew he had?

Added to all this is the thought that if the defence of liberty is truly the poet's adequate consolation, then the relishing of continental fame rings distastefully hollow as a supposed climax following it. Perhaps this is why it is hard to escape an impression of pathos rather than of triumph as the sonnet moves to its muted conclusion. Of course we know that Milton *does* have a better guide than 'This thought', so we may wonder with some justice why indeed he makes that thought into the climax of the sonnet. It is, finally, strange that for so devout a poet as Milton, 'Heaven's hand or will' seems only the source of the affliction, rather than appearing in any other more positive role.

The great sonnet 'When I consider' is helpfully read in conjunction with an early one (Sonnet VII), also on the poet's own career:

How soon hath time the subtle thief of youth,
  Stol'n on his wing my three and twentieth year!
  My hasting days fly on with full career,
  But my late spring no bud or blossom sheweth.
Perhaps my semblance might deceive the truth,
  That I to manhood am arrived so near,
  And inward ripeness doth much less appear,
  That some more timely-happy spirits indueth.
Yet be it less or more, or soon or slow,
  It shall be still in strictest measure even
  To that same lot, however mean or high,
Toward which time leads me, and the will of Heaven;
  All is, if I have grace to use it so,
  As ever in my great task-master's eye.

The poem begins as a lament on the speaker's slowness to mature and achieve. Like all famous laments over creative sterility, it carries its own inherent paradox; but it warrants treatment as more than simply an exercise in humility. We know that Milton both looked younger than his years and felt younger than his peers.

On turning twenty-four (rather than twenty-three, as scholars generally agree on reading line two), Milton felt that he had little to show for his time, and that others of his age were already 'timely-happy spirits' doing impressive things with their lives and talents. The people Milton had in mind for invidious comparison with himself are unknown: guesses vary from his good friend Charles Diodati to the poet Thomas Randolph and to the newly famous boy-wonder Abraham Cowley, who had published his *Poetic Blossoms* at the age of fifteen.

But it is not, after all, the poet's predicament that dominates the sonnet so much as his answer to it. It is characteristic of Milton to begin with a problem or sorrow or misgivings of some sort, and then to turn about in the sestet and end on a note, if not of triumph, at least of some firm determination or reassurance. Likewise here, the sestet resolves the problem by dismissing earthly considerations of pace, and embracing the pace set by 'the will of Heaven'.

As we began the sonnet, time was hasting; as we begin the sestet it seems to slow down; by the time we end the poem, it is as if movement has become an irrelevance under the divine eye which gazes in eternal stasis at the poet (and us), yet provides the grace which it is the poet's choice to use in order to transform his relationship to time and ambition.

Comparison of 'How soon hath time' with Sonnet XIX is fruitful and revealing:

When I consider how my light is spent,
  Ere half my days, in this dark world and wide,
  And that one talent which is death to hide,
  Lodged with me useless, though my soul more bent
To serve therewith my maker, and present
  My true account, lest he returning chide,
  Doth God exact day-labour, light denied,
  I fondly ask; But Patience to prevent
That murmur, soon replies, God doth not need
  Either man's work or his own gifts; who best
  Bear his mild yoke, they serve him best; his state
Is kingly. Thousands at his bidding speed
  And post o'er land and ocean without rest:
  They also serve who only stand and wait.

In each we have the paradox of a fine poem dealing with lack of productive achievement; in each the octave is devoted to lamentation (of, respectively, immaturity and frustration due to blindness); in each the sestet utters the answer to that lament; and in each case it is obviously *for* the sestet's resolution that the sonnet is written. Patient attendance upon God's will is in each case the stance deeply felt and affirmed; and each sonnet ends in a statement of positive assurance. But there are illuminating structural differences.

Perhaps the most important initial observation to be made about 'When I consider' is its structure as a narrative with question-and-answer dialogue. The question of line seven at first sounds rhetorical, in the tone of complaint rather than query; yet the responding voice of the sestet nevertheless offers a firm answer. Spent light, or the light the speaker initially thinks of as spent, naturally includes his creative talent and energies, but clearly and primarily includes his eyesight, as line seven shows. The apparent or alleged unfairness of God is a motif familiar to many writers on spiritual matters (we see plenty of it in George Herbert), and Milton in *Paradise Lost* deals with it so powerfully through Satan as to mislead (with some help from the critics) many of his readers. In the sonnet, the anguished question is fully prepared for by the syntactic suspense of the octave's extended *when* clause: he still has, or should have, most of his working life before him; he fears being like the unprofitable servant in the parable of the talents; he is eager to serve God. Much appears to validate his question, but the moment it is asked he firmly labels it as foolish ('I fondly ask'), and so the sestet's reply is in effect under way before the octave ends.

Insofar as we have a small drama enacted here, it is concentrated by the syntactic skeleton in the middle of the sonnet: 'I. . .ask' and 'Patience . . . / . . . replies'. But Milton uses the flexibility of the octave-sestet asymmetry (as in Italian models like Della Casa) to begin the sestet, as it were, slightly early: as if personified Patience can hardly wait (another paradox) before offering her answer. This deliberate asymmetry has the further paradoxical effect of virtually dividing the poem into seven-line halves, each culminating in one representative and memorable utterance: 'Doth God exact day-labour, light denied?' and 'They also serve who only stand and wait'. The apparent validity of the question is undermined twice even before Patience speaks: once by the 'fondly', and then by the notion that Patience seeks to 'prevent' (forestall and so negate as pointless) the poet's plaint. And Patience's answer both is and is not an answer. She does not answer yes or no to the question about God's exaction; yet she *does* answer by showing that the questioner has failed to understand the true nature of 'labour'.

It is worth asking 'Who is the central figure of this sonnet?' if only because the question sends us back to look at further details. The poet of the octave is very much aware of his God and his obligation (not to mention his eagerness) to serve; it is certainly not accidental that a first-person pronoun occurs eight times before the middle of line eight; and when Patience begins replying, it is natural that *I/me/my* disappears entirely from the rest of the poem, and that the characteristic pronoun becomes the *he/him/his* of God. 'Man' appears generically and reappears as 'they' ('thousands' may include human beings but seems primarily to signify angels). The sonnet ends by speaking about the relationship of God to human and perhaps angelic creation as a whole, *not* to John Milton exclusively – and yet he is answered. A welter of people, tasks, and services offers itself to our imaginations, whereas the first half of the sonnet created the impression of a world comprising Milton and God. What was described so hauntingly as 'this dark world and wide' because it was the world of the physically blind, can now be re-read as the lonely and menacing world of the *spiritually* blind who fail to see beyond themselves and their own pains. To the spiritually enlightened, the burden of personal affliction becomes Christ's 'mild yoke' as in the gospel, and waiting – attending in patience and without ambitious repining – becomes service.

As we stand aside from the sonnet and watch it unfold, we know of course that Milton knew the answer to his question before he asked it, and that the entire little drama is a way both of commemorating an insight and of communicating it to others. The poet, that is, becomes the object of his own moralizing. (While we know that he did *not* in fact 'only stand and wait', what mattered was his achieved readiness to do so if God so willed.) And while Patience in one sense speaks on behalf of God, in another she is a personified part of the poet's own personality and understanding. The central figure of the sonnet is in this sense really the personified Patience, since she is where God and poet meet.

In his sonnets, Milton celebrates, describes, attacks, or advises his contemporaries, but does so in a crystallizing way that tends to turn them into universals. 'When I consider', which alludes to no contemporaries, is really no different: it crystallizes the poet's predicament and turns him into a universal figure for our contemplation. The voice throughout these sonnets, no matter how private or personal their topic, is always essentially a public voice in the sense of being consciously overheard, of turning speaker, hearer, and occasion into matter for meditation both by contemporary readers and by those who come after. This is surely the transforming nature of all art that succeeds: we in effect become Milton's contemporaries, because he becomes ours.

FURTHER READING

Campbell, Gordon, ed., *John Milton: Complete English Poems, Of Education, Areopagitica*, 4th edn rev. (London, 1990)

Carey, John and Alastair Fowler, eds., *The Poems of John Milton* (London, 1968)

Darbishire, Helen, ed., *The Poetical Works of John Milton* (London, 1958)

Honigmann, E. A. J., ed., *Milton's Sonnets* (New York, 1966)

Hughes, Merritt Y., ed., *John Milton: Complete Poems and Major Prose* (New York, 1957)

Leonard, John, ed., *John Milton: The Complete Poems* (London, 1998)

Prince, F. T., *The Italian Element in Milton's Verse* (Oxford, 1954)

ed., *Milton: 'Comus' and Other Poems* (London, 1968)

Smart, John, ed., *The Sonnets of Milton* (Glasgow, 1921)

Spiller, Michael R. G., *The Development of the Sonnet* (London, 1992)

Woodhouse, A. S. P. and D. Bush, eds., *A Variorum Commentary on the Poems of John Milton*, vol. 2 (New York, 1972)

8

BARBARA KIEFER LEWALSKI

The genres of *Paradise Lost*

The Renaissance is a period of heightened genre consciousness in literary theory and poetic practice, and Milton is arguably the most genre-conscious of English poets. His great epic, *Paradise Lost*, is preeminently a poem about knowing and choosing – for the Miltonic Bard, for the characters, for the reader. One ground for such choices is genre, Milton's own choice and use of a panoply of literary forms, with their accumulated freight of cultural significances shared between author and audience.

Critics have long recognized and continue to discover in Milton's poem an Edenic profusion of thematic and structural elements from a great many literary genres and modes, as well as a myriad of specific allusions to major literary texts and exemplary works. Almost everyone agrees that *Paradise Lost* is an epic whose closest structural affinities are to Virgil's *Aeneid*, and that it undertakes in some fashion to redefine classical heroism in Christian terms (Bowra; Di Cesare; Hunter; Steadman 1967). We now recognize as well how many major elements derive from other epics and epic-like poems. From Homer's *Iliad*: a tragic epic subject – here, the death and woe resulting from an act of disobedience; a hero (Satan) motivated like Achilles by a sense of injured merit; and the battle scenes in heaven. From the *Odyssey*: Satan's wiles and craft and Satan's Odysseus-like adventures on the perilous seas (of Chaos) and in new lands. From Hesiod's *Theogony*: many aspects of the war in heaven between the good and evil angels. And from Ovid's *Metamorphoses*: the pervasiveness of change and transformation – diabolic and divine – in the Miltonic universe (Blessington 1979; Mueller; Aryanpur; Steadman 1968, 194–208; Hughes 1965; Revard; Harding 1946; Lewalski 1985, 71–6; Martz).

Other elements derive from romantic epics or other Renaissance varieties of that kind. From Ariosto's *Orlando Furioso*: the Paradise of Fools. From the *Faerie Queene*: the Spenserian allegorical characters, Sin and Death. From Tasso's *Gerusalemme Liberata* and Camoes's *Lusiads*: allusions to contemporary voyages of exploration and imperialism in Satan's voyage to earth through Chaos. From Du Bartas's massive hexameron (creation epic), *The Divine Weeks and Works*: Milton's brief epic of creation in Book 7 (Hughes 1967; Shumacher; Greenlaw; Hieatt; Williams; Quilligan; Quint; Evans; Snyder, 1: 82–8; Taylor). In more general terms, Milton's Eden is in some respects a romance garden of love in which a hero and heroine must withstand a dragon of sorts; it is also a colony of heaven planted by God and attacked by Satan (Giamatti; Evans 1996). Moreover, because heroic values have been so profoundly transvalued in *Paradise Lost*, the poem is sometimes assigned to categories beyond epic: pseudomorph, prophetic poem, apocalypse, anti-epic, transcendent epic (Spencer; Steadman 1973; Wittreich 1975; Tolliver; Webber).

Many dramatic elements have also been identified: some vestiges of Milton's early sketches for a drama entitled *Adam Unparadiz'd*; some structural affinities to contemporary epics in five 'acts', such as Davanant's *Gondibert*; and tragic protagonists who fall from happiness to misery through *hamartia* (Barker; Rollin; Sirluck). Others include the tragic soliloquies of Satan and Adam, recalling those of Dr Faustus and Macbeth; the morality-play 'Parliament of Heaven' sequence in the debate of God and the Son (3.80–343); the scene of domestic farce in which Satan first vehemently repudiates and then fawns upon his reprehensible offspring, Sin and Death (2.643–883); the scenes of domestic tragedy in Books 9 and 10 which present Adam and Eve's quarrel, Fall, mutual recriminations, and (later) reconciliation; and the tragic masques or pageants of Books 11 and 12, portraying the sins and miseries of human history (Demaray; Gardner; Grossman; Hunter, 72–95; Kranidas; Samuel).

The panoply of kinds includes pastoral: landscape descriptions of Arcadian vistas; pastoral scenes and eclogue-like passages presenting the *otium* (ease, contentment) of heaven and unfallen Eden; and scenes of light georgic gardening activity (Daniells; Empson, 149–94; Frye 1965; Knott). Also, several kinds of lyrics embedded in the epic have received some critical attention: celebratory odes, psalmic hymns of praise and thanksgiving, submerged sonnets, an epithalamium (wedding song), love lyrics (*aubade*, nocturne, sonnet), laments and complaints (Summers, 71–86; McCown; Johnson; Nardo; Blessington 1986; Radzinowicz). There are also many rhetorical and dialogic kinds which have not been much studied from the perspective of genre: Satan's several speeches of political oratory in Books 1 and 2; God's judicial oration defending his ways (3.80–134); the parliamentary debate in hell over war and peace (2.11–378); the Satan-Abdiel debate over God's right of sovereignty (5.772–895); a treatise on astronomical systems (8.15–178); a dialogue on human nature between God and Adam (8.357–451) and another on love between Raphael and

Adam (8.521–643); Michael's lectures on Christian historiography in Books 11 and 12; Satan's temptation speech to Eve in the style and manner of 'some orator renowned / In Athens or free Rome' (9.670–732; Amorose; Broadbent; Burden; MacCallum; Steadman 1968, 241–62; Steadman 1969, 67–92).

If we ask why Milton incorporated so complete a spectrum of literary forms and genres in *Paradise Lost*, a partial answer must be that much Renaissance critical theory supports the notion of epic as a heterocosm or compendium of subjects, forms, and styles. Homer's epics, Rosalie Colie has reminded us (22–3), were widely recognized as the source and origin of all arts and sciences – philosophy, mathematics, history, geography, military art, religion, hymnic praise, rhetoric – and of all literary forms. Renaissance tradition also recognized the Bible as epic-like in its comprehension of all history, all subject matters, and many genres – law, history, prophecy, heroic poetry, psalm, allegory, proverb, hymn, sermon, epistle, tragedy, tragicomedy, and more (Lewalski 1966, 10–36; Lewalski 1979, 31–71; Wittreich 1979, 9–26).

Responding to this tradition, Renaissance poets devised epics on inclusivist lines. Tasso, whom Milton recognized as the premier epic poet and theorist among the moderns, observed that Homer and Virgil had intermingled all forms and styles in their great epics, but claimed for Renaissance heroic poems (with obvious reference to his own *Gerusalemme Liberata*) an even greater range and variety, imaging the entire created universe (Tasso, 78). Moreover, the major sixteenth-century English narratives with claims to epic status – Sidney's *New Arcadia* and Spenser's *Faerie Queene* – were quite obviously mixtures of epic, romance, pastoral, allegory, and song. But if contemporary theory and practice gave Milton ample warrant to comprehend a very broad spectrum of literary kinds within *Paradise Lost*, he did not make of it a mausoleum of dead forms. On the contrary, all of Milton's major poems are invested with an imaginative energy which profoundly transforms the genres themselves, creating new models which profoundly influenced English and American writers for three centuries.

Attention to Milton's generic strategies can also highlight some important ways in which Renaissance poetic theory and practice intersect with contemporary critical concerns: intertextuality, the springs of poetic creativity and authority, the responses of the reader (Bloom; Greene; Kerrigan; Fish). In regard to genre, Milton's poem manifests several of the so-called 'novelistic' characteristics the Russian genre-theorist Mikhail Bakhtin finds in many Renaissance and post-Renaissance prose narratives: multiple genres, including extra-literary kinds, which create multiple perspectives upon the subject; the dialogic interaction of forms; the 'polyglossia' of several generic languages within the work; strong connectives linking the poem to contemporary reality; the valorization of process. Yet while these characteristics give Milton's modern epic enormous complexity, they do not produce the indeterminacy and inconclusiveness Bakhtin associates with them. In pursuing these and other suggestive connections between Renaissance and contemporary poetic theory we need to recognize some fundamental differences in assumptions about poetry and the poet, grounded chiefly in the Renaissance and Miltonic conception of the poet as teacher and rhetor.

Milton's complex use of the Renaissance genre system serves in part to enable his own poetic vision, since it is only through such literary forms, which embody the shared imaginative experience of Western man and woman, that the Miltonic Bard is able to imagine and articulate his vision of the truth of things. But also, it is only through such forms that he can accommodate that vision to readers present and future, educating them in the complex processes of making discriminations which are at once literary and moral. Milton's comments about poetry in *The Reason of Church-Government* and the pedagogic ideal he sets forth in *Of Education* suggest that as teacher and rhetor he wishes to advance our understanding through a literary regimen at once intellectually demanding and delightful (*YP* 1: 801–23; 3: 366–79). In *Paradise Lost* his method is to build upon and let his readers refine their responses to the cultural values and assumptions encoded in the genre system – about man and woman, God, nature, language, heroism, virtue, pleasure, work, and love (Lewalski 1985).

Since terms relating to genre have often been used inconsistently, we need a few definitions which accord with the concepts of major Renaissance and modern genre-theorists (Scaliger; Minturno 1559, 1564; Puttenham; Sidney; Frye; Fowler). In the Renaissance, the familiar triad of narrative, dramatic, and lyric normally carried meanings deriving from Plato's and Aristotle's three kinds of imitation or presentation, so I shall refer to them here as *literary categories* or *strategies of presentation*. The term *Genre* (or *kind*, the usual Renaissance word) is reserved for the historical genres – epic, tragedy, sonnet, funeral elegy, hymn, epigram, and many more – which are identified in classical and Renaissance theory and poetic practice by specific formal and thematic elements, topics, and conventions. Alastair Fowler (37–74) discusses these historical genres as families whose members share several (but not always the same) features, among them formal structure, metre, size, scale, strategy of presentation, subject, values, mood, occasion, attitude, style, motifs. *Subgenres* are formed by further specification of subject matter and topics – for example, the revenge tragedy is a subgenre of tragedy. The term *Mode* is appropriate for several expressive literary kinds – pastoral, satiric, comedic, heroic, elegiac, and tragic, among others which are identified chiefly by subject matter, attitude, tonality, and motifs, and which interpenetrate works or parts of works in several genres. For example, we may have a *pastoral* comedy or novel or song, a *tragic* epic, or short story, or ballad, a *satiric* verse epistle or epigram or essay.

Milton's 'Preface' to Book 2 of the *Reason of Church-Government* (1642) provides some indication of his complex approach to the Renaissance genre system. Referring to the epic-dramatic-lyric triad, he deliberates about a wide range of genre choices and notable models – classical, biblical, or contemporary – within each category:

> Time servs not now, and perhaps I might seem too profuse to give any certain account of what the mind at home in the spacious circuits of her musing hath liberty to propose to her self, though of highest hope, and hardest attempting, whether that Epick form whereof the two poems of *Homer*, and those other two of *Virgil* and *Tasso* are a diffuse, and the book of *Job* a brief model . . . Or whether those Dramatick constitutions, wherein *Sophocles* and *Euripides* raigne shall be found more doctrinal and exemplary to a Nation, the Scripture also affords us a divine pastoral Drama in the Song of *Salomon* consisting of two persons and a double *Chorus*, as *Origen* rightly judges. And the Apocalyps of Saint *John* is the majestick image of a high and stately Tragedy, shutting up and intermingling her solemn Scenes and Acts with a sevenfold *Chorus* of halleluia's and harping symphonies . . . Or if occasion shall lead to imitat those magnifick Odes and Hymns wherein *Pindarus* and *Callimachus* are in most things worthy, some others in their frame judicious, in their matter most an end faulty: But those frequent songs throughout the law and prophets beyond all these, not in their divine argument alone, but in the very critical art of composition may be easily made appear over all the kinds of Lyrick poesy, to be incomparable. (*YP* 1: 812–16)

Remarkably, Milton incorporates virtually the entire genre system in *Paradise Lost*, achieving effects which can only be suggested here through a few examples.

Milton employs specific literary modes in his epic to characterize the various orders of being: the heroic mode for Satan and his damned society; mixed for the celestial society of the angels; pastoral (opening out to georgic and comedic) for prelapsarian life in Eden; tragic (encompassing at length postlapsarian georgic, pastoral, and heroic) for human life in the fallen world. These modes establish the affective quality of the several segments of the poem, through appropriate subject matter, motifs, tone, and language, and each mode is introduced by explicit literary signals. As the narrative begins, the epic question and answer present Satan and hell in heroic terms, with reference to a range of epic passions, motives, and actions: 'pride', 'glory', 'ambitious aim', 'impious war in heaven', 'battle proud' (1.34–44). The Edenic pastoral mode is introduced by reference to the garden as 'A happy rural seat of various view' (4.247). The forthright announcement 'I now must change / These notes to tragic' (9.5–6) heralds the Fall sequence. And the claim that this tragic subject is 'not less but more heroic' than traditional epic themes (9.14) leads into the mixed modes of postlapsarian but regenerate human life.

These several modes import into the poem the values traditionally associated with them: great deeds, battle courage, glory (*aristeia*) for the heroic mode; love and song, *otium*, the carefree life for pastoral; responsibility, discipline, the labour of husbandry for georgic; the easy resolution of difficulties through dialogue and intellect for the comedic; the pity and terror of the human condition for the tragic. These contrasting modes and their modulations, together with the mixed modes which present life in the heavenly society, engage us in an on-going critique of the various perspectives on human life which they provide.

Within this structure of literary modes Milton incorporates a great many narrative, dramatic, lyric, and discursive genres. The longer narrative and dramatic kinds – epic and romance, tragedy and comedy – are incorporated through what I term generic paradigms, identified by characteristic themes, motifs, conventions, and structural patterns associated with the given genre. These generic paradigms are further reinforced by verbal allusions, plot analogies, and references to scenes, episodes, and motifs in major classical and Renaissance works in each kind. By this means we are invited to identify certain genres and certain poems as subtexts for portions of Milton's poem, and then to attend to the completion or transformation of those allusive patterns as the poem proceeds. Let us examine some of these paradigms.

Satan, we soon discover, enacts the generic paradigms of one after another of the heroic genres (epic of strife, quest epic, romance): he is thereby measured against the most notable heroes in all these kinds, promoting an exhaustive examination of the meaning of heroism. The opening scene in hell displays the distinctive topics and conventions of the epic of wrath and strife: Homeric catalogues of leaders, epic games, a council of war, addresses to armies. In relation to this paradigm, Satan reveals himself by degrees as a debased version of Achilles and Aeneas, the most notable heroes in that kind. Like Achilles (though without his justification) Satan prides himself on his obduracy, his 'fixed mind / And high disdain, from sense of injured merit' (1.97–8); and like Aeneas he escapes from a flaming city to seek a better kingdom. The *Iliad* pattern develops through several flyting matches (epic taunts), single combats, and epic battle scenes in heaven in which Satan, unlike Achilles, is ignominiously defeated. The *Aeneid* pattern continues through Satan's adventures and successful conquest in Eden, though (unlike Aeneas) he can find no new homeland because he brings hell with him everywhere: 'my self am hell' (4.75). The epic-of-wrath paradigm culminates in Satan's self-designed scene of epic triumph in Book 10, a triumph which turns to abject humiliation as Satan and his followers are abruptly transformed to serpents, enduring the thirst of a Tantalus in the Virgilian underworld.

Intersecting with this paradigm is that of the quest epic, which extends to include romance, the quintessential quest form. Milton incorporates a 'mini-Odyssey' into his epic as Satan is measured against the crafty Odysseus. The *Odyssey* pattern begins as Satan sets forth on his journey to earth through Chaos; it develops in Chaos and Eden as he continually proves himself a skilled rhetorician and a master of disguises (Steadman 1968, 194–208); and it finds completion when he returns to hell in Book 10, liberating his wife and son (Sin and Death) from captivity by his notable victory. But unlike Odysseus, whose entire adventure is a journey home, Satan at the very outset of his travels (in Book 2) is reunited with, but ironically fails to recognize, his reprehensible daughter-wife Sin, and the hideous offspring of their incestuous union, Death. And the honour they accord him at his return to hell in Book 10 soon gives way to the universal hiss of his followers turned into snakes.

Again, Milton's poem incorporates the basic narrative paradigm of romance: the continual wandering and multiple quests of knights-errant, as their ultimate goals or principal quests are almost indefinitely postponed or only partially achieved (Parker). In Satan and the fallen angels this romance paradigm is perverted as the wandering (intellectual and physical) becomes an absolute. In hell the fallen angels explore the hardest philosophical questions – 'Fixed fate, free will, foreknowledge absolute' – but find 'no end, in wandering mazes lost' (2.560–1). And instead of a wandering wood or labyrinthine landscape, Satan in Chaos traverses 'a dark / Illimitable ocean without bound, / Without dimension' (2.891–3), where he has no control whatsoever over his own motions or directions but 'swims or sinks, or wades, or creeps, or flies' (2.950) as he can, subjected entirely to the winds of chance.

Certain of Satan's adventures are specifically associated with episodes in particular romances or romantic epics, but again we recognize the perversions. Spenser's Red Crosse Knight defeats the serpent Error and (at last) the serpentine Duessa, but Satan embraces the Spenserian allegorical monsters he meets (Sin and Death) as his own progeny. Satan's journey to the Paradise of Fools is a darker version of Astolfo's journey to the Limbo of Vanities in Ariosto; however Satan comes on no rescue mission but because he is himself the source of all the vanities soon to be housed in that place. In Eden, Satan perverts all the familiar romance roles of knights in gardens of love, for he cannot win love there, nor find sensual delight, nor enjoy sensuous refreshment: instead he sees 'undelighted all delight' (4.286) and feels more intensely than before the agony of his own loneliness, lovelessness, and unsatisfied desire. A perverse Guyon (*Faerie Queene* 2. Canto 12), he destroys in Eden not a wantonly sinful but a joyously innocent Bower of Bliss and Love. In Book 10 this romance paradigm also finds its fitting resolution, as Satan – a truly perverse St George – does not slay but turns into the dragon.

Milton also incorporates the paradigms of several forms of tragedy. Satan enacts at the outset a parodic version of heroic tragedy, portraying himself in Book 1, with particular reference to Aeschylus's *Prometheus Bound*, as the noble and indomitable victim of an irrational, tyrannical, and wrathful God (Werblowsky). But Satan himself admits that he was motivated to rebel by pride and ambition – not, like Prometheus, by an intention to benefit mankind. Satan's great soliloquy on Mount Niphates (4.32–113) casts him briefly as a Faustean tragic hero, voicing the spiritual agonies of the damned soul and forced to acknowledge his guilt – his paradigmatic scene of suffering, as John Steadman notes (1976, 103–4). In subsequent soliloquies in Book 4 Satan takes on first the posture of the villain hero driven by ambition (a Macbeth or a Richard III), and at length that of an Elizabethan revenge hero – a Barabbas or an Iago wracked with envy and jealousy, devising plots and exulting in evil plans: 'O fair foundation laid whereon to build / Their ruin!' (4.521). However, as he sets his revenge plot in motion in Book 9, he perverts the usual Elizabethan paradigm, for he cannot harm his true enemy, God, and the human beings he ravages have done him no wrong whatsoever.

When Satan imbrutes himself in the serpent he recognizes how radically he is reversing the usual tragic paradigm. He is not felled by fate or his own *hamartia* for seeking to soar above humanity; rather he here chooses to sink far below it:

> O foul descent! That I who erst contended
> With gods to sit the highest, am now constrained
> Into a beast, and mixed with bestial slime,
> This essence to incarnate and imbrute,
> That to the highth of deity aspired;
> But what will not ambition and revenge
> Descend to? (9.163–9)

He also sees clearly that the revenge he seeks must be self-destructive: 'Revenge, at first though sweet, / Bitter ere long back on it self recoils' (9.171–2). Satan has now moved outside both the classical and Elizabethan paradigms of tragedy, since for him there can be no catharsis of any kind, not even the release of meeting the worst at last, but only a continual declining and falling. At last, when Satan's involuntary transformation into a serpent in Book 10 makes him the butt of scorn and derision, we see God rewriting the Satanic revenge tragedy as black comedy.

By contrast with Satan's parodic revenge tragedy, Milton devised the Fall of Adam and Eve to conform to Aristotle's prescriptions for the best kind of classical tragedy (Aristotle; Steadman 1976). The plot involves a change in the protagonists' fortunes from happiness to misery, precisely articulated in Adam's outcry – 'O miserable of happy!' (10.720). As Aristotle recommended, the protagonists are persons better than ourselves who fall through *hamartia* (in this case, culpable errors of judgement); and the plot is complex, developed through several highly dramatic scenes: the marital dispute, the two temptations, reactions to the Fall (9.192–10.862). There are several *peripeteia* (reversals) with attendant tragic ironies. There is an explicit *anagnorisis* (discovery) when Adam and Eve awaken from their lust-induced sleep and realize their loss: 'good lost, and evil got . . . naked thus, of honour void, / Of innocence, of faith, of purity' (9.1072–5). And there is a long scene of suffering as Adam and Eve voice shame, fear, guilt, remorse, torments of conscience, and mutual recriminations, culminating with Adam's poignant complaint, prostrate and paralyzed by despair, 'from deep to deeper plunged' (10.844).

At this point, the Aristotelian tragic paradigm gives way to the paradigm of Christian tragedy, drawn essentially from the Book of Revelation. Catastrophes in this paradigm are not averted: like Christ himself, the elect suffer trials, sicknesses, catastrophes, deaths, martyrdoms, but they are enabled through grace to endure their suffering in patience and to wait in faith and hope for the reversal which will occur only at the Apocalypse (King). In Milton's poem the turn from classical to Christian tragedy is the literary manifestation of the action of grace: God works a reversal by clothing Adam and Eve's physical and spiritual nakedness; and Eve's act of begging Adam's forgiveness does so on the human plane, restoring the community of human love. God's directive to Michael concerning the emotional state he is to induce in Adam and Eve defines precisely the catharsis appropriate to this new Christian tragedy: Adam and Eve are to go forth from the Garden, and we from the poem, 'not disconsolate', 'sorrowing, yet in peace' (lines 113–17).

The lyric and discursive genres are present in Milton's epic through another strategy of inclusion. Rhetorical and dialogic kinds are embedded in *Paradise Lost*: rhetorical speeches in the three classical genres (judicial, deliberative, demonstrative); several kinds of dialogue (Platonic, Boethian, biblical); and also formal debates. These embedded discursive genres engage us in careful discriminations concerning the uses and the perversions of speech and language. Also, many lyrics are embedded in the narrative, set off by specific generic conventions, signals of commencement and closure, and integrity of structure, tone, and subject matter. Milton's epic employs a much more complete spectrum of lyrics, for a larger array of purposes, and in a more complex and conscious way, than does any previous epic. The Bard voices many apostrophes, four hymnic proems (to Books 1, 3, 7, and 9), and an epithalamium, 'Hail wedded love' (4.750–5). Satan and the fallen angels often fall into laments but cannot sustain them long, and they can only pervert lyrics of praise. The angels celebrate all divine activities with hymnic praises, but they produce their most elaborate and most exalted hymns when divine love and divine creativity are manifested (3.372–415; 7.182–91; 7.565–73; 7.602–32). And prelapsarian and postlapsarian man and woman exhibit their psychological and spiritual states through a great variety of odes, love lyrics, laments, complaints, prayers, and hymns, the most elaborate and eloquent of which is their magnificent morning hymn of praise (5.160–208; McColley, 106–51). In *Paradise Lost* characters reveal their natures and their values through the lyrics they devise.

To illustrate how some of these embedded lyric forms function in Milton's epic, we might examine the rich significances which attach to Adam and Eve's love lyrics and laments. Eve devised the first love lyric in prelapsarian Eden, an exquisite, rhetorically complex, sonnet-like poem of eighteen lines, celebrating the sweetness and beauty of Eden through elaborate patterns of repetition, and building to the final half-line which proclaims Adam the essence of Eden for Eve:

> With thee conversing I forget all time,
> All seasons and their change, all please alike.
> Sweet is the breath of morn, her rising sweet,
> With charm of earliest birds; pleasant the sun
> When first on this delightful land he spreads
> His orient beams, on herb, tree, fruit, and flower,
> Glistering with dew; fragrant the fertile earth
> After soft showers; and sweet the coming on
> Of grateful evening mild, then silent night
> With this her solemn bird and this fair moon,
> And these the gems of heaven, her starry train:

But neither breath of morn when she ascends
With charm of earliest birds, nor rising sun
On this delightful land, nor herb, fruit, flower,
Glistering with dew, nor fragrance after showers,
Nor grateful evening mild, nor silent night
With this her solemn bird, nor walk by moon,
Or glittering starlight without thee is sweet. (4.639–56)

Lovely as this is, Adam's *aubade* or dawn song (5.16–22) is presented as a finer love poem, characterized by vibrant imagery, freer form, more intense feeling; verbal echoes identify it as a prototype of the Bridegroom's song to the Bride (Song of Sol. 2: 10–13), often said to be the most exquisite of all love songs (Lewalski 1979, 67):

Awake
My fairest, my espoused, my latest found,
Heaven's last best gift, my ever new delight,
Awake, the morning shines, and the fresh field
Calls us; we lose the prime, to mark how spring
Our tended plants, how blows the citron grove,
What drops the myrrh, and what the balmy reed,
How nature paints her colours, how the bee
Sits on the bloom extracting liquid sweet. (5.17–25)

But in the fallen world the situation is reversed: Adam inaugurates the tragic lament-complaint while Eve transforms and perfects that kind. Adam voices several tragic lyrics: desperate laments for what is lost, and bitter complaints seeking some remedy or relief. His first sight of the fallen Eve evokes an anguished interior lament for her ruin and for the bleakness of life without her, 'O fairest of creation, last and best / Of all God's works . . .' (9.896–916). His longest 'sad complaint' which begins 'O miserable of happy! Is this the end / Of this new glorious world' (10.720–844), vainly seeks relief in outcries, apostrophes, and agonized questions. In structure and tone, Adam's tragic lyrics most closely resemble such classical models as Ovid's *Heroides*, culminating in despair.

By contrast, Eve inaugurates a better kind of tragic lyric, the true archetype of the penitential psalms in substance and in structure. Echoing especially Psalms 38, 51, and 102, her prayer to Adam for forgiveness fully expresses the misery, grief, and agony of the fallen condition, but also voices repentance for sin, desire to make amends, hope of reconciliation:

Forsake me not thus, Adam, witness heaven
What love sincere, and reverence in my heart
I bear thee, and unweeting have offended,

Unhappily deceived; thy suppliant
I beg, and clasp thy knees; bereave me not,
Whereon I live, thy gentle looks, thy aid,
Thy counsel in this uttermost distress,
My only strength and stay: forlorn of thee,
Whither shall I betake me, where subsist?
. . .
On me exercise not
Thy hatred for this misery befallen,
On me already lost, me than thy self
More miserable; both have sinned, but thou
Against God only, I against God and thee,
And to the place of judgment will return,
There with my cries importune heaven, that all
The sentence from thy head removed may light
On me, sole cause to thee of all this woe,
Me me only just object of his ire. (10.914–36)

Eve's eloquent psalmic prayer begging forgiveness of the husband she has wronged begins her redemptive role as type of the Second Eve whose seed is the Messiah, even as she echoes the Son's proposal in the dialogue in heaven to assume mankind's guilt unto himself (3.236–7). E. M. W. Tillyard was right to stress the importance of Eve's prayer, though not I think in his claim that it replaces the Fall as the true climax of the poem (8–44). Rather, Milton makes it the point at which the Fall as classical tragedy, eventuating in despair and death, gives way to Christian tragedy, in which catastrophes and suffering can be endured in hope. Eve's prayer prepares for the couple's repentant prayer to God at the close of Book 10, but at that point they can produce only mute sighs of remorse. Accordingly, Eve's psalmic prayer to her husband is the archetype for the highest form of tragic lyric in the fallen world.

In Book 12, Eve reclaims the genre of the love song from its Petrarchan perversions by Satan (5.38–47, 9.532–48). When Eve awakens from her prophetic dream and meets Adam returned from the mountain she voices a love poem appropriate to the fallen world. In substance and tone it echoes Ruth's loving and faithful promise to follow her mother-in-law Naomi to another homeland (Ruth 1: 16–17). Eve's postlapsarian love lyric is much simpler than her elegant poem in Book 4, but it retains some artful rhetorical schemes, and it develops the same theme – that Adam is her true Eden:

In me is no delay; with thee to go,
Is to stay here; without thee here to stay,

Is to go hence unwilling; thou to me
Art all things under heaven, all places thou,
Who for my wilful crime art banished hence. (12.615–19)

Along with their other rich significances, these embedded lyrics highlight Milton's portrait of Eve as lyric poet. Some feminist theory maintains that the foundation texts of our culture deny to women any place in literary creation, and exclude them particularly from the use of metaphoric language and poetry (Landy; Gilbert). *Paradise Lost*, certainly a foundation text, does not inscribe that cultural myth. Milton's Eve 'invents' the love sonnet and also (in her story about her creation, 4.449–91) the first autobiographical narrative in Eden, as well as perfecting the tragic lament. Though in some respects inferior to Adam in the hierarchy of being, prelapsarian and postlapsarian Eve is imagined as sharing not only in all the georgic responsibilities and duties of the garden but also in all the arts of speech and song and dialogue which pertain to humankind. The final words spoken in Eden are Eve's, and in them she rises above lyric and above her role as tragic protagonist to become, along with Adam, a new kind of epic hero. Earlier, Adam affirmed the new ideal of Christian heroism (12.561–73); now Eve embraces her divinely appointed and even more central role in the epic of redemption: 'though all by me is lost, / Such favour I unworthy am vouchsafed, / By me the promised seed shall all restore' (12.621–3).

Paradise Lost is, then, an encyclopedia of literary forms which also affords a probing critique of the values those forms traditionally body forth. Most literary forms are present in *Paradise Lost* in several versions – celestial and infernal, prelapsarian and postlapsarian, Christian and pagan – inviting discriminations which are at once literary and moral. Some kinds are closely associated with the Satanic order and the diabolic consciousness – classical epic, deliberative rhetoric, soliloquy, Petrarchan sonneteering. However, this association is not exclusive. All these kinds have also their nobler versions: Christ is an Achilles-like hero in the battle in heaven; Christ's speeches in the dialogue in heaven have a persuasive dimension; Abdiel soliloquizes just before engaging Satan in battle; unfallen Eve composes a magnificent love sonnet to Adam. But some literary kinds and their values are not available to Satan – true dialogue, hymnic praise, the *otium* of pastoral – and that literary deprivation testifies to the impoverishment of the damned consciousness. By contrast, Milton suggests the plenitude and abundant life of the highest orders of being, the angels and most especially God, through the mixture and multiplicity of the genres and modes associated with them. And he indicates humankind's potential for growth and development both in the prelapsarian and the postlapsarian state as Adam and Eve take on the languages and the life-styles pertaining to one after another of the literary genres and modes.

The mixture and multiplicity of literary forms in Milton's epic are an index of its comprehensiveness and vitality. As cultural signposts common to author and reader, they also provide an important key to the interpretation of *Paradise Lost*. No poet has ever exploited them more extensively and more deliberately than Milton.

FURTHER READING

Amorose, Thomas, 'Milton the Apocalyptic Historian: Competing Genres in *Paradise Lost*, Books XI–XII', in Wittreich and Ide, eds., *Composite Orders*

Aristotle, *Poetics*, translated by S. H. Butcher as *Aristotle's Theory of Poetry and Fine Art*, 4th edn (New York, 1951)

Aryanpur, Manoocher, '*Paradise Lost* and the *Odyssey*', *Texas Studies in Language and Literature* 9 (1967), 151–66

Bakhtin, M. M., *The Dialogic Imagination: Four Essays*, ed. Michael Holquist, translated by Caryl Emerson and Michael Holquist (Austin and London, 1981)

Barker, Arthur E., 'Structural Pattern in *Paradise Lost*', *Philological Quarterly* 28 (1949), 16–36

Blessington, Francis C., *'Paradise Lost' and the Classical Epic* (Boston and London, 1979)

'"That Undisturbed Song of Pure Concent": *Paradise Lost* and the Epic-Hymn', in *Renaissance Genres: Essays on Theory, History, and Interpretation*, ed. Barbara K. Lewalski, *Harvard English Studies* 14 (Cambridge, MA, 1986)

Bloom, Harold, *A Map of Misreading* (New York, 1975)

Bowra, C. M., *From Virgil to Milton* (London, 1944)

Broadbent, J. B., 'Milton's Rhetoric', *Modern Philology* 56 (1958–9), 224–42

Burden, Dennis, *The Logical Epic: A Study of the Argument of 'Paradise Lost'* (Cambridge, MA, 1967)

Colie, Rosalie L., *The Resources of Kind: Genre-Theory in the Renaissance* (Berkeley, 1973)

Daniells, Roy, 'A Happy Rural Seat of Various View', in *'Paradise Lost': A Tercentenary Tribute*, ed. Balachandra Rajan (Toronto, 1967)

Demaray, John G., *Milton's Theatrical Epic: The Invention and Design of 'Paradise Lost'* (Cambridge and London, 1980)

Di Cesare, Mario A., '*Paradise Lost* and Epic Tradition', *Milton Studies* 1 (1969), 31–50

Empson, William, *Some Versions of Pastoral* (London, 1935), 149–94

Evans, J. M., *Milton's Imperial Epic: 'Paradise Lost' and the Discourse of Colonialism* (Ithaca and London, 1996)

'Paradise Lost' and the Genesis Tradition (Oxford, 1968)

Fiore, Amadeus P., ed., *Th'Upright Heart and Pure* (Pittsburgh, 1967)

Fish, Stanley, *Surprised By Sin: The Reader in 'Paradise Lost'* (London and New York, 1967)

Fowler, Alastair, *Kinds of Literature: An Introduction to the Theory of Genres and Modes* (Cambridge, MA, 1982)
Frye, Northrop, *Anatomy of Criticism: Four Essays* (Princeton, 1957)
The Return of Eden (Toronto, 1965)
Gardner, Helen, 'Milton's Satan and the Theme of Damnation in Elizabethan Tragedy', rpt. in *A Reading of 'Paradise Lost'* (Oxford, 1965)
Giamatti, A. Bartlett, *The Earthly Paradise and the Renaissance Epic* (Princeton, 1966)
Gilbert, Sandra, 'Patriarchal Poetry and Women Readers: Reflections on Milton's Bogey', *PMLA* 93 (1978), 368–82
Greene, Thomas M., *The Light in Troy: Imitation and Discovery in Renaissance Poetry* (New Haven and London, 1982)
Greenlaw, Edwin, 'Spenser's Influence on *Paradise Lost*', *Studies in Philology* 17 (1920), 320–59
Grossman, Marshall, 'Dramatic Structure and Emotive Pattern in the Fall: *Paradise Lost* IX', *Milton Studies* 13 (1979), 201–19
Hanford, James Holly, 'The Dramatic Element in *Paradise Lost*'; rpt. in *John Milton: Poet and Humanist*, ed. John S . Diekhoff (Cleveland, 1966)
Harding, Davis P., *Milton and the Renaissance Ovid* (Urbana, 1946)
The Club of Hercules: Studies in the Classical Background of 'Paradise Lost' (Urbana, 1962)
Hieatt, A. Kent, *Chaucer, Spenser, Milton: Mythopoeic Continuities and Transformations* (Montreal and London, 1975), 153–270
Hughes, Merritt Y., 'Milton's Celestial Battles and the Theogonies', rpt. in *Ten Perspectives on Milton* (New Haven, 1965)
'Milton's Limbo of Vanities', in Fiore, ed., *Th'Upright Heart*
Hunter, G. K., *Paradise Lost* (London, 1980)
Ide, Richard S., 'On the Uses of Elizabethan Drama: The Revaluation of Epic in *Paradise Lost*', in Wittreich and Ide, eds., *Composite Orders*
Johnson, Lee M., 'Milton's Blank Verse Sonnets', *Milton Studies* 5 (1973), 129–53
Kerrigan, William, *The Prophetic Milton* (Charlottesville, 1974)
King, John N., *English Reformation Literature: The Tudor Origins of the Protestant Tradition* (Princeton, 1982)
Knott, John R., *Milton's Pastoral Vision: An Approach to 'Paradise Lost'* (Chicago and London, 1971)
Kranidas, Thomas, 'Adam and Eve in the Garden: A Study of *Paradise Lost*, Book V', *Studies in English Literature* 4 (1964), 71–83
Landy, Marcia, 'Kinship and the Role of Women in *Paradise Lost*', *Milton Studies* 4 (1972), 3–18
Lewalski, Barbara K., *Milton's Brief Epic: The Genre, Meaning, and Art of 'Paradise Regained'* (Providence and London, 1966)
'Paradise Lost' and the Rhetoric of Literary Forms (Princeton, 1985)
Protestant Poetics and the Seventeenth-Century Religious Lyric (Princeton, 1979)
MacCallum, H. R., 'Milton and Sacred History: Books XI–XII of *Paradise Lost*', in *Essays in English Literature from the Renaissance to the Victorian Age, Presented to A. S. P. Woodhouse*, ed. M. Maclure and F. W. Watt (Toronto, 1964)
McColley, Diane Kelsey, *A Gust for Paradise: Milton's Eden and the Visual Arts* (Urbana and Chicago, 1993)

McCown, Gary M., 'Milton and the Epic Epithalamium', *Milton Studies* 5 (1973), 39–66

Martz, Louis L., *Poet of Exile: A Study of Milton's Poetry* (New Haven and London, 1980), 203–44

Minturno, Antonio Sebastiano, *De Poeta* (Venice, 1559) *L'Arte Poetica* ([Venice], 1563 [1564])

Mueller, Martin, '*Paradise Lost* and the *Iliad*', *Comparative Literature Studies* 6 (1969), 292–316

Nardo, A. K., 'The Submerged Sonnet as Lyric Moment in Miltonic Epic', *Genre* 9 (1976), 21–35

Parker, Patricia A., *Inescapable Romance: Studies in the Poetics of a Mode* (Princeton, 1975), 114–58

Puttenham, George, *The Arte of English Poesie* (London, 1589)

Quilligan, Maureen, *Milton's Spenser: The Politics of Reading* (Ithaca and London, 1983)

Quint, David, *Epic and Empire: Politics and Generic Form from Virgil to Milton* (Princeton, 1993)

Radzinowicz, Mary Ann, *Milton's Epics and the Book of Psalms* (Princeton, 1989)

Revard, Stella P., *The War in Heaven: 'Paradise Lost' and the Tradition of Satan's Rebellion* (Ithaca and London, 1980)

Rollin, Roger E., '*Paradise Lost*: "Tragical-Comical-Historical-Pastoral"', *Milton Studies* 5 (1973), 3–37

Safer, Elaine B., 'The Use of Contraries: Milton's Adaptation of Dialectic in *Paradise Lost*', *Ariel* 2 (1981), 55–69

Samuel, Irene, 'The Dialogue in Heaven: A Reconsideration of *Paradise Lost* III.1–417', *PMLA* 72 (1957), 601–11

Scaliger, Julius-Caesar, *Poetices libri septem* (Geneva, 1561)

Shumacher, Wayne, '*Paradise Lost* and the Italian Epic Tradition', in Fiore, ed., *Th'Upright Heart*

Sidney, Philip, *The Defense of Poesie* (London, 1595)

Sirluck, Ernest, '*Paradise Lost*': *A Deliberate Epic* (Cambridge, 1967)

Snyder, Susan, ed., *The Divine Weeks and Works of Guillaume De Saluste Sieur Du Bartas*, translated by Joshua Sylvester, 2 vols. (Oxford, 1979)

Spencer, T. J. B., '*Paradise Lost:* The Anti-Epic', in *Approaches to Paradise Lost*, ed. C. A. Patrides (Toronto, 1968)

Steadman, John M., *Milton and the Renaissance Hero* (Oxford, 1967)

Milton's Epic Characters: Image and Idol (Chapel Hill, 1968)

'Milton's Rhetoric: Satan and the "Unjust Discourse"', *Milton Studies* 1 (1969), 67–92

'The Epic as Pseudomorph: Methodology in Milton Studies', *Milton Studies* 7 (1973), 3–25

Epic and Tragic Structure in 'Paradise Lost' (Chicago, 1976)

Summers, Joseph, *The Muse's Method: An Introduction to 'Paradise Lost'* (Cambridge, MA, 1962)

Tasso, Torquato, *Discourses on the Heroic Poem*, translated by Mariella Cavalchini and Irene Samuel (Oxford, 1973)

Taylor, George C., *Milton's Use of Du Bartas* (Cambridge, MA, 1934)

Tillyard, E. M. W., *Studies in Milton* (London, 1951)

Tolliver, Harold E., 'Milton's Household Epic', *Milton Studies* 9 (1976), 105–20
Webber, Joan, *Milton and His Epic Tradition* (Seattle and London, 1979)
Werblowski, Zwi, *Lucifer and Prometheus* (London, 1952)
Williams, Kathleen, 'Milton, Greatest Spenserian', in Wittreich, ed., *Milton and the Line of Vision*
Wittreich, Joseph A., *Visionary Poetics: Milton's Tradition and his Legacy* (San Marino, 1979)
ed., *Milton and the Line of Vision* (Madison, 1975)
Wittreich, Joseph A., and Richard S. Ide, eds., *Composite Orders: The Genres of Milton's Last Poems*, *Milton Studies* 17 (Pittsburgh, 1983)

9

JOHN LEONARD

Language and knowledge in *Paradise Lost*

In Book 8 of *Paradise Lost*, Adam recalls his first experiences on waking into life:

> My self I then perused, and limb by limb
> Surveyed, and sometimes went, and sometimes ran
> With supple joints, and lively vigour led:
> But who I was, or where, or from what cause,
> Knew not; to speak I tried, and forthwith spake,
> My tongue obeyed and readily could name
> What e'er I saw. Thou sun, said I, fair light,
> And thou enlightened earth, so fresh and gay,
> Ye hills and dales, ye rivers, woods, and plains,
> And ye that live and move, fair creatures, tell,
> Tell, if ye saw, how came I thus, how here? (8.267–77)

It is surprising to hear the newly created Adam speak so 'readily'; we might have expected him to take more time in finding words with which to express himself. We might even say that Adam takes speech and language for granted, but he is right to do so – precisely because they *are* granted to him. Unlike his descendants, Adam has no need to acquire language laboriously. In a word, Adam's language is natural, not conventional.

The distinction may become clearer if we turn from *Paradise Lost* to a different kind of text: Locke's *Essay Concerning Human Understanding*. In Book 3 of the *Essay*, entitled 'Of Language', Locke considers the case of an explorer encountering strange plants and animals in a newly discovered country:

> He that in a new-discovered Country, shall see several sorts of Animals and Vegetables, unknown to him before, may have as true *Ideas* of them, as of a Horse or a Stag; but can speak of them only by a description, till he shall either take the Names the Natives call them by, or give them Names himself. (3.10.32)

At first sight, this explorer's situation might seem much like Adam's, though in fact it is quite different. Adam doesn't just follow – or even institute – a conventional usage: he recognizes the inherent appropriateness of a certain name to a certain creature. For Locke, however, there is no necessary relation between names and their referents – all is a matter of custom and convention. Where Locke's explorer has a licence to impose names at a whim, Adam names 'readily' from a perfect understanding.

Milton's concept of Adamic language is largely indebted to Plato's *Cratylus*, though it finds some biblical warrant in Adam's naming of the animals in Genesis:

> And out of the ground the LORD God formed every beast of the field, and every fowl of the air; and brought them unto Adam to see what he would call them: and whatsoever Adam called every living creature, that was the name thereof. (2: 19)

Like most of his contemporaries, Milton takes this text as sanctioning the inherent correctness of Adam's names. Adam recalls how he saw 'each bird and beast'

> Approaching two and two, these cowering low
> With blandishment, each bird stooped on his wing.
> I named them, as they passed, and understood
> Their nature, with such knowledge God endued
> My sudden apprehension. (8.350–4)

The effortlessness of Adam's naming ('sudden apprehension') testifies to the completeness of his understanding. In the *Christian Doctrine*, Milton remarks that Adam 'could not have given names to the animals in that extempore way, without very great intelligence' (*YP* 6: 324). He makes the point still more forcefully in *Tetrachordon:* 'Adam who had the wisdom giv'n him to know all creatures, and to name them according to their properties, no doubt but had the gift to discern perfectly' (*YP* 2: 602). To name creatures in Paradise was to know their essences, not just to assign convenient designations.

Adam's names bring him self-knowledge as well as knowledge about the animals. He continues: 'but in these / I found not what me thought I wanted still' (8.354–5). Seeing the animals grouped 'two and two', Adam becomes suddenly aware of his own need for fit companionship. He goes on to employ the animals' names carefully and deliberately in his request for a companion:

> of fellowship I speak
> Such as I seek, fit to participate
> All rational delight, wherein the brute

2. Medici Tapestries (*c.* 1550), *Adam Names the Animals* (Accademia, Florence)

> Cannot be human consort; they rejoice
> Each with their kind, lion with lioness;
> So fitly them in pairs thou hast combined;
> Much less can bird with beast, or fish with fowl
> So well converse, nor with the ox the ape;
> Worse then can man with beast, and least of all. (8.389–97)

Adam pairs the names of species and genera experimentally, by sound as well as sense, to attest to the fitness or unfitness of the creatures' possible unions. After the perfect fit of 'lion with lioness', the alliterations in 'bird with beast, or fish with fowl' reflect a less than perfect match, while the union of 'man with beast' does not even have alliteration to recommend it. Adam's concluding rhyme of 'beast' with 'least' resolutely dismisses any thought of fit society between himself, 'the masterwork' of Creation (7.505), and these, the least of sentient creatures. In this context of sound and sense, the rhyme of 'speak' with 'seek' – 'of fellowship I speak / Such as I seek' affirms the bond between language and knowledge.

When he finally consents to Adam's request, God makes plain that his demurral had only been a test 'to see how thou couldst judge of fit and meet' (8.448). By giving 'fit and meet' names to the animals, Adam has gained knowledge of what is fitting for him. As God says:

> Thus far to try thee, Adam, I was pleased,
> And find thee knowing not of beasts alone,
> Which thou hast rightly named, but of thy self,
> Expressing well the spirit within thee free,
> My image, not imparted to the brute. (8.437–41)

There are limits to Adam's powers of naming. He encounters the first and greatest limit to his language immediately after naming the animals:

> O by what name, for thou above all these,
> Above mankind, or aught than mankind higher,
> Surpassest far my naming, how may I
> Adore thee, author of this universe? (8.357–60)

Adam cannot name or know God as easily as he had 'named . . . and understood' the animals, and yet his very inability to name here brings him the greatest recognition of all.

Names and naming are more important to *Paradise Lost* than at first appears. Adam's ability to call things by their proper names was one expression of the perfect wisdom which was his birthright in Paradise. Milton (unlike most of his contemporaries) even extends this wisdom to Eve, for she names the flowers (11.277). One consequence of the Fall was the loss of this ability to name things rightly, since reason was now clouded and the will perverted. The fallen angels fall so completely as to forfeit the names which had once befitted them:

> of their names in heavenly records now
> Be no memorial blotted out and razed
> By their rebellion, from the books of life.
> Nor had they yet among the sons of Eve
> Got them new names. (1.361–5)

I have argued elsewhere (*Milton Studies* 21) that such names as 'Belial', 'Beelzebub', and 'Moloch' are 'new names' the fallen angels have not yet got at the time of their Fall. Suspended, as it were, in a limbo between their old and new identities, the devils do not yet have new names and are powerless to speak their old ones:

> If thou beest he; but O how fallen! how changed
> From him, who in the happy realms of light
> Clothed with transcendent brightness didst outshine
> Myriads though bright. (1.84–7)

The 'he' here recognized by Satan is not yet 'Beelzebub'. Satan's followers are indeed quite nameless in *Paradise Lost*. No devil ever addresses another one by name.

Satan alone among the devils has a name. 'Satan' means 'enemy' in Hebrew. Before his followers have 'got them new names', before even the Fall of Man, Satan is the 'arch-enemy' and is 'thence in heaven called Satan' (1.82). But he is not called 'Satan' *in hell*. (The devils see God, not Satan, as their 'great enemy'.) Satan, like his fellows, had had a 'former name' (5.658), a name which Milton (following patristic tradition) associates with 'Lucifer', the morning star (5.760, 7.131, 10.425; the allusion is to Isa. 14: 12: 'How art thou fallen from heaven, O Lucifer, son of the morning!'). An awareness of this 'former name' brings out a pointed irony when Satan speaks his name for the first (and only) time:

> Fair daughter, and thou son and grandchild both,
> High proof ye now have given to be the race
> Of Satan (for I glory in the name,
> Antagonist of heaven's almighty king). (10.384–7)

Is this just a casual gloss upon the name? Or is it an unprecedented recognition by Satan of who and what he has become? Satan had not been so forthcoming when the good angels had asked after his name in Paradise:

> Know ye not then said Satan, filled with scorn,
> Know ye not me? Ye knew me once no mate
> For you, there sitting where ye durst not soar. (4.827–9)

It had been as 'Lucifer' that Satan had aspired to 'sit . . . upon the mount of the congregation' (Isa. 14: 13, *PL* 5.760–6). If 'Lucifer' is the name with which he now scorns his captors, the poet's 'said Satan' is not a neutral comment.

Milton builds into his poem a sustained distinction between prelapsarian and postlapsarian nomenclature. He often cites exotic and beautiful names in order to dismiss them. This is most apparent in the negative similes which recur throughout *Paradise Lost*:

Not that fair field
Of Enna, where Proserpine gathering flowers
Her self a fairer flower by gloomy Dis
Was gathered, which cost Ceres all that pain
To seek her through the world; nor that sweet grove
Of Daphne by Orontes, and the inspired
Castalian spring, might with this Paradise
Of Eden strive. (4.268–75)

These place names with their mythical associations are drawn from a splintered, fragmentary, fallen world quite alien to the pristine clarity and passionate immediacy of Paradise. Introducing the names in a supposed attempt to apprehend Edenic beauty, Milton tactfully confesses that his own nomenclature is powerless to bring the kind of 'sudden apprehension' Adam had enjoyed before the Fall.

How, then, does Milton represent Adamic language? Latinisms play a part. In Book 7 Adam asks Raphael:

what cause
Moved the Creator in his holy rest
Through all eternity so late to build
In Chaos, and the work begun, how soon
Absolved. (7.90–4)

Christopher Ricks has drawn attention to the peculiar meaning of Adam's 'Absolved': 'before sin was, *absolution* was no more than completion' (115). By using words in their original, Latin sense, Milton 'takes us back to a time when there were no infected words because there were no infected actions' (110). Ricks sees the same kind of playing of fallen against unfallen meanings in the account of the river which moves 'with serpent error wandering' (7.302): 'it is surely easier to believe in a slightly ingenious Milton than in one who could be so strangely absent-minded as to use both "serpent" and "error" without in some way invoking the Fall' (110). What, then, of 'Absolved'? Ricks asks: 'is Milton deliberately setting aside, and asking us to see that he has set aside, the application to sin because he is describing a sinless world?' (115). Milton is doing this, but Adam is not. Unlike the fallen poet, Adam remains unconscious of the ominousness we read into (and out of) his vocabulary. Milton's prelapsarian play at this point reaches 'back to an earlier purity' (Ricks), but it is free from the kind of melancholy or pejorative tone we hear in 'serpent error wandering'.

Adam's request to hear of Creation has implications for prelapsarian knowledge as well as language. Just what is Adam asking? Milton's early editors took 'late' ('eternity so late to build / In Chaos') as meaning 'after the time'. Thus understood, Adam is asking why God created the universe at so late a date. Such a question, prying curiously into God's secrets, was felt to be impious. Here is Milton's first editor, Patrick Hume (from his edition of 1695):

> Why God was not pleased to create the World 100,000 Years before he did, and how he employed his infinite Power, Wisdom and other unaccountable Perfections before the Creation, are some of those vain and Atheistical Enquiries of impertinent and daring Men, who, little acquainted with the turns and motions of their own frail and unruly Wills, would pry into the Secrets of the Eternal Mind, and ask an account of that *Almighty Will* which created all things how and when he pleas'd . Such Doubts are unresolvable, as not coming within the compass of Human comprehension, for the Question will at last run up to Eternity it self, and the Enquiry will come to this impious and absurd Demand, why God did not make the World co-eternal with himself? (214)

Hume's reading might be supported by an allusion to the Book of Job in 'magnify his work'. Elihu exhorts Job to

> Remember that thou magnify his work,
> Which men behold.
> Every man may see it;
> Man may behold it afar off.
> Behold, God is great, and we know him not,
> Neither can the numbers of his years be searched out.
> (Job 36: 24–6)

On Hume's reading, Adam (unlike Job) is trying to search out the number of God's numberless years.

This interpretation continues to be delivered by Milton's modern editors. Alastair Fowler notes:

> It is curious that Milton should put Adam's question so absurdly – as if he were to ask, like a child, what moved the prime mover. In *De Doctrina* 1.7 Milton calls it 'the height of folly' to enquire into 'the actions of God before the foundation of the world'. (*Poems*)

It would indeed be 'the height of folly' for Adam to ask the question his editors foist upon him; however, he does not ask it. Hume and Fowler have forgotten that 'late' can mean 'recently' (*OED* 4). Thus understood, Adam makes no enquiry about the timing of Creation. 'Late' most often means 'recently' in *Paradise Lost* – and this is its meaning on every other occasion where 'late' follows 'so' (compare 5.675; 10.721, 941; 12.642). This sense is surely uppermost in Adam's 'what cause / Moved the Creator . . . so late to build / In Chaos'. Milton is as aware as Jonathan Richardson (another early editor) that 'Eternal Ages pass'd makes This seem late, though had it been Millions and Millions of Ages Before, it had been Late with Regard to what was Past' (196). Adam might add (in effect he does add): 'though it had been millions of ages before, it would be late (recent) with regard to me'. Adam's question is accordingly both daring and humble. It is even more daring than Milton's editors recognize, for it amounts to 'Why Creation?' not just 'Why Creation now?'

Adam's whole speech is remarkable for the way in which it frees itself from curiosity while asserting a bold spirit of enquiry:

> Deign to descend now lower, and relate
> What may no less perhaps avail us known,
> How first began this heaven which we behold
> Distant so high, with moving fires adorned
> Innumerable, and this which yields or fills
> All space, the ambient air wide interfused
> Embracing round this florid earth, what cause
> Moved the creator in his holy rest
> Through all eternity so late to build
> In chaos, and the work begun, how soon
> Absolved, if unforbid thou may'st unfold
> What we, not to explore the secrets ask
> Of his eternal empire, but the more
> To magnify his works, the more we know. (7.84–97)

Note that there is no question-mark anywhere in these lines. The positioning of 'ask' after 'not' (95) calls into question whether Adam is really asking a *question* at all. (The meaning would be different were he to say 'what we ask, not to explore'.) Placed at the line-ending, 'ask' assumes an emphatic boldness and directness, yet it also strengthens the implied antithesis between 'ask' and 'magnify' ('not to . . . ask . . . but to magnify his works'). Even the repeated 'how' ('how first began . . . how soon / Absolved') is not truly interrogative, for both 'how's follow on from the imperative 'relate'. Adam's whole speech is pregnant with curious questions, but between 'unfold' and 'magnify', it unfolds into a wondering celebration of the magnificence of God's works. Like the 'ambient air' which 'yields or fills / All space', Adam fills a space in his knowledge by yielding to it. He does not search out the number of God's years, but (anticipating Job), remembers to magnify his works.

The purity of Adam's prelapsarian request emerges when we compare it with Satan's very different way of asking about Creation:

> Chaos and ancient Night, I come no spy,
> With purpose to explore or to disturb
> The secrets of your realm, but by constraint
> Wandering this darksome desert, as my way
> Lies through your spacious empire up to light
> . . .
>
> direct my course;
> Directed no mean recompense it brings
> To your behoof. (2.970–82)

Where Adam asserts his will by setting limits to it, Satan is tactlessly blunt ('direct my course'). He tries to placate Chaos and Night by appealing to their self-interest, but it is clear that Satan's interest is not just in magnifying their works. Bentley's emendation of 'disturb' to 'disclose' (on the grounds that 'secrets' cannot be *disturbed*) even brings out a veiled threat. Satan promises not to 'disturb', not to breach the peace of, a realm which peals with disruption as 'loud and ruinous (to compare / Great things with small)' as 'if this frame / Of heaven were falling' (2.921–2, 924–5)! In surroundings which make redundant all talk of disturbing, Satan hints darkly at his own disruptive powers. Nothing could be further in tone and mood from the graceful amplification of Adam's bold humility.

Paradise Lost is a poem peopled with strong presences and many voices, each distinguished from the others, yet all distinctively Milton's. Adam's 'what cause / Moved the creator' picks up the voice of Milton's epic invocation six books earlier, and yet the two voices are quite different:

> Say first, for heaven hides nothing from thy view
> Nor the deep tract of hell, say first what cause
> Moved our grand parents in that happy state,
> Favoured of heaven so highly, to fall off
> From their creator, and transgress his will
> For one restraint, lords of the world besides?
> Who first seduced them to that foul revolt?
> The infernal serpent . . . (1.27–34)

Here, as in Adam's lines, 'what cause' is placed at the line-ending and followed by 'Moved'. The presence of 'creator' also serves to tie the two passages together. In part, the cross-reference works to present Adam's lines as an epic invocation. But it also points to a contrast: our 'grand parents' were moved to fall off, whereas God (with the full weight of the paradox) moved in rest. To recall Fowler, 'it is curious that [Adam] should . . . ask, like a child, what moved the prime mover'. However, Adam does not ask 'what moved the prime mover'; he asks 'what cause / Moved the Creator in his holy rest'. God moved *in* his rest; he did not move from it. It is possible to see this too as an absurdity, but it is not the absurdity Fowler puts in Adam's mouth. Adam's version does not question God's identity as prime mover, but asserts a majesty and self-sufficiency of will which are absurd only when claimed by someone other than God.

The poet's invocation (as the repeated question-marks confirm) is a real question, not a seeming question magnified into something greater. Strictly, there are two questions, not one. Only the second question ('who first seduced them?') is fully answered: our 'grand parents' were seduced by the 'infernal serpent'. The question 'what cause?' is barely glanced at by this response. As Stanley Fish writes: 'the answer to the question, "what cause?" is given in the first line, "Of Man's First Disobedience" . . . The reader who finds a cause for the Fall denies it by denying its freedom' (259). The poet's 'what cause?' is finally unanswerable. Here, as in his negative similes and catalogues of proper names drawn from the fallen world, the poet quietly acknowledges his inability to arrive at first causes. Adam, however, arrives at the First Cause through a direct perception of the immediacy of Creation.

The question 'what cause?' is important to Satan's temptation of Eve. The serpent's argument takes a step forward when he claims to recognize (among other things) the cause for God's forbidding Adam and Eve to eat the apple:

> O sacred, wise, and wisdom-giving plant,
> Mother of science, now I feel thy power
> Within me clear, not only to discern
> Things in their causes, but to trace the ways
> Of highest agents, deemed however wise.
> Queen of this universe, do not believe
> Those rigid threats of death. (9.679–85)

Satan's use of the plural in 'causes' and 'agents' prepares the way for his shift from 'God' ('Indeed? Hath God then said . . . ?') to 'gods': 'ye shall be as gods', 'And what are gods that man may not become / As they?' (9.656, 708, 716). Satan has always been reluctant to speak of 'God' in *Paradise Lost*. (In hell, the devils had used such circumlocutions as 'our supreme foe', 'he . . . whom I now / Of force believe almighty', or just 'he'). The effect here of the serpent's 'gods' is to offer the word as a title available to man: 'so ye shall die perhaps, by putting off / Human, to put on gods' (713–14). Soon it is dressed specifically for Eve: 'Goddess humane, reach then, and freely taste' (732).

While avoiding (so far as possible) any mention of 'God', Satan does sometimes drop a singular pronoun into his talk of 'the gods':

> What can your knowledge hurt him, or this tree
> Impart against his will if all be his?
> Or is it envy, and can envy dwell
> In heavenly breasts? (9.727–30)

Discerning 'things in their causes', Satan here arrives most cunningly at his alleged cause for the prohibition. As Thomas Newton noted in 1749, Satan 'generally speaks of Gods when the sentiment would be too horrid, if it was spoken of God' (2: 186). Satan uses the plural to allege divine malevolence, and the singular to reassure Eve that God will not hurt her. To this end, he will even speak of 'God': 'will God incense his ire / For such a petty trespass?' (9.692–3). Eve must not feel too soon that she is being asked to repudiate the one God she has known and loved. Yet when (three lines later) Satan next speaks of 'God', it is to cancel the word: 'God therefore cannot hurt ye, and be just; / Not just, not God' (700–1). This is the last time 'God' passes Satan's lips in the poem.

What we witness throughout the temptation is a contest (unconscious on Eve's part) between herself and Satan for the authority to interpret prelapsarian language. The serpent first stakes a claim upon Eve's language through the seeming miracle of his ability to speak:

> he glad
> Of her attention gained, with serpent tongue
> Organic, or impulse of vocal air,
> His fraudulent temptation thus began.
> Wonder not, sovereign mistress . . . (9.528–32)

Milton's demurral as to whether Satan actually employs the serpent's tongue is not mere pedantry. Satan finds words for his temptation, but it is not certain that he finds a tongue to speak them: his snake-speech might involve illusion within illusion ('impulse of vocal air'). Eve, however, believes herself to be hearing a 'serpent tongue / Organic' which obeys its owner as 'readily' as Adam's tongue had obeyed him when first giving names. She is amazed to hear a serpent speak.

Here Milton departs significantly from Genesis, which offers no explanation for the serpent's speaking. (It doesn't even identify the serpent as

Satan, though this identification was made from pre-Christian times.) Milton's contemporaries were much interested in Eve's lack of surprise in Genesis. Thomas Browne inferred that Eve's own grasp of Adamic language must have been weak:

> She might not yet be certain that onely man was priviledged with speech, and being in the novity of the Creation, and inexperience of all things, might not be affrighted to hear a serpent speak: Besides she might be ignorant of their natures who was not versed in their names, as being not present at the generall survey of Animalls, when Adam assigned unto every one a name concordant unto its nature. (1.238–9)

In *Paradise Lost*, Eve reflects directly on the serpent's name and nature: 'Thee, serpent, subtlest beast of all the field / I knew, but not with human voice endued' (9.560–1). Browne implies that for Eve to feel surprise would be an advantage. Yet surprise need not entail vigilance. When Milton's Eve replies: 'What may this mean? Language of man pronounced / By tongue of brute?' (553–4), she reacts in just the way Satan had hoped for. To be sure, her wonder creates a dangerous moment for Satan, an opportunity for Eve to exercise special vigilance. However, it is an opportunity Eve misses, and a moment that Satan turns to his advantage with what is a dramatic masterstroke by Milton: the serpent speaks specifically about his speaking and attributes this supposedly new power to some as yet unspecified fruit.

The serpent's most persuasive argument is his ability to argue. His seeming participation in language not only argues a miraculous change; in a world where names correspond to natures, language is knowledge. The illusion of a 'serpent tongue / Organic' implies Satan's whole case that the forbidden fruit confers knowledge. However, language on the serpent's lips becomes an instrument of deception and so a means of replacing knowledge with ignorance.

Throughout the temptation, Satan bestows names amiss so as deliberately to deceive Eve. We have seen how he abuses the terms 'God' and 'gods'. Another term, still more central to the serpent's argument, is the name of the forbidden Tree. As Arnold Williams has shown, the name 'Tree of Knowledge of Good and Evil' received much attention from biblical commentators. Because God speaks the name at Genesis 2: 9 and 2: 17, it was most widely held that he had given it before the Fall. This is certainly the view incorporated in *Paradise Lost* (8.323–4). Milton agrees with Andrew Willet that the Tree cannot be 'so called because of the lying and enticing words of Satan' (28). Thomas Newton noted that 'our first parents were created with perfect understanding, and the only knowledge that was forbidden was the knowledge of evil by the commission of it' (2: 59). Properly, the Tree's name is a warning against evil. Yet Satan speaks it as a promise of good. Eating, he claims, will lead

> To happier life, knowledge of good and evil;
> Of good, how just? Of evil, if what is evil
> Be real, why not known, since easier shunned? (9.697–9)

Though many theologians have denied evil any real existence in Nature, none has thought it unimportant. Tucked away in a parenthesis, Satan's 'if what is evil / Be real' implies that evil is nothing to worry about. And yet the 'if' does not make for a complete dismissal. While reassuring Eve, Satan also excites her curiosity and suspicion by hinting that God has planted evil in Nature. Hume comments:

> *If what is Evil be real*: if there be any thing really Evil in this World, wherein God the Creator made all, and acknowledged all that he made was *Good* . . . Eve had been forewarn'd of the dangerous Evil of Temptation and Sin, there was no other Evil in nature to be dreaded or avoided by her, though slyly here insinuated by Satan. (259)

Evil, in Milton's universe, is a vitiation of Nature; it is not a nature created by God. Satan manages to cast doubt upon the goodness of the Creator by insinuating that evil is created. He even implies that it would be dangerous for Eve *not* to know this evil. In just two lines Satan has (1) awakened Eve's suspicions about God, (2) titillated her curiosity about 'evil' (supposedly an unexplored part of Nature), and (3) reassured Eve that no harm will befall her if she eats the apple.

Twenty lines later, the serpent promises Eve knowledge of good and evil in the gods' (not God's) despite: 'if they all things, who enclosed / Knowledge of good and evil in this tree, / That whoso eats thereof, forthwith attains / Wisdom without their leave?' (9.722–5). Contemplating these words (and the serpent's ability to speak them), Eve then accepts Satan's interpretation of the Tree's name:

> Great are thy virtues, doubtless, best of fruits
> . . .
> Whose taste, too long forborne, at first assay
> Gave elocution to the mute, and taught
> The tongue not made for speech to speak thy praise:
> Thy praise he also who forbids thy use,
> Conceals not from us, naming thee the tree
> Of knowledge, knowledge both of good and evil;
> Forbids us then to taste, but his forbidding
> Commends thee more, while it infers the good

> By thee communicated, and our want:
> For good unknown, sure is not had, or had
> And yet unknown, is as not had at all.
> In plain then, what forbids he but to know,
> Forbids us good, forbids us to be wise?
> Such prohibitions bind not. (9.745–60)

Eve thus comes to see the 'tree of knowledge, knowledge both of good and evil' as the tree of 'good'. 'Evil' drops quietly away. Governing 'good', the words 'not had at all' are dramatically ironic: Eve means that good must be known to be possessed, but her 'Knowledge of good' is to be 'bought dear by knowing ill' (4.222). Eve is to gain knowledge *of* good, but good itself is not to be had at all. As Adam later cries: 'our eyes / Opened we find indeed, and find we know / Both good and evil, good lost, and evil got' (9.1070–2).

Eve would have done well to heed the Tree's whole name, not just that part stressed by Satan. Despite the seeming miracle of 'language of man pronounced by tongue / Of brute', the serpent's language is not Eve's. He insinuates himself into her language in order to bestow names amiss and so deceive her. She surrenders her language too readily to him and so forfeits that pure and natural speech which Adam had spoken as a birthright on first waking into life. The corrupting of innocence begins with a corrupting of language.

FURTHER READING

Bentley, Richard, *Milton's 'Paradise Lost'* (London, 1732)
Browne, Thomas, *Pseudodoxia Epidemica* (London, 1650)
Fish, Stanley E., *Surprised By Sin: The Reader in 'Paradise Lost'* (London and New York, 1967)
H[ume], P[atrick], *Annotations on Milton's 'Paradise Lost'* (London, 1695)
Leonard, John, '"Though of thir Names": The Devils in *Paradise Lost*', *Milton Studies* 21 (1985)
Locke, John, *An Essay Concerning Human Understanding* (1690), ed. P. H. Nidditch (Oxford, 1975)
Newton, Thomas, *'Paradise Lost': A Poem in Twelve Books*, 2 vols. (London, 1749)
Richardson, Jonathan (father and son), *Explanatory Notes and Remarks Upon Milton's 'Paradise Lost'* (London, 1734)
Ricks, Christopher, *Milton's Grand Style* (Oxford, 1963)
Willet, Andrew, *Hexapla: A Sixfold Commentary on Genesis* (London, 1608)
Williams, Arnold, *The Common Expositor: An Account of the Commentaries on Genesis, 1527–1633* (Chapel Hill, NC, 1948)

10

DENNIS DANIELSON

The Fall and Milton's theodicy

Milton's presentation of his various literary characters can be controversial because so many people still believe in, or worry about, the actual existence of some of his most important ones: Adam, Eve, Satan, Jesus. But Milton's God is especially controversial. For all Milton's 'language of accommodation' (see *PL* 5.572–4, 6.893, 7.176–9), Milton never presents *his* God as if he is not really God, the eternal and almighty Being who created the heavens and the earth, who reveals himself in the Bible and in the life and person of Jesus Christ, and to whom all beings owe thanks and worship for his goodness and greatness. Moreover, to believe or not to believe in this God is such a fundamental thing that one cannot realistically join the conversation created by *Paradise Lost* and expect one's belief or unbelief to go unaddressed. Nevertheless, Milton does not force the issue concerning belief in God's mere existence, for that is something he simply assumes; for him God's existence is a premise much more than a conclusion (see *YP* 6: 130–2). In spite of the radical polarities of belief about God in *Paradise Lost*, its humans and devils and angels are united in this: they all believe that he is.

The theological apologetic that *Paradise Lost* does undertake concerns not God's existence but his nature, or character. Milton ends the first paragraph of his epic by asking the Muse to raise him 'to the highth of this great argument' so that he may 'assert eternal providence, / And justify the ways of God to men' (1.24–6). Milton thus announces that he will attempt a *theodicy*, a defence of God's justice. This attempt, in the course of the epic, requires that Milton perform a series of balancing acts. The so-called theological problem of evil – the problem that a theodicy sets out in some degree to solve – can itself be seen as a problem concerning how to balance three fundamental propositions to which virtually all Christians, and perhaps others, assent:

1 God is all powerful (or omnipotent).
2 God is wholly good.
3 There is evil in the world.

3. Albrecht Dürer (1471–1528), *Adam and Eve* (Gallerie degli Uffizi, Florence)

The question, some of whose formulations date from antiquity, is: if we assert any two of these three propositions, how can the remaining one make any sense? If God is all powerful and wholly good, how can there be evil in the world he created? But we know there *is* evil in the world, so how can we believe God to be both all powerful and wholly good? Is he able to remove evil but unwilling? Or is he willing but unable?

Historically there have been those who have 'solved' the theological problem of evil by tacitly abandoning its premises. Some 'dualists' have so defined and straitened God's power as to deprive omnipotence of its meaning. Some 'voluntarists' have defined God's goodness merely as a function of God's will, or power, so that a thing is good merely by virtue of the fact that God wills it – a manoeuvre whereby *goodness* as predicated of God loses its ordinary meaning. And still others, like the eighteenth-century 'optimists' mocked by Voltaire and Samuel Johnson, have defined evil in the world in such a way that it is not to be seen truly as evil after all but rather as a necessary part of some universal good. None of these wafflings, however, is acceptable to Milton, and it is a measure of his theodical courage that he sets out to tell the story of 'all our woe' in a way that none the less asserts God's power (his 'eternal providence') *and* justifies God's ways.

This philosophical balancing act that Milton knows he must perform also entails a rhetorical balancing act. For if God's ways are justifiable not only in the abstract but also to actual human beings ('justifiable to men'; *SA* 294), then part of Milton's job is to respect, and to avoid alienating, readers whom he must at the same time accuse of being sinful and limited in their understandings. To undertake a theodicy at all presupposes that we have *some* right or ability to arrive at judgements concerning God's nature and character. Yet no religious theodicist may ever forget that the God thus being 'judged' is himself the Author and Judge of all Things. Without the first assumption, an attempt to explain God's ways to human beings would be ridiculous. Without the second, it would be blasphemous. So Milton begins *Paradise Lost* by declaring our and his solidarity in the Fall of Man, in its effects, and in the need to be redeemed from its effects (1.1–5). He also confesses his own 'darkness' and 'lowness' and his need to be illuminated, raised, and supported before he can adequately tell his story and present his theodicy (1.22–6). Yet throughout his epic he not only provides us with repeated reminders that we are fallen creatures ourselves, but also presupposes and appeals to our ability truly to recognize that which is good. I will return to some of the ways in which Milton, by appealing to that recognition of good, draws his readers into his conversation. For now, it is enough merely to recognize how *Paradise Lost* as a theodicy demands of both its author and its reader a delicate balance between *chutzpah* and humility.

Now the Fall (traditionally called 'the Fall of Man') refers to the first human transgression of the divine command. It can be conceived narratively, embodied in an account of the transgression, including both the events leading up to it, and its consequences; or conceived in doctrinal terms concerning the cause and nature of humanity's wickedness, suffering, and estrangement from God. Although the narrative and the doctrinal may obviously influence each other, historically they have often not been particularly integrated, and *Paradise Lost* is remarkable for the extent to which Milton seeks to establish a balance between the interests of narrative and those of doctrine, with each enriching the other.

Biblically, the Fall narrative appears in Genesis 2 and 3: the Lord God, having created man (Adam) and placed him in the garden of Eden, commands him, 'thou shalt not eat' of the tree of the knowledge of good and evil, adding, 'for in the day that thou eatest thereof thou shalt surely die' (2: 17). After woman is created, the serpent speaks to her, denies that if they eat of the forbidden fruit they shall surely die, and ascribes to God a jealous motive for his interdiction: 'God doth know that in the day ye eat thereof, then your eyes shall be opened, and ye shall be as gods' (3: 5). The woman then eats of the fruit and gives some also to her husband, who likewise eats. This eating is followed immediately by their knowing themselves to be naked (3: 7), and not long after by the Lord God's arriving to curse the serpent with crawling upon its belly, the woman with sorrow in bearing children and in being dominated by her husband, and the man with sorrow and sweat in his obtaining food from the ground (3: 14–19).

Some modernist critics have viewed this story 'as a straightforward aetiological myth, designed to explain why a man cleaves to his wife and why he is the senior partner in the union, why he has to labour in the fields and she in childbirth, why we wear clothes, why we dislike snakes, and why they crawl on their bellies' (Evans 1968, 9), and, of course, also why we must die. In any case, the rest of the Old Testament makes no clear mention of the story of Adam and Eve, and its only biblical interpretation is given in the New Testament by St Paul, who reads it typologically, thus amplifying and universalizing the significance of Adam and of his transgression by seeing them as the backdrop for Jesus Christ's acts of redemption. Adam's sin and its effects are symmetrical with the non-sin and life-giving sacrifice of Christ, whom Paul calls 'the last Adam' (1 Cor. 15: 45): 'For since by man came death, by man came also the resurrection of the dead. For as in Adam all die, even so in Christ shall all be made alive' (1 Cor. 15: 21–2; see also Rom. 5: 19).

Although such doctrine and such typology play an important role in Milton's works, for him the narrative also informs doctrine. His epic medium is itself narrative; it must respect the details of its ur-narrative, and must also inevitably impose some concrete, literary limitations of its own upon doctrine. Particularly because *Paradise Lost* vastly expands the biblical story of Adam and Eve, it brings into view narrative details which, when seen only from afar, might not even appear doctrinally significant. Milton's magnifying lens, however, focuses attention on a whole series of questions about the Fall story: how can we talk about *the* Fall when there really were two falls, Adam's and Eve's? How can we talk about Adam being tempted by Satan when Satan tempted only Eve? What motivations operated in each of their falls? How did it come about that they were tempted separately? Was Eve's fall inevitable? Once Eve had fallen, was Adam's fall inevitable? If they were ignorant of good and evil, how could they have been expected to avoid evil? If God knew they were going to be tempted, could he not have forewarned them? Why would the serpent have wanted to have Adam and Eve disobey God anyhow? These and many other questions which Genesis leaves in the background are brought by Milton's detailed narrative into the foreground where their answers can be inspected for both literary and doctrinal coherence.

One of the most notable difficulties Milton encounters in thus seeking to meld things narrative and doctrinal is the issue of divine foreknowledge and human free will. A vital component of Milton's theodicy is the 'Free Will Defence', the model or argument according to which God, for reasons consistent with his wisdom and goodness, created angels and human beings with freedom either to obey or disobey his commands. Such an act of creation represents a self-limitation on God's part: it means that he cannot manipulate the free choices of angels and humans, though this claim is no mark against his omnipotence, because the 'cannot' is a logical entailment of his own exercise of power. The Free Will Defence, furthermore, claims that, although innumerable such free creatures have in fact disobeyed God's commands and so created an immense amount of evil, the amount of goodness that presupposes the exercise of freedom ultimately *outweighs* the total amount of evil. For without freedom, what value would things such as honesty, loyalty, and love possess? From Tertullian on, freedom has been valued also theologically as an indication in human beings 'of God's image and similitude . . . the outward expression of God's own dignity', freedom being the 'primary postulate of goodness and reason' (*Adversus Marcionem* 2.6, 2.5). Milton himself stresses in *Areopagitica* that freedom is an essential quality for any moral or rational creature:

> Many there be that complain of divin Providence for suffering *Adam* to transgresse, foolish tongues! when God gave him reason, he gave him freedom to choose, for reason is but choosing; he had bin else a meer artificiall *Adam*, such an *Adam* as he is in the motions [puppet shows]. We our selves esteem not of that obedience, or love, or gift, which is of force. (*YP* 2: 527)

God of course could merely have created automata, puppets. But except in a depreciated, mechanical way, no honesty or loyalty or love could ever have been predicated of such beings. Therefore, it is at least plausible to claim that free will, though also the necessary condition of a huge amount of moral evil, is worth it – and therefore, too, that God's choosing to make creatures with that potential for going wrong is consistent with his being both all powerful and wholly good.

Accordingly, in *Paradise Lost* Milton's God declares:

> I made [human beings] just and right,
> Sufficient to have stood, though free to fall.
> Such I created all the ethereal powers
> And spirits, both them who stood and them who failed;
> Freely they stood who stood, and fell who fell.
> Not free, what proof could they have given sincere
> Of true allegiance, constant faith or love,
> Where only what they needs must do, appeared,
> Not what they would? What praise could they receive?
> What pleasure I from such obedience paid,
> When will and reason (reason also is choice)
> Useless and vain, of freedom both despoiled,
> Made passive both, had served necessity,
> Not me. (3.98–111)

Most readers of *Paradise Lost*, I think, can accept, provisionally at least, the logic of the Free Will Defence – can accept it, in other words, as a reasonable *doctrine*. However, Milton has the doctrine appear in a speech delivered by God within a dramatic context. The most obvious problem that results is that of anthropomorphism, of God sounding like a human being vociferously defending his own actions. Such a context thus makes it very difficult for us not to feel the same scepticism regarding this speaker's motivations that we would feel in any analogous human situation.

But even ignoring what might be called the dramatic problem – even if we can take God's words simply at face value – we encounter a more serious clash as we read on: a clash between doctrine and narrative. In Book 3, God carries on to say that angels and human beings were thus created truly free, so that if they fall, they cannot blame

> Their maker, or their making, or their fate,
> As if predestination overruled
> Their will, disposed by absolute decree
> Or high foreknowledge; they themselves decreed
> Their own revolt, not I: if I foreknew,
> *Foreknowledge had no influence on their fault,*
> *Which had no less proved certain unforeknown.*
> So without least impulse or shadow of fate,
> Or aught by me immutably foreseen,
> They trespass, authors to themselves in all
> Both what they judge and what they choose.
>
> (3.113–23; italics added)

The doctrinal or philosophical question of whether God's foreknowledge and human free will can coexist remains an interesting and keenly debated one – as it was in Milton's day. For Milton and for many of his contemporaries, to accept any kind of determinism was to abandon free will, and to abandon free will was to abandon theodicy. One must conclude, says Milton in *Christian Doctrine*, that 'neither God's decree nor his foreknowledge can shackle free causes with any kind of necessity'. For otherwise, God himself is made 'the cause and author of sin'; and to refute this conclusion 'would be like inventing a long argument to prove that God is not the Devil' (*YP* 6: 166).

In so defending free will, however, Milton was not prepared to restrict God's omniscience. In the seventeenth century the Socinians, for example, argued that just as omnipotence can do only that which it is logically possible to do, so omniscience can know only that which it is logically possible to know; future free actions are in principle not knowable; and what is not knowable is therefore not *fore*knowable, even by God. By contrast, orthodox Calvinists saw God's foreknowledge as *based on* his decrees, so that if anything is said to be divinely foreknown, one can infer that it is also divinely decreed, and thus predetermined. Milton denies both of these extremes: 'We should feel certain that God has not decreed that everything must happen inevitably. Otherwise we should make him responsible for all the sins ever committed, and should make demons and wicked men blameless. But we should feel certain also that God really does foreknow everything that is going to happen' (*YP* 6: 164–5; *CM* 14: 84).

However, if God's foreknowledge implies no determinism, why does God in Book 3 of *Paradise Lost* say that humankind's fault 'had no less proved certain unforeknown' (119)? Seventeenth-century theologians carefully distinguished certainty from necessity, the latter relating to events in themselves, the former relating to knowledge of the events. Thomas Pierce complains about those writers who, failing 'to distinguish *necessity* from *certainty* of *events* . . . call that *necessary* which is but *certain* and *infallible*' (1657, 60; see *YP* 6: 165 and *CM* 11: 48–50). 'What God decreed to *effect*', says Pierce, 'will come to pass *unavoidably*, and by *necessitation* . . . But what he *only* decreed to *permit*, will *contingently* come to pass; yet . . . with a *certainty* of *event*, because his *foreknowledge* is *infallible*' (1658, 128). 'What is contingently come to pass', says Henry Hammond, 'being done, is certain, and cannot be undone, and God sees it, as it is, therefore he sees it as done, and so certain, yet as done contingently, and so as that which might not have been' (*Works* 1674, 586). An inelegant but accurate paraphrase of line 119, therefore, would be: 'the fall would have been known certainly (but not as something necessary) after the fact even if I hadn't known it certainly (but not as something necessary) before the fact'.

In this way, for Milton and some of his contemporaries, God's *fore*knowledge is no more indicative of any kind of determinism than is that certainty which an event proves to have once it becomes a *fait accompli*. That *we* know an event with certainty does not preclude its having occurred as a result of free choice. Boethius's *Consolation of Philosophy*, which contains what is still the most famous and influential treatment of divine foreknowledge, declares that indeed all of God's knowledge is analogous to our knowledge of things present – it is properly *scientia* rather than *praescientia*, since God dwells in an eternal present that transcends our categories of time and tense. 'Divine knowledge', says Boethius, 'resides above all inferior things and looks out on all things from their summit' (116). And in *Paradise Lost* Milton tells us that God looks down on the world, 'beholding from his prospect high, / Wherein past, present, future he beholds' (3.77–8).

One can thus recognize a Boethian element in Milton's presentation of divine foreknowledge, and one can accept the possible coherence of Hammond's and Pierce's and Milton's insistence that God foreknows with certainty human choices that are nevertheless genuinely free – and yet still have profound misgivings as one reads, in Book 3 of *Paradise Lost*, God's words about the Fall. For as Martin Evans points out, 'the abstract idea of an "eternal present" is simply not translatable into narrative terms' (Evans 1973, 178). The 'mistranslation' Milton thus has to settle for renders a view of things as temporally present or past and hence already accomplished. In Book 3, where we 'see God foreseeing', God's speech very quickly shifts into the past tense. We are told that man '*will* fall' (95), but then that he *had* sufficient means to avoid falling (97), that 'foreknowledge *had* no influence on their fault' (118), and so on. Accordingly, the notion of free will upon which Milton's theodicy is based takes on an ambiguity that it would not have possessed had God uttered his judgement only after the Fall, epic time. Because narrative is a time-bound medium, a God thus narratively presented cannot help but sound prejudiced when he speaks of the supposedly 'unnecessary' future Fall as if it were a *fait accompli.* Although the difficulty may be literary and not ultimately doctrinal, one cannot readily justify Milton for placing God in what appears such a doctrinally awkward situation.

Yet overall, Milton's intrepidity in trying to fuse narrative and doctrine produces much more clarity than confusion. Quite apart from the issue of foreknowledge, Milton in justifying God's ways must also render credible the claim that theologically, psychologically, sexually, and environmentally the Fall was not necessary. But he must also make credible the Fall's *possibility.* Though the latter claim may appear obvious, historically within Christianity there has been a tendency to glorify the prelapsarian condition in such superlative terms that one is made to wonder how the Fall could have happened at all. Clearly, if Adam and Eve's perfection before the Fall were defined in such a way that they appeared supremely and immutably good, then the Fall – especially when one tried to imagine it concretely and narratively – would appear utterly inexplicable. Yet historically within Christianity there has also been a separate, somewhat lesser tendency to see the Fall as inevitable (perhaps because of some innate, unavoidable flaw in human nature), or else as necessary to the greater glory of God and the fuller development of humankind. For Milton none of these alternatives is acceptable. If the Fall is in principle inexplicable, then a narrative account of it will lack credibility, and Milton's reader will either give up hope of hearing any rational theodicy, or even perhaps cultivate a suspicion that humankind did not fall but was somehow pushed. Similarly, if the Fall appears as inevitable, then Milton's reader, in spite of God's disclaimers, will indeed blame humankind's 'maker, or their making, or their fate' (3.113) – with similarly disastrous results for theodicy. Finally, of course, if the Fall appears desirable, then it will not be seen or lamented as a fall at all.

To put the matter technically, Milton had to build into his narrative both the necessary conditions for Adam and Eve's falling *and* the necessary conditions for their standing. One of the main ways he does this is to expose Adam and Eve to some kind of trial or temptation before they must face *the* temptation. Eve, for example, almost becomes infatuated, Narcissus-like, with her own image in the lake; but she hears and responds to the Voice that leads her to Adam, and she moves from being attracted to a two-dimensional image to loving a real person whose image she shares (4.449–91). Some critics have thought that this episode and others like it –

such as Eve's dream and Adam's flutterings of infatuation for Eve – are evidence that Adam and Eve are 'fallen before the Fall'. But what Milton is doing is presenting Adam and Eve's potential for falling, their *fallibility*, not their fallenness. Without that potential, nothing in the poem would make sense. And yet even given that potential, the Fall is not inevitable. Indeed, the discipline and moral exercise occasioned by that potential for evil are themselves good and help constitute Adam and Eve's potential for not falling. As Milton puts it in *Areopagitica*:

> Wherefore did [God] creat passions within us, pleasures round about us, but that these rightly temper'd are the very ingredients of vertu? They are not skilfull considerers of human things, who imagin to remove sin by removing the matter of sin . . . *This justifies the high providence of God*, who though he command us temperance, justice, continence, yet powrs out before us ev'n to a profuseness all desirable things, and gives us minds that can wander beyond all limit and satiety. Why should we then affect a rigor contrary to the manner of God and of nature, by abridging or scanting those means, which books freely permitted are, both to the *triall of vertue*, and the exercise of truth . . . Were I the chooser, a dram of well-doing should be preferr'd before many times as much the forcible hindrance of evill-doing. For God sure esteems the *growth and compleating* of one vertuous person, more then the restraint of ten vitious. (*YP* 2: 527–8; italics added)

In this passage Milton not only recapitulates the Free Will Defence, according to which the good that presupposes freedom *outweighs* the evil that restraint or a deterministic control of human behaviour could prevent; he also adumbrates what is sometimes called a 'soul-making' theodicy, one that in part explains possibilities of both natural and moral evil as necessary ingredients in an environment for what Milton elsewhere in *Areopagitica* calls 'the constituting of human vertue' (*YP* 2: 516). In *Paradise Lost* Milton takes this dimension of theodicy much further, for here the demands of narrative for concreteness and coherence lead him to imagine a prelapsarian environment that is interesting, challenging, even at times frightening. Eve is tempted to fall for her own image, Adam is tempted to fall for his image, and both Adam and Eve are told the story of how Satan does fall for Sin, who is his image. They hear how Abdiel resists the temptation of Satan, who also enters Paradise and inspires in Eve a bad dream, which makes Eve cry and for which Adam and Eve must seek at least a partial explanation. They must work in the garden, organize their chores, and show hospitality to angels. They converse with, and compose poetry for, God, the angel, and each other. Adam must name the animals, and Eve the plants. And of course, again, there is one plant whose fruit, on pain of death, they are forbidden to eat. In this environment they thus face 'challenges, dangers, tasks, difficulties, and possibilities of real failure and loss' (Hick 1967; 3: 139) – which God is nevertheless justified in allowing them to face because of the conspicuous richness of life that such an environment makes possible. Milton imagines an unfallen life for Adam and Eve that seems very far indeed from what E. M. W. Tillyard unaccountably calls 'the hopeless position of Old Age pensioners enjoying perpetual youth' (quoted in Evans 1968, 244).

For Adam and Eve before the Fall, Paradise was a beginning, not a dead end. Their perfection was a perfection capable of enrichment and increase. One of the most exquisite examples of that perfection is provided by their sexual relationship with each other. Throughout history, many commentators have seen sexual intercourse as a result of the Fall, or have seen the Fall itself as resulting from sexual temptation. However, Milton not only assumes but also boldly presents prelapsarian sexual relations that take place fully within the divine plan of creation. The goodness Adam and Eve enjoy is from God. 'Their blissful bower . . . was a place / Chosen by the sovereign planter, when he framed / All things to man's delightful use' (4.690–2). And we are reminded by the couple's evening prayers, which immediately precede their gentle love-making, that their union is at once significant for the rest of humankind and conducive to the further declaration of the goodness of God, who has 'promised from us two a race / To fill the earth, who shall with us extol / [His] goodness infinite' (4.732–4).

The connection between sex and theodicy is clear: we have no trouble seeing the abuses of sex as postlapsarian; but if also the glories of sex are envisaged as resulting from the Fall, then how can we look on the Fall as regrettable, and how can Milton declare the goodness of a Creator who would withhold so great a gift from his sinless creatures? In trying to depict the Fall and life before it concretely and narratively, Milton had to assume that if every good gift came from the very God whose goodness and power he was setting out to declare, then loving physical union between man and woman must be an essential component of Paradise.

Furthermore, though prelapsarian sex was good, and better than postlapsarian sex (compare 9.1011–58), it could have become better still – as could all of human enjoyment. As Milton presents it, the scope of unfallen experience was to expand as Adam and Eve grew and persisted in obedience. Raphael tells them:

> Your bodies may at last turn all to spirit,
> Improved by tract of time, and winged ascend
> Ethereal, as we, or may at choice
> Here or in heavenly paradises dwell;
> If ye be found obedient, and retain

> Unalterably firm his love entire
> Whose progeny you are. (5.497–503; see also 7.155–61)

This unfallen scenario includes a great increase in humankind's mobility and spirituality. And part of what Raphael implies is that Adam and Eve's bodies may become more like his body and those of the other angels, who even as spiritual beings enjoy all the pleasures of the body – eating, for example, and also sexual union.

In one of the most remarkable scenes in *Paradise Lost* Adam asks Raphael how angels express their love. And Raphael,

> with a smile that glowed
> Celestial rosy red, love's proper hue,
> Answered. Let it suffice thee that thou know'st
> Us happy, and without love no happiness.
> Whatever pure thou in the body enjoy'st
> (And pure thou wert created) we enjoy
> In eminence, and obstacle find none
> Of membrane, joint, or limb, exclusive bars:
> Easier than air with air, if spirits embrace,
> Total they mix, union of pure with pure
> Desiring; nor restrained conveyance need
> As flesh to mix with flesh, or soul with soul. (8.618–29)

Contrary to popular idiom, human beings in coitus do not go *all the way*. But Milton's angels do – and so eventually might Adam and Eve and their progeny, were it not for the Fall.

In constructing his theodicy, then, Milton's imagination is at work seeking to present recognizably good things – both actual joys and prospects of even greater – as the Creator's gifts, and so also to establish the undesirability of humankind's falling. 'Soul-making' and Free Will Defence work together to explain how the relative riskiness and decision-dependence of Adam and Eve's perfection create the necessary (though not the sufficient) conditions of their falling; the Fall is conspicuously possible. And at the same time, through Milton's dynamic presentation of life in Eden, they provide grounds for believing that the risk may have been worth it.

Yet the Fall did take place – as God knew it was going to. Was God thus simply thwarted? Or was the Fall really, at some secret level, something he willed? Perhaps the most famous response to these questions is the so-called paradox of the Fortunate Fall, according to which the sin of Adam and Eve was a happy fault, a *felix culpa*, because 'if it had never occurred, the Incarnation and Redemption could never have occurred' (Lovejoy,

164). Without fully entering the debate here I would simply suggest that this theory has become an unfortunate cliché of Milton criticism. When Adam in Book 12 hears of the Redemption and glorious future that God will make available to the fallen human race, he confesses:

> Full of doubt I stand,
> Whether I should repent me now of sin
> By me done and occasioned, or rejoice
> Much more, that much more good thereof shall spring,
> To God more glory, more good will to men
> From God . . . (12.473–8)

To read Adam's confession of doubt as a normative expression of doctrine, and to read the rest of *Paradise Lost* in the light of that doctrine, is highly uncritical. For here too Milton performs a balancing act. The future that God will provide is a glorious one, and he is much to be praised for providing it. That future may even offer something more glorious and happy than Adam and Eve's original condition (12.464–5). Yet the unfallen scenario Milton presents in *Paradise Lost* suggests that, however great our future, it will never match the still greater future that Adam and Eve and their offspring might have enjoyed in a world without sin. God in his mercy and might does bring good out of evil, but 'the alternative might have been *more* glorious' (Mollenkott, 3). As the words of God himself indicate in *Paradise Lost*, things would have been still 'Happier, had it sufficed [man] to have known / Good by it self, and evil not at all' (11.88–9).

Nor should the Fall be seen as necessary to God's greater glory. For, as Milton's contemporary John Goodwin puts it:

> God is not so poorely or meanely provided, in, and of himself, for the exaltation of his Name and Glory, as to stand in need of the dunghill of sin to make a foot-stoole for him whereby to ascend into his Throne. If the *goodnesse* and *righteousnesse* of man be nothing unto God, *profit* not him, much lesse can the sins of men claime *part and fellowship* in such a businesse. So then the sins of men [are] . . . contriveable to his glory, but no wayes requisite or necessary hereunto. (*Redemption Redeemed* 1651, 40)

God is to be glorified. He is all powerful. He is wholly good. But there *is* evil in the world – evil that no juggling with optimistic paradoxes can rationalize away.

For Milton, a large proportion of the evil that persists in the world is represented by the loss of real human beings who will not accept the salvation that God offers them by grace through the work of his Son. Although free will is impaired by the Fall, Milton, in accordance with his belief in God's justice, declares that 'prevenient' grace (11.3) 'to all / Comes unprevented, unimplored, unsought' (3.230–1), grace that enables the fallen will to turn to God. Some, of course, will 'neglect and scorn' God's sufficiently and universally offered grace, though 'none but such' will be excluded from mercy (3.185–202). In this way Milton suggests that God, both before and after the Fall, does everything he can for the sake of humankind short of violating free will or the conditions necessary for 'the constituting of human vertue'.

In this way too Milton confronts the problem of evil at the practical level. His theodicy responds not only to the concrete demands of narrative, but also to the spiritual needs of human beings. The goodness of God has to be asserted not simply out of a kind of theological purism, but out of a recognition that actual worship of God, if it is to have any integrity, is predicated on a conviction that the object of worship is wholly worthy of being worshipped. Moreover, if such worship, along with obedience, is essential to human felicity, then to encourage it is also to perform a pastoral ministry. The preface to *God's Goodness Vindicated*, a pastoral theodicy published by Richard Baxter in 1671, puts the issue thus:

> How much the Glory of God and the Salvation of Men is concerned in the right understanding of his Goodness . . . is evidently seen by all that have any true Notion of the Divine Excellency and Mans Felicity. God's Goodness is his most solemnly proclaimed Name and Glory. It is his Goodness duly known, that leads Sinners to Repentance, and unites their Hearts to fear his Name, and excites . . . that Love which is our Holiness and Happiness to Eternity. It is also too well known, how much this amiable Divine Goodness is denied or doubted of. (*The Practical Works* 1707, 2: 923)

Milton's theodicy similarly has an evangelical and pastoral dimension. It performs this role not merely by declaring the goodness of God, but by doing so in the face of evil, which experientially is theodicy's first datum, as it is of *Paradise Lost*: 'first disobedience', 'mortal taste', 'death', 'woe', 'loss'. Poetically and actually, we are thrust not only into the midst of things but into the midst of evils – including, of course, the evil of sin.

Integral with Milton's theodicy, therefore, is his attempt to help us to come to grips with sin. In this attempt, his narrative and pastoral and rhetorical skills are all essential. As Baxter says in *God's Goodness Vindicated*, 'with the Melancholy' – with those worried about the problem of evil – 'the greatest Difficulty lieth in making them capable to receive plain Truths: For [the truth] will work, not as it is, but as it is received' (2: 924). Theodicy therefore needs to address the problem of evil not just from above, abstractly, but also from below, from the point of view (so to speak) of the consumer, addressing what Stanley Fish has called the 'defects' of the reader (1–22). Again, that is one of the reasons why those last two words of the first invocation are so important. For, at least in Milton's theodicy, the job is to 'justify the ways of God *to men*' – to human beings with real needs and real sins.

Finally, Milton provides us with literary models, pastoral examples, of characters who in the midst of their fallenness come to remember the benevolence of the one who created and judged them. But just as a recognition of God's benevolence facilitates Adam and Eve's confession of sin, so the confession of sin in turn enhances their freedom to confess God's goodness. The first words we hear Adam speak in Book 11, after his and Eve's prayers of repentance are heard, emphasize the divine benevolence. 'Eve', says Adam,

> easily may faith admit, that all
> The good which we enjoy, from heaven descends;
> But that from us aught should ascend to heaven
> So prevalent as to concern the mind
> Of God high-blest, or to incline his will,
> Hard to belief may seem. (11.141–6)

If Adam was earlier surprised by sin, he is here also in a sense surprised by forgiveness. Clearly, the spontaneity of the unfallen Adam – who in Book 8 leaps to his feet and declares at once God's 'goodness and power preeminent' (279) – is gone; but then so is ours. We *recognize* this more tentative Adam and perhaps also feel with him that, after the acknowledgement of our own sin, the next hardest thing is to believe that a holy God would forgive it.

Here then, once more, is the balancing act between *chutzpah* and humility. In a peculiar way, in Milton, these two apparently opposed attitudes end up nurturing each other. As Job's demand to put his case to God ends with his repenting in dust and ashes, and as Charles Wesley's 'And can it be that I should gain an interest in the Saviour's blood' leads to 'Bold I approach th'eternal throne', so Adam's recognition of divine goodness leads to an astonishment at the gulf that separates us from it; and so an acknowledgement of humankind's fallen condition, as in the first paragraph of *Paradise Lost*, can eventuate in a project of theodicy. The two attitudes – like doctrine and narrative, like the potential for evil and the potential for good, like prelapsarian innocence and experience – can be integral. Perhaps naturally, a consideration of the Fall humbles, whereas theodicy emboldens. But as we know, Milton undertakes the two simultaneously. And it is an indication of the wholeness he aims at, that in concerning himself with the justification of God, he is also concerned with the justification of sinners.

FURTHER READING

Boethius, *The Consolation of Philosophy*, translated by Richard Green (New York, 1962)

Burden, Dennis, *The Logical Epic: A Study of the Argument of 'Paradise Lost'* (London, 1967)

Danielson, Dennis, 'Timelessness, Foreknowledge, and Free Will', *Mind* 86 (1977), 430–2

Milton's Good God: A Study in Literary Theodicy (Cambridge and New York, 1982)

'Through the Telescope of Typology: What Adam Should Have Done', *Milton Quarterly* 23 (1989), 121–7

Empson, William, *Milton's God* (London, 1961)

Evans, J. Martin, *'Paradise Lost' and the Genesis Tradition* (Oxford, 1968)

ed., *'Paradise Lost': Books* IX–X (Cambridge, 1973)

Fish, Stanley Eugene, *Surprised By Sin: The Reader in 'Paradise Lost'* (London, 1967)

Hick, John, *Evil and the God of Love* (London, 1966)

'Evil, The Problem of', *Encyclopedia of Philosophy*, ed. Paul Edwards (New York, 1967)

Kirkconnell, Watson, *The Celestial Cycle: The Theme of 'Paradise Lost' in World Literature with Translations of the Major Analogues* (Toronto, 1952)

Lewalski, Barbara Kiefer, 'Innocence and Experience in Milton's Eden', in *New Essays on 'Paradise Lost'*, ed. Thomas Kranidas (Berkeley, 1969)

Lovejoy, Arthur O., 'Milton and the Paradox of the Fortunate Fall', *ELH* 4 (1937), 161–79, rpt. in *Critical Essays on Milton from ELH* (Baltimore, 1969)

McColley, Diane Kelsey, *Milton's Eve* (Urbana, 1983)

Mollenkott, Virginia R., 'Milton's Rejection of the Fortunate Fall', *Milton Quarterly* 6 (1972), 1–5.

Pierce, Thomas, *The Divine Philanthropie Defended* (London, 1657)

Self-Condemnation (London, 1658)

Plantinga, Alvin, *God, Freedom and Evil* (London, 1974)

Radzinowicz, Mary Ann, '"Man as Probationer of Immortality": *Paradise Lost* XI–XII', in *Approaches to 'Paradise Lost': The York Tercentenary Lectures*, ed. C. A. Patrides (Toronto, 1968)

Ulreich, John C., Jr, 'A Paradise Within: The Fortunate Fall in *Paradise Lost*', *JHI* 32 (1971), 351–66

Williams, Norman Powell, *The Ideas of the Fall and of Original Sin* (London, 1927)

11

JOHN CAREY

Milton's Satan

The controversy about Milton's Satan provides an opportunity to inspect the relationship between a literary text and critical reaction to it. This is instructive because it shows how literature works (or has worked), and how it should not be expected to work.

A word, first, about the generation of Milton's Satan. There is very little in the Bible about Satan. In *Christian Doctrine* Milton collects all the available biblical evidence in a few sentences. It amounts to little more than that Satan is the author of all evil and has various titles (*YP* 6: 349–50). As Kastor has shown, it was not until about AD 200 that official Judaism began to absorb popular concepts of Satan. From then on appearances of Satan in literature, sub-literature, and theology multiplied. Scores of literary Satans evolved, and some of them – notably those created by Du Bartas, Andreini, Grotius, and Vondel – possibly influenced Milton. However, no convincing single source for Milton's Satan has been found.

The need to create a Satan figure arises from a Manichaean view of the moral universe. Within this mentality, as Jung has pointed out (Werblowsky, x–xii), the evolution of God as a *summum bonum* necessitates the evolution of an *infimum malum*, to account for the presence of evil in the world. It was to combat Manichaeanism that the early church launched its doctrine that evil had no real being but was merely *privatio boni* (privation of good).

This sophistical tenet had no appeal for Milton. He presents evil as real and traceable to a single Evil One. The wish to isolate evil in this way argues a particular mental configuration which seems to be associated with the belief that, once isolated, evil may become containable or punishable. Hence has arisen the urge to locate evil in a single kind of being, which has borne fruit throughout history in pogrom, ghetto, and racial massacre. In Freudian terms it may be identified as an effort of the severe and critical superego which subjugates the recalcitrant id. From a literary viewpoint, the isolating effort of the purifying and punitive will is the opposite of the mentality we think of as Shakespearean, which accepts the fact that evil is inextricably enmeshed in collective human experience.

Milton's effort to encapsulate evil in Satan was not successful. That is, those readers who have left their reactions on record have seldom been able to regard Satan as a depiction of pure evil, and some of the most distinguished have claimed that he is superior in character to Milton's God. It is sometimes supposed that critical support for Satan began with the Romantics, but this is not so. Sharrock (463–5) has shown that the notion of Satan as the true hero of Milton's epic goes back to Dryden and was a commonplace of eighteenth-century literary opinion both in France and England. Barker (421–36) finds that eighteenth-century admirers of the sublime praised Satan's 'high superior nature', and so came into conflict with Addison and Johnson, who declared Satan's speeches 'big with absurdity'. Among Romantic critics, Blake, Byron, Shelley, and Hazlitt championed Satan, whereas Coleridge identified him with Napoleonic pride and sensual indulgence (see Newmeyer). These critics certainly intensified and politicized the controversy, but they did not start it – nor, of course, did they finish it. In the twentieth century, anti-Satanists such as Charles Williams, C. S. Lewis, S. Musgrove, and Stanley Fish have been opposed by A. J. A. Waldock, E. E. Stoll, G. Rostrevor Hamilton, William Empson, and others.

The correct critical reaction to this dispute is not to imagine that it can be settled – that either Satanists or anti-Satanists can be shown to be 'right'. For what would that mean but ignoring what half the critics of the poem have felt about it – ignoring, that is, half the evidence? A more reasonable reaction is to recognize that the poem is insolubly ambivalent, insofar as the reading of Satan's 'character' is concerned, and that this ambivalence is a precondition of the poem's success – a major factor in the attention it has aroused. Other texts generally recognized as 'great' literature manifest similar ambivalence in their central characters. The critics who strive to prove that Shakespeare 'really meant' Shylock to be essentially bad, or essentially good, would, supposing either side could prevail, destroy much of the play's power and interest. A similar ambivalence characterizes Isabella, Prospero, Othello, Lear, Falstaff, and so on. Within liberal bourgeois culture, disputability is generally advantageous to a text since it validates individual reinterpretation and so functions, from the consumer viewpoint, as an anti-obsolescence device.

To recognize that the character of Satan is essentially ambivalent is not to say that we must agree with everything the Satanists or the anti-Satanists propose. Both sets of critics misrepresent or overstate in their bid to strengthen their case. Among anti-Satanists there is a tendency to jeer at

Satan and become sarcastic at his expense, as if he really existed. Williams and Lewis both manifest this. Pro-Satanists are likewise seduced into anger and indiscretion – as when E. E. Stoll (124), replying to Lewis, deplores the fact that criticism is nowadays 'complicated by scholarship'. The power to entangle and excite readers is an observable feature of the Satan figure.

Satanist critics generally emphasize Satan's courage, anti-Satanists his selfishness or folly. These simplified versions of Satan ignore or evade the evidence within the poem that fails to square with them. If we wish to find a single term for the character attribute which Satan's ambivalent presentation, taken as a whole, generates, then the most suitable term seems to be 'depth'. Depth in a fictional character depends on a degree of ignorance being sustained in the reader. The illusion must be created that the character has levels hidden from us, the observers. By comparison with Satan, the other characters in *Paradise Lost* – Adam, Eve, even God – exist simply and transparently at the level of the words they speak. Satan does not – partly because his habitual mode is dissimulation, partly because, unlike the other characters, he exists, or has existed, within the historical span the poem covers, in a number of different modes.

These different modes are partly inherent in the biblical and post-biblical Satan material. The traditional Satan story, as it eventually took shape, involves Satan in three separate roles – an Archangel, before and during the war in heaven; a Prince of Devils in the council in hell; a serpent-tempter in the garden. Satan is thus not a single concept, but a trimorph. In the earliest records of the Satan myth, the Pseudepigrapha and Apocrypha of the Old Testament, the three roles were, as Kastor notes (1–17, 69–71), performed by three different figures. The ambivalence of Milton's Satan stems partly from his trimorphic conception; pro-Satanists tend to emphasize his first two roles, anti-Satanists his third.

Further, Milton has compounded the ambivalence by making the division between the roles uncertain. Satan as Archangel, before his fall, is never shown by Milton, but this stage of his existence is often alluded to, as is the fact that some of his archangelical powers remain, though we cannot be quite sure which. Hence Satan, as fictional character, gains a hidden dimension and a 'past'. Also, Satan as Prince of Devils is still present within Satan-as-Tempter, as is shown when Ithuriel touches the toad with his spear, and Satan springs up 'in his own shape' (*PL* 4.819). This means that Satan's bestial disguises need not be regarded as debasement or degradation, as some critics have viewed them, since he retains his inner consciousness despite his disguises – or seems to. This qualification has to be added, for the precise state of Satan's consciousness at various points in the action is problematic (for example, at the point where, in the debate with Abdiel, he denies that he and the other angels were created by God; see below). The reader cannot solve these problems, because no textual evidence is available which will provide him with access to Satan's 'true' state of mind. By this device of narrative occlusion, Satan gains depth; whereas with the other characters no such interesting possibility of discrepancy opens up between inner state and outward profession or appearance.

The one part of the poem where access is provided to the 'true' Satan is his soliloquy at the start of Book 4 (32–113). The impression of depth is maintained throughout this because, although Satan's mind is no longer hidden, his inner debate and self-criticism reveal him as a creature of dynamic tensions, such as the other characters of the poem notably lack. This is partly because the soliloquy is a generic transplant. Edward Phillips, Milton's nephew, tells us it was written as part of a drama, not an epic, at a time when Milton intended to write a tragedy on the Fall. The soliloquy has the immediacy of drama, not the distance of epic. In it, Satan concedes his own criminality, and his own responsibility for his fall. He vacillates between remorse and defiance. He confesses that his rebellion was completely unjustifiable, that he had the same 'free will and power to stand' as all God's creatures, and that he therefore has nothing to accuse but 'heaven's free love dealt equally to all'. Since heaven's love means his own damnation, he curses it ('Be then his love accursed'), but then, rationally, turns his curse against himself ('Nay, cursed be thou'). Satan could be called evil at this point in the poem only in some attenuated sense, since he speaks the truth and curses himself as God curses him. He and God are in accord. The function of the speech within the poem's argument is to justify God; even Satan, we are meant to see, admits God was right. But paradoxically this admission redeems Satan in the reader's eyes, so that the response elicited is, as usual with Satan, ambivalent.

As part of his 'official' task of exculpating God in the soliloquy, Satan explains that even if he could repent and get back to heaven 'by act of grace', it would do him no good, since, once back there, he would grow proud again ('how soon / Would highth recall high thoughts'), and this would lead to a 'worse relapse' and 'heavier fall'. The intent of this argument, within the poem's apparent didactic strategy, is to make it seem merciful of God not to have mercy on Satan and allow him back. However, ambivalence once more surrounds the issue. For it is reasonable for the reader to ask why Satan should not learn from his fall, and be forgiven without any risk of his falling again. Why should a hypothetical but inevitable recurrence of his fall be built into his nature as part of the poem's case? The question is important, since whether Satan might ultimately be forgiven was a doctrinal issue; one church father, Origen, had opined that he would, though Milton disagreed (see Robins). Patrides argues that at this juncture in the poem the dramatic context demands that Satan's redemption should be entertained at least as a possibility, and it is of course true (within Christian doctrine) that Satan's redemption could not be regarded as impossible for God, since this would infringe God's omnipotence. To retrieve the situation, Milton has to make Satan's irredeemability his own fault, and the soliloquy effects this. He emerges as a creature trapped within his own inevitably and repeatedly fall-prone nature. But this means, of course, that he is trapped within Milton's fiction, of which that 'nature' is a part. The fiction leads him towards a doom from which he sees a way of escaping ('But say I could repent'). Hence Satan appears to possess, from the reader's viewpoint, an autonomy which is another attribute of fictional 'depth'. The illusion is created that he is independent of the fiction that contains him, and unfairly manipulated by that fiction.

The most obvious sense in which Satan is trapped within an alien fiction is that the fiction requires him, though an archangelically rational creature, to take up arms against a God who is axiomatically omnipotent. Much has been made of this by anti-Satanist critics, who take Satan's hostility to Almighty power as a sign of folly. The pro-Satan critics, on the other hand, produce it as evidence of his supreme courage, since even his adversary's omnipotence does not daunt him. Neither response can, of course, be pronounced 'right'; the potential of Satan to elicit both is simply a product of his habitual ambivalence. Folly and courage are, however, strictly inadequate terms for describing the behaviour of Satan and the rebel angels in relation to God's omnipotence, since these terms relate to human behaviour, and the fiction places Satan and his followers in a situation for which we can find no precise human counterpart. Comparison with Napoleon and other earthly conquerors (such as Coleridge suggests) is inaccurate, since Satan's situation is more curious than any such parallel would allow. The situation the devils are in is clearly enunciated by Belial during the council in Pandaemonium in Book 2. Belial acknowledges that God is not only omnipotent, and therefore proof against any attack the devils can make, but also omniscient, so that he cannot be outwitted. Neither force nor guile, Belial concludes, can be effective against such an adversary. God 'views all things at one view', and 'sees and derides' the devils' council even while it is in progress. The devils are performing before God as their audience, and are aware of his presence even as they discuss outwitting him. This means that their behaviour is not just 'foolish' or 'courageous'; it has an inherent fictive improbability. In order to make their behaviour credible, the reader has to assume that the devils make an at least temporarily successful effort at self-deception or willed oblivion: that they forget, or pretend that they are ignorant of, the predicament Belial has described. Otherwise it is not evident how they could keep up the momentum of their action.

Milton indicates that this is how he requires us to read the processes of diabolic intelligence by the way he writes about Satan at the start of Book 4. As Satan flies up from hell to earth, we are told that he does not rejoice in his speed. 'Horror and doubt distract' his thoughts when he remembers that 'of worse deeds worse sufferings must ensue'. But if Satan knows his mission is bound to make things worse for him, why, we may ask, does he undertake it? The answer, strictly, is that he cannot escape the terms of the fiction he finds himself in. He is the victim of a breakdown of fictional logic inherent in the terms of the myth Milton is transcribing. For he is cast in a poem with an axiomatically omniscient and omnipotent God, and this means that every hostile move he makes must be self-defeating. Yet his fictional function is precisely to make hostile moves: he is the fiend, the enemy.

The unlikelihood of Satan's rebellion against God had worried biblical commentators. They were especially puzzled by Isaiah 14: 14 where 'Lucifer, son of the morning' is depicted as saying 'I will ascend above the heights of the clouds; I will be like the most High.' This text was generally taken as a reference to Satan, but it caused difficulties since it would have been irrational for Satan to aspire to be equal in power with God. As Stella Revard shows (45–6), both Anselm and Aquinas argued that Satan could not, despite the apparent meaning of the text, have wished directly for equality with God, for as a rational and perfect being he would have known this was impossible. Partly because of these interpretative problems, Protestant theologians tended to deny that the Isaiah text referred to Satan at all. Calvin and Luther both read it as alluding to the King of Babylon.

Milton, however, could not evade the terms of the story by an exegetical manoeuvre of this sort. In the narrative he adopts, the omnipotence of God, which must have been evident to an archangelically intelligent Satan, coexists incongruously with a Satanic rebellion. Milton disguises this insuperable narrative difficulty partly by omitting any depiction of the unfallen Satan from his account. In this way he sets aside the problem of showing perfect intelligence operating imperfectly. He also makes the story seem more likely by adapting the fallen Satan's psychology. Satan's states of awareness, we are given to understand, are murky and changeable. Thus his realization, at the start of Book 4, that worse deeds will lead to worse sufferings, is presented as something he managed previously to forget. 'Now conscience wakes despair / That slumbered' (4.23–4). Satan, then, manages genuinely to hope at times, though after these respites despair reasserts itself. The fallen Satan is, we gather, a creature of moods, apprehending reality through mists of self-deception and forgetfulness. This wavering, slumbering, deceptive state of consciousness is another factor that gives Satan fictional depth, concealing him from our full knowledge. It also lends credibility to his unlikely story, since the reader tends to assume that the fallen Satan's indecisiveness about God's omnipotence (perhaps, he sometimes thinks, God is only 'Almighty styled' (9.137) not really Almighty) also characterized the unfallen Satan, and led to his revolt. In fact, of course, the unfallen Satan could not, by definition, have been fallible in this way. But Milton's narrative strategy conceals the logical flaw.

The fallen Satan's ability to dismiss unattractive facts from his consciousness is a feature which complicates the interpretation of his argument with Abdiel about the creation of the angels in Book 5, lines 835–64. In response to Abdiel's declaration that the angels were created by the Son, Satan insists that they were, on the contrary, 'self-begot, self-raised', and that Abdiel's theory is a 'strange point and new'. When soliloquizing, however, in Book 4, lines 42–4, he admits to himself that it was 'heaven's matchless king' (meaning, presumably, God the Father not the Son) who created him. Some critics (Lewis, for example) have seen this later admission as proof that Satan was simply lying in the Abdiel episode. Others (such as Waldock and Empson) have interpreted it as a new perception by Satan, or a resurgence of something he has chosen to forget. We cannot adjudicate between these interpretations with any confidence, since either would be reconcilable with Satan's mental processes as the poem elsewhere shows them. It is certainly odd that the other angels present at the debate accept Satan's, not Abdiel's, version of the creation. Presumably this means either that they never had any intuitive knowledge of their creation by the Son, or that they have wilfully suppressed or simply lost it. Steadman (166) suggests that Abdiel, like Adam, may have worked out by means of reasoning the fact that God created him. But Abdiel would have intuitive, not discursive reason, so would not need to work things out. The crux remains insoluble. Satan may be lying, he may be deceiving himself, he may have genuinely lost touch with the truth. That he never knew the truth does not seem a probable interpretation, since it would contradict his archangelical knowledge (though, of course, archangels did not know everything, nor, even, did the Son, according to Milton in *Christian Doctrine* (*YP* 6: 227) – full knowledge was the Father's alone).

The depth and ambivalence Satan gains from this episode issue from an uncertainty of interpretation. The facts are not fully ascertainable. More often it is the moral evaluation of his actions which generates disagreement among readers. Three episodes have proved particularly divisive. The first occurs in Book 1, when he weeps at the sight of his fallen followers, and cannot speak for tears:

> Thrice he essayed, and thrice in spite of scorn,
> Tears such as angels weep, burst forth. (1.619–20)

Pro-Satanist critics interpret the tears as magnanimous compassion. But anti-Satanists point out that angels were not supposed, in orthodox theology, to weep, since tears were a sign of passion, which angels were not subject to. Fowler annotates the lines with a quotation from Marvell ('only humane Eyes can weep'). The tearlessness of angels certainly seems to be emphasized by Milton in Book 11, where Michael shows Adam the effects that death and disease will have upon mankind in the future. Adam weeps, but Michael remains composed and dry-eyed, and Milton remarks rather pointedly on the contrast between them. The future fate of mankind was

> Sight so deform what heart of rock could long
> Dry-eyed behold? Adam could not, but wept,
> Though not of woman born; compassion quelled
> His best of man, and gave him up to tears. (11.494–7)

'Though not of woman born' echoes *Macbeth* (v.vii), and, as Fowler notes, the echo is more than just a verbal reminiscence, for one of the chief themes of *Macbeth* is the evil that ensues from a drying up of compassion – the 'milk of human kindness'. This point does not, of course, redound to the credit of Michael or other tearless angels, and, though Fowler fails to note it, Milton's phrase 'Tears such as angels weep' in the description of Satan weeping also has a Shakespearean original. In *Measure for Measure* Isabella proclaims that

> man, proud man,
> Dress'd in a little brief authority,
> Most ignorant of what he's most assur'd,
> His glassy essence, like an angry ape,
> Plays such fantastic tricks before high heaven
> As makes the angels weep; who, with our spleens
> Would all themselves laugh mortal. (11.ii. 117–23)

This Shakespearean original might be taken (by a pro-Satan critic) as removing any culpable passion from Satan's weeping. Weeping, it seems, is what angels do in situations where men, being coarser and more splenetic, would laugh. Anti-Satan critics might point out, on the other hand, that the 'proud man' in Isabella's speech is remarkably like Satan, an 'angry ape' of God, so that if the echo is to be taken as more than a chance reminiscence, it would become anti-Satanic in its reverberations, and would, indeed, highlight the ambivalent responses Satan's 'tricks' evoke – laughter in some readers, tears in others. As usual there is no deciding between these evaluations of Satan's action, which remains essentially disputable – though the Shakespearean echo, coming from such a context, probably enhances his depth for most readers. By weeping 'tears such as angels weep' he seems more grief-stricken than mere human weepers.

A second instance of Satanic action – or reaction – which seems at first creditable, but can be claimed as evidence by both Satanists and anti-Satanists, occurs when he sees Eve in Eden and is so enraptured by her beauty that he becomes momentarily good (9.460–79). He is deprived of his 'fierce intent' as he watches her, 'abstracted' from his own evil:

> and for the time remained
> Stupidly good, of enmity disarmed,
> Of guile, of hate, of envy, of revenge. (9.464–6)

But he snatches himself back from the brink of innocence, 'recollects' his hatred, and 'excites' himself to evil once more:

> Thoughts, whither have ye led me, with what sweet
> Compulsion thus transported to forget
> What hither brought us, hate, not love. (9.473–5)

The passage seems to indicate that Satan's natural tendency, when caught unawares, is to love. Beauty and delight are his natural element. Hatred is an effort of his will. This could be seen as making him either more, or less, sympathetic. Like his angelic tears, it shows his capacity for a role different from the one the fiction assigns him to. From the viewpoint of his function within the plot, the incident is extraneous. Milton did not need to include it to advance his narrative. It is a gratuitous piece of 'characterization', and seemingly favourable. On the other hand, since Satan chooses not to escape his diabolism, although he has the opportunity, he could be seen as the more damnable. The incident shows that he is not a destructive automaton, but a creature who chooses to destroy the human race against the promptings of his better nature. Milton echoes, in the passage, both himself and Shakespeare. 'Sweet compulsion' is from the vision of universal harmony described by the Genius in *Arcades* ('Such sweet compulsion doth in music lie'; 68); and 'whither have ye led me' echoes the ruined Antony after Actium ('O whither hast thou led me, Egypt?'; *Antony and Cleopatra* III.xi.51). Both echoes can be seen as 'lifting' Satan, setting him in the context of tragic love and the music of the spheres, which is what the Genius is listening to. But both echoes are also, by implication, critical of Satan, since Antony chooses to lose the world for love, whereas Satan does the opposite, and the music of the spheres signifies universal harmony, which Satan is about to destroy. As usual, he moves within a cloud of ambivalence.

A third prominent example of Satan's attaining depth through ambivalence occurs earlier in the poem's action than his 'stupidly good' response to Eve, and is (if read as pro-Satanists read it) the most surprising and poignant of his utterances. When he first sets eyes on Adam and Eve in Eden he is stricken with wonder at the human pair – not spirits, he perceives, yet 'little inferior' to heavenly spirits – and feels, or says he feels, an inclination to love them. They are creatures

> whom my thoughts pursue
> With wonder, and could love, so lively shines
> In them divine resemblance. (4.362–4)

Satan's reason for feeling he could love Adam and Eve – that they look so like God – naturally surprises the reader, since we have been led to suppose it is God Satan hates. Though there is nothing here so clear as an echo, there seems to be a recollection of the incident in Marlowe's *Doctor Faustus* where Mephistophiles, asked by Faustus how he comes to be out of hell, replies:

> Why, this is hell, nor am I out of it.
> Think'st thou that I, who saw the face of God,
> And tasted the eternal joys of heaven,
> Am not tormented with ten thousand hells,
> In being deprived of everlasting bliss?

The similarity lies in the unexpected revelation of love or desire for God in a figure we believed to be wholly committed to the opposition. Not all critics are prepared to grant that Satan really feels any inclination to love at this point. Whereas pro-Satanists (Raleigh, Stoll, Hamilton) take his response to 'divine resemblance' to be sincere, anti-Satanists (Lewis, Musgrove) interpret his words as brutal irony. Since he is soliloquizing, irony is perhaps unlikely – but not impossible. As usual, we cannot take the simple step of declaring one reading correct. But we can see that Satan gains fictional depth from the dubiety surrounding the point, as well as from the possibility of his underlying love for God.

These three examples all help to make Satan seem inscrutable. So, too, does his imaginativeness. As a dissimulator, he displays imagination in ways that are unavailable to God or the other good characters. Unlike him, they do not depend on lies, so the constant imaginative effort by which Satan sustains himself is foreign to them. They remain, from the viewpoint of imagination, relatively undeveloped beings. It is no doubt true, in a doctrinal sense, that God 'imagined' the universe, since he created it out of his mind. But he is not presented, in the poem, as an imaginative being. Satan is – as we note, for example, when the snake tells Eve how he found the forbidden fruit:

> Till on a day roving the field, I chanced
> A goodly tree far distant to behold
> Loaden with fruit of fairest colours mixed,
> Ruddy and gold: I nearer drew to gaze;
> When from the boughs a savoury odour blown,
> Grateful to appetite, more pleased my sense
> Than smell of sweetest fennel or the teats
> Of ewe or goat dropping with milk at even,
> Unsucked of lamb or kid, that tend their play.
> To satisfy the sharp desire I had
> Of tasting those fair apples, I resolved
> Not to defer; hunger and thirst at once,
> Powerful persuaders, quickened at the scent
> Of that alluring fruit, urged me so keen.
> About the mossy trunk I wound me soon,
> For high from ground the branches would require
> Thy utmost reach or Adam's: round the tree
> All other beasts that saw, with like desire
> Longing and envying stood, but could not reach.
> Amid the tree now got, where plenty hung
> Tempting so nigh, to pluck and eat my fill
> I spared not, for such pleasure till that hour
> At feed or fountain never had I found. (9.575–97)

This is all lies, of course. Satan does not like milk or apples; he never climbed a tree. But he has imagined himself into the snake's existence so vividly that we almost forget he is lying. He even takes the trouble to make the tree 'mossy', imagining that would make it more comfortable for a snake to wind around. (Is this where Keats got his 'mossed' apple trees in 'To Autumn'?) Of course, being inside a snake may have enabled Satan to take over the snake's sensibility, which would aid his imagination. We cannot tell. Nor can we tell whether his rapt musing on unsucked teats and fair apples is prompted by the naked woman he is gazing at. (Some critics have suggested that 'ewe' is a Freudian slip: 'the teats / Of you'.) Maybe. As usual we cannot locate Satan's state of consciousness within a firm reading. But however we read him, his imaginativeness is impressive, and allies him, of course, with the creator of the poem, Milton, who had to imagine it all.

Satan's imagination is crucial because it inaugurates the whole divergent history which is *Paradise Lost* and the story of the human race – a narrative divergent from God's original perfect creation, and a narrative which began when Sin, Satan's imagining, jumped out of his head. The episode with Sin and Death at the gate between Hell and Chaos (2.648–870) is one of the most puzzling in the poem, and the one that seems to carry us furthest into the half-light of Satan's subconscious. As he talks to Sin she reveals a buried phase of his life, and one which, even when she has recounted it, it seems he has no recollection of. He is, she tells him, her father, but also her mother. He went through birth pangs in heaven and she sprang from an opening in the side of his head. She became his accomplice against God, but she was also his image, as the Son is the image of the Father. He had a child by her, Death, who, once born, pursued his mother and raped her. That rape begot the 'yelling monsters' that now surround her.

We can recognize in all this a perverted rewriting of several of the poem's motifs. Adam is father and mother to Eve, since she was taken from his side, as Sin from Satan's head. He pursues her and unites sexually with her, as Death does Sin. In this murk of rape and incest and male birth pangs, the themes and actions of the poem swim about guiltily transformed. We have here, as it were, not just Satan's but the poem's subconscious. Its myths of origin are here released from narrative decorum, and parade in spectral shapes. The theme of lethal eating (the deadly apple) finds its counterpart in this underworld sequence in cannibalism. Death wants to eat Sin, but she warns him she would 'prove a bitter morsel, and his bane' (2.808). What adds to the strangeness and profundity of the sequence is that it has not only perversion to offer but also wifely and (as nowhere else in the poem) motherly love, shown when Sin rushes between Satan and Death to prevent their fighting.

Of course, readers are at liberty to insist that the sequence is 'just allegory', and that we should not bother with any of its deeper shades. However, even readers who take this line need to explain what it is an allegory of – what are the actual events that its various details correspond to? It does not take much thought to see that we are in no position to answer such a question. The status of the sequence in terms of the poem's 'reality', and the level on which we are to read it, are not matters about which we can obtain any firm directives. This means that, in this strange episode as in much else, Satan slips from our knowledge. We can see that he is implicated in depths, but the nature of them eludes our understanding.

The emergence of Sin from Satan's head was Milton's way of dealing with the poem's (and Christianity's) most difficult question – how evil originated. The problem of how evil could have been created spontaneously from good exercised, as Revard points out (35–6), the minds of the church fathers, and Manichaeanism grew from the belief that the evil factor, Satan, was created from a kingdom of darkness over which God had no authority. Christianity could not allow this solution, since it had an omnipotent God. But the church fathers who, like Cyril of Jerusalem, simply asserted that Satan became evil of his own free will, though created good, did not have to show it happening. Milton, too, found this impossible, and retreated into the cloudy region at hell's gate where Sin tells of events which took place somewhere other than in the poem's usual narrative mode, though we cannot tell where.

Finally, the relation of Satan to Milton's intentions (was Milton of the Devil's party? or not? or only subconsciously so?) has interested critics. Such questions are all clearly unanswerable since we have no access to Milton's mind, let alone his subconscious, at the time of writing. That does not, of course, prevent speculation about them. We can, moreover, be sure that Satan was originally the product of Milton's psychology (he was certainly, that is, not the product of anyone else's psychology), and critics who oppose the psychological approach are usually participating in it without realizing they are doing so. Merritt Hughes, for instance, asserts that the interpretation of Satan must be cleared of all 'modern psychologism' that makes him a reflection of irrational depths in Milton's nature. Milton created him, Hughes lays it down, 'as an example of the self-deception and the deception of others which are incident to the surrender of reason to passion' (177). Hughes's interpretation is of course flatly intentionalist, since it assumes access to Milton's mind, and is therefore an instance of the 'psychologism' he believes himself to be opposing.

Though originally the product of Milton's psychology, Satan, as he is read and interpreted, is also the product of the reader's psychology. *Paradise Lost*, like other texts, reads the reader, and Satan, as I have shown, divides readers into opposed camps. Most readers, probably, can feel sympathy with both the Satanists and the anti-Satanists. We feel that by suppressing a part of ourselves we can disown and denounce Satan, but we also feel the power of that part of us which is having to be suppressed. This situation has encouraged critics to see the character of Satan as built over a dichotomy in Western – or human – consciousness. Werblowsky (53) associates Satan with the drive towards science and rationalism in Western culture, and away from the female womb chaos (the Jungian *mater devorans*). Maud Bodkin (38–44) sees *Paradise Lost* as rendering in symbol the conflict between aspiration and a sense of one's own nothingness, basic to human experience. Isabel MacCaffrey (182–3) maintains that all arguments about where our sympathies lie in *Paradise Lost* are vain, since they lie both with the fallen and with the rigours of discipline necessary for our survival as reasonable beings.

Freud's analysis of the modern psyche seems particularly applicable to Satan's disputable nature, as well as to the recognition that Satan is a 'great' (that is, widely significant) creation. At the end of *Civilization and Its Discontents* Freud speaks of the exorbitant development of the superego in modern culture, and particularly the ethical demands the superego makes on the individual. It requires the individual habitually to suppress his aggressiveness and his hunger for self-satisfaction:

> In the severity of its commands and prohibitions it troubles itself too little about the happiness of the ego . . . It, too, does not trouble itself enough about the facts of the mental constitution of human beings. It issues a command and does not ask whether it is possible for people to obey it. On the contrary, it assumes that a man's ego is psychologically capable of anything that is required of it, that his ego has unlimited mastery over his id. This is a mistake; and even in what are known as normal people the id cannot be controlled beyond certain limits. If more is demanded of a man, a revolt will be produced in him, or a neurosis. (80–1)

Freud goes on to argue that the unappeasable commands of the civilized cultural superego in modern man lead to whole civilizations, 'possibly the whole of mankind', becoming neurotic. The controversy about Milton's Satan – what I have called Satan's essential ambivalence – is, I would suggest, evidence of that neurosis.

FURTHER READING

Barker, Arthur E., '". . . And on His Crest Sat Horror": Eighteenth-Century Interpretation of Milton's Sublimity and his Satan', *University of Toronto Quarterly* 11 (1942), 421–36

Bodkin, Maud, 'Literature and the Individual Reader', *Literature and Psychology* 10 (1960), 38–44

Darbishire, Helen, ed., *The Early Lives of Milton* (London, 1932)

Empson, William, *Milton's God* (London, 1961)

Evans, J. Martin, *'Paradise Lost' and the Genesis Tradition* (Oxford, 1968)

Fish, Stanley E., *Surprised By Sin: The Reader in 'Paradise Lost'* (London and New York, 1967)

Freud, Sigmund, *Civilization and Its Discontents*, translated by Joan Riviere, revised and newly edited by James Strachey (London, 1979)

Hamilton, Rostrevor, *Hero or Fool? A Study of Milton's Satan* (London, 1961)

Hughes, Merritt Y., *Ten Perspectives on Milton* (New Haven and London, 1965)

Kastor, Frank S., *Milton and the Literary Satan* (Amsterdam, 1974)

Kirkconnell, Watson, *The Celestial Cycle: The Theme of 'Paradise Lost' in World Literature with Translations of the Major Analogues* (Toronto, 1952)

Langton, Edward, *Satan, A Portrait: A Study of the Character of Satan Through All the Ages* (London, 1946)
Lewis, C. S., *A Preface to 'Paradise Lost'* (Oxford, 1942)
MacCaffrey, Isabel Gamble, *'Paradise Lost' as 'Myth'* (Cambridge, MA, 1959)
Milton, John, *Christian Doctrine*, ed. Maurice Kelley, translated by John Carey (*YP* vol. 6)
Musgrove, S., 'Is the Devil an Ass?', *Review of English Studies* 21 (1945), 302–15
Newmeyer, Edna, 'Wordsworth on Milton and the Devil's Party', *Milton Studies* 11 (1978), 83–98
Patrides, C. A., 'The Salvation of Satan', *JHI* 28 (1967), 467–78
Revard, Stella Purce, *The War in Heaven: 'Paradise Lost' and the Tradition of Satan's Rebellion* (Ithaca and London, 1980)
Robins, Harry F., *If This Be Heresy: A Study of Milton and Origen*, Illinois Studies in Language and Literature 51 (Urbana, 1963)
Rudwin, Maximilian, *The Devil in Legend and Literature* (London, 1931)
Sharrock, Roger, 'Godwin on Milton's Satan', *N&Q*, New Series 9 (1962), 463–5
Steadman, John M., *Milton's Epic Characters: Image and Idol* (Chapel Hill, 1968)
Stoll, E. E., 'Give the Devil His Due: A Reply to Mr Lewis', *Review of English Studies* 20 (1944), 108–24
Waldock, A. J. A., *'Paradise Lost' and Its Critics* (Cambridge, 1947)
Werblowsky, R. J. Zwi, *Lucifer and Prometheus: A Study of Milton's Satan*, with an introduction by C. G. Jung (London, 1952)
Williams, Charles, ed., *The Poetical Works of Milton* (Oxford, 1940)

12

DIANE K. MCCOLLEY

Milton and the sexes

When the Archangel Michael in *Paradise Lost* foresees the church attacked from without by persecution and from within by 'specious forms' so that 'truth shall retire / Bestuck with slanderous darts' (12.534–6), he summons along with the figure of Truth a picture of St Sebastian stuck full of arrows: who, however, did not die of those wounds but had to be executed repeatedly. Milton's epic is similarly susceptible to recurrent volleys; and his figure of Woman brought to life in Eve has been a primary target, with similar resurgent vitality.

Thirty years ago, a largely 'masculinist' critical consensus thought that Milton conformed to a traditional reading of the biblical Eve as inherently trivial, vain, and inclined to fall, thus denying Milton's assertion of eternal providence. Since then much work has been done – by Joan Bennett, Francis Blessington, Barbara Lewalski, Mary Ann Radzinowicz, Stella Revard, James Turner, Irene Samuel, Kathleen Swaim, Joan Webber, and Joseph Wittreich, to name a few – showing how Milton shatters this stereotype. More recently in the vanguard of attack have been feminists offended by Milton's partial acceptance of Pauline tradition concerning the subordination of wives and the misogynous diatribes he allows some of his dramatis personae. 'Resistant' readers writing from the point of view of gender – for example, Jackie DiSalvo, Sandra Gilbert, Christine Froula, Marcia Landy, Mary Nyquist, Patricia Parker, and Maureen Quilligan (178), some of whom admire Milton in other ways – challenge what Nyquist calls 'Western bourgeois or liberal feminism'; Nyquist interrogates the 'historically determined and class-inflected discourse of "equal rights"' (99), shows that Milton's contemporaries of both sexes offered less gender-specific interpretations of Genesis, and finds that Milton's contractual interpretation of God's provision of meet help, contrasted with Rachel Speght's view of Adam as a 'passive recipient' of divine grace, serves 'an individualism paradigmatically masculine' (114–15). Joseph Wittreich relates that eighteenth- and early nineteenth-century women applauded

4. Gerard de Jode, *Thesaurus Sacrorum historiarum veteris testamenti*, Antwerp, 1585.
An engraving of the Creation of Eve with Admonition, by Jan Sadeler after Crispijn van den Broeck

Paradise Lost as conducive to their honour and dignity. David Boocker replies that later nineteenth-century women charged Milton with upholding patriarchy because his portrait of marital bliss was recommended to women to keep them in their place. A note in the new *Riverside Milton* skips over three decades of reassessment by stating that 'There is no evidence in *Paradise Lost* that Eve's proper role according to Milton is anything other than "meek submission"' (708).

Amid the volleys, those who love Milton's poems find that his high regard for the quality of human beings of both sexes offers more toward mutual respect than the problem of equality can undo. His dramatic characters represent a spectrum of opinion and experience that provokes free debate on just about every issue we debate today. He incorporates in Adam and Eve the fusion of nature and spirit – not allegorically divided between them, but processive in each and reciprocal in their marriage – that for him defines human (and all) life. Like the apostles, he considered it his calling to prepare for 'an extraordinary effusion of *Gods* Spirit upon every age, and sexe' (*YP* 1: 566; Acts 2: 17–18); and although his hope of spiritual rebirth for the body politic was disappointed, he never abandoned his hope for the rebirth of the specific men and women who would read his poem.

Milton does not need to be defended by means of allowances for the assumptions of his time; Milton himself struck off the chains of custom. Nevertheless, it is useful to know that in seventeenth-century England women did not hold official civil or ecclesiastical positions, attend universities, or engage in the major professions, though they did write and prophesy. Milton did not assault these limitations, but provided prose arguments and poetic experience designed to expand the disciplined liberties of a regenerate people. He did not deny women perfectibility in any spiritual or moral gifts, and redefined marriage as mutual help through spiritual companionship as well as assistance in all '*the helps and comforts of domestic life*'. He did not think wifehood coextensive with womanhood; rather he found 'the properties and excellencies of a wife set out only from domestic vertues; if they extend furder, it diffuses them into the notion of som more common duty then matrimonial' (*YP* 2: 612–13).

Milton represented the relations of the sexes in *Paradise Lost* and other poems, in a series of 'divorce tracts', and in *Christian Doctrine* 1.10, 'Of the Special Government of Man before the Fall' – which adds a defence of polygamy on scriptural grounds – and 2.15, of 'Private Duties'. All are rooted in Genesis 1–3, conferred with other biblical passages, and much expand the conception of meetness in the words of the Creator, 'It is not good that the man should be alone; I will make him an help meet for him'

(2: 18). Milton's representation of the first man and woman advances the 'Renaissance' confluence of classical and Christian thought by interpreting Genesis with a high regard for both human dignity and the goodness of the visible creation, including sexuality, as a divine gift.

In Hesiod's *Theogony* Zeus creates Woman in revenge for Man's acquisition of forbidden knowledge from Prometheus; her name is Pandora, and she comes equipped with a box of evils. The Hebrew creation story differs radically from the Greek: instead of gods of both sexes who are a part of nature, and hence unreliable and sometimes hostile to humankind, it represents a transcendent but provident maker of nature who 'created man in his own image . . . male and female created he them', pronounced the whole creation good, and blessed it; and instead of producing Woman as punishment, it represents her as fit help in the callings to care for and to populate the earth. That little word *help*, however, with the description in Genesis 2 of God making Eve from Adam's rib, suggests a sex that is subordinate, perhaps created only secondarily in God's image and so spiritually inferior. That suggestion coupled with the story that Eve first disobeyed God and enticed her husband to do likewise affords excuses for misogyny in spite of God's original blessing on both male and female. Milton believed that the Bible was divinely inspired but open to interpretation by the individual conscience guided by the Holy Spirit and the rule of charity. He believed also that next to the relation between each person and God, the relation of husband and wife was the chief source of personal happiness or misery. His matrimonial ideals and especially his representation of the first marriage in *Paradise Lost* reflect his libertarian belief in the original goodness – now wounded by sin but recoverable by grace and hard work – of creation, including man, woman, and sexuality. The *quality* of this goodness depends partly on Milton's sense that to be a 'help' is not servile, but a calling and pleasure that men, women, and angels share with their maker. *Paradise Lost*, though painfully acknowledging evil and loss, celebrates the problematically complex original and regenerable excellence of both sexes.

The Hebrew Bible continues with the epic of the monotheistic and patriarchal Israelites who established a theocracy ordered by holy laws amidst enemies who worshipped deities of both sexes, some of whom required child sacrifice, mutilation, ritual prostitution, sumptuous shrines, and other violations of human dignity, which Milton personified as Moloch, Belial, and Mammon. This history, once seen as unifying the human family under one 'Father' and freeing it by divine law from the inequities of human power, is now sometimes viewed as establishing the rule of invisible (paternal) over visible (maternal) power. John Rogers argues, however, that Milton's account of Earth's womb bringing forth in *Paradise Lost* 'clear[s] an independent and almost exclusively feminine space of creative power . . . the feminine earth had been "form'd" from the start to function efficiently without assistance from paternal authority'. 'The focus on a self-sufficient feminine process works to reorient the ethos informing the traditional rhetoric of agency: in avoiding the conventional scientific figuration of the imposition of masculine force upon passive feminine matter, it functions to reconfigure the authoritarian dynamic of power in the world at large' (117–18).

The leaders of the Reformation used patriarchal language in treating the Hebrew Testament typologically and removed from church decoration and liturgy much of the feminine imagery associated with the Virgin Mary and other women saints. On the other hand, they dethroned the scepticism toward women and marriage of the early 'Fathers of the Church', promoted women's spiritual equality, commended marriage to all (including priests), and regarded the family as a 'little church and a little state', hierarchical to be sure but valuing each member. Writers of conduct books stressed Paul's teaching that the husband should love his wife as Christ loved the church and cherish her as his own body – advice meant to protect and honour women but given in figures of subordination and inapplicable to arenas 'more common . . . th[a]n matrimonial'. By refusing to divide body from spirit and by making both Adam and Eve 'the church', Milton jostles these analogies. He is also remarkable, as Dayton Haskin shows, in his attention to Mary in *Paradise Regained* as a Protestant saint, not mediatrix but teacher, pondering and transmitting to her son not only the content of Scripture but also, by 'conferring place with place', a method of interpretation.

Thanks to three centuries of progress toward liberty which Milton helped to promote, the idea that woman was made for man, or that any segment of the human family is necessarily subordinate to any other, has been discredited. Milton himself narrowed the gender gap considerably. To follow out the paths he mapped is to proceed toward a fuller awareness of the plenitude of potentiality in each human being and each relationship. He broke the stereotypical scapegoating of Eve as essentially a temptress and uniquely gave her responsible motives for her independent movements on the morning of the Fall: her sense of responsibility for the Garden, the epitome of the whole natural world, that flourishes in response to her maternal but unmanagerial attention, and her refusal to let the existence of evil destroy the processes of a free community. Problematic as her departure may be, these motives are not proleptic of the Fall, but of human responsibility to repair both the human community and the Earth, which the Fall into consumerism – beginning with the consumption of the fruit of one sacred tree – would wound. Thus Milton gives unfallen Eve an unprecedented role in seeking the complex harmony of authentic individuality (not egocentrism or Satanic desire for autonomous power), authentic community (not tyrannous conformity), and the relation of human beings to other beings in a comprehensive ecology. The Fall interrupts this process; Eve's plea for reconciliation (10.914) and Adam's reasoned response resume it.

Milton was born into an age when poets spent a great deal of ink and breath on the proposition that although some women are unattainable divinities, few are, in Donne's proverbial words, both 'true, and faire'. Milton vowed early to celebrate those in whom 'good and faire in one person meet', emulating Dante and Petrarch, 'who never write but honour of them to whom they devote their verse' (*YP* 1: 890). His first English poem, at age seventeen, undertakes the difficult task of consoling his sister on the death of her infant daughter. His early 'Epitaph on the Marchioness of Winchester' places her 'high . . . in glory' next to Rachel; 'Methought I saw my late espoused saint' commemorates a wife of whom he trusts to have 'full sight . . . in heaven'; although in his blindness he can not see her face, 'Love, sweetness, goodness in her person shined / So clear, as in no face with more delight'. 'Lady, that in the prime', 'Daughter to that good Earl', and 'When faith and love which parted from thee never' commend the spiritual victories of actual women, a refreshing change from the prevailing fictions of complaint and compliment.

In addition, Milton praised women in six Italian sonnets and three Latin epigrams, especially for their speech and singing; and an accolade, in *Arcades*, to the Dowager Countess of Derby for her patronage of the arts. Stella Revard traces his affirmations and forswearings of love in the Latin Elegies, the affirmations blossoming again in the epic, where 'Mother Eve is likened to the divinities of the flowering Mother Earth' (23). *A Masque Presented at Ludlow Castle* ('*Comus*') gives its young heroine a spirited resistance to evil and receptivity to grace that embody and adumbrate Milton's most serious and consistent themes. Milton's graces and muses link what might be called the feminine principle to the act of poetic creation itself. The Celestial Muse appears to be a female persona of the Holy Spirit – 'spirits when they please / Can either sex assume' (*PL* 1.423–4) – or an offspring of the inspiring Spirit and the aspiring mind, the matrix wherein the divine begetting and the human conception of the poem fuse.

A good deal of attention has been given to Milton's monstrous figure of Sin and to Dalila as the embodiment of meretricious female sexuality used to exploit and entrap. (There are plenty of masculine horrors, too: Satan, Death, Moloch, Belial, Mammon, Chemos, and Comus caricature cruelty, deception, and rapacity.) Whereas some readers have seen fear of birth or sexuality in the dreadful spectacle of Sin giving birth to Death and the Hellhounds, Louis Schwartz studies the terrors of seventeenth-century obstetrics and finds compassion in Milton's imagery of childbirth. Mary Adams discusses Milton's cosmic, unfallen and fallen wombs, the latter being the 'most moving emblem of the fallen condition' (178). A lively debate on both Dalila and Eve runs through the collections edited by Walker, McColgan and Durham, Labriola, and Stanwood. Stella Revard gives Dalila the stature of a Euripidian heroine; Joan S. Bennett argues cogently that in his encounter with Dalila 'Samson voices a growing vision that his God is not only tribal, but universal, and that God's moral law extends beyond national rules to all people', while when Dalila defends her 'private sin . . . as a public virtue, then she surrenders herself entirely to the service of tyranny' (134 and 141).

Milton's five 'divorce' tracts are part of his programme to advocate religious, civil, and domestic liberty for sober and religious men – and, to an extent, women – written, one supposes, under some pressure from his own difficult marital situation. The first of these tracts was *The Doctrine and Discipline of Divorce: Restor'd to the Good of Both Sexes, From the bondage of the Canon Law, and other mistakes, to Christian freedom, guided by the Rule of Charity*, published unsigned and unlicensed in 1643, during the deliberations of the Westminster Assembly, and again, augmented and initialled, in 1644. Annabel Patterson deftly unpacks interpenetrating and conflicted layers of autobiographical subtext, reading the tracts' 'narrative stratagems' as 'the ruses of a self in process of sexual and social reconstruction' (88). Milton's proposals were rejected and attacked in print, in Parliament, and from the pulpit – without, he complained, being carefully read or answered with reasoned argument. When he learned that the respected reformer Martin Bucer had expressed similar views, he translated them, expecting to be 'fully justified' by so notable an authority, but still with little success. In 1645 he produced *Colasterion*, an angry reply to his detractors, and *Tetrachordon*, whose title means a four-stringed instrument, the four strings being the four chief places in Scripture concerning marriage: Genesis 1:27–8 and 2:18, 23–4; Deuteronomy 24:1–2; Matthew 5:31–2 and 19:3–11; and 1 Corinthians 7:10–16. The purpose of *Tetrachordon* is to show that, despite canonical interpretation of the words of Christ in Matthew as stricter than the law of Moses, these four 'strings' are really in tune with each other. The hostility with which this exercise in case divinity was received elicited two sonnets, 'I did but prompt the age to quit their clogs' and 'A book was writ of late called *Tetrachordon*; / And woven close, both matter, form and style.'

The arguments in these tracts are both close-woven and extensive, but their gist is that Christ did not abrogate the law of Moses permitting divorce, which would put God in the position of having colluded with sin, but spoke specifically to the arrogance of the Pharisees. Marriage was given by God for the good of man; a marriage that fulfils none of its purposes is not 'what God hath joined together'. Since the spiritual relation of husband and wife is its true form, followed by the procreation of children and the 'mutual benevolence' of the marriage bed, to allow divorce for physical infidelity but not for fundamental spiritual discord turns upside down the purposes of the marriage covenant. To the charge that liberalizing divorce laws would give trivial and licentious persons an excuse to change partners at whim, Milton replies that the liberties of good and serious persons are more important than the restraint of the vicious, who are unfaithful to their marriage vows anyway, while good people in intolerable marriages are robbed of the energy to serve their families, callings, and countries.

In the course of these arguments Milton uses what we now call 'sexist' language. He calls canonists who thought that the divorce laws were only for abused wives 'Palpably uxorious! who can be ignorant that woman was created for man, and not man for woman; and that a husband may be injur'd as insufferably in mariage as a wife' (*YP* 2: 324). He explicates Genesis 1:27 by arguing from 1 Corinthians 11 that 'the woman is not primarily and immediatly the image of God, but in reference to the man . . . not he for her, but she for him'. With only partial mitigation he adds, 'Nevertheless man is not to hold her as a servant, but receives her into a part of that empire which God proclaims him to, though not equally, yet largely, as his own image and glory: for it is no small glory to him, that a creature so like him, should be made subject to him. Not but that particular exceptions may have place, if she exceed her husband in prudence and dexterity, and he contentedly yeeld, for then a superior and more naturall law comes in, that the wiser should govern the lesse wise, whether male or female.' But, he continues, God cannot have meant 'that man the portraiture of God, joyning to himself for his intended good and solace an inferiour sexe', should become the thrall of one 'whose wilfulnes or inability to be a wife frustrates the occasionall end of her creation' and yet not exercise 'that indeleble character of priority which God crown'd him with' to obtain his freedom; 'She is not to gain by being first in the transgression, that man should furder loose to her, because already he hath lost by her means' (*YP* 2: 589–90).

Despite this stung resort to convention, however, Milton redefines marriage in language of thorough mutuality as 'meet and happy conversation' with 'a fit conversing soul', conferring the 'dignity & blessing' of the 'mutual enjoyment' of a love 'begot in Paradise by that sociable & helpful aptitude which God implanted between man and woman toward each other'. Each is 'the copartner of a sweet and gladsome society', fed by a 'coequal & *homogeneal* fire' which 'cannot live nor subsist, unlesse it be mutual'. Marriage was ordained 'when man and woman were both perfect' and is still meant to fulfil God's promise 'in proportion as things now are' (*YP* 2: 246, 251–5, 308–9). Marriage is a covenant in which 'There must be first a mutuall help to piety, next to civill fellowship of love and amity, then to generation, so to household affairs, lastly the remedy of incontinence'; its causes 'are all mutual' (*YP* 2: 599, 630). This is the 'essential form' of marriage in *Paradise Lost*.

The epic as a whole gives at least as much praise to qualities traditionally considered 'feminine' as to those considered 'masculine', and this redress is part of Milton's radical re-evaluation of prevailing concepts of power. He casts scorn on the traditional epic hero's acquisitive will to power, represented by Satan and his fellow terrorists, and commends as more heroic the virtues of 'Subverting worldly strong, and worldly wise / By simply meek' (12.568–9), as he does again in *Paradise Regained*. He ridicules the notion that one can pursue fame and glory by flinging hardware and maiming flesh, and makes nurturing the earth and the growth of living souls the shared concern of both sexes.

The obvious way to represent man and woman 'when man and woman were both perfect' would have been to let Adam and Eve represent traditionally gendered virtues. But to bring them closer to a 'conjugall fellowship' of beings more 'like' than convention allowed – and yet keep the pattern by which, as Lewalski (1985) notes, 'each individual is stimulated to intellectual and literary expression . . . in conference with a superior' (218) – Milton chooses instead to show Eve and Adam in their dialogues both capable, in proportion, of all sorts of virtue. Traditionally 'manly' virtues like fortitude, clear-headed justice, fidelity to principle, and reason unswayed by passion, and 'womanly' ones like sympathy, gentleness, and fidelity are not strictly divided between them. In the separation colloquy principles very like Milton's own move Eve to decline to let Satan's threat interfere with their liberties and the pursuit of their callings; Adam's respect for open dialogue and true relation, needing freedom, move him to accede to her wish. At the Fall these qualities run to excess in Eve's ambition and Adam's 'effeminacy', when he puts the immediacy of personal relations above the long-term claims of truth.

The form and imagery of *Paradise Lost* balance masculine and feminine constructs. Its language combines linear logic with circumferential awareness; the design is sturdily architectural, but the radiant consciousness so suffuses it with dance that subsequence and precedence are constantly transposed. Its male and female imagery is inscribed in Raphael's astronomical discourse (8.66–178) just before Adam's uneasy though delighted attempt to square Eve's theoretical inferiority with his sense of her 'greatness of mind' (8.521–59). What Raphael says about heavenly bodies should free Adam and us from such polarities, including the supposition that the 'greater should not serve / The less':

> consider first, that great
> Or bright infers not excellence: the earth
> Though, in comparison of heaven, so small,
> Nor glistering, may of solid good contain
> More plenty than the sun that barren shines,
> Whose virtue on it self works no effect,
> But in the fruitful earth; there first received
> His beams, unactive else, their vigour find. (8.87–97)

If, in fact, the whole heavens circle the earth, their swiftness serves 'thee earth's habitant'. But what if the earth 'industrious of her self fetch day', her light and the moon's 'Reciprocal', and the whole universal dance be so too, 'other suns perhaps / With their attendant moons . . . Communicating male and female light, / Which two great sexes animate the world'? (8.99, 137, 142–51). This 'new philosophy' throws in doubt ancient sexual archetypes and opens the concepts of inferiority and service to 'various' interpretations. While we can no longer easily divide human sexuality into two kinds, Cosmic Eros is broadly conceived, or learned from the Celestial Muse. As Stevie Davies, Michael Lieb, James Turner, John Rogers, Joseph Summers, and others have variously shown, the sexes, both great, both in their natural innocence communicating light, constitute the universe and the fabric of the poem. Its characters and its bardic voice are sexually distinct, but the *poem* is androgynous.

With these matters in mind, let us examine four critical cruxes – a discordant tetrachord of places in *Paradise Lost* most likely to disturb – asking questions, exercising reason, and debating alternatives as Adam and Eve do when they read the book of nature. The first, in which we look over Satan's shoulder, begins by assuming a greater physical, spiritual, and moral equality for Eve than she had ever enjoyed before; but it ends with the lines that have, perhaps, most offended gender-oriented readers:

> Two of far nobler shape erect and tall,
> Godlike erect, with native honour clad

In naked majesty seemed lords of all,
And worthy seemed, for in their looks divine
The image of their glorious maker shone,
Truth, wisdom, sanctitude severe and pure,
Severe but in true filial freedom placed;
Whence true authority in men; though both
Not equal, as their sex not equal seemed;
For contemplation he and valour formed,
For softness she and sweet attractive grace,
He for God only, she for God in him. (4.288–99)

Both are 'lords of all', full of divine attributes, and placed in filial freedom. Eve is included, even, in 'true authority'; later, though the narrator assigns dominion less largely to Eve than to Adam, the animals of Eden are 'duteous at her call' (9.521). We should note, too, Milton's improvement on the 'he not for her, but she for him' of *Tetrachordon*. We might be pleased, and his first readership startled, if Milton had written 'Both equal, though their sex not equal seemed' and 'Each for God, and for God in each other', levelling domestic hierarchy in one blow. Since he did not, we might ask whether his 'two' represent kinds of goodness that can in each reader go, like Adam and Eve, hand in hand.

Equality under the law is remedial for a fallen race not much given to rejoicing in the goodness, much less the superiority, of others, to rectify injustices that no one in a state of sinless blessedness would commit. If we are to read Milton's poem with candour we need to avoid Satan's dreary habit of thinking himself impaired by another's goodness. Postlapsarian wrongs occur when people think *themselves* superior, or any being is exploited or scorned. Does Milton's poetry contribute to such injustices, or work to dissolve them? What seems to matter most to him is the *eachness* of each being. Each angel has individual talents, like Dante's, 'Ciascun distinto de fulgore et d'arte' (*Paradiso* 31.132–3); each human being is jointly fashioned by herself or himself and God. This celebration of particularity – Ingram and Swaim's *Concordance* lists 151 uses of *each* in *Paradise Lost* – honours each created being regardless of hierarchical place. We have discarded some of the hierarchies Milton had to deal with, but we need not discard love of the distinct lustre of particular persons where each self is fuller of light the more it rejoices in other selves.

The second string of our chord or discord is Adam's perplexed avowal that though he knows Eve 'the inferior, in the mind / And inward faculties',

Authority and reason on her wait,
As one intended first, not after made
Occasionally; and to consummate all,

Greatness of mind and nobleness their seat
Build in her loveliest, and create an awe
About her, as a guard angelic placed. (8.541–59)

Adam's state is more complex than either Raphael or psychologists of 'erotic valuation' give him credit for. Clearly, he needs to retrieve his balance. Yet Paul exhorts 'all the saints' to be 'of one accord, of one mind', as Adam says he and Eve are (8.603–5), and adds 'in lowliness of mind let each esteem other better than themselves' (Phil. 1:1; 2:2–3). Adam and Eve are 'all the saints' and their marriage is the type of the early church to be reformed. So Milton needs to express through them both the scriptural not-quite-equality of husband and wife and the scriptural more-than-equality of a holy community – and on top of that, the erotic delight and mutual exaltation of lovers, with the risk of idolatry and the need for a responsive relation to the rest of creation by those who enjoy that 'sum of earthly bliss' (8.522). As a family Adam and Eve participate (but only verbally) in a hierarchy that gives the male 'greater authority'. As a holy community, each esteems the other 'better'. A society in which each person cares 'for the things of others' (Phil. 2:4) and rejoices in *each* other's goodness is a heavenly banquet, a *sacrum convivium*.

The third string is a double one. Eve's own views of her position shift even more radically than unfallen Adam's as she moves from naively innocent to wiser to fallen perceptions. 'My author and disposer', she says to Adam in Book 4, 'what thou bid'st / Unargued I obey; so God ordains, / God is thy law, thou mine: to know no more / Is woman's happiest knowledge and her praise' (635–8). Is this allegation to be taken as the ventriloquization of a poet who thought that 'all believers' are 'living temples, built by faith to stand, / Their own faith not another's' (12.52–8), and that 'fellowship . . . fit to participate/ All rational delight' (8.389–91) is the true form of marriage? But after she bites the fruit, Eve reverses her earlier over-simplification, wondering whether to 'keep the odds of knowledge in my power':

So to add what wants
In female sex, the more to draw his love,
And render me more equal, and perhaps,
A thing not undesirable, sometime
Superior; for inferior who is free? (9.820–5)

If we set aside the fact that Eve is entirely deluded about the nature of the fruit, does her question have any validity? One answer to it is 'everybody', since in a universe constituted of plenitude and gradation for the sake of diversity and unity, every being is 'inferior' in some sense to someone, yet all are free 'Till they enthrall themselves' (3.125). But in fact Eve is as self-governing as Adam. He needs her, she consents; and she (naturally and regularly) goes off alone on errands of art, nurture, or hospitality. Moreover, Milton often calls attention to the moral power of subordinates: Eve; Abdiel; the mocked, blind, and imprisoned Samson; the politically powerless young Hebrew hero of *Paradise Regained* – none is impaired while they keep intact their will to goodness.

Apart from eating the fruit of one tree – which God has forbidden in order to remind them that 'it is he who hath made us, and not we ourselves', that there should be a limit to consumption, and that passions and pleasures need to be tempered – is there any honest and non-violent activity or pursuit of knowledge that Adam and Eve cannot both enjoy? They cannot be lawyers, physicians, or clergymen, because these treat effects of the Fall, but they can create good government, health, liturgy, and pastoral care. They do not engage in armed warfare, but spiritual valour is surely requisite to both sexes, with the Spirit of Darkness aping animals and entering through mists unseen. Unlike many predecessors, Milton did not think sensuous pleasure wicked nor that Adam and Eve fell because of sexual love. James G. Turner demonstrates the unique amplitude of Milton's erotic version of Genesis. Their sexual bliss is matched by the spiritual intimacy of their prayers; and these set to music, along with their work and conversation, represent all wholesome arts and sciences. Their work is mutual – only once does it fill typical gender roles, when Eve 'within, due at her hour / Prepared . . . dinner' while Adam 'sat' (5.299–304) – and unfallen Eve's love of fruits and flowers that 'at her coming sprang' is as needful as Adam's 'studious thoughts abstruse' (8.40–7) to ensure that their employments keep earth glorious. Sin can only impede these freedoms.

The fourth string, because it issues from their maker and redeemer, is the 'fundamental' of the chord, and so least explicable on grounds of multiplicity of voices or the gradual education of the reader. The Judge asks Adam,

> Was she thy God, that her thou didst obey
> Before his voice, or was she made thy guide,
> Superior, or but equal, that to her
> Thou didst resign thy manhood, and the place
> Wherein God set thee above her made of thee,
> And for thee, whose perfection far excelled
> Hers in all real dignity[?] (10.145–51)

These are salient lines for a reading family to wrestle with. What husband who had got this far in the poem would dare to gloat at them? It was this husband's 'part / And person' to 'bear rule' instead of falling, since his wife did not surpass him in prudence. But should we suppose that the Judge is also alluding to Adam's allowing Eve to leave his side? The 'filial freedom' in which both are created would then have been abrogated as a pattern for human institutions. The Judge censures Adam 'Because thou hast hearkened to the voice of thy wife, / And eaten of the tree concerning which / I charged thee' (10.198–200), making Eve his 'guide' at the moment of the Fall, and so transmitting sin to all posterity and losing his chance to transmit grace to Eve. This passage, like the first, improves the language of the divorce tracts, in which he 'lost by her means'; here the responsibility belongs to both, though more to him. If we acknowledge the biblical, Dantean, Miltonic patterns for the growth and perfection of all protagonists, whatever their gender – that status has no effect on fullness of joy, that humility exalts, that service frees – then we will not see this passage as a statement authorizing male arrogance. If we have noted Milton's dramatic decorum, his sense of limitless process in the works of this very Creator-Redeemer, and the interchange of attributes Eve and Adam have experienced in their unfallen lives together, then we will not suppose that these words dashing Adam's disastrous dependency on the opinion of fallen Eve apply to all people through all time. Yet for male readers looking for ways to justify tyranny or female ones looking for reasons to abandon charity – which either could do only by ignoring the rest of the poem – this passage is prime grist, and we would do Milton an injustice if we neglected to point out the misuses that can be made of it in new contexts, or the ways in which both the failures and the graces of both characters can apply to all of us. The epic poet lets us not only hear but *be* each character in turn. While each of us is mimetically being Eve and Adam, we gather in the possibilities of both.

Curiously, some people object to Eve's derivation from Adam, in spite of her original truth, beauty, wisdom, and sanctitude, who are unalarmed by the news that we are all derived from hairy bipeds called *Australopithecus afarensis*. Some resent her service to 'God in him' who recommend the narrower confines of 'self-servience' and have no interest in service of God at all. Some censure the slight imparity of perfections of Eve and Adam without lamenting our general inferiority to them both. Some think Eve unfree who do not protest the oppression of psychological theories that put each person and all affection into a few sexual categories and locate the genesis of civilization in the vicinity of that portion of the male body on which 'Adam sat'. Some denounce Milton's fidelity to the scriptural idea of the family who accept the stupendous repression of spirit with which much criticism paves over the wellspring of holiness from which all value issues in *Paradise Lost*.

The 'woman question' in Milton will never be *decided*; good poems never end. Milton was radical in making Eve an ardent caretaker of the natural world, a passionate, sensuous, and pure erotic partner, a spontaneous composer of exquisite lyric and narrative poetry, a participant in numerous kinds of conversation including political debate, and the leader in peacemaking after the Fall. He was probably more serious about the relations of the sexes, more careful of their resonances, and more hopeful of their happiness and holiness than any other poet of his or perhaps any other time. He was radical in his insistence on women's spiritual completeness, responsibility, and fitness for 'all rational delight' and in his celebration of erotic bliss in the morning of Creation. Perhaps no one else has depicted sexual happiness at once so lavishly and so purely. His loving portrait of Eve, not excusing her sin on any grounds, certainly not incapacity, but portraying her as a person of delightful mind as well as beautiful form, honour as well as charm, sanctitude as well as radiant looks and graceful gestures, moral searching as well as artistic creativity, political combativeness as well as sweet compliance, asperity as well as gentleness, and a capacity for repentance and forgiveness as well as rash default, raises her immeasurably above other Eves of art and story, opening new possibilities of dialogue for the reading family at every turn. To the small degree that Adam and Eve are 'higher' and 'lower' they are as two strings tuned to different pitches, to make harmony. It would be rude to ignore Milton's interest in showing how good Adam and Eve both are, and how many ways they are good, and sad to miss his harmonies, in an argument about precedence, as if jostling for a high place at the table kept us from enjoying the feast. The last shall be first, in any case. But it would be untrue to Milton, as well, not to give him the honest argument, based on thorough and thoughtful reading, that he looked for in vain from his early opponents. Such a reading can bring reader and text together in 'meet and happy conversation'.

FURTHER READING

Adams, Mary. 'Fallen Wombs: The Origins of Death in Miltonic Sexuality', *Milton Studies* 29 (1992), 165–79.

Aers, David, and Bob Hodge, '"Rational Burning": Milton on Sex and Marriage', *Milton Studies* 13 (1979), 3–33

Barker, Arthur, 'Christian Liberty in Milton's Divorce Pamphlets', *Modern Language Review* 35 (1940), 153–61

Benet, Diana Treviño, 'Abdiel and the Son in the Separation Scene', *Milton Studies* 18 (1983), 129–43

Benet, Diana Treviño, and Michael Lieb, eds., *Literary Milton: Text, Pretext, Context* (Pittsburgh, 1994)

Bennett, Joan S., *Reviving Liberty: Radical Christian Humanism in Milton's Great Poems* (Cambridge, MA, 1989)

Blessington, Francis C., *'Paradise Lost' and the Classical Epic* (Boston, 1979)

Boocker, David, '"Women Are Indebted to Milton": Milton and Woman's Rights in the Nineteenth Century', in McColgan and Durham, eds., *Arenas of Conflict*, 51–64

Braden, Gordon, and William Kerrigan, 'Milton's Coy Eve: *Paradise Lost* and Renaissance Love Poetry', *ELH* 53 (1986)

Davies, Stevie, *The Feminine Reclaimed: The Idea of Woman in Spenser, Shakespeare, and Milton* (Lexington, KY, and Brighton, 1986; published in the UK as *The Idea of Woman in Renaissance Literature*)

Di Pasquale, Theresa M., '"Heav'ns last best gift": Eve and Wisdom in *Paradise Lost*', *Modern Philology* 95 (1997), 44–67.

DiSalvo, Jackie, *War of Titans: Blake's Critique of Milton and the Politics of Religion* (Pittsburgh, 1983)

Dobranski, Stephen B., and John P. Rumrich, *Milton and Heresy* (Cambridge, 1998)

DuRocher, Richard, *Milton and Ovid* (Ithaca, NY, 1985)

Evans, J. M., *'Paradise Lost' and the Genesis Tradition* (Oxford, 1968)

Farwell, Marilyn R., 'Eve, the Separation Scene, and the Renaissance Idea of Androgyny', *Milton Studies* 16 (1982), 3–20

Flannagan, Roy, ed., *The Riverside Milton* (Boston, 1998).

Fleming, Ray, '"Sublime and Pure Thoughts Without Transgression": The Dantean Influence in Milton's "Donna leggiadra"', *Milton Quarterly* 20 (1986), 38–44

Fresch, Cheryl H., '"And brought her unto the man": The Wedding in *Paradise Lost*', *Milton Studies* 16 (1982), 21–33

Friedman, Donald M., 'Divisions on a Ground: "Sex" in *Paradise Lost*', in Stanwood, *Of Poetry and Politics*, 203–12

'The Lady in the Garden: On the Literary Genetics of Milton's Eve', *Milton Studies* 35 (1997), 114–33

Froula, Christine, 'When Eve Reads Milton: Undoing the Canonical Economy', *Critical Inquiry* 10 (1983), 321–47

Frye, Northrop, 'The Revelation to Eve', in *'Paradise Lost': A Tercentenary Tribute*, ed. B. Rajan (Toronto, 1969), 18–47

Gallagher, Philip J., *Milton, the Bible, and Misogyny*, ed. Eugene R. Cunnar and Gail L. Mortimer (Columbia, 1990)

Gilbert, Sandra M., 'Patriarchal Poetry and Women Readers: Reflections on Milton's Bogey', *PMLA* 93 (1978), 368–82

Gregerson, Linda, *The Reformation of the Subject: Spenser, Milton, and the English Protestant Epic* (Cambridge, 1995)

Gulden, Ann Tornay, 'Milton's Eve and Wisdom: The "Dinner Party" Scene in *Paradise Lost*', *Milton Quarterly* 32 (1998), 137–43

Hagstrum, Jean, *Sex and Sensibility: Ideal and Erotic Love from Milton to Mozart* (Chicago, 1980)

Halkett, John G., *Milton and the Idea of Matrimony* (New Haven and London, 1970)

Haller, William and Malleville, 'The Puritan Art of Love', *Huntington Library Quarterly* 5 (1941–2), 235–72

Haskin, Dayton, *Milton's Burden of Interpretation* (Philadelphia, 1994)

Hobby, Elaine, *Virtue of Necessity: English Women's Writing, 1649–88* (Ann Arbor, 1989)
Kelso, Ruth, *Doctrine for the Lady of the Renaissance* (Urbana, 1956)
Kerrigan, William, *The Sacred Complex: On the Psychogenesis of 'Paradise Lost'* (Cambridge, MA, 1983)
'Milton's Kisses', in Dobranski and Rumrich, eds., *Milton and Heresy*, 117–35
Kim, Julie H., 'The Lady's Unladylike Struggle: Redefining Patriarchal Boundaries in Milton's *Comus*', *Milton Studies* 35 (1997), 1–20
Labriola, Albert C., ed., *The Miltonic Samson* (*Milton Studies* 23, Pittsburgh, 1997)
Landy, Marcia, '"A Free and Open Encounter": Milton and the Modern Reader', *Milton Studies* 9 (1976), 3–36
Le Comte, Edward S., *Milton and Sex* (London and New York, 1978)
Leonard, John, *Naming in Paradise: Milton and the Language of Adam and Eve* (Oxford, 1990)
Lewalski, Barbara K., 'Milton on Women – Yet Once More', *Milton Studies* 6 (1974), 3–20
'Paradise Lost' and the Rhetoric of Literary Forms (Princeton, 1985)
Lieb, Michael, *The Dialectics of Creation: Patterns of Birth and Regeneration in Paradise Lost* (Amherst, 1970)
'"Two of Far Nobler Shape": Reading the Paradisal Text', in Benet and Lieb, *Literary Milton*, 114–32
McChrystal, Deidre, 'Redeeming Eve', *ELR* 23 (1993), 490–508
McColgan, Kristin Pruitt, '"God is also in Sleep": Dreams Satanic and Divine in *Paradise Lost*', *Milton Studies* 30 (1993), 135–48
McColgan, Kristin Pruitt, and Charles W. Durham, eds., *Arenas of Conflict: Milton and the Unfettered Mind* (Selinsgrove, 1997)
Spokesperson Milton: Voices in Contemporary Criticism (Selinsgrove, 1994)
McColley, Diane K., 'Free Will and Obedience in the Separation Scene of *Paradise Lost*', *Studies in English Literature* 12 (1972), 103–20
Milton's Eve (Urbana, 1983)
A Gust for Paradise: Milton's Eden and the Visual Arts (Urbana, 1993)
Miller, Dorothy Durkee, *'Eve'*, *JEGP* 61 (1962), 542–7
Miller, Leo, *John Milton Among the Polygamophiles* (New York, 1974)
Mollenkott, Virginia, 'Some Implications of Milton's Androgynous Muse', in *Bucknell Review: Women, Literature, Criticism*, ed. Harry R. Garvin (Lewisburg, PA, 1978)
Nyquist, Mary, 'The Genesis of Gendered Subjectivity in the Divorce Tracts and in *Paradise Lost*', in Nyquist and Ferguson, eds., *Re-membering Milton*, 99–127.
Nyquist, Mary, and Margaret W. Ferguson, eds., *Re-membering Milton: Essays on the Texts and Traditions* (New York, 1987)
Parker, Patricia, 'Eve, Evening, and the Labor of Reading in *Paradise Lost*', *ELR* 9 (1978), 319–42
Patterson, Annabel, 'No Meer Amatorious Novel?' in David Loewenstein and James Grantham Turner, eds., *Politics, Poetics, and Hermeneutics in Milton's Prose* (Cambridge, 1990)
Pechter, Edward, 'When Pechter Reads Froula Pretending She's Eve Reading Milton; or, New Feminist Is But Old Priest Writ Large', *Critical Inquiry* 11 (1984), 163–70

Peczenik, F., 'Fit Help: The Egalitarian Marriage in *Paradise Lost*', *Mosaic* 17 (1984), 29–48

Quilligan, Maureen, *Milton's Spenser: The Politics of Reading* (Ithaca, NY, 1983)

Radzinowicz, Mary Ann Nevins, 'Eve and Dalila: Renovation and Hardening of the Heart', in *Reason and Imagination: Studies in the History of Ideas, 1600–1800*, ed. J. A. Mazzeo (New York and London, 1962)

Revard, Stella P., 'Eve and the Doctrine of Responsibility in *Paradise Lost*', *PMLA* 88 (1973), 69–78

'Dalila as Euripidean Heroine', *Papers in Language and Literature* 23 (1987), 291–302.

Milton and the Tangles of Neaera's Hair: The Making of the 1645 'Poems' (Columbia, 1997)

Rogers, John, *The Matter of Revolution: Science, Poetry, and Politics in the Age of Milton* (Ithaca, NY, 1996)

Rudrum, Alan, 'Polygamy in *Paradise Lost*', *Essays in Criticism* 20 (1970), 18–23

Samuel, Irene, *Dante and Milton* (Ithaca, NY, 1966)

Schwartz, Louis, '"Conscious Terrours": Seventeenth-Century Obstetrics and Milton's Allegory of Common Sin in *Paradise Lost*, Book 2', in McColgan and Durham, eds., *Arenas of Conflict*

Shawcross, John, 'The Metaphor of Inspiration', in *Th'Upright Heart and Pure*, ed. Amadeus P. Fiore (Pittsburgh, 1967)

Shullenberger, William, 'Wrestling with the Angel: *Paradise Lost* and Feminist Criticism', *Milton Quarterly* 20 (1986), 69–85

Stanwood, P. G., ed., *Of Poetry and Politics: New Essays on Milton and His World* (Binghamton, 1995)

Summers, Joseph H., *The Muse's Method* (London and Cambridge, MA, 1962), especially chapter 4, 'The Two Great Sexes'

Swaim, Kathleen, 'Flower, Fruit, and Seed: A Reading of *Paradise Lost*', *Milton Studies* 5 (1973), 155–76

'"Hee for God Only, Shee for God in Him": Structural Parallelism in *Paradise Lost*', *Milton Studies* 9 (1976), 121–49

Thickstun, Margaret Olofson, *Fictions of the Feminine: Puritan Doctrine and the Representation of Women* (Ithaca, NY, 1988)

Treip, Mindele Anne, *Allegorical Poetics and the Epic: The Renaissance Tradition to 'Paradise Lost'* (Lexington, 1994)

Turner, James Grantham, *One Flesh: Paradisal Marriage and Sexual Relations in the Age of Milton* (Oxford, 1987)

Walker, Julia, ed., *Milton and the Idea of Woman* (Urbana, 1988)

Webber, Joan Malory, 'The Politics of Poetry: Feminism and *Paradise Lost*', *Milton Studies* 14 (1980), 3–24

Wittreich, Joseph, *Feminist Milton* (Ithaca, NY, 1987)

'"Inspir'd with Contradiction": Mapping Gender Discourses in *Paradise Lost*', in Benet and Lieb, *Literary Milton*, 133–60

'Milton's Transgressive Maneuvers: Reception (Then and Now) and the Sexual Politics of *Paradise Lost*', in Dobranski and Rumrich, eds., *Milton and Heresy*, 244–61

13

GEORGIA CHRISTOPHER

Milton and the reforming spirit

The Reformation was an important part of England's national identity in the seventeenth century and an important part of Milton's identity. While England defined itself as a Protestant nation over against the largely Roman Catholic Continent, Milton defined himself over against Protestant opponents at home, turning his antipapal rhetoric first against prelates in the Church of England, whom he called 'more Antichristian than Antichrist himselfe' (*YP* 1: 850), and later against the Scots Presbyters.

Milton did not consider Luther's break with Rome to be the important watershed in western history it is now regarded, and usually he did not speak of *the* Reformation. In his prose tracts, however, he repeatedly writes of 'reformation', by which he means the work of returning the English Church – and the English nation – to the purity and simplicity of the Gospel. Milton views the work of reformation as a recurring task. In *The Reason of Church-Government*, for example, he refers to the plight of Old Testament prophets 'that liv'd in the times of reformation', to a 'more perfect reformation under Christ', and to the reforming message of the Lollards and Hussites who had anticipated Luther (*YP* 1: 799, 757). England's role in the modern reformation is for Milton a point of particular pride, and he firmly believes that England has been chosen to complete the Reformation, in which he feels called to participate. Near the beginning of *The Reason of Church-Government*, he explains that he is personally hesitant:

> But when God commands to take the trumpet and blow a dolorous or a jarring blast, it lies not in mans will what he shall say, or what he shall conceal. If he shall think to be silent, as *Jeremiah* did, because of the reproach and derision he met with daily . . . he would be forc't to confesse as he confest, *his word was in my heart as a burning fire shut up in my bones, I was weary with forbearing and could not stay.* (*YP* 1: 803)

Milton goes on to argue that the prelates – especially the bishops and archbishops – are rich, greedy, and corrupt, interested in anything but the care of souls. This hierarchical system of governance, he argues, should be replaced by assemblies of divines *and* laymen – the form of church government that he finds the New Testament advocating. It is, not coincidentally, an arrangement that embodies a cardinal point of Reformation theology – the Priesthood of Believers. Milton says, 'Christians ought to know, that the title of Clergy S. *Peter* gave to all Gods people' until 'the succeeding Prelates took it from them' (*YP* 1: 838). Therefore he maintains that 'the functions of Church-government ought to be free and open to any Christian man though never so laick' (*YP* 1: 844).

To advocate complete change in church governance was in Milton's day politically radical because church leaders had been part of the political establishment since the time of Henry VIII. Accordingly, religious discourse was integrated with political discourse in a seamless rhetorical bond that now we have difficulty seeing whole. Milton and the Puritans were not devoid of political or economic motivation, and we catch occasional glimpses of an economic grudge, as when Milton berates the prelates for their wealth and lordliness, even claiming that prelacy 'shall spoil and havock your estates' (*YP* 1: 851). Nevertheless, public discourse was primarily – and passionately – doctrinal, that is, cast in Protestant categories of thought inherited from the continental reformers – from Luther, Calvin, Melanchthon, among others – and from systematized versions of that thought compiled by English scholastics like William Ames and William Perkins. Milton stands squarely in this evangelical Protestant tradition, as opposed to the more Thomistic Protestant tradition espoused by Richard Hooker and Archbishop Laud.

Little in Protestantism was not already present in the medieval Catholic tradition, but Luther's emphases amounted to a new configuration in which religious life took on a distinctively 'literary' cast. Accordingly, there were marked modifications in how sin was perceived, what composed a sacrament, and what comprised devotional life. One need not be a Protestant in order to read *Paradise Lost*, because the basic story and much of its religious language is common to several religious traditions, the word 'saint' for ordinary believers being one of the few terms given a peculiarly Protestant meaning. Nevertheless, Protestant thought profoundly shaped Milton's poetry and helps to explain its distinctive features. Unlike Dante, Milton represents God by a discursive voice, not by a sensuous symbol. The Virgin is absent from the enthronement scene in heaven, and Purgatory has disappeared altogether from the cosmos.

More particularly, Protestant thought helps explain the shape of Milton's hell and his presentation of evil. The Catholic tradition dealt with a precisely calibrated hierarchy of venial and mortal sins; and though the plan in Dante's *Inferno* is not exactly a map of the seven deadly sins, it is arranged hierarchically beginning with the most sympathetic sin – adultery between book lovers – and descending in rational sequence toward the bestial and heinous, down to the depths of usury, and finally to Judas and the betrayers. In Milton's hell, however, the terrain is more exegetical than judicial; that is to say, the varied terrain, with its ever burning sulphur and contrasting regions of ice, does not signify gradations of sin, but evidence of the delusional character of the devil's discourse, in particular Belial's assertion that the devils can adjust and become 'inured' to the flames. Although Satan addresses his fellows in misery by titles that seem to presume a ranking by degree – 'Princes, potentates, / Warriors, the flower of heaven' (*PL* 1.315–16) – these titles are primarily honorific and rhetorical. There are effectively only two degrees in Milton's hell – fallen Archangel and his compatriots. The demonic council embodies a two-step hierarchy, rather like a parodic version of the church governance Milton advocated (minister-and-lay-leaders). Dramatically speaking, at least, the orators seem to be peers, differing only in forensic acuity, age, and individual temper. Elsewhere, Milton is explicit about the levelling of evil. There are, he says, but 'two degrees' of evil: 'a reprobat conscience in this life, and hell in the other world' (*YP* 1: 835).

The elision of degree in hell reflects the Protestant abolition of confession and of precisely calibrated penances. To be sure, Protestants developed their casuists, but their piety purported to erase gradations of sin and concentrate upon the heart's primary orientation. Moral calculus began with faith. The biblical underpinning for this point, cited by Milton as by Luther before him, was Romans 13: 23: 'Whatsoever is not of faith is sin' (*YP* 6: 639; *Luther's Works* 26: 250). This view no longer localized sin in careful categories, but spread it into all areas of existence, including those normally reserved for virtue. The most 'virtuous' action without faith was sinful; conversely 'sloth' (or merely standing and waiting) might be a most heroic act of faith. This 'either-or' shaping of sin is the most misunderstood point about Milton's devils, who are conspicuous for their virtue. In Book 2 of *Paradise Lost* we see a fearless warrior, a staunch intellectual ('who would lose, / Though full of pain, this intellectual being . . . ?' (2.146–7)), an architectural wizard, and a forensic champion. Unlike the denizens of Dante's *Inferno*, not one devil belongs in a state prison. They are epitomes of sin for one reason only: they lack faith.

Faith, in Milton's tradition, furthermore has an irreducible 'literary' component, for it is defined by reception of divine words that constitute a 'verbal sacrament'. This verbal sacrament is a 'scripture within scripture', or the promise of redemption in Christ in any of the lexical forms in which it recurs throughout the Bible, both in the New Testament and more obliquely in the Old Testament. Indeed, the promise *of* redemption can be inferred simply by the mention of Christ. The difference between the Catholic and Protestant traditions has often been located in the question of free will, but a more basic distinction concerns authority, which Protestants place, not in the institution of the church or its hierarchy, but in Scripture – 'the only true theologie' (*YP* 7: 306) – and in the Holy Spirit that makes it 'piercing'.

In a notably Protestant gesture, accordingly, Milton constructs an episode in Book 5 to initiate the entire action of *Paradise Lost* with a pronouncement – a verbal sacrament – paraphrasing Psalm 2: 7:

> This day I have begot whom I declare
> My only Son . . .
>   whom ye now behold
> At my right hand; your head I him appoint. (5.603–6)

The speech concludes with a promissory emphasis: 'Under his great vice-regent reign abide / United as one individual soul / For ever happy' (5.609–11). It is Satan's refusal to accept the sacramental promise, his refusal to 'hear' God's words, that constitutes the primal sin. Once Satan strikes this posture, any virtue or courage he may display partakes of sin. A similar verbal sacrament obtains in the Garden of Eden. Milton takes pains to show that Adam and Eve make glorious love before the Fall, because it is important to show that their primal sin does not derive from sexuality, does not cast suspicion on the goodness of Creation. Rather, their sin, like Satan's, consists in a disregard of divine words. In accordance with the same principle, Adam and Eve's redemption is occasioned by a *reception* of divine words.

The divine promise that comes to Adam and Eve after the Fall, however, is veiled in the sentence of judgement that the Son pronounces in Book 10:

> Between thee and the woman I will put
> Enmity, and between thine and her seed;
> *Her seed shall bruise thy head, thou bruise his heel.*
> (10.179–81; italics added)

Any well catechized Puritan would recognize this as a redaction of Genesis 3: 15, known as the *protevangelium*, the first Messianic promise, the first utterance of the Gospel (see *YP* 6: 515). Adam and Eve, however, do not at first see anything promissory in the *protevangelium*. Only at line 1030, after an emotional reconciliation with Eve – and in response to her suggestion that they abstain from lovemaking to prevent the curse on future generations – does Adam partially solve the *protevangelium*. He seizes upon the right referent for the word *Serpent* in the judicial sentence and instantly grasps that it signifies the death of 'our grand foe Satan' (1033–4).

This moment in *Paradise Lost* is susceptible of several interpretations. Readers in the tradition of Aquinas and Hooker will emphasize an apparent reasoning process in Adam's words, 'then let us seek / Some safer resolution . . .' (1028–9), whereas readers in the evangelical tradition will emphasize the sudden access of memory and argue that identifying the *Serpent* calls for a daring leap of reference that cannot merely be deduced by the knowledge available to Adam in this scene. In either case, the moment of eureka! marks the passage of the couple from despair to faith. Once Adam sees something of the promise in the *protevangelium*, he begins to see promise in the labour that is to come in the fields, and in childbed.

Adam's experience here also fits the Reformation archetype of a lonely encounter with Scripture and follows the pattern set by Luther's account of how the meaning of Romans 1:17 ('The just shall live by faith') was for him suddenly transformed – from an impossible demand for goodness into a promise of bestowed righteousness. 'Here I felt that I was altogether born again and had entered paradise itself through open gates', Luther explains (*Luther's Works* 34: 337). The turning point in Book 10 is also very like Christian's experience in *The Pilgrim's Progress* when he is about to commit suicide in the Dungeon of the Giant Despair. Suddenly he remembers that in his pocket he has had the Key of Promise with him all along. He draws it out, turns the lock, and soon is on his way again toward the Celestial City. And so are Adam and Eve, though they still have a great deal more to learn about the *protevangelium* under the tutelage of Michael in Books 11 and 12.

That Milton depicts in minute detail Adam and Eve's experience with God's oracular promise and that he gives it emphasis of place – Books 9, 10, 11, and 12 – is consistent with the assumption in Protestant hermeneutics that Adam and Eve are the first Christians and that, as Milton puts it, the mystical church 'includes people from many remote countries, and from all ages since the creation of the world' (*YP* 6: 500). Accordingly, Milton's Adam and Eve relate to the sacramental promise in the same way as did Milton's contemporaries, that is, as verbal *report*, albeit an anticipatory one. Milton's choice not to narrate the crucifixion in a poem that includes all time and space reflects the Protestant view that it is the (promise-bearing) *report* of the event, not its repetition in the Mass, that is sacramental. If Milton pushed 'Christian' experience back to the Garden of Eden, he was following in the exegetical footsteps of Luther, Calvin, and other reformers, but he was also making a political gesture, defending

Protestantism against the claim that it was a new-fangled religion (Patrides 1982, 102).

If there is no priest in the Edenic Church, who then administers the verbal sacrament? The answer, as Calvin elaborated it, was that the proclamation of God's Promise is made effectively sacramental by the operation of the Holy Spirit. Milton thus presents the *protevangelium* as having no immediate effect upon Adam and Eve during the judgement scene when it is pronounced. Only later in the midst of a marital quarrel is the promise embraced. As the Father explains, their reception of it is a result of 'My motions in him' (*PL* 11.91).

For Calvin, the work of the Spirit was virtually confined to the reception of Scripture, and the sheer fact of belief was the only reliable token of the Spirit's presence. In seventeenth-century England, however, the question of the Spirit's operation was variously understood. For the Cambridge Platonists, the Spirit's work was all but equated with the working of human reason. For the radical sectaries of the 1640s, the Spirit's work was that of prompting a man to specific actions, which might range from choosing a certain text to inciting a bizarre action. For the Quakers, the Spirit was certified both by inner impulse and by a Meeting's consensus, one which might go beyond or counter to Scripture. Milton finds no scriptural warrant for the Holy Spirit as a *Person* within the Trinity, but his *Christian Doctrine* assembles many verses about 'the spirit of God'. Interior 'motions' and the urging of conscience to speak out comprise a prominent theme in Milton's tracts and poetry alike. His shorter poems begin to resolve themselves when a sudden voice supplies an answer. These voices are tactfully designated as 'Patience' in 'When I consider how my light is spent' and as 'Phoebus' in *Lycidas*. In *Paradise Lost*, Adam reveals to Eve the content of the 'persuasion' that grew in him when he remembers the word about the Seed: 'the bitterness of death / Is past, and we shall live' (11.157–8). In *Samson Agonistes* the poet does not supply the content of the 'intimate impulse' that comes to the hero (223, 1382), but in *Paradise Lost* the content of the Spirit's tutelage is fine doctrinal discrimination.

Milton generally refers to the Spirit's work in a restrained and reticent way. Sometimes his assertions seem to identify the Spirit with human reason, as when he insists that Truth should undergo 'the triall and inspection of the Understanding' (*YP* 1: 830). Sometimes reason and divine prompting seem indistinguishable, as when Milton, on the eve of the Restoration, advocates an unpaid clergy. He writes, 'I promisd then to speak further, when I should finde God disposing me, and opportunity inviting. Opportunity I finde now inviting; and apprehend therein the concurrence of God disposing' (*YP* 7: 278). At other times the Spirit is implicitly an enemy of reasoning, as when Milton says, 'the quick and pearcing word . . . throw[s] down the weak mightines of mans reasoning' (*YP* 1: 827). Sometimes the Spirit is credited only with the task of scriptural interpretation (*YP* 6: 583). And on occasion, Milton claims urgent divine prompting, as in *The Reason of Church-Government* when he advocates abolishing the entire episcopal system: 'Were it the meanest under-service, if God by his Secretary conscience injoyn it, it were sad for me if I should draw back . . .' (*YP* 1: 822). If a 'Secretary' here means one 'entrusted with the secrets or commands of God' (*OED*), then the assertion is a bolder claim to divine intimacy than it first appears.

The question of Milton's inspiration is a vexed one, but it has a bearing upon the dramatic role of the Son, who fights with the 'Sword of the Spirit' in *Paradise Regained*. Milton has been accused of claiming that heavenly dictation supplanted his own writing skill, of claiming that he was privy to God's innermost secrets, or, alternatively, that he was invoking the heavenly muse as a pro forma bow to the epic tradition. The reality lies somewhere between these extremes. As to poetic skills, the role of the Spirit seems to be an additive one – that of a 'supreme inlightning *assistance*'. As opposed to the heat of youth or the fume of wine, Milton claims reliance upon prayer and 'that eternall Spirit who can *enrich* with all utterance' and send a Seraph to purify the lips with a coal (*YP* 1: 749, 820–1; italics added). What may now seem to be an arrogant presumption of knowing God's mind was, within the Puritan ethos, a witness to faith. Milton's confident tone signals his depth of conviction. When, for example, he claims to be 'incorporate into that truth whereof I was perswaded' (1: 871), he is simply taking the Priesthood of Believers seriously. As he explains in *Christian Doctrine*, the communion that obtained between man and God in his tradition was the kind of union that occurs in 'persuasion' (see *YP* 6: 471–5): agreement of mind and heart and soul, unity in the Spirit.

One can easily read *Paradise Lost* without being conversant with Protestant theology, because the poem transcends its doctrinal roots. When reading *Paradise Regained*, however, one needs to take account of the 'literary' operations Calvin and Milton credited to the Holy Spirit – belief in the promise of the Redeemer, a faithful interpretation of Scripture, its right application on a given occasion, and the prompting to preach or speak. Calvin, to whom Milton stands closest on 'the question of the Spirit', holds Jesus to be the unique bearer and sender of the Holy Spirit. (Calvin so emphasizes the association between Christ and the Spirit that his position has sometimes been labelled a 'Spirit-Christology'.) In *Paradise Regained* the Father affirms Jesus as his 'son beloved' (1.85) when he rises from the baptismal waters, and this pronouncement initiates the action of the brief epic. The descent of the dove at this moment signals the *full* donation of the Spirit, but Satan sees only a dove, and does not understand that now the hero possesses a secret weapon that will enable him to win any scriptural battle. In short, the hero possesses what Bunyan was to call the Interpreter.

The lack of anything numinous in the hero's presence or his speech tends to mislead us along with Satan, for we expect an emotional effusion to accompany an access of the Spirit. We tend to expect 'heart burnings' of the sort found in Puritan diaries. Instead, the hero's forensic precision is almost chilling, and his failure to defend himself makes him appear emotionally empty. But this absence of the claims of the self is an important indication of the hero's hidden identity as Bearer of the Spirit. As Milton pointed out, to be in the Spirit 'is also called self-denial' (*YP* 6: 478). In *Christian Doctrine* the Son and the Holy Spirit are both defined by their dialogue: of each, Milton says that he 'never speaks anything of himself but always refers to the authority of God the Father' (*YP* 6: 259–60). Hence it is revelatory that Satan never manages to engage the hero in discussion as to the 'degree' of his sonship, and that the hero withstands all Satan's attempts to have him speak *as himself*.

Ironically, the Tempter comes very close to the Son's hermeneutic secret when he offers him all the wisdom of the ancients: 'These rules will render thee a king complete / Within thyself' (*PR* 4.283–4). However, Reformation thought considered self-mastery, not sensuality, the quintessence of flesh, to which it opposed self-denial, or self-emptying in favour of the governance of the Spirit. To surrender the egoistic flesh to the governance of the Holy Spirit therefore required, not self-mastery, but an opening of oneself to 'Light from above, from the fountain of light' (*PR* 4.289).

The final temptation on the pinnacle of the Temple demonstrates the supernatural 'inlightning' that helps the hero to defeat Satan. The Tempter's rhetoric presents a dilemma. Once atop the temple spire, he says, 'To stand upright / will ask thee skill' (4.551–2), indicating by his understatement that the feat of standing on the spire is physically impossible. If the hero stands, he will reveal his supernatural identity. Then the Tempter says, 'Now show thy progeny; if not to stand, / Cast thyself down' (4.554–5). The hero must, according to the categories of the natural world, either stand or fall. Yet anything he does will be obeying Satan. The dilemma appears to be an infallible temptation; it invites the despairing conclusion that life in this world necessarily defeats faith. The Son, however, does not betray the smallest tremor of anxiety. He confidently strikes back with a verse from Deuteronomy 5:16: 'Also it is written, / Tempt not the Lord thy God, he said and stood' (4.560–1). The reply is a denunciation of Satan's perverse application of Scripture, but it is also the most spectacular of all the hero's verbal gestures of self-denial. Once again he refers the Satanic challenge to higher authority, and climactically identifies himself (to those who are doctrinally informed) as a hero fighting with the Sword of the Spirit.

Thus Milton reforms, or recasts, the aggressive warrior-Christ of his first epic into a character more like Abdiel, one who withstands and triumphs over interrogation, verbal attack, and misrepresentation of scriptural truth. The important discriminations in Milton's universe are finally 'literary' ones, for Milton's hell, heaven, 'Edenic Church', and ultimate hero all are defined by the reception of divine words. And that reception, when positive, is credited to the work of a secret agent – the Holy Spirit – whose agency is the beginning of all true reformation.

FURTHER READING

Barker, Arthur E., *Milton and the Puritan Dilemma* (Toronto, 1942)
Calvin, J., *Institutes of the Christian Religion*, ed. John T. McNeill, 2 vols. (Philadelphia, 1960)
Christopher, Georgia, *Milton and the Science of the Saints* (Princeton, 1982)
Danielson, Dennis, *Milton's Good God: A Study in Literary Theodicy* (Cambridge and New York, 1982)
Haller, William, *The Rise of Puritanism* (New York, 1955)
Hill, Christopher, *Milton and the English Revolution* (London, 1977)
Kerrigan, William B., *The Prophetic Milton* (Charlottesville, VA, 1975)
Lieb, Michael, *The Poetics of the Holy* (Chapel Hill, NC, 1981)
Luther's Works, ed. Jaroslav Pelikan and Helmut T. Lehmann, 55 vols. (St Louis, 1955–76)
Patrides, C. A., *Milton and the Christian Tradition* (Oxford, 1966)
Premises and Motifs in Renaissance Thought and Literature (Princeton, 1982)
Rajan, Balachandra, *'Paradise Lost' and the Seventeenth-Century Reader* (London, 1947)

14

MARY ANN RADZINOWICZ

How Milton read the Bible: the case of *Paradise Regained*

Milton read Scripture with a commitment to its themes, genres, and style. He read its two Testaments *thematically* as forming one body of saving truth, consistent but gradually becoming clearer to the understanding. He read it *generically* as consisting of law, story, prophets, and poetry, the poetry divisible into further genres. He read the poetry as composed, *stylistically*, with greater skill and purity than any other ancient national poetry. These three modes of reading influenced his own poems from the beginning to the end of his career, as he took scriptural themes, events, or doctrines for them, adapted scriptural genres to them, and echoed biblical style in them.

The earliest of his poems Milton thought worth saving were English paraphrases of Psalms 114 and 136, the first carrying the headnote 'This and the following Psalm were done by the Author at fifteen years old' (*Poems* 6). The last of his poems, *Paradise Regained*, published when he was sixty-three, was a debate poem like Job, with a plot taken from Luke, expounding an interpretation of Christ's redemptive work drawn from Hebrews, framed by angelic hymns, and foregrounded by human laments modelled on Psalms. That last poem is a particularly good place to see what reading the Bible meant to Milton, since it engages with Jesus at the moment when by his own reading of Scripture he understands his messiahship and holds to it throughout Satan's temptations. At that moment, the New Testament interprets the Old, changing, for Milton, the way the Hebrew Bible should thereafter be understood.

Milton explained how to read Scripture thematically in *De doctrina christiana* in Book 1, the book about beliefs: his analytic method was both comparative and linguistic. He 'proved' his points in that work by arranging citations from the Old Testament in the order of its canonical books and then from the New Testament in the order of its canonical books; he took that canonical order to be the arrangement God made for our understanding of the working out of his providential plan for human beings in history, more or less chronological and increasingly clear if read habitually from beginning to end, Genesis to Revelation. To read in this way is to read *typologically*, subjecting the Old Testament to a Christian hermeneutic, according to which events and persons of the Old are seen as foreshadowing or predicting those of the New Testament (see *YP* 6: 581; Budick, 198–212; Lewalski 1979, 111–44).

In that same chapter 30 of Book 1, Milton also distinguished the Old and New Testament, or as he sometimes called them, the Hebrew and Greek Testament, into broad genres using the terms 'the law of Moses', 'the prophets', and 'the historical books'. In *The Reason of Church-Government*, he not only found lyrical poetry in the Bible, referring to the frequent songs throughout the law and prophets; he also found dramatic and heroic poetry in it, calling The Song of Solomon a divine pastoral with a double chorus, Revelation a tragedy with a sevenfold chorus, and Job a brief model of epic poetry (*YP* 1: 813). He further distinguished the poetry of the Bible into the genres of psalms in *De doctrina christiana* in Book 2, the book about worship. There he explained that God ought to be worshipped by 'methods which he himself has prescribed' (*YP* 6: 666), methods found in the Bible patterns or models of such psalm genres as hymn, thanksgiving, lament, and wisdom song (which he called witness, or 'an open profession of the true faith'). Milton thought that God spoke divine truths to chosen individuals who later wrote down what he had said. He knew that certain parts of the Bible showed textual corruption and thought some books lost, but believed the Old Testament better preserved than the New. Of the accuracy of Old Testament history he wrote, 'It is true that the . . . historical [books] cannot be certainly ascribed to a particular date or author, and also that the chronological accuracy of their narrative often seems suspect. Few or none, however, have called in doubt their doctrinal part.' He took the speech formulae of Scripture to offer imitable forms, not prescriptions, explaining: 'Even the Lord's Prayer is a pattern or model, rather than a formula to be repeated verbatim' (*YP* 6: 670).

Finally, both in *The Reason of Church-Government* as a young man and in *Paradise Regained*, Milton commented on the style of biblical poetry. In the former, he said that the Bible's songs were incomparable not in their divine argument alone, but in their very art of composition (*YP* 1: 816). In *Paradise Regained*, Satan proposes that Jesus study at 'Athens . . . mother of arts / And eloquence' (4.240–1) in order to 'learn the secret power / Of harmony in tones and numbers hit / By voice or hand, and various-measured verse' (4.254–6). Jesus refuses, having a better model of the power of harmony in mind:

if I would delight my private hours
With music or with poem, where so soon
As in our native language can I find
That solace? All our Law and story strewed
With hymns, our psalms with artful terms inscribed,
Our Hebrew songs and harps in Babylon,
That pleased so well our victor's ear, declare
That rather Greece from us these arts derived;
Ill imitated, while they loudest sing
The vices of their deities, and their own
In fable, hymn, or song, so personating
Their gods ridiculous, and themselves past shame.
Remove their swelling epithets thick-laid
As varnish on a harlot's cheek, the rest,
Thin-sown with aught of profit or delight,
Will far be found unworthy to compare
With Sion's songs, to all true tastes excelling,
Where God is praised aright, and godlike men,
The Holiest of Holies, and his saints;
Such are from God inspired, not such from thee;
Unless where moral virtue is expressed
By light of nature not in all quite lost. (4.331–52)

Jesus commends Hebrew poetry in an imitation of its 'artful terms': the binary rhetorical schemes of balance, antithesis, and parallelism (Alter, 3–27; Berlin, 18–30,127–34; Frye, 199–214; Kugel, 49–58). Jesus thinks that the Old Testament is inspired truth; he thus infers that all its poetical figures too are significant. He treats its parallelism as a device of intellectual complementarity and he praises its purity. He frames a moral antithesis that pits a luxuriant style against a plain style by means of such contrasting pairs as 'remove': 'compare', 'thick-laid': 'thin-sown', 'their gods ridiculous': 'themselves past shame'. He epitomizes the luxuriant by the metaphor of cosmetics and disease ('swelling epithets' are like harlot's varnish) and the plain by the literalized metaphor of clear sight (those praise aright who are inspired by the light of God or the 'light of nature'). His moral antithesis accordingly forms an aesthetic antithesis – good men have good taste and prefer biblical to Hellenic poetry.

Milton was habituated to these three modes of reading – thematic, generic, stylistic – and practised them simultaneously. Since he read both Hebrew and Greek and used both the Junius-Tremellius Latin Bible and the *Biblia Sacra Polyglotta* of Brian Walton, he was not committed to a particular translation and did not signal the importance of Scripture to his poetry merely by echoing the language of the King James Version (Sims, in

Hunter; Shawcross; but see Sims 1962). What Milton uniquely did among the seventeenth century's great religious poets was to become as far as possible a biblical poet himself, not reproducing the language but reconstituting the themes, genres, and stylistic figures of Scripture within his own religious poetry. What he uniquely did in *Paradise Regained* was to use the lyric genres of Psalms to foreground, highlight, or emotionally colour the important moments in a debate between Satan and Jesus; to take his plot from an event in the life of Jesus as given in Luke's Gospel in preference to the others (Pope); to shape that plot like a judicial debate modelled on the testing of Job (Lewalski 1966); and to centre the debate on a conflict between Jesus and Satan over the interpretation of messiahship derived from the Letter to the Hebrews. The debate instances how Milton read Scripture for its themes.

Theme: Satan and Jesus discuss sonship

In *Paradise Regained* Satan quotes Scripture in his own cause and the Son responds with interpretations that wrest Scripture back from him again. Milton constructs a dramatic conflict by opposing to Satan's literal but worldly reading of the biblical theme of messiahship an evolving higher reading of the theme by the Son (Radzinowicz 1984; Martz 1960). Satan, who apparently has read through the Hebrew Bible with an inquiring but cold eye, makes an adversarial or ironic use of scriptural quotations, seeking to persuade the Son that they define the Messiah as an earthly king, for on that basis Jesus might betray the spiritual values in Holy Writ. Jesus replies with an inspired reading of scriptural quotations to defeat Satan's strategy; he not only eludes entrapment, he enunciates the true meaning of messiahship by his truer hermeneutic.

At the beginning of the poem, Jesus, newly baptized in the Jordan, walks out into the desert in deep thought, reviewing the course of his life. He recollects his first delighted boyhood reading in Scripture and then a further reading, after Mary has told him how at his birth the angels proclaimed him Messiah, 'searching what was writ / Concerning the Messiah, to our scribes / Known partly, and soon found of whom they spake / I am' (1.280–3). What he knows of himself is what has been revealed in the Old Testament. Then Satan comes to the contest with him, straight from a council of the fallen angels called after the baptism, at which he reported that when Jesus rose out of the Jordan a voice from heaven was heard to say, 'This is my son beloved, in him am pleased' (1.85). That proclamation is a mixture of Psalm 2: 7, 'I will declare the decree: . . . Thou art my Son, This day have I begotten thee', and Isaiah 42: 1, 'Behold my servant, whom

I uphold; mine elect, in whom my soul delighteth.' What Satan knows of the Son is also what *he* has read in the Old Testament. But since he reads literally Psalm 2: 6, 'Yet have I set my King upon my holy hill of Zion', he construes the next verse, 'Thou art my Son', just as literally: Jesus is of the line of King David: *ergo* the 'decree' is a coronation formula. Hence Satan's attack on the Son is double: one prong is to strike a treaty with the claimant Son; all knees may bow to him, if he will bow to Satan. The other prong is subversive: to alienate Father from Son by showing him unworthy of inheritance. But Jesus already has read:

> that my way must lie
> Through many a hard assay even to the death,
> Ere I the promised kingdom can attain.
> Or work redemption for mankind, whose sins'
> Full weight must be transferred upon my head. (1.263–7)

He knows, that is, that his messiahship includes priesthood, also an office once dependent on lineage and inheritance (Lev. 8: 1–13) but now on calling and merit (Heb. 5: 4–10). The 'decree' for him is therefore an appointment not to worldly kingship but to high priesthood and self-sacrifice.

The contest between Satan and the Son concludes in the epic as it concluded in Luke 4: 9–13, with a last tussle over Scripture. Satan places the Son on the highest pinnacle of the temple and scornfully invites him to stand:

> For it is written, [God] will give command
> Concerning thee to his angels, in their hands
> They shall uplift thee, lest at any time
> Thou chance to dash thy foot against a stone. (4.556–9)

That taunting quotation of Psalm 91: 11 assumes that Jesus, only a perfect man, will not be saved by means of angelic levitation. Jesus rebukes Satan from Deuteronomy 6: 16: 'Also it is written, / Tempt not the Lord thy God, he said and stood. / But Satan smitten with amazement fell' (4.560–2). Jesus resists Satan's temptations to abdicate his spiritual mission by constantly rebutting Satan's Scripture-laced arguments through better readings of Scripture. Milton took the pattern for Jesus' self-understanding from Hebrews, having praised its exposition of sonship in *De doctrina christiana*: 'The generation of the divine nature is by no one more sublimely or more fully explained than by the apostle to the Hebrews' (*YP* 6: 211).

The dispute between Satan and the Son over how to interpret Scripture on the meaning of sonship ranges throughout *Paradise Regained*; but one instance may stand for the whole, that where Satan turns Psalm 82: 6, 'I have said, Ye are gods and all of you are children of the Most High', against the Son. In Book 4 Jesus rejects the kingdoms of the world offered by Satan in exchange for worship of himself, Jesus' indignation being fully aroused by Satan's audacity '[to] offer them to me the Son of God, / To me my own, on such abhorred pact' (4.190–1). In response to that outraged self-identification, Satan quotes Psalm 82: 6:

> Be not so sore offended, Son of God;
> Though Sons of God both angels are and men,
> If I to try whether in higher sort
> Than these thou bear'st that title, have proposed
> What both from men and angels I receive
> . . .
> God of this world invoked and world beneath.
> (4.196–200, 203)

Satan reads the verse just as Milton read it in *De doctrina christiana*: it is 'God's own words when he was addressing kings and magnates . . . kings are said to be gods, and yet no one would conclude from this text that the saints were of one essence with God' (*YP* 6: 213). To Satan too 'Sons of God' is God's formula for the delegation of power, analogous to the titles bestowed on him by men and angels, 'God of this world invoked and world beneath'. Hence when Jesus withstands the terror of the storm, Satan recurs to the verse to test him with a final reading:

> Then hear, O Son of David, virgin-born;
> For Son of God to me is yet in doubt
> . . .
> [I] Heard thee pronounced the Son of God beloved.
> Thenceforth I thought thee worth my nearer view
> And narrower scrutiny, that I might learn
> In what degree or meaning thou art called
> The Son of God, which bears no single sense;
> The Son of God I also am, or was,
> And if I was, I am; relation stands;
> All men are Sons of God; yet thee I thought
> In some respect far higher so declared. (4.500–1, 513–21)

But Milton went on to say, 'We should notice . . . that the name "God" is by the will and permission of God the Father, not infrequently bestowed even upon angels and men (*how much more, then, upon the only begotten Son, the image of the Father!*)' (*YP* 6: 233; italics added). Both in Hebrews and to Milton the Psalm does bear one single sense, and Satan's summary of the action reaches that one sense although he himself misreads it:

[I] have found thee
Proof against all temptation as a rock
Of adamant, and as a centre, firm
To the utmost of mere man both wise and good,
Not more; for honours, riches, kingdoms, glory
Have been before contemned, and may again:
Therefore to know what more thou art than man,
Worth naming Son of God by voice from heaven,
Another method I must now begin. (4.532–40)

To be 'the utmost of mere man both wise and good' stands in Satan's hermeneutic as insufficient evidence that Jesus is 'more than man / Worth naming Son of God'. But that was the evidence by which Hebrews identified the redeemer priest: 'For we have not a high priest which cannot be touched with the feeling of our infirmities; but was in all points tempted like as we are, yet without sin' (Heb. 4: 15). The unique priest is the one who 'Though he were a Son, yet learned . . . obedience by the things which he suffered; and being made perfect, he became the author of eternal salvation unto all them that obey him' (Heb. 5: 8–9). The uniqueness of the Son's priesthood is his willing choice of a life of the most extreme humiliation and suffering. Milton understood the single sense of that heroic self-sacrifice as removing the need of any other mediation, 'if Christians would but know thir own dignitie, thir libertie, thir adoption, and let it not be wondered if I say, thir spiritual priesthood, whereby they have all equally access to any ministerial function whenever calld by thir own abilities and the church' (*YP* 7: 320).

Milton's thematic consideration of Psalms, Luke, and Hebrews supplied him not only with the language and interpretation for the Son and Satan in their debate over sonship, but also with an interpretation of sonship that emphasized priesthood over kingship, freeing Christians of his own day from the pretensions of the prelates. To follow the trail of his thinking through his biblical sources is to arrive at an understanding of the exemplary and salvatory action of the Son in standing fast against temptation, which makes that action a sufficient atonement and example for all men.

Style: the Old Testament and the Son's dream

In Jesus' preference for Hebrew poetry over Greek, Milton signalled his intention to imitate biblical hymns and psalms in *Paradise Regained* by imitating recognizably scriptural 'artful terms'. The artful terms he chose are the binary structures of balance, repetition, and antithesis, and the rhythms of natural emphasis that reinforce those parallel structures. He imitated a scriptural style in this way throughout the poem, but again one instance may stand for many.

Having rejected the first temptation to turn stones into bread, in Book 2 of *Paradise Regained*, after forty days in the wilderness Jesus for the first time is conscious of hunger as he prepares to sleep, but resolved not to 'mind it, fed with better thoughts that feed / Me hung'ring more to do my Father's will' (2.258–9). Meanwhile Satan, discomfited by the failure of the first temptation, after a second council of his peers skulks nearby with some of them. Surrounded by those hostile beings, Jesus lay down and 'slept, / And dreamed, as appetite is wont to dream / Of meats and drinks' (2.263–5). Satan takes advantage of the dream to bring on the banquet that concludes the temptation to appetite. The banquet scene is a Miltonic invention, not suggested by any of the Gospels; the dream episode, however, is dense with scriptural echoes, and its style is demonstrably parallelistic.

Milton invented the dream episode to exemplify Jesus' sense of mission represented in John 4: 34 – 'My meat is to do the will of him that sent me, and to finish his work' – and thus typologically in the New Testament to complete his earlier use of Deuteronomy 8: 3: 'Man lives not by bread only, but each word / Proceeding from the mouth of God; who fed / Our fathers here with manna' (1.349–51). Milton created the scene from Psalms 3 and 4 translated by him in 1653 (Radzinowicz 1978, 198–208), from two incidents in the life of Elijah (1 Kings 17: 5–6 and 19: 4–8), and from one incident in the life of Daniel (Dan. 1: 3–21).

In Psalm 3, the speaker seeks and receives God's help against enemies surrounding him by night. Its subtitle, 'A Psalm of David when he fled from Absalom his son', linked it to an occasion when David 'passed over the brook Kidron . . . *toward the way of the wilderness*' (2 Sam. 15: 23) pursued by the rebellious army of his son. Milton translated it as a dramatic monologue:

Lord how many are thy foes
    How many those
  That in arms against me rise
    Many are they
  That of my life distrustfully thus say,
No help for him in God there lies.
But thou Lord art my shield my glory,
    Thee through my story
  The exalter of my head I count
    Aloud I cried

Unto Jehovah, he full soon replied
And heard me from his holy mount.
I lay and slept, I waked again,
For my sustain
Was the Lord. Of many millions
The populous rout
I fear not though incamping round about
They pitch against me their pavilions.
Rise Lord, save me my God for thou
Hast smote ere now
On the cheek-bone all my foes,
Of men abhorred
Hast broke the teeth. This help was from the Lord
Thy blessing on thy people flows.

The passionate declamation has a strong forward rhythm. It is divided into four stanzas, each translating two verses of the original, rhyming a a b c c b, with a stress pattern 4 2 4 2 5 4. The poem on the page is not printed in strophes, however, and while the stress pattern is identical in each stanza, the syllabic pattern is very different indeed, running 7 4 7 4 10 8 / 9 5 7 3 10 8 / 8 4 8 5 10 10 / 8 4 7 4 10 8. Because the unaccented syllables are dominated by a strong idiomatic speech-stressing, the rhythmic structure of the verse sounds very much more important than its metrical structure. Spoken English stress and the allowable variations in English prosody override a metre of feet; Milton's translation emphasizes as its musical principle a counterpointed rhythm of natural stress over the rhythm of quantity or feet. His willingness to translate eight psalms in a wide variety of metres suggests that he thought Hebrew verse observed an ancient freedom, privileging rhythm over metre. His version does not echo the words of previous translations; it imitates the parallelism of biblical poetry and its stress-rhythms.

In *Paradise Regained* Milton makes Jesus' beleaguered desert situation – when Satan 'takes a chosen band / Of spirits likest to himself in guilt / To be at hand' (2.236–8) – comparable to that of David in the wilderness; those versicles (4 10 4 syllables rhyming a b a) even pick up the rhythmic effect of his psalm translation. The Son sleeps conscious of hunger. During the night he dreams of God's feeding Elijah and Daniel in the wilderness; the dream is borrowed from Psalm 4, Milton's translation of the relevant verses reading:

Into my heart more joy
And gladness thou hast put
Than when a year of glut

Their stores doth over-cloy
And from their plenteous grounds
With vast increase their corn and wine abounds.
In peace at once will I
Both lay me down and sleep
For thou alone dost keep
Me safe where'er I lie
As in a rocky cell
Thou Lord alone in safety mak'st me dwell.

In the episode in *Paradise Regained*, Milton in effect reverses those two stanzas, imagining a sleep in which joy at God's presence is figured as a dream of receiving food from his storehouse (2.252–78); he fills the gap in the account of David's experience in Psalm 3 between 'I lay and slept, I waked again' with an experience drawn from Psalm 4 which accounts for the emotion with which David in the original and Jesus in *Paradise Regained* awoke: 'I fear not though camping round about / They pitch against me their pavilions.' Satan interprets Jesus' dream literally and provocatively: he reminds Jesus how God fed others who hungered in the wilderness, adding 'Of thee these forty days none hath regard.' The Son challenges his logic – 'what conclud'st thou hence?' – and rebuts it with a pithy antithesis: 'They all had need, I as thou seest have none' (2.315–18).

Milton recounts the Son's dream in the third person as a narrator's summary; he does not enter the sleeper's consciousness, but glosses the dream in advance as wish-fulfilment – Jesus 'dreamed, as appetite is wont to dream'. And he presents it as temptation – Jesus imagines that 'with Elijah he partook'. The summary, although plainstyle, artfully creates complex metrical effects:

Him thought, he by the brook of Cherith stood
And saw the ravens with their horny beaks
Food to Elijah bringing even and morn,
Though ravenous, taught to abstain from what they brought.
(2.266–9)

The quatrain, three pentameters and one casual hexameter unsupplied with elisions, within the envelope rhyme 'Him thought': 'they brought', is bound together by the internal rhyme 'thought . . . though . . . taught' and half rhymes 'brook . . . stood . . . food'. Milton then summarizes the feeding of Elijah in an even plainer and pithier style than that of his source. 1 Kings 19: 5–8 reads:

And as he lay and slept under a juniper tree, behold, then an angel touched him, and said unto him, Arise and eat. And he looked, and behold there was a

> cake baked on the coals, and a cruse of water at his head. And he did eat and drink, and laid him down again. And the angel of the Lord came a second time, and tended him, and said, Arise and eat; because the journey is too great for thee. And he arose, and did eat and drink and went in the strength of that meat forty days and nights unto Horeb the mount of God.

Milton uses fewer than half as many words as the biblical scenario to create the spaceless placeless specificity of dreams in another plain but rhetorically artful passage:

> He saw the prophet also how he fled
> Into the desert, and how there he slept
> Under a juniper; then how awaked,
> He found his supper on the coals prepared,
> And by the angels was bid rise and eat,
> And eat the second time after repose,
> The strength whereof sufficed him forty days. (2.270–6)

Among its devices are medial and terminal slant rhymes 'prophet': 'desert': 'fled' / 'slept'; sound repetitions in 'prophet', 'juniper', 'supper', 'prepared', and 'repose'; anaphora in 'how he fled . . . how there he slept . . . then how awaked', and ploche in 'and eat, / And eat'. Milton adopts the linguistic register of the King James Version – 'juniper', 'coals', 'arise and eat', 'strength', 'forty days' – and extends it – 'fled', 'supper', and 'awaked'. If he seems to have overlooked the most resonant phrase in 1 Kings – 'because the journey is too great for thee' – he has actually reserved it for a later echo and variation. If wish-fulfilment, the dream incorporates Jesus' hope for God's material aid as the faithful in the past received it. The salvation theology of Psalms 3 and 4 makes a different point: God sustains the believer by his inner presence, not by literal food.

Thus 'wore out night'; and Milton glosses the Son's awakening as vulnerable:

> As lightly from his grassy couch uprose
> Our Saviour, and found all was but a dream,
> Fasting he went to sleep, and fasting waked. (2.282–4)

Satan reads the awakening as disappointed: an angel came to Elijah with food, an unfulfilled dream came to the Son. Then Milton closes his account, rhythmically echoing but overturning the meaning of that resonant line in 1 Kings. Elijah was fed 'because the journey is too great for thee'; the Son's case is different: 'they all had need, I as thou seest have none' (2.318). Whether the Son rest on grassy couch in the wilderness or in rocky cell in exile, the Father fulfils his promise; and in the Son the fulfilment is total trust. His response to Satan has parallelistic pith – 'They

. . . had need, I . . . have none'; seconding alliteration in 'They': 'thou', 'all': 'as', 'have': 'had', 'need': 'none'; and medial near rhyme 'need': 'seest': 'none'.

The metaphorical plainness of *Paradise Regained* has been frequently remarked – as have the exceptions in images of light and dark, desert and pastoral life, the society of heaven and the solitude of the wilderness; and in scripturally derived key words that work both literally and metaphorically, nouns like 'hand', 'sheep', 'head', 'root', 'fruit', 'light' and verbs like 'stand', 'fall', 'feed', 'guide' (Robson, 124–37; Elliott, 227–42; Fowler; Ferry). But the poem's richly biblical parallelism of structure and rhythm has perhaps been insufficiently remarked.

Genre: wisdom song and the Son as autobiographer

Imitating biblical genres, Milton framed *Paradise Regained* within two angelic hymns, based on Luke's New Testament songs conflated with Old Testament psalms. Luke incorporated in the chapters before he treated the temptation in the wilderness four non-canonical psalms made in imitation of Old Testament psalmody (Mowinckel, 2: 122–5): Mary's Magnificat, Zacharias's Benedictus, the angels' Gloria, and Simeon's Nunc Dimittis. Milton framed his poem by combining the Benedictus and the Gloria with topoi from hymnic psalms. At the end of the first temptation, he wrote two laments by those closest to Jesus, left behind while he sojourned in the wilderness, one by Mary and one by the disciples, which preface the long second temptation and intensify its emotional power. For Mary's lament, he put the Magnificat in the past and reinforced it by psalmic lament formulae; for the disciples, he used Zacharias's Nunc Dimittis in a similar manner. For the self-characterization of the Son (but see Nohrnberg; Kerrigan), he imitated an Old Testament poetic form, the wisdom song, and his use of that genre may illustrate the value of his generic analysis of the Bible (Radzinowicz 1987).

Wisdom songs are found in Proverbs, Ecclesiastes, Job, Psalms, and many of the prophets. Typically in wisdom song, a learned poet introduces himself as a scribe, refers to his words as a private meditation, confesses that he speaks from his own insight, asks God's approval of his thoughts, and then delivers moral truths, rooting his motive for morality in his fear of God. A blend of wise saws and personal religious awareness, his moral wisdom is typically couched in linked proverbs coupled with exhortations and offered within a stylized autobiography. The scribe emphasizes God's law: its revelation began his enlightenment and he often contrasts his former foolishness with his present understanding by way of the formula 'then I knew'. Sometimes but not often a personality may be discerned behind the stylized autobiography; usually the speaker mentions only his age and general situation. His three main themes are (1) the contrast between the two 'ways', 'roads', or 'paths' of life – worldly, deceitful, and barrenly prosperous versus pious, honest, and ultimately favoured by God; (2) the doctrine of the proper or ripe time or season for human acts and of man's responsibility to discern that time; and (3) the testimony of creation and history to God's justice and concern with man's moral life. Its stylistic signature is the proverb: its pith, clarity with gnomic suggestiveness, memorability promoted often by enumeration (Von Rad, 24–53). Elihu (Job 32: 4–10, 18–20) instances its autobiography, proverbs, and themes:

> I am young, and ye are very old; wherefore I was afraid, and durst not show you mine opinion.
> I said, Days should speak, and multitude of years should teach wisdom.
> But there is a spirit in man: and the inspiration of the Almighty giveth them understanding.
> Great men are not always wise: neither do the aged understand judgment.
> Therefore I said, Hearken to me; I also will show mine opinion . . .
> For I am full of matter; the spirit within me constraineth me.
> Behold my belly is as wine which hath no vent; it is ready to burst like new bottles.
> I will speak that I may be refreshed: I will open my lips and answer.

So does Jesus in Luke 10: 22, 'All things are delivered to me of my Father: and no man knoweth who the Son is, but the Father; and who the Father is but the Son, and he to whom the Son will reveal him.' Wisdom song is composed to attest to the scribe's personal faith and ethos quite as much as to his learning and reason; in *Paradise Regained*, Jesus' opening 'holy Meditations' (1.196–293) imitate both its witness and autobiography.

Alone, Jesus thinks through the chronological course of his intellectual history, beginning and ending with his present state of mind. He begins with a 'multitude of thoughts' that 'swarm', while he 'considers what he feels, hears, and knows of his role'; and he ends calmly, 'led' by 'a strong motion' that he does not yet understand but accepts, 'For what concerns my knowledge God reveals.' These contrasting states encompass the common wisdom themes, 'where is wisdom to be found?' and 'trust in the Lord', the first seen, for example, in Proverbs 4: 26, 'Ponder the path of thy feet, and let all thy ways be established'; and the last in Proverbs 3: 5, 'Trust in the Lord with all thine heart; and lean not unto thine own understanding.'

Between these moods, Jesus passes through two stages of insight common to sages and then two unique to the Son (Stein, 36–47); the stages are intrinsic to wisdom song. The first concerns childhood vocation. When Jesus recalls that as a child 'all my mind was set / Serious to learn and know' and that – 'therefore above my years, / The Law of God I read, and found it sweet, / Made it my whole delight' (1.201–8), he divulges a youth much like the psalmist's in Psalm 119: 9, 14, and 16:

> Wherewithal shall a young man cleanse his way? By taking heed thereto according to thy word . . .
> I have rejoiced in the way of thy testimonies, as much as in all riches . . .
> I will delight myself in thy statutes: I will not forget thy word.

His decision to 'do / What might be public good' reflects a second stage in his conception of his role in the world – 'by winning works to conquer willing hearts' (1.203–4, 222) – also much like the psalmist's in Psalm 78: 2 and 72:

> I will open my mouth in a parable: I will utter dark sayings of old . . .
> So he fed them according to the integrity of his heart; and guided them by the skilfulness of his hands.

Wisdom autobiography is impersonal because it claims that the speaker testifies to God, not simply as someone who stepped forward, but as someone sent (Ricoeur, 119–54). Jesus' soliloquy of witness follows God's declaration that He sends and inspires the 'humiliation and strong sufferance' of 'This perfect man, by merit called my Son' (1.160,165). Isaiah 43: 8–10 represents God's calling of a witness (or *martus*):

> Bring forth the blind people that have eyes, and the deaf that have ears.
> Let all the nations be gathered together, and let the people be assembled:
> Who among them can declare this, and show us former things?
> Let them bring forth their witnesses, that they may be justified: or let them hear, and say, it is the truth.
> Ye are my witnesses, saith the Lord, and my servant whom I have chosen,
> That ye may know and believe me, and understand that I am he.

The witness is a teacher, but more than that he is a servant, ultimately the suffering servant. Hence the chosen one acknowledges in his impersonal autobiography that what matters is not how he is a particular human being (he might be blind or deaf), but that he is a witness (yet he has eyes or ears). The consequences of accepting the role of witness or *martus* are 'humiliation and strong sufferance', as in Psalm 44: 22: 'Nay for thy sake we are slain all the day long, and accounted as sheep for the slaughter.' Hence Milton shows Jesus move on from the resolve to teach to an acceptance of the role of witness 'through many a hard assay even to the death' (1.264).

In a final stage of insight in the autobiographical soliloquy, Jesus having accepted his role as suffering servant – 'Yet neither thus disheartened or dismayed / The time prefixed I waited' (1.268–9) – arrives at the conclusion, 'I knew the time / Now full, that I no more should live obscure, / But openly begin' (1.286–8). The Son's cognizance of the ripeness of his time adapts the final wisdom theme.

As a wise person Jesus learnt about himself and his role by meditating on the world God created, on his historical moment, and on revelation in history. He inferred his messiahship and read in it his role both as a wise teacher and heroic martyr; he witnessed God in those inferences and proposed for himself a period of wisdom-teaching followed by perfect obedience in suffering. His inference does not foreclose further revelation; indeed Jesus anticipates that what he now begins openly as teaching must end silently and in pain. Milton adapted wisdom song to impersonal autobiography to display the resolution of *two* questions, 'how is man to live?' and 'who is the messiah?' In *Paradise Regained* it is true both that Jesus knows, in advance of trial, the essential form of his mission and that he is capable of attaining to profounder understanding. To hold fast to both these truths is to respond to Milton's biblicism, which would reject an interpretation of Jesus' life in the poem whereby the search for identity and the exemplification of moral choice are incompatible alternatives.

For Milton the reading of Scripture in the case of his brief epic confirmed or authorized his themes as truthful and reasonable; gave him a style expressive of resilience, toughness, shrewdness, and pith; and put him in touch with a genre capable also of an abstract serenity conveying the moral equipoise of purposes long maturing. These effects were the rewards of listening for biblical resonances to the poet who prayed that his last poem would be a

> prompted song else mute
>
> of deeds
> Above heroic, though in secret done,
> And unrecorded left through many an age,
> Worthy t'have not remained so long unsung. (1.12, 14–17)

Milton's attitude towards his scriptural sources inheres in those words: the poet takes strength from his inspiration to rerecord heroic biblical deeds, and sings them anew for his own times, for in Sion's songs 'God is prais'd aright, and Godlike men.' The spirit that led Jesus into the desert inspires Milton's hoped-for 'Song to Generations' (*YP* 1: 706).

FURTHER READING

Alter, Robert, *The Art of Biblical Poetry* (New York, 1985)

Berlin, Adele, *The Dynamics of Biblical Parallelism* (Bloomington, IN, 1985)

Boitani, Piero, and Anna Torli, eds., *Medieval and Pseudo-Medieval Literatures* (Cambridge, 1984)

Budick, Sanford, 'Milton and the Scene of Interpretation: From Typology toward Midrash', in Hartman and Budick, eds., *Midrash and Literature*

Cook, Eleanor, and Chaviva Hosek, eds., *Centre and Labyrinth: Essays in Honour of Northrop Frye* (Toronto, 1983)

Elliott, Emory, 'Milton's Biblical Style in *Paradise Regained*', *Milton Studies* 6 (1974), 227–42

Ferry, Anne Davidson, *Milton's Epic Voice* (Cambridge, MA, 1963)

Fisher, Alan, 'Why is *Paradise Regained* So Cold?', *Milton Studies* 14 (1980), 195–217

Fowler, Alastair, '*Paradise Regained*: Some Problems of Style', in Boitani and Torli, eds., *Medieval and Pseudo-Medieval Literatures*

Frye, Northrop, *The Great Code* (New York, 1982)

Hartman, Geoffrey H., and Sanford Budick, eds., *Midrash and Literature* (New Haven, 1986)

Hunter, William B., Jr, *A Milton Encyclopedia* (Lewisburg, PA, 1978–81)

Kelley, Maurice, ed., *Christian Doctrine*, translated by John Carey, *YP* vol. 6

Kermode, Frank, ed., *The Living Milton* (London, 1960)

Kerrigan, William, 'The Riddle of *Paradise Regained*', in Woycik and Frontain, eds., *Poetic Prophecy*

Kugel, James L., *The Idea of Biblical Poetry* (New Haven, 1981)

Lewalski, Barbara K., *Milton's Brief Epic* (Providence, RI, 1966)

Protestant Poetics and the Seventeenth-Century Religious Lyric (Princeton, 1976)

'Paradise Lost' and the Rhetoric of Literary Forms (Princeton, 1985)

MacKellar, Walter, ed., *Paradise Regained*, vol. 4, *A Variorum Commentary on the Poems of John Milton* (New York, 1975)

Martz, Louis L., '*Paradise Regained*: The Meditative Combat', *ELH* 27 (1960), 223–47

The Paradise Within (New Haven, 1964)

Poet of Exile: A Study of Milton's Poetry (New Haven, 1980)

Mowinckel, Sigmund, *The Psalms in Israel's Worship*, 2 vols. (Oxford, 1962)

Nohrnberg, James, 'Paradise Regained By One Greater Man: Milton's Wisdom Epic as a "Fable of Identity"', in Cook and Hosek, eds., *Centre and Labyrinth*

Patrick, J. Max, and Roger Sundell, eds., *Milton and the Art of Sacred Song* (Milwaukee, 1979)

Pope, Elizabeth Marie, *'Paradise Regained': The Tradition and the Poem* (Baltimore, 1947)

Radzinowicz, Mary Ann, *Towards 'Samson Agonistes': The Growth of Milton's Mind* (Princeton, 1978)

'*Paradise Regained* as Hermeneutic Combat', *University of Harvard Studies in Literature* 16 (1984), 99–107

Milton's Epics and the Book of Psalms (Princeton, 1989), Part I

Rajan, Balachandra, ed., *The Prison and the Pinnacle* (Toronto, 1973)

Revard, Stella, 'The Gospel of John and *Paradise Regained:* Jesus as "True Light"', in Sims and Ryken, eds., *Milton and Scriptural Tradition*
Ricoeur, Paul, *Essays on Biblical Interpretation*, ed. Lewis S. Mudge (London, 1981)
Robson, W. W., 'The Better Fortitude', in Kermode, ed., *The Living Milton*
Shawcross, John T., 'Bibles', in Hunter, *A Milton Encyclopedia*
Sims, James H., *The Bible in Milton's Epics* (Gainesville, FL, 1962)
'Milton and the Bible', in Hunter, *A Milton Encyclopedia*
Sims, James H., and Leland Ryken, eds., *Milton and Scriptural Tradition: The Bible into Poetry* (Columbia, MO, 1984)
Stein, Arnold, *Heroic Knowledge* (Minneapolis, 1957)
Von Rad, Gerhard, *Wisdom in Israel* (London, 1972)
Woycik, Jan, and Raymond-Jean Frontain, eds., *Poetic Prophecy in Western Literature* (Rutherford, NJ, 1984)

15

JOAN S. BENNETT

Reading *Samson Agonistes*

In 1671, when Milton published *Paradise Regained*, he had another piece printed along with it in the same volume. The title-page read: 'PARADISE REGAIN'D, A POEM In IV Books. To which is added *Samson Agonistes*'. Although Milton is reported to have composed his brief epic during the four years that had passed since the publication of *Paradise Lost* in 1667, no one knows when he wrote his tragedy. In *Paradise Lost* and *Paradise Regained* we hear the voice of the poet, a strong presence, pursuing 'Things unattempted yet in prose or rhyme' (*PL* 1.16), sharing with his readers his prayers for inspiration (*PL* 3.1–3) and his judgements of the poem's actions. In *Samson Agonistes*, however, we make no contact with that authoritative voice except in the preface, entitled 'Of that Sort of Dramatic Poem which Is Call'd Tragedy', an 'epistle' to the reader requesting that his dramatic poem (which he did not intend to have performed on stage) be read in the context of Aeschylus', Sophocles', and Euripides' works, recognizing the power of ancient Greek tragedy to inscribe central truths.

It has been suggested that Milton chose the genre of drama for *Samson Agonistes* in order to let a wide range of readers share in the rich paradoxes and dilemmas of his poetic vision of human experience without requiring of every reader a 'fit' understanding of his religious and intellectual beliefs (Hale, 193; cf. *PL* 7.31). Nevertheless, Milton's preface indicates that in the tragedy we will find ourselves in the same Christian humanist world of the epics – the world as viewed by the philosopher Cicero and 'the Apostle Paul himself' – and that, in submitting ourselves to this tragedy, we will enter an experience graver, more moral, and to our greater spiritual growth than even that of *Paradise Lost* or *Paradise Regained*; for, however we are able to receive it, the tragedy will work directly on our innermost selves, addressing the roots of sin and suffering in us.

To clarify the experience that a reader of his tragedy should expect to undergo, Milton offers the traditional Aristotelian analogy for the experience of tragic art, that of medical 'purging' or 'tempering'. To explain

PARADISE
REGAIN'D.
A
POEM.
In IV *BOOKS.*
To which is added
SAMSON AGONISTES.

The Author
JOHN MILTON.

LONDON,
Printed by *J. M.* for *John Starkey* at the
Mitre in *Fleetstreet*, near *Temple-Bar.*
MDCLXXI.

5. Title page from *Paradise Regained* (Courtesy University of Delaware Library)

tragic catharsis by a similar analogy from today's medicine we could refer to inoculation: when injected with a controlled dose of the antigen of a disease, our own immune system produces antibodies that restore homeostasis (that 'temper and reduce to just measure') and that remain in us to fight powerfully for homeostasis against that disease when we meet it again in its full force and naturally occurring form. What is the 'disease' for which Milton wants his tragedy to prepare his readers once they have witnessed the loss and recovery of paradise? It is 'pity and fear, or terror' and 'such like passions', that is, all pain – both positive (pity) and negative (terror) – that afflicts our emotional life as a result of sin. We should expect, then, that by entering into Samson's experience we will emerge strengthened in mind and spirit to meet such suffering directly in its full and complicated force in our world and in ourselves.

As a tragic hero, Samson is not constructed nor held up as an exemplar for readers to emulate; rather, tragic heroes relate to us as 'persons like ourselves . . ., doing and suffering terrible things, with respect to those closest to them' (Hale, 193). In place of heaven, hell, paradise, or even the wilderness, the drama shows us a familiar world: of family (parent, lover, wife); of friendship (colleagues, countrymen); of conventional beliefs and values (religious, societal, political); of glimpses of human intersection with the divine. It is the world of personal discovery and of commitment to an individual life's meaning; of exhilaration in the achievement of goals against the odds; of betrayal and abandonment; of personal failure and despair; of deep guilt, of the struggle for religious faith, of liberation, of the purest individual freedom within the confines of history.

It is also, very importantly, the political world; and the protagonist's struggle is not separable from the difficult national and international context within which he bears responsibility. Reading *Samson Agonistes*, we face issues not only of personal spiritual suffering and growth but of corporate humanity's struggle to exist with meaning as well. We can be alert to this fact by recognizing that these issues were not distant history or myth but lived experience for Milton, who was as deeply concerned for England's liberation as the Judges were for Israel's: its people had been divinely chosen to establish a just society through the Revolution and attempted Commonwealth, had failed, and had now to find a will and a way, under oppression, to continue (Hill; Achinstein).

Although the world of twelfth-century B.C. Palestine is consistently close to us as the worlds of *Paradise Lost* and *Paradise Regained* are not, and although Samson is more ordinarily 'human' than either Jesus or Adam, the protagonist we meet at the play's opening is still not someone whom we may readily feel to be 'one of us'. His violent life and his suffering have made him not likeable or even approachable. We meet him – a prisoner of war in forced labour – in rags, filthy, with the stench of 'air imprisoned also', eyes gouged out, living 'a life half dead', his own 'sepulchre, a moving grave' (102). His pain and humiliation are so excruciating, his potential violence so terrifying – poised on the brink of 'sudden rage to tear thee joint by joint' (953) – that when we see him we might wish 'like the choruses of many Greek tragedies, to cry out and to turn away our eyes' (Summers, 156).

But we are not to *look* at this play – it was 'never intended' to the stage; rather, we are to *listen* for the language of the spirit complicating the words spoken by all the characters, words such as 'strength', 'dark', 'light', 'blindness', 'vision', 'prison', 'liberty', 'choice', 'promise', 'reason', 'fool', 'random', 'chance', 'necessity', 'love', 'law', 'deliverance'.

What kind of person is Samson as Milton conceives him? He has been a tremendous warrior but not an effective leader, as evidenced by his own people's acceptance of their oppression. The famous battle at Ramath-Lechi (142–5 and 263–6) is a case in point. There two very important events occurred. First Samson, alone and with only a bone weapon, defeated, indeed decimated, an entire, well equipped, top-flight, Philistine army division, clearing the way for Hebrew independence and the end of the Philistine occupation. Second, not one Hebrew tribe or individual joined Samson in the resistance effort, and Israel remained a subject nation.

In the course of the tragedy, Samson comes to realize two truths that have impaired his divinely given mission to liberate Israel. The first he has learned before the opening of the play: that his own people have failed their divine calling, have grown 'to love bondage more than liberty, / Bondage with ease than strenuous liberty' (269–71). Milton had experienced the same abandonment of the revolutionary cause in England where, after twenty years' labour to which he believed God had called him and other leaders of the attempted Commonwealth, the English people, preferring 'bondage with ease', chose to recall the heir to the deposed British monarchy from his exile in France – just as if, Milton exclaimed in *The Ready and Easy Way to Establish a Free Commonwealth* (1659), the Israelites of the exodus, for whom God had parted the Red Sea waters, were to call themselves back a captain out of Egypt.

The second truth about his failure, however, comes to Samson as utterly new knowledge. It comes unevenly, in deep pain, in the course of the tragedy, as Samson, the loyal but unreflecting strong man, by facing his own moral weakness, enters into the spiritual core of his political mission and is thereby reborn as the liberator he was destined to be, though in the moment of his death.

I

Both Milton's Chorus of Hebrews in *Samson Agonistes* and readers of the drama witness Samson's ordeal of faith. Milton may well have intended for his readers to measure their own ability to respond to Samson's experience against the ability of that Chorus of ordinary citizens. Although these Hebrews have not had the clarity of vision or the courage to join Samson in political revolution, they also do not abandon him personally; but they remain ignorant of how to help him or themselves, struggling with pity and in fear but without success to understand the meaning of their experience. In the end both witnesses – they and we – are purged. What are the temperings that occur?

Samson's perceptions are very much like the Chorus's when we first meet him. He feels the agony of his life's mission betrayed:

> Promise was that I
> Should Israel from Philistian yoke deliver;
> Ask for this great deliverer now, and find him
> Eyeless in Gaza at the mill with slaves. (38–41)

Although it was God who had promised Israel's deliverance, Samson is hesitant simply to blame providence for his present plight, considering: 'what if all foretold / Had been fulfilled but through mine own default. . . ?' (44–5). If he had kept his strength sacred to God, he would still have his sight and his freedom to continue the fight for Israel's liberation. Yet, he asks, if God had a mission for his great physical strength to accomplish, why did God create him with such a simple mind and weak will that he could be won over by a woman's temptations? 'But what is strength without a double share / Of wisdom? . . . Proudly secure, yet liable to fall / By weakest subtleties' (53–6). Dalila, Samson allows himself to feel, though physically 'weakest', had really been too psychologically subtle and emotionally powerful for him, whose only human resource was physical. Why did not God make him wiser? Samson remains, in his suffering, a man of faith and tries not to 'quarrel with the will / Of highest dispensation' (60–1); but he is prepared at this point to consider God's will for him, in spite of prophecies, to be 'above my reach to know' (62). His faith is blind.

It is worthwhile here to recall Milton's earlier published work. That God's human creatures cannot reason toward knowing God's will for them is an idea quite contrary to the spirit of *Paradise Lost*, which was written to 'assert Eternal Providence' (1.25). Providence does not foretell specific outcomes; rather, Providence grounds an understanding of God's ways toward human beings. In Milton's Heaven and in his Eden before the fall, the entire working laws of their universe are known intuitively to the angels and to the man and woman who live in harmony with the divine ordering. Just as material bodies interact with no need to understand the physical laws of nature that underlie their movements, so also in unfallen worlds do rational and spiritual beings interact perfectly with no need to articulate, to separate out and analyze, the moral laws that guide their interaction. There are no written laws in Heaven because the angels have 'reason for thir Law' (*PL* 6.41); angelic and human minds continually make moral choices in perfect accordance with the universal Good. Milton shows us angelic hymns and dances and Edenic perfection in his epic because he wants our imaginations to reach for a vision of the sheer elegance, at once mystical and mathematical, the heart-stopping beauty of the spiritual wholeness of God's creation. Only in vision, prayer, and poetry will we glimpse the whole, of course. But having seen it, we are better able to grasp how very fragmented our own moral experience is, and how that fragmentation is reflected in our need for individually expressed laws to govern our behaviour.

After his fall into sin, Adam has trouble imagining how God, who is Perfection, can remain in relationship with sinners. How can Perfection incorporate into itself evil? Adam's question is answered by the Archangel Michael (*PL* 12.280–306); and we need to hold his answer as firmly as possible in our minds when we share Samson's struggle with this same question. For Milton's God will not send an angel for every crisis; like Samson, we will have to draw on what has already been given us.

Michael answers that God remains in relationship with sinners, rather than abandoning them to evil, by extracting and giving individual expression to selected moral dimensions of the whole Law of being, which sin has shattered. These articulated moral and spiritual principles are given their first expression as the Mosaic commandments, 'so many and so various', which serve first of all to preserve the moral sense, the human capacity for moral awareness. We are given the fragmented, but explicit, commandments so that we can continue to recognize a sin when we meet it. In all of Milton's portrayals of temptation, evil's most formidable strength is its ability to be attractive, to assault all of our senses, emotions, and rationality with the powerful claim that it is really not evil but good. God articulates laws for human beings, then, as graspable pieces of reality for them to hold onto in the midst of this assault.

It is no easy contest, however, because what abets evil's attractiveness for us is the pain of our own guilt. If only we truly did not know that our actions were sinful, then we would be free from this guilt. But here is the crux of the answer to Adam's question: consciousness of guilt is what keeps the way open for the sinner's relationship with goodness. That very pain is God's loving gift to a fallen people of a continuing knowledge of the truth. To remain, after sin, in relationship with God, they must attain a full awareness of their own guilt, or depravity:

> And therefore was law given them to evince
> Their natural pravity, by stirring up
> Sin against law to fight . . . (*PL* 12.287–9)

Then will come a corresponding awareness of the sheer power of the Good, of God who can take this full consciousness of guilt and turn it into faith.

How this process will work out in human history, Michael explains, is through the self-offering of Christ for human sin; the Son's incarnation and atonement will abrogate the Mosaic law. God's people are thus to come through a strict belief that they *must* keep the law to a realization and full admission that they *cannot*. The moral depth gained by such an admission will then yield the ultimate insight: that this collection of laws itself is imperfect because it can 'discover sin, but not remove' (12.290). The law is still their link to the divine: better to stumble blindly but faithfully in attempting adherence to it, like the Hebrews and Samson, than to live cut off from Truth, without that law and its attendant suffering, like the Philistines. But ultimately, 'in full time', when they have been 'disciplined . . . from flesh to spirit', the law will lead its truest followers to transcend its own limits, taking them from God's 'imposition of strict laws' to their own 'free / Acceptance of large grace'. When they have persevered to a full awareness of their own impossible, but highly desired, relationship to perfection, then their efforts to observe the commandments – those articulated fragments of the original order – are redeemable by God. Then their 'works of law' become, like the deeds of the unfallen angels, 'works of faith', genuine expressions of the nature given them by God at creation (12.301–6).

Most importantly, what a reader of Milton's tragic drama must understand is that the second function of the law can come into being only after the first function has had its full effect. This does not happen for the Chorus in *Samson*: they are servants under bondage, not yet fully aware of the sin in themselves which the law discovers but cannot remove, pious followers of their Lord, but incapable of faith. Samson, however, reaches the limit of the law and hence is able to transcend and fulfil it. As Samson becomes capable of facing in himself a tremendous sense of guilt, so he proves capable finally of a relentless belief in the existence of that justice which includes within itself the mercy of a chastising Father (see Heb. 8: 5–10).

That belief is hard-won, through a struggle with Samson's own physical, emotional, and moral pain. To such a struggle Milton typically subjects his characters. Their dilemma is always to distinguish pain from evil and good from pleasure. Samson, when we meet him at the play's beginning, feels his own miseries to be 'So many, and so huge, that each apart / Would ask a life to wail' (65–6) – his blindness, his captivity and slavery, his humiliation. His friends and his father Manoa attempt to help Samson ward off a serious psychological depression that would add to his troubles. 'Deject not then so overmuch thyself / Who hast of sorrow thy full load besides' (213–14), the Chorus says, 'wisest men / Have erred, and by bad women been deceived; / And shall again, pretend they ne'er so wise' (210–12). This is the world's wisdom: nobody, after all, is perfect. Manoa, in his own pain, tries to fit God to the world's scheme according to which Samson's suffering is out of proportion to his offence:

> Alas methinks whom God hath chosen once
> To worthiest deeds, if he through frailty err,
> He should not so o'erwhelm
> Be it but for honour's sake of former deeds. (368–71)

For Samson's spiritual struggle, Manoa's slight impiety, his readiness to argue with the Lord, is more helpful than the attempted worldly wisdom of the Chorus, who view Samson's case as a 'mirror of our fickle state' – just one of those things – and who view God's will for human beings on such an occasion as being 'justifiable', but only inscrutably and dreadfully so.

When he hears his own thoughts reflected in the words of his friends and father, Samson is able to gain some perspective on what they imply. Their way of believing in God's inscrutability in effect denies God's justice. This is a very important insight for Samson. A just God does not reward evil or punish virtue; the spiritual fall of a moral creature is always the result of sin. If a person feels an affliction to be from God – that is, if one experiences during tribulations a sense of heaven's desertion – then one must accept one's suffering as merited, and its justice as comprehensible; one must seek out its cause and its cure. This is not to say that human beings can attain an understanding of God's own *being*; this is the knowledge that is 'forbidden' in Eden, forbidden because it is impossible. It is to say, however, that humans can stay in a true, non-arbitrary relationship with a God whose *ways* toward created beings are reliably consistent and sufficiently revealed. (For readings that operate outside of this Christian humanistic paradigm, God's philosophical inscrutability can still be seen as liberating in an existential and psychological sense; see Fish and Cable.)

Instead of accepting an unjust or unknowable God, then, Samson is able to continue to look for justice accessible to human understanding and available as a moral guide; he is thus led to admit into his understanding, from the magnitude of the punishment, the magnitude of his offence:

> Appoint not heavenly disposition, father,
> Nothing of all these evils hath befall'n me
> But justly; I myself have brought them on,
> Sole author I, sole cause: if aught seem vile,
> As vile hath been my folly, who have profaned
> The mystery of God given me under pledge
> Of vow. (373–9)

The Chorus also looks to the law to discover the causes of Samson's punishment. However, all it can find is a double breach of the law which forbids intermarriage with non-Jews. One consequence of the Chorus's own failure to see how its sin of servility breaches the spirit of the law is its inability to sense how the law embodies the unified 'mystery of God'. The Chorus holds many fragments, the 'letters' of the law, but cannot discriminate higher and lower, central and derivative. It cannot glimpse the law's wholeness, its 'spirit'. The expression it gives to its confusions about the law, however, helps Samson to straighten out his own responsibilities.

Thus, Samson has easily understood that his first non-Jewish marriage – to the Timnan woman – God allowed in order to fulfil the very purpose of the law against intermarriage, that is, to preserve God's people from falling captive to false gods and morals, in this case by seeking Israel's political liberation and religious freedom. Thinking from letter to spirit, Samson is led then to realize that in his second marriage he violently broke the spirit of that same law – not in marrying Dalila, but in profaning to her the mystery of his strength. This illumination yields only fuller pain, since Samson is now able to see not merely how the ceremonies being held to honour the idol Dagon in celebration of his captivity are Philistine breaches of the Hebrew ceremonial code, but also, more importantly, how they result from his betrayal of his own God-given relationship to the Hebrew people (448–57). For while their political captivity is their own fault, the same moral weakness that binds them in political subjection renders them all the more vulnerable to a spiritual confusion from which he, as their leader, has an even greater responsibility to protect them.

At the end of Manoa's visit, both the Chorus and Samson are near despair, but for different reasons. The Chorus suffers fear or 'dread' (Lieb) because it worships a God whom it believes to be unjust (667–709):

> God of our fathers, what is man!
> That thou towards him with hand so various,

> Or might I say contrarious,
> Temper'st thy providence through his short course. (667–70)

Samson, on the other hand, has clearly seen the depth of his own sin, his betrayal of God's trust; and this guilt is the truth that binds him to God's justice. He is at last ready, in his ensuing encounters with the Philistines, to learn that God operates by a law even more perfect than that by which Samson now, truthfully and accurately, judges himself.

II

Milton's Philistian Dalila is an extraordinary woman, a beautiful, passionate, intelligent, life-filled person who is, however, spiritually anchorless and hopelessly adrift, 'the sumptuous Dalila floating' (1072). She has turned her foreign husband over to the authorities of her country, enjoying the role of civic heroine – 'how honourable, how glorious'; 'how meritorious with the gods' – as well as relief from the pressures to which the authorities had been subjecting her. Her public image, her mental ease, her emotional and physical pleasure – these are all good things. And she wants to accumulate the greatest possible number of such goods, to which, she must presume, her very gifted nature entitles her.

Since Samson is in prison, however, she has been frustrated in her attempt to have it all. Wanting Samson back, she recognizes 'I was . . . mistaken / In what I thought would have succeeded best' (907–8). But she has no real sense that she was morally wrong, for Dalila lives outside the law that enables one to distinguish the good from pleasure and evil from pain. Thus she cannot comprehend Samson's notion of freedom when he says, 'This jail I count the house of liberty / To thine' (949–50).

Dalila's relationship to the Mosaic law is ambiguous. Although she is married to a Hebrew, she herself comes from a nation not bound to Jehovah or his decrees. The Hebrew Chorus sees no ambiguity in Dalila's case. According to its interpretation of God's giving the man headship in marriage, the man possesses 'despotic power / Over his female in due awe' (1054–5). Its view of the marriage relationship is an extension of its view of its own relationship to a God whom it is ready to consider likewise despotic, a God who behaves in a contradictory way but is all-powerful and therefore not to be questioned. Samson, by contrast, is prepared to relate to Dalila not despotically but by requiring of her moral liberty, that spiritual state into which he himself is growing during the course of this drama.

Before his fall, Samson too, like Dalila, had unthinkingly believed that he could and should have it all – public glory and private pleasure to match his considerable giftedness. He had been fighting for God and against oppression without understanding the justice of his cause or of his Lord. His actions were not morally contradictory, like Dalila's, but they were unexamined. In examining Dalila's actions now, Samson finds within himself a growing vision of his own God as a universal and not merely national deity; he glimpses the law in its wholeness.

Although he refers to the custom by which a foreign wife adopts the country of her husband, Samson does not make custom the basis of his own thought. Instead, he intuits that Dalila, while his wife, could have retained her 'Philistine' nationality and even her worship of 'Dagon' if those names had represented conditions that were genuinely national and genuinely religious. When her rulers demanded, however, that in service to her nation Dalila should dishonour her own marriage, they – in that very demand – violated the right purpose for any government, which is 'to train up a Nation in true wisdom and vertue', as Milton had asserted in *Of Reformation* (1641; *YP* 1: 571):

> if aught against my life
> Thy country sought of thee, it sought unjustly,
> Against the law of nature, law of nations. (888–90)

Since their request revealed them to be violators of the universal purpose of government, they were accordingly not to be regarded as valid governors:

> No more thy country, but an impious crew
> Of men conspiring to uphold thir state
> By worse than hostile deeds. (891–3)

From the reasoning by which Samson judges the crime of Dalila and her governors, we can see how his love for her and his campaign against the Philistines need never have entailed moral contradiction. While using his position as Dalila's husband to oppose the Philistine tyranny, he would not have acted against *her*, would not have sought 'aught against [her] life', in violation of his marriage.

As Samson insists, the Philistine 'politician lords' (1195) and not Israel have been Philistia's true foe. If the Philistines had practised true nationhood, permitting religious and civil liberty, Samson's revolution could have ceased; Israel would have been liberated peacefully, and the marriage of Dalila and Samson could have developed a ground for being. Their divorce, though it enacts a necessary sorting and separation of the destructive elements of their chaotic relationship, records a terrible loss in this dark tragedy. Remembering the vision Milton showed in *Paradise Lost* of the marriage bond as the basis for individual human identity and for all human relationships, we can be even more aware than from the drama alone of the cost to Samson's person and mission of this failed bond, a bond which Milton's unfallen Adam had seen as part of his own soul and which had drawn fallen humanity toward redemption (*PL* 4.487, 10.915–61; cf. DiSalvo).

At Dalila's departure, Samson finds himself obliquely aware that God has been at work with him during Dalila's visit: 'God sent her' (999). His second Philistine visitor is, like Dalila, spiritually adrift. He is 'a storm' (1061); a 'wind hath blown him hither' (1070). Samson's emotional energy is returning, and his wish is to fight this enemy soldier, a desire which he formulates as a proposal to test 'whose God is strongest' (1155). The form of Harapha's refusal serves to draw Samson quickly beyond this unthinking stance, however. 'Presume not on thy God', Harapha sneers (1156).

While Samson's service to God before his fall had been loyal, it had also been presumptuous. But the opposite of presumption is not, as the 'tongue-doughty' Harapha imagines, a retreat into despair. Presumption and despair are two sides of the same coin – of willed ignorance of God. The opposite of such blindness is faith, which seeks genuine understanding, trusting that experience of the Truth is attainable.

Harapha seeks to cow Samson with the world's wisdom: 'Is not thy Nation subject to our Lords?' The rest of Judah had indeed succumbed to this expediency. 'Knowest thou not that the Philistines are rulers over us?' the heads of tribes had said to him before Ramath-Lechi (Judges 15: 2). This had been the royalists' argument during the English revolution: one must obey the King absolutely, even if he is a tyrant, simply because he is the ruler in power. The royalists had quoted Romans 13: 'There is no power but of God'. Milton replied, however, that these words of St Paul 'must be understood of lawfull and just powers, els we read of great power in the affaires and Kingdoms of the World permitted to the Devil' (*Tenure of Kings and Magistrates* (1649), *YP* 3: 209–10).

Your cause is illegal and your God, 'whate'er he be', has disowned you, Harapha charges (1156–63). But Harapha, like Dalila, is a tool of Providence for Samson. In divorcing Dalila, Samson has come to realize how fully his own private sin has fought against his public cause. He is left, at her departure, feeling that not only Dalila, but also he is hopelessly guilty. Now, however, in the political confrontation with Harapha, Samson envisages a contrary possibility. For as he defends his past public acts he finds a basis for the hope that God may yet again use him in a public role, simply because of the justice of his cause, which exists regardless of Samson's or the Hebrews' unworthiness. And this hope is identical with a hope for Grace: God's 'ear is ever open; and his eye / Gracious to readmit the suppliant' (1172–3).

Samson's courage in the encounter with Harapha has inspired the Chorus: 'Oh how comely it is and how reviving' (1268). But they are unable to understand exactly what Samson has experienced, for he has proven 'victor' not merely 'over all / That tyranny or fortune can inflict', but also over these as the appearance of God's desertion (1290–1). Samson rejects the notion of the arbitrariness of 'fortune', while relentlessly pursuing a full knowledge of his own and others' guilt. And that discovery brings with it victory over the ultimate enemy, over Samson's own sin and despair. Therefore, he is now ready to meet in his future not what will 'chance' to become of him (1294–6) but what God will offer.

With the coming of the next visitor, God speaks at last to Samson directly, though not to the Chorus or to us. A Philistine officer requires Samson's athletic performance at the feast of Dagon, initiating a scene that works through the questions faced by Milton himself and other religious dissenters during the Restoration period in which *Samson Agonistes* was published (Achinstein, 139). In loyalty to the Hebrew law and his own conscience, Samson refuses to yield to religious compulsion. But as soon as he has thought through his options for dealing with this demand, a new sense of the Law's wholeness comes upon him in 'some rousing motions . . . which dispose / To something extraordinary' his thoughts (1382–3). His moral reason has led him to a statement of the hierarchy of values inhering in God's law. God 'may dispense with me or thee / Present in temples at idolatrous rites / For some important cause' (1377–9). Then he knows that he will go to the temple. There, having submitted like a wrestler (an *agonist*) to the Philistines' demand for circus-like shows of strength, in an enormous feat done 'of [his] own accord' (1643), he pulls down the pillars of the temple on all the Philistines' 'choice nobility' (1654) and on himself.

Thus death, for which Samson had earlier prayed as an escape from shame, is given to him instead as the enactment of his own spiritual liberation, as well as the prophesied freeing of Israel. The poet does not let us share that moment with Samson but requires us to stay with the Chorus, against whose reaction we must weigh our own. The men of the Chorus have been sufferers both of the enemy's oppression and, worse, of the fear that God had departed from their leader and from them, leaving no meaning to their suffering. This had been Samson's 'chief affliction, shame and sorrow' (457), that his own sin, in combination with their cowardice, had brought his people to 'diffidence of God' (454), to the brink of spiritual chaos. That Chorus, because it has not faced its own guilt, has likewise not shared Samson's vision of the Law's wholeness. It has been purged by its experience; it has acquired a 'calm of mind, all passion spent' (1758). But a more lasting tempering, a stronger immunity to the ravages of pity and terror, will be experienced only by those readers who can share Samson's vision at the pillars.

III

For a growing number of readers, however, an obstacle to such a reading is present in the play's catastrophe itself, where the physical vehicle for Samson's spiritual victory involves the violent deaths of hundreds of people. Teachers have observed how very differently the drama is experienced by Jewish students whose relatives faced the Holocaust and by Palestinian students who live in Israeli-occupied territories, as each set of readers deals with a tendency toward literal identification with the Hebrew or Philistine side of Milton's biblical source. Some readers, believing that Milton could not – as a Christian and a humanist – in any context have condoned such violence, argue that he intended to show Samson not as the New Testament man of faith, but rather as an unthinking strong man bent on a personal revenge which may have been justified by an Old Testament partisan morality but which Milton meant to contrast to a newer, humanistic morality portrayed in *Paradise Regained* in the character of Jesus, who patiently endures the onslaughts of his enemy, eschewing violence (Wittreich). Still others, whose materialist paradigm precludes both spiritual and political freedom, have no way of seeing law as freeing, and so they elaborate a view of Samson as terrorist rather than liberationist (Guillory).

Although Milton wrote *Samson Agonistes* to stand in relationship to the post-revolutionary period of English history in which he lived, we may profitably seek in our own recent history other contexts in which to understand the tragedy. Certainly the twentieth century offers many analogous situations of extreme oppression, but I would suggest we compare the world of Milton's Samson with that of a Christian theologian and freedom fighter from the period of the Second World War, Dietrich Bonhoeffer, whose religious and political philosophy resembles Milton's. While Bonhoeffer was not a pacifist, he is also not generally considered a terrorist. Let us follow his thought for a moment.

Bonhoeffer did not believe that Christ calls people to 'a new ethical system'. When we renounce the world's demands on us, he says in *The Cost of Discipleship* (1937; New York, 1963), 'it should not be as though . . . we were exchanging a lower ideal for a higher one'. The law of God is eternally the same. It is 'the call of [God] regarded not as an ideal, but as the word of a Mediator, which effects in us this complete breach with the world' and which calls us to love others, even our enemies; and not just those enemies who hate us as individuals or nationals but those who embody that enmity 'which exists between the People of God and the world' (163), those such as the Philistines or the Nazis. 'The will of God . . . is that men should defeat their enemies by loving them' (164). However, for Bonhoeffer as for Milton, such love does not mean passive endurance of evil.

Milton's treatise *Of Civil Power in Ecclesiastical Causes* (1659), which argues against the civil government's penal authority in matters of religious belief and expression, has been read as if it were a pacifist tract. But Milton's argument is against using force in matters of conscience. Samson destroys the Philistine temple not to force the Philistines' conscience but to stop their evil and to free the Israelites from their religious and political oppression. In this drama it is the Philistines who are 'forcers of conscience', tyrants whom free people have an obligation to resist. In *Of Civil Power*, Milton discusses Jesus' words in Gethsemane: 'If my kingdom were of this world, then would my servants fight' (John 18: 36). This 'disproves not', Milton warns, 'that a Christian commonwealth may defend itself against outward force in the cause of religion as well as in any other; though Christ himself, coming purposely to dye for us, would not be so defended' (*YP* 7: 258).

While Bonhoeffer never lost his early belief that 'men should defeat their enemies by loving them', he found no contradiction between this faith and his own activism. 'We must take our full share of responsibility for history . . . because we know that it is a responsibility laid upon us by God', Bonhoeffer wrote just before his imprisonment at the end of 1942, ten years after he had made his first public statement of opposition to Hitler's National Socialism and five years after, as a well known international figure, he had refused asylum in the United States and England and returned to Germany at the outbreak of war to offer leadership to the German church (*Letters and Papers From Prison*, ed. E. Bethge (London, 1969), 138).

Bonhoeffer's leadership took the form simultaneously of intensive moral and theological teaching and of intensive underground attempts to overthrow the Nazi government. After 1939, he did not believe, as Milton shows the young Christ of *Paradise Regained* imagining, that he could 'make persuasion . . . teach the erring Soul' (1.221–4; see Wittreich, 324). 'Folly', Bonhoeffer wrote in 1944 in reference to the German people's support of Hitler, 'is never amenable to reason . . . it is a moral rather than an intellectual defect . . . the fool cannot be saved by education. What he needs', Bonhoeffer concludes, as does the mature Jesus of *Paradise Regained*, 'is redemption' (*Letters and Papers*, 139–40).

'At the cost of his own slavery', Milton wrote, Christ 'put our political freedom on a firm foundation' (*A Defense of the English People*; *YP* 4, 1: 376). Especially during the last years of his own struggle for political freedom, Bonhoeffer wrote on 21 July 1944, he 'had discovered . . . that it is only by living completely in this world' – not by trying to be an untainted 'saint' awaiting the apocalypse – 'that one learns to believe. It is in such a life that we throw ourselves utterly into the arms of God and participate in his sufferings in the world and watch with Christ in Gethsemane' (124–5). These words can be taken as a guide to understanding the relationship between *Samson Agonistes* and *Paradise Regained*. 'How can success make us arrogant or failure lead us astray, when we participate in the sufferings of God by living in this world?' (*Letters and Papers*, 125). Milton's deeply repentant Samson, after 'arrogance' in success and 'straying' in failure, in the end realizes in himself the pure love of God by taking action. How can he know that his rousing motion comes from God? He can know from the depth of his own repentance and from his sense of God's return.

Of course, Samson dies, and the success of his cause is short-lived. Where then is his freedom?

'Helpless and forlorn', Bonhoeffer wrote, accurately foreseeing his own imminent death following the failed attempt by the German resistance to assassinate Hitler on 20 July 1944, 'you see the end of your deed. Yet . . . you resign your cause to a stronger hand, and are content to do so.' Bonhoeffer's meditation shows how naturally the action undertaken 'of one's own accord', that is, in freedom, is simultaneously of God's accord. 'For one brief moment you enjoyed the bliss of freedom, only to give it back to God, that he might perfect it in glory.' To perfect human freedom in glory is the task of the Jesus of *Paradise Regained*. Reading Milton's paired brief epic and tragedy in this context, we may see the process by which God's Son invests all deaths – including Samson's and the Philistines' – with the meaning that death held for Bonhoeffer and for Milton's Samson as the last of the 'stations' on the road to eternal freedom (*Letters and Papers*, 161).

FURTHER READING

Achinstein, Sharon, '*Samson Agonistes* and the Drama of Dissent', *Milton Studies* 33 (1996), 133–58

Bennett, Joan S., *Reviving Liberty: Radical Christian Humanism in Milton's Great Poems* (Cambridge, MA, 1989), ch. 5

'Asserting Eternal Providence: John Milton Through the Window of Liberation Theology', in *Milton and Heresy*, ed. Stephen B. Dobranski and John P. Rumrich (Cambridge, 1998)

Cable, Lana, *Carnal Rhetoric: Milton's Iconoclasm and the Poetics of Desire* (Durham, NC, 1995), ch. 6 'Samson's Transformative Desire'

DiSalvo, Jackie, 'Intestine Thorn: Samson's Struggle With the Woman Within', in *Milton and the Idea of Woman*, ed. Julia Walker (Champaign, IL, 1987)

Fish, Stanley, 'Question and Answer in *Samson Agonistes*', *Critical Quarterly* 11 (1969), 237–64

'Spectacle and Evidence in *Samson Agonistes*', *Critical Inquiry* 15 (1989), 555–86

Guillory, John, 'The Father's House: *Samson* in Its Historical Moment', in *Remembering Milton: Essays on the Texts and Traditions*, ed. Mary Nyquist and Margaret W. Ferguson (New York and London, 1987)

Hale, John K., *Milton's Languages: The Impact of Multilingualism on Style* (Cambridge, 1997), ch. 10 'Hebrew Meets Greek in *Samson Agonistes*'

Hill, Christopher, *The Experience of Defeat: Milton and Some Contemporaries* (London and New York, 1984)

Kerrigan, William W., 'The Irrational Coherence of *Samson Agonistes*', *Milton Studies* 22 (1987), 217–32

Labriola, Albert, and Michael Lieb, eds., *The Miltonic Samson, Milton Studies* 33 (Pittsburgh, 1996)

Lewalski, Barbara K., 'Milton's *Samson* and the "New Acquist of True [Political] Experience"', *Milton Studies* 24 (1988), 233–51

Lieb, Michael, '"Our Living Dread": The God of *Samson Agonistes*', *Milton Studies* 33 (1996), 3–25

Loewenstein, David, *Milton and the Drama of History: Historical Vision, Iconoclasm, and the Literary Imagination* (Cambridge, 1990)

Low, Anthony, *The Blaze of Noon: A Reading of 'Samson Agonistes'* (New York, 1974)

Mueller, Janel, 'Just Measures? Versification in *Samson Agonistes*', *Milton Studies* 33 (1996), 47–82

Radzinowicz, Mary Ann, *Toward 'Samson Agonistes': The Growth of Milton's Mind* (Princeton, 1978)

Samuel, Irene, '*Samson Agonistes* as Tragedy', in *Calm of Mind: Tercentenary Essays on 'Paradise Regained' and 'Samson Agonistes' in Honor of John S. Diekhoff*, ed. Joseph A. Wittreich (Cleveland, 1971), 237–57

Summers, Joseph, 'The Movements of the Drama' in *The Lyric and Dramatic Milton: Selected Papers From the English Institute*, ed. Joseph Summers (New York, 1965)

Wittreich, Joseph, *Interpreting 'Samson Agonistes'* (Princeton, 1986)

16

NICHOLAS VON MALTZAHN

Milton's readers

Milton idealizes the reader, and to this idealization his many readers have often consented. In part this follows from the idealization of himself that so drove Milton's endeavours from an early age. His careers as teacher, pamphleteer, civil servant, and poet were all founded in his passion for learning – a college friend teased him about his 'inexcusable perseverance, bending over books and studies day and night', and he was later proud to recall 'that from my twelfth year scarcely ever did I leave my studies for my bed before the hour of midnight' (*YP* 1: 337, 4: 612). Such learning he encourages his readers to share. Later literary and educational tradition made much of this legacy by giving *Paradise Lost* a central place in the canon, and finding in the epic a valuable store of cultural capital. But Milton exalts the reader in another still more compelling way: by setting his learning aside and, out of respect for individual reason, asking readers to experience wholly their being in the world in relation to the divine. Here his success is more difficult to chart, but finds expression in the rich diversity of responses to his works over the last four centuries.

I

Milton's suspicion of the very educational tradition in which he would become so implicated colours *Paradise Regained*. There he has the Son of God resist the 'temptation of Athens', in which Satan offers the Son all that classical learning might lend his 'empire'. Learning includes more, the tempter claims, than just Jewish law and prophecy: 'The Gentiles also know, and write, and teach' (4.227). Rebuking Satan, the Son provides the fullest critique of reading in Milton's poetry:

who reads
Incessantly, and to his reading brings not
A spirit and judgment equal or superior,
(And what he brings, what needs he elsewhere seek)

Uncertain and unsettled still remains,
Deep-versed in books and shallow in himself. (*PR* 4.322–7)

Readers who are less 'equal' the Son describes as 'children gathering pebbles on the shore'. But the need to bring to reading 'A spirit and judgment equal or superior' can seem to make the act of reading itself unnecessary. The difficulty follows from Protestant self-doubt about the effect of human learning unaided by the Holy Spirit. How could the misdirected will freely assent to divine grace? Humility was needed. Faith was prior to understanding. Hence the scriptural core of Protestant reading, evoked in the Son's earlier affirmation that 'The law of God I read, and found it sweet, / Made it my whole delight, and in it grew' (*PR* 1.207–9).

Milton had often been much readier to proclaim the joys of reading openly and of responding decisively. Against press controls past and present, his *Areopagitica* (1644) 'defies conventional communicative structures that he regards as repressive in order to galvanize his readers into imagining new structures' (Norbrook, 27). This liberal impulse promotes the benefits, to person and to community, of readers freely judging and examining with a proper spirit (*YP* 2: 511). Notwithstanding the 'all-sufficiency' of Scripture (*YP* 1: 625), Milton read and wrote very widely beyond it. He at first insisted on the needlessness of any supplement to holy text, owing to its supposedly unique capacity for self-interpretation. But interpretation and guidance were soon to take a much more central place in his description of the community of readers, and in his own role within it. The tension in Milton has been described as a persistent one (Fish 1990). On one hand there is his impatience with subjection to another's mastery, with the limits of 'alwaies learning and never knowing, [being] alwaies infants' (*YP* 7: 320); on the other, there is the charity of open dialogue needed in the long work of reformation, imagining change, speaking into action.

Awareness of audience was a distinctive part of the rhetorical tradition within which Milton was educated, both in English and Latin. Performance and persuasion were supposed to have a strongly ethical and practical direction, especially in preparation for the ministry, to which Milton had been consecrated. His schooling fostered an ethos that associated excellence with eloquence, and linked both to salvation; the resulting self-consciousness shows in Milton's earliest correspondence (*YP* 1: 311–32). His *Of Education* (1644) shows comparable ambitions for his students. His was the humanist service of instructing his province in classical culture, and of representing it in Latin abroad. Seventeenth-century England was in effect a colony of a lasting Latin cultural empire, which might demand subaltern deference to its values from those at its margins. And in his onslaught upon Salmasius, who had attacked the English republic for the execution of Charles I, there is something of the subaltern's thrill at insurgency against the imperial centre, and at finding it not so central after all.

Milton's concerns about his readership govern his shifting rhetorical strategies. In writing against bishops in 1641–2, his is already a volatile relation to his potential audience. The underlying impulse to court readers reveals itself in his changing modes of address, whether in the first of these pamphlets, presented as 'Written to a Freind', or in the last, addressed to its 'Readers' throughout (*YP* 1: 517, 868 ff.). The proliferation of such references shows him constructing a public as never before: 'heare me out now Readers . . . I beseech ye friends' (*YP* 1: 876, 890–6). Although Milton seldom addresses his readership so directly in other publications, he 'persisted in his attempts to formulate an image of the public' (Achinstein, 8). In part this was to propose an ideal reader, through commendation and condemnation of different reading practices. Thus he prefers strenuous readers, whose activity is an expression of virtue and a promotion of liberty: these he styles 'ingenuous', 'ingenious', 'acute', 'intelligent', 'diligent', 'attentive', 'judicious', 'knowing', 'learned', 'elegant', 'equal', 'charitable'. By contrast, others read only 'meanly', 'ignorantly', and are 'vulgar' or 'common', and 'credulous'. He praises 'good intellects' and condemns 'the stall-reader' ('On the Detraction'). An energetic reading public is essential to Milton's ideal commonwealth, and helps to define the republicanism that emerges in 1644 in *Of Education* and *Areopagitica* (Smith 1990, 105–6; Norbrook, 10–11; Dzelzainis 1995b, 10–14).

Between Milton's implied and his actual audience there was of course some difference. His idealization of himself and his readers succeeded less with his contemporaries than with later generations. Within his lifetime, most of his works in prose and verse found a limited readership. Only a few of them were successful enough to warrant even second editions; only his Latin *Defensio* against Salmasius (1651) enjoyed wide circulation at home and abroad. Some reactions to Milton's early pamphlets did appear in the anti-episcopal controversy, and again after he wrote in favour of divorce in the early 1640s. There are not many other contemporary responses to these works, however. Notwithstanding his bad reputation as a 'divorcer', for example, the many such gibes at his expense seldom indicate much familiarity with the divorce tracts themselves. His *Areopagitica* (1644), so famous in times since, did not occasion much contemporary comment, although like his *Of Education* it found some notice in progressive educational circles. One reader just observed that, despite its merits, *Areopagitica* is too satirical and elaborate (Miller).

Milton himself shows a lifelong sensitivity to responses to his work, and he reacted to his failure to forge a better readership in the early 1640s. His glowing confidence in *Areopagitica* about a nation heroic in its reading does not find renewed expression. Instead, he seems to withdraw from the public sphere later in that decade (*YP* 2: 763). Only in 1649, at the time of the execution of Charles I, were his adversarial skills again engaged. A less colourful rhetoric now features in his breakthrough work promoting resistance against the crown. *The Tenure of Kings and Magistrates* (1649) helped Milton win his appointment to the governing Council of State after the regicide, but although the pamphlet appeared in a second edition, there is little other sign of its finding many readers. Only when he applied this political theory to his attack in *Eikonoklastes* (1649) on the 'King's Book', the *Eikon Basilike*, does Milton begin to find a broader market. He is pessimistic about any wider readership by this time, noting the effectiveness of the best-selling *Eikon* in deceiving 'the common Reader' (*YP* 3: 373), whom he contrasts with 'understanding' or 'wise men' (*YP* 3: 376, 600–1).

Even as Milton lost confidence in English readers, he met with his greatest success in a Latin work that gave him fame at home and abroad. His *Defensio* of the English people resulted from an official commission to argue the justice of the proceedings against Charles I. Now Milton entered the European market for the first time, and his accomplishment there helped him find more recognition in England. He delighted in this, boasting that he had triumphed 'in liberty's defence, my noble task, / Of which all Europe talks from side to side' ('To Mr Cyriack Skinner'). The Latin *Defensio* appeared in edition after edition from a number of presses English and Continental, and in different formats – folio, quarto, duodecimo – for different markets. Such was the triumph that piracies multiplied to meet the demand. It found wide notice, including some substantial responses, and reaction was fierce – in France, it was banned and burned (French, 3: 38 ff.). Readers admired Milton's work for its fund of learned Latin, a prized commodity that long won admiring comment, whatever the notoriety of Milton's argument. The *Defensio* was also translated into Dutch and English, although it is striking that the English translation did not find publication, a fact suggesting that, for domestic circulation, Milton's rhetoric may have given unease to his less revolutionary masters (in 1653 the Leveller John Lilburne would quote from the *Defensio* to chide the government for failing its mandate; French, 3: 217–19). His fame in controversy also helped sell his *Defensio secunda* (1654), and the more personal *Defensio pro se* (1655), to Latin readers at home and abroad. His

Ciceronian role in saving the state, he was glad to think, had been applauded by 'the best citizens of my own and of foreign lands' (*YP* 4: 537). He had secured his position as mouthpiece for the Commonwealth, with a high profile in the European republic of letters.

Milton's triumph was very nearly his undoing. If he had set out to create a 'revolutionary reader', it was his own prominence as a revolutionary that almost cost him his life in 1660, and that much coloured the reception of his works in the Restoration and after. But his success as a servant of successive interregnal regimes had already lost him his more radical readership, increasingly disenchanted by Cromwellian rule. It was against Cromwellians and not just Cromwell that the plotter Edward Sexby made his death-threats in 1657, and hence against Milton the Cromwellian orator. Where Lilburne had sardonically cited 'their valiant and learned Champion Mr. Milton' against 'the Lord Generall and his Confederates', Sexby promised violence against those 'who are Confederates with Tyrants, and will side with them, and but appear to defend them, or allow them'. For the 'learned Milton' to be named just down the page was full of menace (cf. French, 4: 148). The suggestion of his apostasy surely increased his unease. Further reformation mattered deeply to him. In 1658, he distances himself from the government he still served (Dzelzainis 1995a, 200–5). In 1659–60, with the end of the Cromwellian regime, he seeks to revive his readership with some more open restatements of his ideals. In the season of press freedom after the fall of the Protectorate, Milton went from publishing with the government printer to the Baptist bookseller Livewell Chapman, at the centre of radical religious politics. As if to free himself from his reputation, he now observes that 'Pomp and ostentation of reading is admir'd among the vulgar: but doubtless in matters of religion he is learnedest who is planest' (*YP* 7: 272). His new direction was noted, for example in a letter to Milton by the millenarian Moses Wall (*YP* 7: 510–12). Wall's correspondence includes bitter reflections on the recent tyranny of Cromwell's Protectorate. To Milton he expresses relief to find him freed of such court leanings, even as he gives him readerly encouragement to publish the second of the 'twin' tracts, *Considerations Touching the Likeliest Means to Remove Hirelings Out of the Church* (1659), with which Milton soon obliged. Chapman and Wall were both keen supporters of Sir Henry Vane, champion of the sects. So too was another admirer of Milton in 1659, Henry Stubbe. Stubbe had previously valued Milton's attack on the 'capricious Paedant[r]ie of hot-liver'd Grammarians'. At issue now was the renewal of the tithes controversy, when a younger generation of readers might go to school in Milton's tracts against the bishops, tracts reissued in the mid-1650s and again advertised for sale. These now presented an anti-episcopal orthodoxy that invited further reformation of the church. Stubbe pursued such interests with his fellow students at Christ Church, Oxford, including another who read Milton's *Of Reformation* at this date, the young John Locke (Shawcross, *Bibliography*, nos. 166, *381*, *383*, *395*, *435*). A more sceptical response to Milton's new direction came from the republican theorist James Harrington (*YP* 7: 518–21).

Just as Milton was gaining new readers, political changes overtook him and his fellow republicans and religious radicals. The season of opportunity occasioned by the breakdown of protectoral government led within eighteen months to the sudden revival of monarchy in 1660, to widespread acclaim. Near the Restoration Milton lost his audience, now replaced by a more hostile royalist readership bent on revenge. The resulting caricature of Milton, drawing on earlier royalist polemic, would predominate in public references to him for a generation, shaping his reputation until his death and beyond. Two of the most vivid voices vilifying Milton were those of Roger L'Estrange, royalist pamphleteer and later the central figure in Restoration censorship, and Samuel 'Hudibras' Butler, whose satirical writings in prose and verse include some of the most knowing attacks on Milton's prose. Mocking Milton for the failure of his cause, for his humanist rhetoric, and for his blindness, these skilful antagonists took advantage of his return to controversy in their lively and influential pamphlets in the spring of 1660. He was characterized as 'Pedantique, and Envenom'd', too 'Peremptory and Magisterial', and as 'an old Heretick both in Religion and Manners, that by his will would shake off his Governours as he doth his Wives'. 'Let us have No Blinde Guides', joked L'Estrange, with others claiming that Milton deserved hanging, unless his blindness was already sufficient judgement upon him. The threat of execution was not an idle one after the Restoration. In 1660 a proclamation went out from Charles II that Milton's books against Charles I be publicly burnt. The law forbade ownership, still less circulation, of *Eikonoklastes* and the *Defensio*. For the next generation, Milton's reputation for republican Latinity yielded to that for sedition. He was the 'needy Pedagogue' whose writings amounted to a 'bloody Schoole of King-killing', and who might be excoriated whenever memorials of Charles I lamented the regicide and rebellion. About Milton there was always a whiff of sulphur. Many Restoration readers might agree with the verdict of one of his first biographers that 'the great Anti-monarchist' was 'a rogue' (Parker 1940, 43–55; French, 4: 298 ff.; von Maltzahn 1994, 157; von Maltzahn 1995, 235; von Maltzahn 1998, 270–6, 281–5).

II

Paradise Lost was published in 1667 to a reading world transformed from that in which Milton had presented his prose works of the 1640s and 50s. There had been a sharp contraction of the public sphere in the Restoration, in which the new regime gained significant controls over parliament, press, and pulpit, as well as over the courts and universities. In the world of print, the constraint was aggravated by the huge losses suffered by the booktrade in the Fire of London (1666). When, in the winter of 1666–7, the recent disruptions of the plague and fire led to a mood of national repentance, Milton brought his epic to the press. Permission to publish came from a licenser suspicious that Milton was still likely to be writing in an anti-monarchical vein; that the poem overcame this difficulty is tribute to its sophistication in justifying 'the ways of God to men'. For the presswork Milton turned to the Simmons family of dissenting printer-booksellers, with whom he had associations going back to the 1640s. While the epic was in the press, the English failure in the Second Anglo-Dutch War further discredited the governing regime and contributed to the slow beginnings of some recovery of public debate, especially about religious policies kinder to Protestants outside the Church of England. By the time *Paradise Lost* appeared in the autumn of 1667 it spoke to this issue of toleration, as well as to the need for moral renewal that was so widely felt. Now it seems Milton might be still more confident that his epic would 'a fit audience find, though few' (*PL* 7.31).

Some of the earliest responses to Milton's epic show its power for its first readers, and its pleasures. Sir John Denham, poet, Member of Parliament, and no friend to Milton's politics, is reported to have come 'into the House [of Commons] one Morning with a Sheet, Wet from the Press', pronouncing *Paradise Lost* 'the Noblest Poem that ever was Wrote in any Language'. There was also intense satisfaction with Milton's epic on the part of another MP, the Presbyterian Sir John Hobart. He exclaimed that he had 'never read any thing more august, & withall more gratefull to my (too much limited) understanding'; he was 'strangely pleas'd' by his 'deleberate and repeated reading' of the work, and more pleased 'the last tyme then the first'. From this primary locus of reading (parliament, London) he circulated the poem to his country cousin, claiming he could 'not injure the author by too advantagious a preoccupation'. This response went against expectations of Milton, whom Hobart refers to as a 'criminall and obsolete person', although he acknowledges that even Milton's worst works were not so 'for want of witt or learning'. Milton's great abilities were often thus contrasted with his regrettable allegiances. The country minister John Beale had in 1667 expressed the hope that Milton could be won to the support of the Royal Society, lest he do 'mischeefe' being so 'full of the Devill' – only then to have his London correspondent send him *Paradise Lost*, which Beale thinks 'excellent' while doubting it will 'beare up into a prevalent example'. Years later, however, he could still propose Milton as the one true poet among the dissenting 'Phanatics' (von Maltzahn 1992, 194; von Maltzahn 1996, 487–97).

We are struck with the immediacy of these first reactions to what since has become a classic. Yet readers are as quick to respond to opinions as to generate them. In January 1668, only a few months after its first appearance, Hobart already reports 'the opinion of the impartiall learned' that *Paradise Lost* is 'not only above all moderne attempts in verse, but equall to any of the Antient Poets'. Likewise Milton's nephew soon advertises to a continental audience that the epic is judged by discriminating readers 'to have reached the perfection of this species of poetry'. Milton himself had done much to prepare this response by so vividly incorporating in his masterpiece many features of classical and subsequent epics, which contribute to his transcendent self-description as inspired bard. Thus his readers might know right away to associate Milton's blindness with that of Homer, with Hobart adding that 'his raptures & fancy bring him uppon a nearer paralele'. Many later readers also applauded Milton's adoption of classical idiom for his Christian epic, agreeing with the conventional praise that he had, in John Dryden's words, joined the 'loftiness' of Homer with the 'Majesty' of Virgil. Milton's ambivalence about this potential in his reception is plain from *Paradise Regained* (1671), which has been described as more obviously 'anti-epic' in its impulse, and as a notably critical self-reading (Rajan).

If Milton's 'handling of allusion is his highly individual and original defense against poetic tradition' (Bloom 1975, 125), this too was a construction of tradition. The enjoyment of Milton's relation to his poetic forebears emerges conspicuously in the poetry of Dryden and Alexander Pope, not least in their translations from the classics, often coloured by knowing references to Milton's own responses to such texts. There were features of *Paradise Lost* – particularly its sometimes archaic diction and its blank verse – that confronted early readers with formal issues more familiar from classical than from English example. Thus Hobart understood the unusual diction to reflect Milton's ambition for his epic, inviting 'the liberty of Homer or Virgill, who resussitated many words (as I have heard) from obscurity'. This was part of the decorum of epic. Later Pope confirmed such judgements, most conspicuously in his translation of the *Odyssey*, where he much drew on Milton's example, valuing the 'just and moderate mixture of old words . . . to give a kind of venerable air' (Pope, 10: 390).

Milton's example eventually revived blank verse as a staple of English poetry. Beale's correspondence shows that the blank verse in *Paradise Lost* was much discussed from the beginning, with Milton himself soon supplying an introductory note justifying his choice in later issues of the first edition (1668–9). Hobart also praises the poem as 'more extraordinary for the matter, then verse', although the latter was far from 'common'. There are few Restoration imitations of Milton's blank verse, but with the growth of his reputation in the 1690s he began to leave his mark, especially on Whig heroic poetry. Now too appeared the first obvious parodies, notably John Philips's influential *Splendid Shilling* (1705). In the first years of the 1700s a more consciously Miltonic style evolved, and *Paradise Lost* soon became a very 'prevalent example' indeed. By the late eighteenth century it had become the predominant one.

Milton's growing popularity came at a time when his Baroque theology was being left behind, particularly in the educational culture in which his poetry came so to prosper. His had been an extraordinary statement of mid-seventeenth-century vitalism, that is an animist materialism asserting the inseparability of body and soul, here based on the emanationist belief that 'one almighty is, from whom / All things proceed, and up to him return, / If not depraved from good' (*PL* 5.469–71; Danielson, 43–57, 212–13; Rogers, 1, 110–29; Rumrich, 118–27). For Milton reason and free will were fundamentally 'Twinned', with 'no dividual being' (*PL* 12.84). This fusion was the mainspring of his poetics, the theology integral to his epic. From early in the Restoration, however, many of his readers evolved strategies for separating the two. Some were unready to make concessions, and collapsed the poetics of freedom with Milton's notorious politics. Although Milton's 'natural parts might deservedly give him a place amongst the principal of our English Poets', claimed one critic, 'his Memory will always stink' (Winstanley, 195). Others, not always out of friendship to Milton, were readier to recuperate the epic from his evil reputation, but chiefly by aestheticizing *Paradise Lost*. The intellectual climate in England and Europe was in a period of rapid change, and Milton's expansion of mid-seventeenth-century poetics – strongly monist (finally all is an expression of just a single kind of being) and apocalyptic – encountered an increasingly mimetic aesthetics, and a much more secular reading of the heroic. It has been argued that 'the philosophical opposition between monism and dualism and the political opposition between freedom and authority simply did not have the same power over Milton as they did over eighteenth-century readers of his work' (Kolbrener 1995, 73).

The change seems to have added to the attractions of *Paradise Lost* in later years. The epic offered a legacy from the Baroque of a broader rationality, worked out of the proportion (*ratio*) between humans and God. Major critics like Richard Bentley and Samuel Johnson might react against Miltonic reason. Very many more readers, however, seem to have been drawn to what they could not quite recover. Some such appetite animates the common eighteenth-century readings in which the claims of reason are superseded by those of experience, especially experience of the Sublime.

It seems that responses to Satan governed seventeenth- and nineteenth-century readings of *Paradise Lost*, whereas responses to Paradise, Adam, and latterly Eve governed eighteenth- and twentieth-century readings. Clearly, the emphasis on Satan follows in part from uncertainties generated by the epic, as well as from suspicions about Milton's politics. Many of his early readers were inclined to see in Satan some version of the author's infamy. That Milton's politics coloured his epic was apparent enough to some readers. Beale, for example, held that Milton 'makes the Devil . . . speak at that rate himself would have done . . . had he thought it convenient' (von Maltzahn 1992, 197); he also thought the Nimrod passage (*PL* 12.24–110) an outrageously bald statement of the antimonarchical Milton's 'old principle'. Those more sympathetic to that principle might be reassured by the degree to which the poem prudently disguised its message while delivering it nonetheless (Benthem, 58). Milton's violence as a critic of Stuart government sharpened the sense of risk in his epic. The tension principally discharged itself in readings of his Satan, which often fused with the autobiographical aspects of the poem. Those who deplored Milton's politics might read *Paradise Lost* as expressing repentance for rebellion, an aggressive interpretation that alleviated anxieties about its claims. Dryden was among those who thought that the Devil had been Milton's 'hero, instead of Adam'. This he may have meant in a formal sense, but it worked as a Tory slur against 'that Grand Whig, Milton'. The commonplace would later be improved upon by the radical William Blake, who famously reversed the valuation and sophisticated it in declaring that 'The reason Milton wrote in fetters when he wrote of Angels & God, and at liberty when of Devils & Hell, is because he was a true Poet and of the Devils party without knowing it' (*Marriage of Heaven and Hell*, plate 6). As long as the legacy of the English Revolution remained an issue, Milton's role in the revolution would colour evaluations of him and his work. This is strongly the case through the 1690s, but remained a significant issue through the eighteenth century and beyond, as for example with such influential readers of Milton as Samuel Johnson, Lord Macaulay, and T. S. Eliot.

That Milton's readers might recoil from Satan appears from the complaint that Milton had 'put such long & horrible Blasphemyes in the Mouth of Satan, as no man that feares God can endure to Read it, or without a poysonous Impression' (von Maltzahn 1992, 194). Such readers were more suspicious than has sometimes been claimed (Fish 1967). Moreover, they could be profoundly concerned about the exact details of Milton's theodicy, especially his elaborate description of Hell and its inhabitants. One set of early annotations, for example, shows close scrutiny of the chronology of the fall of the angels and the creation of the world, as if to make sure of the truth claims of the poem (*Paradise Lost* 1674, at Case Western Reserve University). A dualist reading of Satan as antagonist features in the plays of John Dryden, Thomas Shadwell, and Nathaniel Lee, who already in the 1670s found in the Miltonic sublime a new way to create impressive effects. The influence of such adaptations would in turn instruct later readers to dwell on Satanic grandeur in *Paradise Lost*. It is notable that Milton's libertarian reasoning is lost in the more libertine logic of such imitations. Dryden's *State of Innocence* (1677), which outsold *Paradise Lost* until the turn of that century, rewrites the epic as a semi-opera fashionably determinist in its explanation of the Fall.

It took some time for *Paradise Lost* to reach a wider readership. The first edition of 1667 sold quite well in quarto. It was improved in several reissues, chiefly with the addition of an introductory set of 'Arguments' summarizing the action of each book, which brought the work more fully in line with the norms for presenting classical epic. The second edition, however, appeared only in 1674, in a less expensive format, with a very similar third edition appearing in 1678. These two editions frame the epic for the Restoration reader with commendatory verses which are themselves revealing readings of the poem – in Latin by Samuel Barrow and in English by Andrew Marvell. Many copies include a frontispiece portrait of Milton, a common feature in such books but in his case suggestive of the beginnings of his rehabilitation, at least in the literary realm. After a lull of one decade the notable fourth edition appeared in 1688: an elaborate subscription folio, impressively illustrated, whose commercial success prepared the way for the more frequent publication of Milton's poetry thereafter.

The new owner of the copyright for Milton's poetry, Jacob Tonson, was one of the great print entrepreneurs of the late seventeenth and early eighteenth centuries. The secret of his success was 'his genius for converting the English poets into classics and the classical poets into English' (Treadwell, 361). In one portrait Tonson appears clasping a copy of his precious *Paradise Lost*. In different formats for different markets the epic far outsold Milton's other poems, with his prose-works appearing still less frequently and from other, more oppositional booksellers. With Shakespeare, Milton was *the* English author who could be presented as a classic to a burgeoning middle-class readership. And unlike Shakespeare, Milton required little editorial labour, although Tonson developed new ways of packaging him, notably with scholarly annotation – on English poetry! – already in 1695. Competing booksellers, who could not contest the Tonson copyright, were quick to promote other products that might cash in on Milton's fame. His name was often adopted and his style adapted to draw on the emerging demand. A still wider readership was further instructed in how to enjoy Milton by the hugely popular and influential critical essays on *Paradise Lost* by Joseph Addison (*Spectator* 1712). Only in the 1730s did Milton's text come into dispute, in a major attempt at modernizing it by the classical critic Richard Bentley. This was published now by the younger Jacob Tonson, despite his having access to disproof of Bentley's claim regarding the corruption of Milton's text. The resulting critical debate sold even more copies of the poem, even as Bentley's claims were refuted.

But the Tonsons' success in promoting Milton and in controlling the copyright for his poetry eventually constrained the market. Despite the many Tonson editions of Milton's poetry in the first half of the eighteenth century, already there were some piracies, and foreign publishers had begun to publish the poem both in English and in translations. That the market was far from saturated appears from such competition, and particularly from the much faster rate of publication of new editions after the lapsing of the Tonsons' ownership of the Milton copyright in the 1750s. Anthologies increasingly included Milton, and selections proliferated, as did simplified and abbreviated versions of the epic, along with a variety of annotated and illustrated editions. Responses to his poetry flourished in other media, notably in the theatre (Dugas), in music (famously in Handel's settings), in gardening (Schulz, 9–18), and in the visual arts (Pointon). Encouragements to reading now included the push to help a wider range of readers, including women (Wittreich 1987), who owing to limits on their education often enjoyed only limited access to classical texts, and also poorer readers, especially through the leadership of John Wesley and his Methodist followers. These together with an ever widening middle-class readership and eventually more economical print technologies made *Paradise Lost* the modern classic, published annually or more often, in Britain and abroad, and in larger and larger print runs. Milton's English epic was distinguished by its wide availability as well as by its great sublimity.

Aestheticization of the epic accommodated most of its anomalous features for educated eighteenth-century readers. This contributed to Satan's status, but also to a wider range of response to other wonders in the poem. A more affective reading encouraged its reception as the national poem, Protestant and English. As much as *Paradise Lost* was a commodity of particular value to the booksellers, it also gained rapidly in importance as cultural capital for its readers in the eighteenth century and since. The phenomenon appears, for example, in the Scottish embrace of English culture after the Act of Union (1707). As Scots sought citizenship in a 'British' republic of letters, it was natural to turn to Milton among the best English authors. Milton had provided his own vernacular epic in subaltern defiance of Latin culture. Subaltern Scots, however, schooled themselves in *Paradise Lost* as the supreme expression of English Protestant poetics. Perhaps the most influential Miltonist after Addison was the Scottish poet James Thomson, who worked his way to the heart of London's metropolitan culture by his devotion to English poetics, and to Milton in particular. In the emergence of university studies in English literature, a vital part was played by this Scottish tradition – that of Lord Kames, Adam Smith, and Hugh Blair in the eighteenth century, and also of Lord Macaulay (if at a remove) and David Masson in the nineteenth. Milton lent himself to its objectives because of his learning, his Protestantism, and his offering in *Paradise Lost* what might be taken as a strenuous native counterpart to Latin, a poetry fit for empire (Crawford, 16–44; von Maltzahn 1999).

But the English, as much as the Scots, might wish to be more English still. Promoting the vernacular invited the consecration of Milton as the great national poet. The result was the ever-broadening circulation of *Paradise Lost*. By the mid-eighteenth century, the educational applications of Milton's poetry were obvious. Thus the ringing endorsement from Thomas Sheridan, in his reforming *British Education: Or the Source of the Disorders of Great Britain* (1756): 'Milton in the poetic . . . may be considered as truly classical, as the Virgil . . . of the Romans; nor is there any reason that [he] should not be handed down as such equally to the end of time' (quoted in Guillory, 100–1). This imperial Milton met with a searching critique from no less a reader than William Blake. Especially in Blake's *Milton*, 'Milton is not only the symbol but the vehicle of the nation's corruption by classical models', and to succumb to his classicizing model was 'to lose native genealogy in imperial typology' (Wright; Newlyn, 257–78). Less able to disembarrass themselves of Milton's authority, however, most readers and writers came instead to internalize him 'as a figure of conscience, wisdom, and restraint' (Newlyn, 25).

The proposal of *Paradise Lost* as a classic, and as central to English Protestantism, found wide embrace in Britain and in its empire. English acculturation was exported more and more widely: witness the young

Francis Parkman, on the Oregon Trail, crossing the American frontier in the 1840s, and there encountering in a remote household a copy of Milton, which he notes as if a last vestige of civilization. Perhaps the example of Thomas Babington Macaulay's famous 'Minute' on Indian education (1835) best shows how dynamically Milton's poetry might be involved in the colonial project. Macaulay himself had loved Milton from an early age, made his name in a famous essay on Milton in the *Edinburgh Review*, and was reputed to know *Paradise Lost* by heart. Against the policy that the British support Indian education in native languages and cultures, Macaulay successfully proposed instead an Anglicist ideal of the 'learned native', among whose distinctions was conversancy with Milton's poetry. For Macaulay it was self-evident that 'a single shelf of a good European library was worth the whole native literature of India and Arabia'. *Paradise Lost* might effect the missionary work that was otherwise restrained by secular policies. Moreover, what classical languages had been in the English Renaissance 'our tongue is to the people of India'. Milton's literary career had taken him from within that classical culture to writing an epic both English and Protestant. One hundred and fifty years later his work played a central part in the determination that, not least for imperial and educational purposes, 'The literature of England is now more valuable than that of classical antiquity' (Clive; Viswanathan).

By the end of the eighteenth century it could be claimed that Milton's epic 'is read with pleasure and Admiration, by Persons of every Degree and Condition' (Newlyn, 19–62). In the next two centuries that 'pleasure and Admiration' were increasingly harnessed to educational objectives, in which the circulation of *Paradise Lost* came to define the frontiers of English Protestant culture, and more broadly of 'traditional Western culture' (Rumrich, 146). Milton's work was made to serve orthodoxies from which modern scholarship has increasingly struggled to free it. The great challenge for Milton's early readers was to divorce his poetry from his prose, and to rescue *Paradise Lost* from scandal, particularly that of his regicide pamphlets. The great challenge for modern scholarship has been to reunite them, and to understand the great epic in terms of the beliefs that animated Milton's career. And yet, vast as the accumulation of Milton scholarship has become, *Paradise Lost* is too good a poem for us to allow all that to get very much in the way. We cannot help but feel the weight of cultural capital and its institutions, within which a great proportion of Milton's modern readers first encounter his epic, and in which the publication of the present essay is much involved. But those need not detain us too long. The reading of Milton's writings always awaits, and with it the chance to experience more wholly our being in the world in relation to the divine, whatever that may be.

FURTHER READING

Achinstein, Sharon, *Milton and the Revolutionary Reader* (Princeton, 1994)
Benthem, Henrich Ludolff, *Engeländischer Kirch- und Schulen-Staat* (Lüneburg, 1694)
Blake, William, *William Blake's Writings*, ed. G. E. Bentley, Jr (Oxford, 1978)
Bloom, Harold, *Anxiety of Influence* (New York, 1973)
A Map of Misreading (New York, 1975)
Campbell, Gordon, *A Milton Chronology* (New York, 1997)
Clive, John, *Macaulay: the Shaping of the Historian* (New York, 1973)
Crawford, Robert, *Devolving English Literature* (Oxford, 1992)
Danielson, Dennis, *Milton's Good God: A Study in Literary Theodicy* (Cambridge, 1982)
Dugas, Don-John, '"Such Heav'n-taught Numbers should be more than Read": *Comus* and Milton's Reputation in Mid-Eighteenth-Century England', *Milton Studies* 34 (1996), 137–57
Dzelzainis, Martin, 'Milton and the Protectorate in 1658', in *Milton and Republicanism*, ed. D. Armitage, A. Himy, and Q. Skinner (Cambridge, 1995), 181–205
'Milton's Classical Republicanism', in *Milton and Republicanism*, ed. D. Armitage et al., 3–24
Fish, Stanley, *Surprised By Sin: The Reader in 'Paradise Lost'* (Berkeley, 1967; 2nd edn London, 1997)
'Wanting a Supplement: The Question of Interpretation in Milton's Early Prose', in *Politics, Poetics, and Hermeneutics in Milton's Prose*, ed. D. Loewenstein and J. G. Turner (Cambridge, 1990), 41–68
French, J. Milton, *The Life Records of John Milton* (New Brunswick, NJ, 1949–58)
Gadamer, Hans-Georg, *Truth and Method*, translated by J. Weinsheimer and D. G. Marshall, 2nd rev. edn (New York, 1990)
Griffin, Dustin, *Regaining Paradise: Milton and the Eighteenth Century* (Cambridge, 1986)
Guillory, John, *Cultural Capital: The Problem of Literary Canon Formation* (Chicago, 1993)
Jauss, Hans Robert, *Toward an Aesthetic of Reception*, translated by T. Bahti (Minneapolis, 1982)
Kolbrener, William, '"In a Narrow and to Him a Dark Chamber": Milton Unabridged', *Common Knowledge* 4 (1995), 72–96
Milton's Warring Angels (Cambridge, 1997)
Miller, Leo, 'A 1647 Critique of *Areopagitica*', *Notes and Queries* 234 (1989), 29–30
Nelson, James G., *The Sublime Puritan: Milton and the Victorians* (Madison, 1963)
Newlyn, Lucy, *'Paradise Lost' and the Romantic Reader* (Oxford, 1993)
Norbrook, David, '*Areopagitica*, Censorship, and the Early Modern Public Sphere', *Cultural Politics* 7 (1994), 3–33
Oras, Ants, *Milton's Editors and Commentators* (Tartu and Oxford, 1931)

Parker, William Riley, *Milton's Contemporary Reputation* (Columbus, 1940)
Milton: A Biography (Oxford, 1968; rev. edn Gordon Campbell, Oxford, 1996)
Pointon, Marcia, *Milton & English Art* (Manchester, 1970)
Pope, Alexander, *The Twickenham Edition of the Poems of Alexander Pope*, eds. John Butt et al. (1938–68)
Rajan, Balachandra, 'The Imperial Temptation', in *Milton and the Imperial Vision*, eds. Balachandra Rajan and Elizabeth Sauer (Pittsburgh, 1999)
Rogers, John, *The Matter of Revolution: Science, Poetry, and Politics in the Age of Milton* (Ithaca, 1996)
Rumrich, John, *Milton Unbound: Controversy and Reinterpretation* (Cambridge, 1996)
Schulz, Max, *Paradise Preserved: Recreations of Eden in Eighteenth- and Nineteenth-Century England* (Cambridge, 1985)
Sensabaugh, George, *Milton in Early America* (Princeton, 1964)
Shawcross, John T., 'A Survey of Milton's Prose Works', in *Achievements of the Left Hand*, eds. Michael Lieb and John T. Shawcross (Amherst, 1974), 291–391
Milton: A Bibliography For the Years 1624–1700 (Binghamton, 1984)
John Milton and Influence: Presence in Literature, History, and Culture (Pittsburgh, 1991)
ed., *Milton: The Critical Heritage*, 2 vols. (London, 1970–2)
Smith, Nigel, '*Areopagitica*: Voicing Contexts, 1643–45', in *Politics, Poetics, and Hermeneutics in Milton's Prose*, ed. D. Loewenstein and J. G. Turner (Cambridge, 1990), 41–68
Literature and Revolution in England, 1640–1660 (New Haven, 1994)
Treadwell, Michael, 'The English Book Trade', in *The Age of William III and Mary II: Power, Politics, and Patronage, 1688–1702*, ed. Robert Maccubbin and Martha Hamilton-Phillips (Williamsburg, 1989), 358–65
Van Anglen, Kevin, *The New England Milton* (University Park, PA, 1993)
Viswanathan, Gauri, *Masks of Conquest: Literary Study and British Rule in India* (New York, 1989)
von Maltzahn, Nicholas, 'Laureate, Republican, Calvinist', *Milton Studies* 29 (1992), 181–98
'Wood, Allam, and the Oxford Milton', *Milton Studies* 31 (1994), 155–77
'The Whig Milton, 1667–1700', in *Milton and Republicanism*, eds. D. Armitage, A. Himy, and Q. Skinner (Cambridge, 1995), 229–53
'The First Reception of *Paradise Lost* (1667)', *Review of English Studies* 47 (1996), 479–99
'From Pillar to Post: Milton and the Attack on Republican Humanism at the Restoration', in *Soldiers, Writers and Statesmen of the English Revolution*, eds. I. Gentles, J. Morrill, and B. Worden (Cambridge, 1998), 265–85
'Acts of Kind Service: Milton and the Patriot Literature of Empire', in *Milton and the Imperial Vision*, eds. Balachandra Rajan and Elizabeth Sauer (Pittsburgh, 1999)
Walsh, Marcus, *Shakespeare, Milton, and Eighteenth-Century Literary Editing* (Cambridge, 1997)
Winstanley, William, *The Lives of the Most Famous English Poets* (London, 1687)
Wittreich, Joseph, *Feminist Milton* (Ithaca, 1987)

ed., *The Romantics on Milton* (Cleveland, 1970)
ed., *Milton and the Line of Vision* (Madison, 1975)
Wright, Julia, '"Greek and Latin Slaves of the Sword": Rejecting the Imperial Nation in Blake's *Milton*', in *Milton and the Imperial Vision*, eds. Balachandra Rajan and Elizabeth Sauer (Pittsburgh, 1999)

17

WILLIAM KERRIGAN

Milton's place in intellectual history

Intellectual historiography as it has commonly been practised is devoted to the formidability of tradition. It seeks to identify enduring suppositions – world-pictures, cosmological principles, models of nature, mind, time, and God – and to view their elasticity over great expanses of cultural history. It does not shy away from apparent examples of radical change. Indeed, some of these examples are its stock subjects – the seeming break between Christianity and antiquity, the rise of scientific empiricism, the self-proclaimed specialness of the various romanticisms. But, armed with concepts such as the 'unit ideas' of Arthur O. Lovejoy and the 'reoccupied positions' of Hans Blumenberg, intellectual historians have generally preferred to craft stories about gradual renovation and substitution rather than rupture and novelty. It is telling in this respect that in *The Legitimacy of the Modern Age*, a work of tremendous scope and originality, and probably the most distinguished contribution to intellectual history in recent years, Blumenberg should keep returning to the oddly provincial point that the idea of progress does not derive from a secularization of Christian history: for a historian of ideas, the challenge of modernity is to get straight on its tradition. It can sometimes seem, in the light of this discipline, as if the course of Western thought were the internal conversation among fifty or so intellectuals dedicated to solving each other's problems while doomed to pass on new versions of them. This vision of thinking as the grandest of human games, self-generated and self-regulating, is responsible for a marked decline today in the authority of classical intellectual history. At the extreme of this suspicion, in the popular new Marxisms, the entire project of intellectual history, the boundary that constitutes its subject matter, appears wishful. Intellect is too flimsy and extravagant, too uneconomical, to have so grim and massive a thing as a history. Ideas are the forms ideology takes when forgetful of its purpose, and intellectual history dissolves into the forces at work in history at large.

Whatever the future may hold for intellectual history, its popularity as an

6. Peter Paul Rubens (1577–1640), *The Fall of the Damned into Hell* (Alte Pinakothek, Munich)

approach to Milton's work, especially *Paradise Lost*, shows no signs of exhaustion. For one thing, *Paradise Lost* is built of the very same materials intellectual historians delight in studying. Other poems take place against the backdrop of a universe. Milton's makes one, producing rather than presupposing its structuring principles: his is an intellectual universe composed of theories, causes, explanations, arguments. Where but to intellectual history, long familiar with these matters, should we turn for enlightenment about this thoughtful poem and its famous puzzlements, such as the appearance of Galileo in a universe that is none the less terracentric and finite? Moreover, the ambitious world-weaving of the epic has as its complement Milton's unrelieved erudition, or it might be better to say, his knowingness. He used with precision, and in the primordial contexts afforded by his myth, those large treacherous words like 'author', 'reason', 'nature', and 'grace' that intellectual history at its most impressive has warned us not to receive naively, since they bear vast networks of interlocking assumptions. These words flowed from every Renaissance pen, of course, but Milton was not off-hand. His frame of reference was *the* frame.

Much like Dante, then, whose work bears a similar affinity to the programme of intellectual history, Milton has repeatedly been 'placed' on the grids of this discipline. We know a good deal about his relationship to science (Curry; Svendsen; Nicolson; Kerrigan), to the various Platonisms, and above all to Protestant and patristic theology. I want to suggest, with all due respect, two difficulties with this approach to *Paradise Lost*.

The mere extent of this knowledge, coupled with the sense of coherent tradition with which it has customarily been offered, encourages us to regard the poem in a certain fashion – as, let us say, a very nice museum. *Paradise Lost* gathers into one text many odd and wonderful snatches of ancient lore, and annotating curators keep enlarging the exhibits. Thus Lactantius, to open yet another exhibit in the name of one of Milton's favourite church fathers (see Hartwell), contended that man alone among creatures was created upright with a swivelling neck so that he could know the heavens. Recounting his birth, Milton's Adam tells of the first use he made of his propitiously hinged head:

> Straight toward heaven my wondering eyes I turned,
> And gazed a while the ample sky, till raised
> By quick instinctive motion up I sprung,
> As thitherward endeavouring, and upright
> Stood on my feet. (8.257–61)

Milton packs the Lactantian nexus of neck, heavenly knowledge, spiritual aspiration, uprightness, and righteousness into a single fluid action: the first action in human history. We have adduced the source; the exhibit is open. But the achievement of intellectual history in such cases does not serve the vitality of the poem, which is ultimately the vitality of its readers, if it leads us to believe that interpretation is now complete.

Often the procedures of intellectual history assume that while passages in *Paradise Lost* are mysteries in need of interpretation, the sources discovered for them are not. Illumination flows in one direction only, from source to poem, and the implied relationship of poem to source becomes the placid one of mere duplication. Should it be made to appear that the meaning of Lactantius is the meaning of Milton's use of Lactantius, we face tradition at its apex of coherence: repetition. But the pieces of lore embedded in Milton's beautifully complex design are extended, questioned, cross-referenced with other themes and symbols. To understand the moment when Adam first leaps to his feet we must work out connections with many other passages; a partial list would include the golden roof of Pandaemonium (1.717), the bowed heads of bedazzled angels (3.381–2), the broken heads of proud angels (6.840), Eve's curiosity about night (4.657–8), the apparent limits placed on human curiosity about the heavens in Book 8, the story of aspiration Satan invents for the snake (9.571–612), the uprightness of the snake (9.494–503), and the punishment God imposes on the uprightness of the snake (10.175–81). There are intriguing metaphorical transformations here. Reaching for knowledge of the stars seems to prefigure reaching for the forbidden fruit. Curiosity about the heavens becomes entwined with the question of the sufficiency of man's original happiness, wealth, and intellectual endowment. Milton sets the gifts of the creator against our problematic need to seek more than we already have, which may itself belong to our endowment, yet also appears to lay down the plot of our depravity. It is above all this interwovenness, the constant pressure of the entirety upon the part, that renders Milton's place in intellectual history a treacherous subject. We have stumbled into a common thicket: how is poetry related to philosophy? Milton's epic is not simply an instance of this general problem. As I will later suggest, *Paradise Lost* actively and deliberately stages the ancient battle between poetry and philosophy.

A second disappointment with the contribution of intellectual history to Milton studies is its relative lack of interest in articulating his position with respect to subsequent philosophy, despite the impressive start made in this direction by one of the early triumphs of modern Milton criticism, Denis Saurat's *Milton, Man and Thinker.* Milton lived at a time when philosophy, theology, science, and poetry were just beginning to feel the extent of their mutual antagonism. A century later the various systems of Romantic philosophy would try to suspend in a unity the fragments of an exploding intellectual universe, and philosophy would establish itself as the queen of disciplines, charged with determining the ultimate sense and good order of the others (see Rorty). As M. H. Abrams demonstrates in his magisterial *Natural Supernaturalism*, philosophies of the self-perfected subject in one sense conquered, but in a profounder sense reinstigated departed Christian myth by claiming as their own the old story of oneness, exile, and return. In figures like Schelling and Hegel, Spirit – the mind in its potential for self-consciousness – traverses its own salvation history. Philosophy must begin somewhere; and in this tradition it wants to set out in the truth, from the rational Eden of an apodictic ground. But the piecemeal business of philosophical exposition must proceed in exile from this initial oneness with the truth. The goal of the system is to recover at the end of its long detour into the partialities of exposition the 'absolute' from which it presumes to have arisen. Viewed in this context, Milton chose to dilate the great cycle of salvation history – to write of 'all', as Marvell noted in his commendatory verses – on the threshold of a major mutation in the history of this myth.

Since the myth survived philosophically in non-incidental metaphors that cannot be dissociated from the conviction Romantic thought both exemplified and inspired, *Paradise Lost* provides us with a master exploration of these key philosophical tropes. Consider, for instance, the summary symbol created by the action of the epic and named in its title. There are three paradises by the time we have arrived at the concluding Expulsion: Eden, the lost paradise; the eschatological 'Paradise' (12.464) toward which Christ leads us; and in between the 'paradise within' (12.587), the interior soul of mortal man cultivated by Christian virtues. At the Expulsion, man bears within him a symbol born of paradise lost and pointed toward paradise regained. In Romantic idealism (to follow Abrams once again) the two paradises on either side of the interior one reappear in the naive oneness prior to systematic thought and the sophisticated oneness regained at its completion. The break characteristic of twentieth-century philosophy occurs when the two framing paradises drop away, leaving us only a paradise within, the symbol of a home that reason never had and can never hope to find. There is just wandering, just discourse or *écriture*.

Exile then becomes the sole condition of thought. Alienation or homelessness, the philosophical afterlife of Milton's summary symbol, is among the pervasive signs of modern culture. We find it in Marxism, in Freudian ideas such as 'displacement' and the 'uncanny' (*unheimlich*, 'un-homely'), in Derrida's 'deferral', 'difference', and '*différance*', and conspicuously in early Heidegger, the ponderous magician of philosophical symbolism who preached alienation with an almost Gnostic intensity.

It is impossible to understand the point of *Being and Time*, its evocation of historical crisis, without appealing to texts like *Paradise Lost* as horizons against which to measure its strange, godless reassertion of traditional theological ideas. Who is Heidegger's *Dasein*? Imagine an Adam for whom the arc of time stretches from the throw of birth to the oblivion of death. Expulsion is his life. He visits rather than dwells, for how can he be at home in a world he must leave? Here is Heidegger preaching a secular sermon on Novalis's 'Philosophy is strictly speaking a homesickness':

> We are without a native land and are restlessness itself, living restlessness: it is because of *this* that it is necessary for us to philosophise. And this restlessness is *our* confinement, we who are finitude itself. And we are not allowed to let it pass away, to comfort ourselves in an illusion about totality and a satisfactory infinitude. We must not only bear this restlessness in us, but accentuate it, and when we are not only confined but entirely isolated, only then do we strive more to incite ourselves to be important, civilized; only then are we in a position to be 'gripped'. And when we thus make ourselves grippable, by handing ourselves over to reality, our homesickness makes us into human beings. (Quoted in Naess, 174)

If, for 'restlessness' and 'homesickness' in this passage, we substitute 'the philosophical fate of Milton's symbolism of paradise', we see where we are in modern thought, which is not to say that Milton's vision yields Heidegger's merely by subtraction. For the gesture by which Heidegger converts this homesickness into an opportunity for authentic existence in the resolute grip of life's finite possibilities is recognizably a version of the therapy Milton's God designs in order to prepare Adam and Eve for their Expulsion: accepting loss and privation as our own, and not as fates chosen once in a mythical past and ever after suffered passively, makes us human beings able to choose a place of rest in the possibilities of our history. Writing a theodicy in the absence of God, early Heidegger resists the illusion of religion while affirming the conventional theological imperative to own up to our privation, dispelling the 'forgottenness' of comfortable repose in this world. It is difficult to see why this sort of reading, breaking into modern thought with Milton and into Milton with modern thought, should be considered less truly critical, and less a matter of historical concern, than the approach through classical and patristic texts. Looking ahead to the mutations of its myth permits the epic to seem, not a museum, but the poem Milton wanted to create, 'so written to aftertimes, as they should not willingly let it die' (*YP* 1: 810).

By some measures the author of *Paradise Lost* was not a particularly philosophical man. I doubt whether he read Descartes. He does not seem to have felt the seventeenth-century urge to nip scepticism in the bud by supplementing Scripture with rational proofs for things divine, although in *Paradise Lost* he follows the fashion of his day in suggesting, with Edward Herbert, Descartes, and the Cambridge Platonists, that God is an innate idea, even that, in a plausible interpretation of the final two books, the Bible as an inspired record still in need of construction is an idea innately planted in fallen man. It is useful in fixing Milton's positions to refer to famous landmarks of seventeenth-century intellectual history, such as the Hobbes-Bramhall debate on free will. Yet I do not think Milton would have had the patience to get down to brass tacks with Hobbes on subjects like this. An almighty God and a free human will were true for Milton because they had to be true, because the meaning of the world he both derived from and imposed on the Bible demanded they be true. 'No man who knows ought', he grumbled in *The Tenure of Kings and Magistrates*, 'can be so stupid to deny that all men naturally were borne free' (*YP* 3: 198). Many, on this view, were his stupid contemporaries. After conceding the sometime complexity of words like 'naturally', we do well to remember that these are also the words used for beliefs impervious to objection. Sheer conviction probably outweighs proposition in Milton's prose. The result is not what we normally think of as rational argument: it is ridicule, Milton describing how stupid opponents look from the point of view of his own exasperated certainty. The compatibility of God and freedom, which has vexed many Christian thinkers, is only a problem in Milton's epic for philosophical devils, and God says all there is to say on the matter in his first speech (3.80–134). When Eve murmurs after her fall, 'for inferior who is free?' (9.825), the entire poem rises up as one voice to shout back at her: 'Everyone free in this universe (save God) is also inferior!'

But Milton does of course have an argument, and a great one. He fuses narrative and theodicy in *Paradise Lost* – a two-sided intention neatly epitomized in the doubleness of the word *argument*, meaning both plot and proposition. The effect of theodicy on such a scale is very near to a recentring of Christianity about the justification of God; and, in fact, Christianity in *Paradise Lost is* invented before our very eyes in response to theodical antinomies brought about by the foreseen fall of man. Dennis Danielson has shown how the early Protestant endorsement of predestination led to seventeenth-century controversies over the power and goodness of God. It is important for modern readers to grasp this background sympathetically, because they are almost certain to bring Enlightenment suspicions to Milton's great argument. Theodicy inevitably takes up the theme of this world's relation to other possible worlds; to justify God means to defend some vision of how things are against other visions of how things might be. The relation of possible worlds to the actual world is a subject of such rarefied difficulty in a theological context that Duns Scotus, its scholastic proponent, had become a laughing-stock to many seventeenth-century thinkers (though not to Milton; see Rumrich), and by the late eighteenth century the fate of Leibniz, author of the most influential theodicy in Renaissance philosophy, was not dissimilar. Voltaire, repelled by the smug hubris of drawing-room theodicy, remarked that God must have given us noses so that we could put spectacles on them. The barb goes deep, since Christians have a longstanding habit of making facts into occasions for appreciating divine wisdom – witness Lactantius on the neck.

In his essay 'On the Failure of All Philosophical Attempts at Theodicy', Kant proposed that insofar as theodicies presume to know the ways of God to men, 'which are inscrutable', all such arguments exemplify the premier human vice of insincerity. We are not sincere with ourselves about knowing and believing. The mind is so prone to self-deceit in the matter of knowledge that many people spend their entire adult lives congratulating themselves on having achieved it: 'In the carefulness to be conscious to one's self of this believing (or not believing), and not to give out any holding-true, of which one is not conscious, the very formal conscientiousness, the ground of veracity, consists' (Kant, 181). Kant had not read Milton. Yet he brilliantly articulates the grudge that Milton's opponents old and new tend to hold against him. There is no theodicy without presumption, and Milton was unquestionably a presumptuous man – by Kant's definition an insincere man, convinced that he knew what no man can know.

Intellectual history should instruct us here. The impressive thing about Milton's case of Kantian insincerity is that we do not find it nakedly before us in the form of unconceded presumption, but marked, pointed out by an elaborate prophetic stance, which could be thought of as a way of confessing within a Christian framework that the argument is beyond human capacity, 'invisible to mortal sight' (3.55). Nor is theodicy for Milton, or for his century, the sugared enhancement of moral complacency it became in the next. Seventeenth-century Protestants did not ask about God's justice as one might the sum of the angles of a triangle or the implications of rebounding billiard balls. Milton reanimated theodicy because he felt that good men, in the current or future state of the world, would be compelled to enquire into the moral vision of the deity; and the impulse to worship, adore, and celebrate God as noble creatures worthy of being his creations could not last if this enquiry were to be denied in principle – denied as Kant was to deny it. What Kant leaves out is sincerity about our need for theodical assurance. Milton's was an argument taken up in the heat and sorrow of disappointment, in the face of apparent evidence of divine injustice. So Milton argues, narrating and contending. At stake is the justice of God, and beyond that the momentous question of whether religion can be made answerable to our moral dispositions.

Sometimes Satan and the divine speakers in *Paradise Lost* seem to be trading rejoinders like warring pamphleteers who will do almost anything for a score and show little interest in the mutual articulation of their positions. This quality has often been noted in Satan's improvised reproaches to God, but it can also be found (the taunt of lowering the stairs of heaven as Satan flies by, the derisive metamorphosis at Satan's return to hell) on the righteous side. Some readers, moved by this spirit of controversy, take up the cudgels for one party or the other. Some in the spirit of Kant find the theodicy pretentious. Yet the grand justification taken in its entirety, which is the entirety of our experience of the poem, is astonishingly tight. Any arguer must be allowed some givens. Once you grant Milton a Christian premise or two, there are not many good ways out, which may be one of the things that drove Blake mad and transformed William Empson into a picky lawyer. The theodicy of *Paradise Lost* is a consummate example of impassioned argument. More than this, like no other argument with which I am familiar, the epic delivers its meaning so as to produce a friendly competition between (Milton might not have used these terms) poetry and philosophy.

That Milton's epic is, in one sense or another, highly 'philosophical', we have the valuable testimony of Lovejoy: 'Now *Paradise Lost* is not merely, as the schoolboy noted with surprise, full of familiar quotations: it is also full of ideas' (3). Milton probably seems to us a more philosophical poet than Spenser, but this judgement has more to do with what seems to us philosophical than it does with the intellectual character of either poet. Spenser's notion of what constitutes philosophically serious talk descends in the main from Italian Neoplatonism. Though generally shunned in Renaissance universities, this philosophy attracted Elizabethan poets in large part because it already resembled poetry. It spoke of cosmology by allegorizing classical myth, and sought to display creation's order in corresponding lists of hierarchical kinds. Its harmonies were often generated through numerology: beholding reflections and graded repetitions in the world demands analogies, and number is the readiest sanction for analogies; anything may be related to anything else simply because there are three of them, or seven, or ten, cosmic homology without end. The early Milton, who would 'unsphere / The spirit of Plato', fell partially under the spell of this tradition. Spenserian allegory remained an alluring model for philosophical poets of the seventeenth century such as Henry More and Edward Benlowes; in his *Conjectura Cabbalistica*, an exegesis of Genesis, More used the numerological tradition to construct an up-to-date Cartesian hexameron. But in philosophy proper these neoplatonic strains were dying out, which is to say that people like Descartes himself were establishing a new idea of 'philosophy proper'. Toward the end of the century we find Leibniz proclaiming that Plotinus and his follower Ficino had responded only to the fanciful Plato, downplaying his severer rationalism, reifying his myths, and freely debasing his thought with curious additions (Cassirer, 155). At last the Platonic tradition, for centuries lagging behind the Aristotelian in the practical matters of textual transmission and plausible commentary, was getting its house in order. This insistence on keeping a distance from myths and magic numbers, which was to culminate in Enlightenment thought, dovetails with the sort of exercise Milton set himself in the *Christian Doctrine*, the work of systematic theology and biblical exegesis that occupied him before and during the composition of *Paradise Lost*.

This treatise proceeds in a medieval manner by proposing flat, gnomic, unmetaphorical *sententiae* which are then broken apart into constituent phrases and justified by proof texts. This is hardly Cartesian philosophy, but in its banishment of cosmological myth, in its suspension of 'literary' elements such as myth and parable, and in the emphatically unintoxicated tone of its exposition, it is far closer to Cartesian philosophy than to Marsilio Ficino. One doubts whether Spenser possessed, or thought it important to possess, such a catalogue of scrubbed axioms for the design of the Christian world. In the preface to *Christian Doctrine* Milton calls the work 'my dearest and best possession' (*YP* 6: 121).

As a poet, however, Milton had in some manner to remythologize these stark doctrines. At times in *Paradise Lost* the factual or philosophical appears almost separate from the figurative or poetic, dividing for a moment the two ambitions linked in the word 'argument'. Thus Chaos is represented first as a wild sea of embryonic atoms and then as a senile monarch. For the reader this is a fateful crossroads. What is the relationship between philosophy and poetry? Are the two representations of Chaos equivalent semantic twins, each the mirror of the other? Associating the propositional with the truthful, we are disposed to assume that the atoms interpret the senile monarch. But could it be the other way around? Does the symbolic Chaos tell us something that the propositional one does not?

It is at moments like this, when we are invited to reach into Milton's representations and make our own sense of them, that *Paradise Lost* transcends philosophy as we have come to know it. For in its journey from Ficino to Descartes, Hobbes, Locke, Hume, and Kant, philosophy gradually aspired to transparency, a clear and explicit language requiring no special act of interpretation because its interpretation is already conveyed in its sense, is its sense; allegory, which requires decoding but seeks to stipulate its correct interpretation, could be viewed as the literary analogue of this dream. But if we decide, as I think we will, that Chaos as personification is not the semantic double of embryonic atoms, then Milton's monarch has broken loose from the moorings of conventional allegory, and becomes – I can think of no better phrase – an authentic symbol. Interpretation in Milton always comes up against realms of adventure. If we have read Augustine, we know in propositional form the argument about evil as privation or non-being. Arguing in two senses, Milton in the opening books of his epic embodies or emplots this idea by appropriating the old literary convention of the parodic devil. Never before has the convention been so charged with intellectual weight, and never before has the idea been so richly imagined. As we watch Satan and hell imitating God and heaven, we strike beneath metaphysical abstractions to recognize in the literary mode of parody, which turns against its source, a way to be while hating being; we see the hard pathos of a rivalry in which the detested God is also the devil's most coveted ideal. Formulations in philosophy proper do not feel like this. After noting that Milton had many ideas, Lovejoy went on to say, 'Scarcely one of them is original with him, though many of them receive a special twist or coloring, or enter into novel combinations, in consequence of personal characteristics of his' (4). The intellectual historian treads softly here. He wants to say that Milton is philosophical, but does not want to say that Milton ranks with the philosophers he has borrowed from. The adjective befits him, yet not the honorific noun. Because Lovejoy assumes that literary texts, when they are full of ideas, duplicate or strive to duplicate philosophy proper, he underestimates the intellectual power of this poet.

A doubleness of meaning, similar to the one that parts Chaos, emerges in Milton's similes. Epic comparisons are 'focused' in that, unlike metaphors and ordinary similes, they state expressly the terms of the analogy. So Satan on the burning lake is 'in bulk as huge / As . . .' (1.196–7). Bulk, we are told as we enter the simile, is the unknown to be determined. These are our instructions: learn how huge Satan is. When we exit from the first simile of *Paradise Lost* thirteen lines later, Milton reiterates the initial lesson plan with the implication that the unknown is now well known: 'So stretched out huge in length the arch-fiend lay' (1.209). But what are we to do with the wealth of information seemingly extraneous to the determination of

Satan's size – the story of the slumbering leviathan, the mistaken pilot, and the ominous lack of closure in this story, which does not say how the beast reacted to that anchor in its scaly rind? Reading has its slavish side. Presented with the signifiers, we adduce the signifieds, and bear the sense of the syntax variously from line to line. But we have no instructions concerning the semantic overspill of the simile. We are, as Milton punningly suggests a few lines later, 'at large' (1.213), freed from the bonds of explicit sense. We have the freedom to make our own rules, and the responsibility to argue about our results with other readers. Look again on the protean face of Chaos. Whatever is said about the incoherence of the atoms, the personification does speak, does express, which might be thought to question creation's claim to a monopoly on Logos; and whatever is implied in *Paradise Lost* or stated in the *Christian Doctrine* about the moral neutrality of the embryonic atoms, the personality of Chaos makes an alliance with Satan (see Schwartz), whose own face, reminding us of his senile partner, undergoes contortions of rage and despair when he lands on earth (4.114–17). The bulk of Satan is to the extraneous story of the pilot what the atoms are to Chaos personified. Meaning in both cases has a double structure, one explicit and one a challenge. As he welcomes ideas into *Paradise Lost*, Milton invites us to rescue them from their calcified formulations in discursive philosophy.

Since our interpretations will translate the surplus of the simile or the symbolic representation of Chaos into new discursive forms, which may then require fresh interpretation of other discursive and symbolic passages in the epic, the meaning of *Paradise Lost* seems forever beyond us, unsettled and in process. Stanley Fish (36) argues that the drama of the mistaken pilot refers to the careless reader who finds a safe harbour in the exposed surface of Satan. I have been suggesting, in line with this view, that the crucial difference in the first simile between what is seen naively and what is submerged betrays a difference throughout *Paradise Lost* between the stated, overt, or discursively known and the symbolized or implied that must be hunted out in the depths of the epic. This second dimension of excess and uncertainty, while allowing Milton's poem to outwit as well as absorb philosophy, brings with it the threat of monstrous chaos. A protean uncertainty of meaning could demote or dismiss truths secured on the discursive surfaces of the work. For this very reason, after all, philosophy has tended to banish literature from its own language, or to enslave it via allegory and example. A major exception to this generalization is the dialogue form, which puts discursive achievements back into process. Suggestively, this is the philosophical genre Milton adapts in the middle and final books of his poem.

Philosophy, in sum, is discourse with a limit. Poetry is chaos. (Philosophy and poetry have other facets in the epic; we are coming in at an angle.)

It might be objected that the effects I have described are common to all instances of philosophy's intrusion into literature. Fair enough: I have been maintaining the inadequacy of the orthodox account of their relationship. But *Paradise Lost is* distinguished by the controlled lucidity with which it releases the double power of 'argument' to fix and free, joining philosophy and literature to their mutual enrichment. The poet is wiser than the philosophers he uses and anticipates. Milton's distinct value in intellectual history derives from the fact that his epic argument is *not* philosophy only, and with respect to the transmutation of sacred history in Romantic idealism, from the fact that his story is *not yet* philosophy. His dictum in *Of Education* that poetry is 'more simple, sensuous, and passionate' than logic (*YP* 2: 403) has often been quoted to discourage readings that might issue in philosophical praise for his literature on the assumption that they would be more likely to uncover philosophical embarrassment. The metaphysicians themselves, however, have taught us that simplicity is the most complex idea of all.

Once, in a metaphysical mood, I played with the notion that Milton's representation of how Adam arrives at God could be reduced to Cartesian epigrams (Kerrigan, 230): I think, therefore I am; I am, therefore I was created; I was created, therefore I am religious; I am religious, therefore I am poetic. The severe compression of this pleases me. But Adam's wondering desire for a maker as he springs upright into the hesiodic space between earth and heaven reveals more about identity and certainty than any attempt to string out Descartes's unimpeachable mental nugget will reveal. As it happens, history presents us with this very choice.

Rhyming Milton's blank verse in *The State of Innocence*, Dryden also tried to regularize his thought. The Adam of *Paradise Lost* bounds to his feet in health and happiness, looks 'about me round' at the landscape and its other inhabitants, inspects his body, exercises in 'lively vigour', and then, aware that he does not know 'who I was, or where, or from what cause', discovers speech in naming and finally addressing his surroundings, searching for the maker who put him there (8.257–82). Dryden knew that this Adam wants for logic. As Wallace Stevens was to note several centuries later, 'Adam / In Eden was the father of Descartes' ('Notes toward a Supreme Fiction'). Immersed in the novelty of how things are, Milton's Adam leaves out a step – a thought he does not make explicit, but necessarily presupposes. Dryden's Adam will not be permitted to elide this truth more certain than the sun, the hills, the rivers, the animals, the body, curiosity or speech. He awakens a professional philosopher:

> What am I? or from whence? For that I am,
> I know, because I think. (Dryden 3: 431)

This Adam is off on the right foot, and before long may be expected to discover the categorical imperative. It can be said in Dryden's favour that he was miltonically correct in placing the *cogito* after the interrogative quest for what and whence; as in *Paradise Regained* (3.106–7), identity is above all else a recognition of having been made. But the passage seems fatally aware of the usual complaint that literature dilutes philosophy. It wants to serve this master impeccably. Giving over the first indicative thought of the first man to the *cogito* of an anxious seventeenth-century Frenchman produces thumping banality because, like all strict allusions, it signals limiting redundance. It says: 'This line means what Descartes means in his *Meditations*.' It implies: 'Descartes figures out this moment in the primordial history of Everyman.'

The poet who designed with palpable relish the Athenian temptation of *Paradise Regained* was never so submissive to philosophy, to the explicit in general. He is a better teacher than Descartes or Kant. They are islands of rock. He is leviathan.

FURTHER READING

Abrams, M. H., *Natural Supernaturalism: Tradition and Revolution in Romantic Literature* (New York, 1971)

Blumenberg, Hans, *The Legitimacy of the Modern Age*, translated by Robert W. Wallace (Cambridge, MA, 1983)

Cassirer, Ernst, *The Platonic Renaissance in England*, translated by James Pettegrove (Austin, 1953)

Curry, Walter Clyde, *Milton's Ontology, Cosmogony and Physics* (Lexington, 1957)

Danielson, Dennis, *Milton's Good God: A Study in Literary Theodicy* (Cambridge, 1982)

Dryden, John, *The Dramatic Works*, ed. Montague Summers, 6 vols. (London, 1932)

Fish, Stanley, *Surprised By Sin: The Reader in 'Paradise Lost'* (New York, 1967)

Hartwell, Kathleen, *Lactantius and Milton* (Cambridge, MA, 1929)

Kant, Immanuel, *An Enquiry Critical and Metaphysical into the Grounds of Proof for the Existence of God, and into the Theodicy*, translated by John Richardson (London, 1836)

Kerrigan, William, *The Sacred Complex: On the Psychogenesis of 'Paradise Lost'* (Cambridge, MA, 1983)

Lovejoy, A. O., *Essays in the History of Ideas* (New York, 1960)

More, Henry, *Conjectura Cabbalistica* (London, 1662)

Naess, Arne, *Four Modern Philosophers*, translated by Alastair Hannay (Chicago, 1968)

Nicolson, Marjorie Hope, *John Milton: A Reader's Guide to his Poetry* (New York, 1963)
Rorty, Richard, *Philosophy and the Mirror of Nature* (Princeton, 1979)
Rumrich, John, 'Milton, Duns Scotus, and the Fall of Satan', *JHI* 46 (1985), 33–49
Saurat, Denis, *Milton, Man and Thinker* (New York, 1925)
Schwartz, Regina, 'Milton's Hostile Chaos: ". . . and the Sea Was No More"', *ELH* 52 (1985), 337–74
Stevens, Wallace, *The Collected Poems of Wallace Stevens* (New York, 1964)
Svendsen, Kester, *Milton and Science* (Cambridge, MA, 1956)

18

R. G. SIEMENS

Milton's works and life: select studies and resources

[Note: Those who wish to use this bibliography on-line may do so by directing their browser to the following Universal Resource Locator: <http: //purl.oclc.org/emls/iemls/postprint/C*CM*2Biblio.html>.]

If Milton's oeuvre itself is daunting, Milton scholarship must appear much more so. Huckabay and Klemp (see 23, below) document some 4,500 studies appearing between the years 1968 and 1988 alone; the *MLA International Bibliography* (see 32, below) records another 1,500 for the ten years prior to 1998; and several hundred items a year continue to be published. Inordinate as this plethora of writings may sometimes seem, it is in fact a measure of Milton's continued vitality, and it offers the student of Milton much good company. Although of course there is no substitute for firsthand engagement with Milton himself, the following list of over three hundred items is intended (complementary to the reading lists at the end of the preceding chapters) as an avenue into the disparate but companionable society of Milton's many editors, expositors, critics, and admirers – and also as a tool with which one may develop one's own links with the ongoing world of Milton scholarship.

For ease of reference, works are listed below by number and arranged in the following categories and subcategories:

- *Editions and Texts* (1–20);
- *Reference Works* (21–61), which includes Bibliographies (21–33), Other Useful Reference Works (34–45), Introductions and Handbooks (46–53), and a section on Background and General Context (54–61);
- *Milton's Life* (62–76);
- *Studies with Multi-Work and Contextual Emphasis* (77–208), including sections on Milton and Other Writers (77–88), Specific Contexts for Interpretation of, and Influences upon, Milton (89–154), Influence on Others, Early Criticism and Note (155–69), Language,

Prosody, Poetics, Imagery, and Style (170–88), and Anthologies and Collections (189–208);
- *Studies with Single-Work Emphasis* (209–325), with sections on *Paradise Lost* (209–73), *Paradise Regained* (274–84), *Samson Agonistes* (285–94), Shorter Poems, *A Masque [Comus]*, *Lycidas* (295–311), Prose (312–25); and
- *Periodicals, Reviews, Discussion Group* (326–35), which includes a short listing of other like resources (331–5).

The section housing works on Specific Contexts for Interpretation of, and Influences upon, Milton (89–154) is further divided into subsections containing the headings Biblical, Religious (89–107); Literary (108–22); Political, Social, Historical (123–43); and Other, Collections (144–54). The section on *Paradise Lost* (209–73) is still further divided into subsections consisting of Broad Studies, Introductions (209–18); Theological Context (219–28); Narrator, Reader, and Argument (229–35); Epic, and Considerations of Form (236–47); the War in Heaven (248–51); Eden, Edenic Life, and the Fall (252–9); Further Considerations (260–9); and Collections (270–3). However, since studies typically overlap a number of such categories, no one should take the latter as definitive. Accordingly, many below are accompanied with liberal cross-references.

In keeping with the importance of reading Milton's writings themselves, a number of editions of his works are here included (1–20). Among the most popular today are editions for student use by Flannagan (6), Carey and Fowler (5), and Campbell (3); likewise profitable is the edition of Hughes (8), used by generations of North American students from the 1950s to the 1990s. In Milton scholarship one finds frequent citation of Fletcher's facsimile edition (7), of Patterson's *Works of John Milton* (14, the 'Columbia Milton', to which the *Variorum Commentary* [39] is keyed), and of Wolfe's *Complete Prose Works* (16, the 'Yale Prose'). In addition to these, a number of electronic editions can be recommended, among them the *Selected Poetry of John Milton* (18, from the University of Toronto's *Representative Poetry* series) and Flannagan's electronic editions of a number of poetic works, especially the 1674 *Paradise Lost* (20). Such texts can of course be read on-screen, but their greatest value is in their use as tools for analysis and research. Facilitated by programs such as *TACT* (with which 18 and 20 are published) one may employ these resources in carrying out close word-oriented scrutiny of a text or texts, much as one would with a concordance of Milton's works (see 34–6) – though with greater flexibility and power.

Further useful tools include *A Milton Encyclopedia* (40), the *Variorum*

Commentary on the Poems of John Milton (39; in progress), and *A Milton Dictionary* (41). Evaluative guides to recent work in Milton studies are available, annually, in the sections devoted to Milton in *The Year's Work in English Studies* (see 29) and in *Studies in English Literature*'s review article 'Recent Studies in the English Renaissance' (see 30). Listings of critical works and other materials from the years 1624–1988 are covered by Fletcher, Huckabay, Huckabay and Klemp, Shawcross, and Stevens (21–5), supplemented by Shawcross's two volumes of *The Critical Heritage* (166–7). Klemp's *The Essential Milton* (26) offers a similar annotation and indexing of select modern studies, as do more focused listings such as Jones's *Milton's Sonnets: An Annotated Bibliography, 1900–1992* (305) and the annotated bibliography on Milton's prose works in preparation by *Milton Quarterly* (326), with others to follow on both *Samson Agonistes* and *Paradise Regained*. Further up-to-date listings of article- and book-length studies on Milton can be found in the print editions of the *MLA International Bibliography* (32) and the *Annual Bibliography of English Language and Literature* (31). Using precise keywords for information associated with author, title, and subject, one can extract more detailed information from the electronic database versions of these works, or from the select *Milton Quarterly Relational Database* (43), which contains searchable information about books reviewed by *Milton Quarterly* (326). Also useful are resources such as those gathered by *OCLC Firstsearch* (33), which includes a database listing of the combined holdings of libraries worldwide and listings of the tables-of-contents of journals.

New article-length studies and reviews appear in *Milton Quarterly* (326), articles are collected in the annual *Milton Studies* (328), and still other reviews are published in the *Milton Review* (327) and *Seventeenth-Century News* (330). Much Milton-related news is announced – and a host of topics of contemporary and long-standing interest are discussed – on the *Milton-L* discussion group (329), whose Internet site offers reliable and useful guides to resources available on the Internet for the study of Milton. Other such resources can be accessed through the Internet sites of the *Milton Review* (327), of *Milton Quarterly* (326), and of the *Luminarium* (332), as well as through those several sections devoted to electronic texts, resources, articles, and the like in *Early Modern Literary Studies* (*EMLS* [331]). Further recommended sites include several created and maintained by Milton scholars and enthusiasts, such as Thomas Luxon's *Milton Reading Room* (333) and Richard Bear's *Renascence Editions* (334). *OCLC Firstsearch* (33), furthermore, contains a searchable database and gathering of Internet resources, while pertinent resources on the Internet can also be located using a number of freely available search engines (a gathering of these is provided by *EMLS* [331]). It should be noted that Internet resources, perhaps even more than print materials, vary greatly in quality and usefulness. However, in evaluating such resources – as in reading Milton generally – one is not merely on one's own (see 335).

Editions and texts

1. Broadbent, John (gen. ed.), *Cambridge Milton for Schools and Colleges*, Cambridge, 1972–.
2. Bush, Douglas (ed.), *The Complete Poetical Works of John Milton*, Boston, 1965.
3. Campbell, Gordon (ed.), *Complete English Poems, Of Education, Areopagitica*, 4th edn rev., London, 1990.
4. Carey, John (ed.), *Complete Shorter Poems*, 2nd edn, London, 1997.
5. Carey, John, and Alastair Fowler (eds.), *The Poems of John Milton*, rev. ed., London, 1980.
6. Flannagan, Roy (ed.), *The Riverside Milton*, New York, 1998.
7. Fletcher, Harris F. (ed.), *John Milton's Complete Poetical Works, Reproduced in Photographic Facsimile*, 4 vols., Urbana, 1943–8.
8. Hughes, Merritt Y. (ed.), *John Milton: Complete Poems and Major Prose*, New York, 1957.
9. Leonard, John (ed.), *John Milton: The Complete Poems, Penguin English Poets*, London, 1998.
10. Orgel, Stephen, and Jonathan Goldberg (eds.), *John Milton. The Oxford Authors*, Oxford, 1991.
11. Patrick, J. Max (ed.), *The Prose of John Milton*, Garden City, 1968.
12. Patrides, C. A. (ed.), *John Milton: Selected Prose*, rev. edn, Columbia, 1985.
13. Patterson, Frank A. (ed.), *The Student's Milton, Being the Complete Poems of John Milton with the Greater Part of his Prose Works*, rev. edn, New York, 1934.
14. Patterson, Frank A. (gen. ed.), *The Works of John Milton*, 18 vols., New York, 1931–8.
15. Shawcross, John (ed.), *The Complete English Poetry of John Milton*, Garden City, 1963; rev. edn, New York, 1971.
16. Wolfe, Don M. (gen. ed.), *The Complete Prose Works of John Milton*, 8 vols., New Haven, 1953–82.

17. Chadwyck-Healey. *Dedicatory poems (1694), A Maske [Comus] (1637), Paradise Lost (1674), Paradise Regain'd (1671), Poems (1645), and Poems Upon Several Occasions (1673)*; in *The English*

Poetry Full-Text Database, Literature Online, Cambridge, 1998–. <URL: http: //lion.chadwyck.co.uk/>

18. Endicott, N. J., Hugh MacCallum, and A. S. P. Woodhouse (eds.), *Selected Poetry of John Milton*; in [Ian Lancashire, electronic text ed.] *Representative Poetry, 1994–98*. <URL: http: //library.utoronto.ca/ www/utel/rp/authors/milton.html>; rptd. [text only, without notes] in Ian Lancashire, in collaboration with John Bradley, Willard McCarty, Michael Stairs, and T. R. Wooldridge, *Using TACT with Electronic Texts*, New York, 1996. <CD File: \br_ir_lt\engl_lit\1600_699\milton_j\poems\mlt_ilrp.txt>.
19. Flannagan, Roy (ed.), *Milton on Disk: The English Poetry of John Milton [Poems* (1645), *Paradise Regain'd* (1671) and *Samson Agonistes* (1671), *Poems* (1673), and *Paradise Lost* (1674)], Clinton Corners, 1990.
20. *Paradise Lost* [1674], [rev. Ian Lancashire]; in Ian Lancashire, in collaboration with John Bradley, Willard McCarty, Michael Stairs, and T. R. Wooldridge, *Using TACT with Electronic Texts*, New York, 1996. <CD Directory: \br_ir_lt\engl_lit\1600_699\milton_j\par_lost\>.

Reference works

Bibliographies:

21. Fletcher, Harris F., *Contributions to a Milton Bibliography, 1800–1930*, Urbana, 1931; rptd. New York, 1967.
22. Huckabay, Calvin, *John Milton: An Annotated Bibliography, 1929–1968*, rev. edn, Pittsburgh, 1969.
23. Huckabay, Calvin (comp.), and Paul J. Klemp (ed.), *John Milton: An Annotated Bibliography, 1968–1988*, Pittsburgh, 1996.
24. Shawcross, John T., *Milton: A Bibliography for the Years 1624–1700*, Binghamton, 1984.
25. Stevens, David H., *Reference Guide to Milton from 1800 to the Present Day*, Chicago, 1930; rptd. New York, 1967.

See also 166–7.

26. Klemp, Paul J., *The Essential Milton: An Annotated Bibliography of Major Modern Studies*, Boston, 1989.
27. Mikolajczak, Michael A., 'Reading Milton: A Summary of Illuminating Efforts', 277–89; in Dennis Danielson (ed.), *The Cambridge Companion to Milton*, Cambridge, 1989.
28. Patrides, C. A., *An Annotated Critical Bibliography of John Milton*, Brighton, 1987.

29. Quint, David, 'Recent Studies in the English Renaissance', *Studies in English Literature* 38 (1998), 173–205.
30. Raymond, Joad, 'Milton', *The Year's Work in English Studies* 76 (1995), 296–309.

31. *The Annual Bibliography of English Language and Literature*, Modern Humanities Research Association, 1921–; rptd. in *Literature Online*, Cambridge, 1998–. <URL: http: //lion.chadwyck.co.uk/>.
32. *MLA International Bibliography of Books and Articles on the Modern Languages and Literatures*, New York, 1922–; rptd. [1963–] Dublin, 1998–. <URL: http://www.oclc.org/>; rptd. [1963–] New York, 1988–. <URL: http://www.ovid.com/>; rptd. [1963–] Norwood, 1988–. <URL: http://www.silverplatter.com/>; rptd. [1963–] New York, 1988–. <URL: www.mla.org>.
33. *OCLC Firstsearch*. Dublin, 1992–. <URL: http://www.oclc.org/>.

Other useful reference works:

34. Cooper, Lane, *A Concordance of the Latin, Greek, and Italian Poems of John Milton*, Halle, 1923; rptd. New York, 1971.
35. Ingram, William, and Kathleen Swaim, *A Concordance to Milton's English Poetry*, Oxford, 1972.
36. Sterne, Laurence, and Harold H. Kollmeier, *A Concordance to the English Prose of John Milton*, Binghamton, 1985.

37. Boswell, Jackson C., *Milton's Library*, New York, 1975.
38. Gilbert, Allan H., *A Geographical Dictionary of Milton*, New Haven, 1919; rptd. Folcroft, 1976.
39. Hughes, Merritt Y. (gen. ed.), *A Variorum Commentary on the Poems of John Milton*, 3 vols. [1, 2, and 4; of a projected 6.], New York, 1970–.
40. Hunter, William B., Jr (gen. ed.), *A Milton Encyclopedia*, 9 vols., Lewisburg, 1978–83.
41. Le Comte, Edward, *A Milton Dictionary*, New York, 1961.
42. *A Dictionary of Puns in Milton's English Poetry*, New York, 1981.
43. *Milton Quarterly Relational Database*, Roy Flannagan (ed.), with Doug Korchinski (prog.) and Jeff Miller (interface), Greg Coulombe (rev.); publ. 1997 in *Early Modern Literary Studies* (331). <URL: http: //purl.oclc.org/emls/iemls/mqlibrary/search.html>.
44. Pecheux, M. Christopher, *Milton: A Topographical Guide*, Washington, 1981.
45. Rogal, Samuel J., *An Index to the Biblical References, Parallels, and Allusions in the Poetry and Prose of John Milton*, Lewiston, 1994.
See also 17–20.

Introductions and handbooks:

46. Broadbent, John, *John Milton: Introductions*, Cambridge, 1973.
47. Bush, Douglas, *John Milton: A Sketch of His Life and Writings*, New York, 1964.
48. Carey, John, *Milton*, London, 1969.
49. Daiches, David, *Milton*, 2nd rev. edn, London, 1971.
50. Hanford, James H., and James G. Taaffe, *A Milton Handbook*, 5th edn, New York, 1970.
51. Miller, David M., *John Milton: Poetry*, Boston, 1978; rptd. [CD] London, 1992.
52. Potter, Lois, *A Preface to Milton*, rev. edn, London, 1986.
53. Wolfe, Don M., *Milton and His England*, Princeton, 1971.
    See also 55.

Background and general context:

54. Corns, Thomas, *Uncloistered Virtue: English Political Literature, 1640–1660*, Oxford, 1992.
55. Duggan, Margaret M., *English Literature and Backgrounds, 1660–1700*, 2 vols., New York, 1990.
56. Keeble, N. H., *The Literary Culture of Nonconformity in Later Seventeenth-Century England*, Athens, GA, 1987.
57. Parry, Graham, *The Seventeenth Century: The Intellectual and Cultural Context of English Literature, 1603–1700*, London, 1989.
58. Patrides, C. A., and Raymond Waddington (eds.), *The Age of Milton: Backgrounds to Seventeenth-Century Literature*, Manchester, 1980.
59. Rogers, John, *The Matter of Revolution: Science, Poetry, and Politics in the Age of Milton*, Ithaca, 1996.
60. Smith, Nigel, *Literature and Revolution in England, 1640–1660*, New Haven, 1994.
61. Wilding, Michael, *Dragon's Teeth: Literature in the English Revolution*, Oxford, 1987.

Milton's life

62. Brown, Cedric, *John Milton: A Literary Life*, New York, 1995.
63. Campbell, Gordon (ed.), *A Milton Chronology*, Basingstoke, 1997.
64. Clark, Donald L., *John Milton at St Paul's School: A Study of Ancient Rhetoric in English Renaissance Education*, Hamden, 1948; [rptd.] 1964.

65. Darbishire, Helen (ed.), *The Early Lives of Milton*, London, 1932, [rptd.] 1965.
66. Diekhoff, John, *Milton on Himself*, New York, 1939, 2nd edn, New York, 1965.
67. Fletcher, Harris F., *The Intellectual Development of John Milton*, 2 vols., Urbana, 1956–61.
68. French, Joseph M. (ed.), *The Life Records of John Milton*, 5 vols., New Brunswick, 1949–58; rptd. New York, 1966.
69. Hanford, James H., *John Milton, Englishman*, New York, 1949.
70. Macaulay, Rose, *Milton*, London, 1933; rptd. New York, 1974.
71. Masson, David, *The Life of John Milton: Narrated in Connexion with the Political, Ecclesiastical, and Literary History of His Time*, 7 vols., London, 1859–94.
72. Parker, William R., *Milton: A Biography*, 2 vols., 2nd edn, rev. Gordon Campbell (ed.), Oxford, 1996.
73. Shawcross, John, *John Milton: The Self and the World*, Lexington, 1993.
74. Thorpe, James E., *John Milton: The Inner Life*, San Marino, 1983.
75. Wilson, A. N., *The Life of John Milton*, Oxford, 1983; rptd. London, 1996.
76. Zagorin, Perez, *Milton, Aristocrat and Rebel: The Poet and His Politics*, Rochester, 1992.
See also 47–9, 98, 133, 203, and 323.

Studies with multi-work and contextual emphasis

Milton and other writers:

77. Esterhammer, Angela, *Creating States: Studies in the Performative Language of John Milton and William Blake*, Toronto, 1994.
78. Ferry, Anne, *Milton and the Miltonic Dryden*, Cambridge, 1968.
79. Frye, Roland M., *God, Man, and Satan: Patterns of Christian Thought and Life in 'Paradise Lost', 'Pilgrim's Progress', and the Great Theologians*, Princeton, 1960; rptd. Port Washington, 1972.
80. Grierson, Herbert J. C., *Milton and Wordsworth, Poets and Prophets: A Study of Their Reactions to Political Events*, London, 1937; rptd. New York, 1962.
81. Guillory, John, *Poetic Authority: Spenser, Milton, and Literary History*, New York, 1983.
82. Hartwell, Kathleen E., *Lactantius and Milton*, Cambridge, 1929; rptd. New York, 1974.

83. Helgerson, Richard, *Self-Crowned Laureates: Spenser, Jonson, Milton, and the Literary System*, Berkeley, 1983.
84. Hieatt, A. K., *Chaucer, Spenser, Milton: Mythopoeic Continuities and Transformations*, Montreal, 1975.
85. Hogan, Patrick C., *Joyce, Milton, and the Theory of Influence*, Gainesville, 1995.
86. Low, Lisa, and Anthony J. Harding (eds.), *Milton, the Metaphysicals, and Romanticism*, Cambridge, 1994.
87. Tillyard, E. M. W., *The Metaphysicals and Milton*, London, 1956; rptd. Westport, 1975.
88. Williams, Meg H., *Inspiration in Milton and Keats*, London, 1982.
See also 56, 58, 93, 97, 101, 108–12, 114–22, 144, 158–9, 162, 165, 168, and 266.

Specific contexts for interpretation of, and influences upon, Milton:

Biblical, religious:

89. Christopher, Georgia B., *Milton and the Science of the Saints*, Princeton, 1982.
90. Driscoll, James P., *The Unfolding God of Jung and Milton*, Lexington, 1993.
91. Egan, James J., *The Inward Teacher: Milton's Rhetoric of Christian Liberty*; *Seventeenth-Century News* (see 330), University Park, 1980.
92. Entzminger, Robert, *Divine Word: Milton and the Redemption of Language*, Pittsburgh, 1985.
93. Fiore, Peter A., *Milton and Augustine: Patterns of Augustinian Thought in 'Paradise Lost'*, University Park, 1981.
94. Fletcher, Harris F., *Milton's Rabbinical Readings*, Urbana, 1930; rptd. Norwood, 1978.
95. *Milton's Semitic Studies and Some Manifestations of Them in His Poetry*, Chicago, 1926; rptd. Norwood, 1979.
96. Gallagher, Phillip, *Milton, The Bible, and Misogyny*, edited by Eugene R. Cunnar and Gail Mortimer, Columbia, 1990.
97. Gregerson, Linda, *The Reformation of the Subject: Spenser, Milton, and the English Protestant Epic*, Cambridge, 1995.
98. Hill, John Spencer, *John Milton, Poet, Priest and Prophet: A Study of Divine Vocation in Milton's Poetry and Prose*, London, 1979; rptd. *Early Modern Literary Studies* (see 331) <URL: http://purl.oclc.org/emls/iemls/postprint/jhill-milt/milton.htm>.
99. Kerrigan, William W., *The Prophetic Milton*, Charlottesville, 1974.

100. Madsen, William G., *From Shadowy Types to Truth: Studies in Milton's Symbolism*, New Haven, 1968.
101. O'Keeffe, Timothy J., *Milton and the Pauline Tradition*, Washington, 1982.
102. Radzinowicz, Mary Ann, *Milton's Epics and the Book of Psalms*, Princeton, 1989.
103. Richmond, Hugh M., *The Christian Revolutionary: John Milton*, Berkeley, 1974.
104. Rumrich, John Peter, and Stephen Dobranski (eds.), *Milton and Heresy*, Cambridge, 1998.
105. Sims, James H., *The Bible in Milton's Epics*, Gainesville, 1962.
106. Sims, James H., and Leland Ryken (eds.), *Milton and the Scriptural Tradition*, Columbia, 1984.
106. Stroup, Thomas B., *Religious Rite and Ceremony in Milton's Poetry*, Lexington, 1968.
107. West, Robert H., *Milton and the Angels*, Athens, GA, 1955.
See also 79, 82, 120, 125, 127, 141, 147, 149, 155, 176, 178, 181, 219–28, 248, 251, 255–8, 262, 268, 287, 307, 316, and 319.

Literary:

108. Burrow, Colin, *Epic Romance: Homer to Milton*, Oxford, 1993.
109. Cullen, Patrick, *Infernal Triad: The Flesh, The World and the Devil in Spenser and Milton*, Princeton, 1974.
110. Demaray, John G., *Cosmos and Epic Representation: Dante, Spenser, Milton and the Transformation of Renaissance Heroic Poetry*, Pittsburgh, 1991.
111. DuRocher, Richard, *Milton and Ovid*, Ithaca, 1985.
112. Falconer, Rachel, *Orpheus Dis(re)membered: Milton and the Myth of the Poet-Hero*, Sheffield, 1996.
113. Grose, Christopher, *Milton and the Sense of Tradition*, New Haven, 1988.
114. Harding, Davis P., *Milton and the Renaissance Ovid*, Urbana, 1946; rptd. Philadelphia, 1978.
115. Mulryan, John, *Through A Glass Darkly: Milton's Reinvention of the Mythological Tradition*, Pittsburgh, 1996.
116. Quilligan, Maureen, *Milton's Spenser: The Politics of Reading*, Ithaca, 1983.
117. Samuel, Irene, *Dante and Milton: 'The Commedia' and 'Paradise Lost'*, Ithaca, 1966.
118. *Plato and Milton*, Ithaca, 1947, [rptd.] 1965.

119. Stevens, Paul, *Imagination and the Presence of Shakespeare in 'Paradise Lost'*, Madison, 1985.
120. Swiss, Margo, and David A. Kent (eds.), *Heirs of Fame: Milton and Writers of the English Renaissance*, Lewisburg, 1995.
121. Whiting, George W., *Milton's Literary Milieu*, Chapel Hill, 1939; rptd. New York, 1964.
122. Wittreich, Joseph A., *Visionary Poetics: Milton's Tradition and His Legacy*, San Marino, 1979.
See also 79, 81–2, 84, 86, 87, 97, 112, 144–5, 149, 155, 180, 187, 194, 223, 226–7, 236, 238, 240, 243, 246–7, 250, 252–3, 266, 279, 290, and 310–11.

Political, social, historical:
123. Achinstein, Sharon, *Milton and the Revolutionary Reader*, Princeton, 1994.
124. Armitage, David, Armand Himy, and Quentin Skinner (eds.), *Milton and Republicanism*, Cambridge, 1995.
125. Barker, Arthur E., *Milton and the Puritan Dilemma, 1641–1660*, Toronto, 1942, [rptd.] 1976.
126. Belsey, Catherine, *John Milton: Language, Gender, Power*, Oxford, 1988.
127. Bennett, Joan S., *Reviving Liberty: Radical Christian Humanism in Milton's Great Poems*, Cambridge, 1989.
128. Davies, Stevie, *Milton*, New York, 1991.
129. Fallon, Robert T., *Captain or Colonel: The Soldier in Milton's Life and Art*, Columbia, 1984.
130. *Divided Empire: Milton's Political Imagery*, University Park, 1995.
131. *Milton in Government*, University Park, 1993.
132. Geisst, Charles R., *The Political Thought of John Milton*, London, 1984.
133. Hill, Christopher, *The Experience of Defeat: Milton and Some Contemporaries*, New York, 1984; rptd. London, 1994.
134. *Milton and the English Revolution*, London, 1977, [rptd.] 1979.
135. Kendrick, Christopher, *Milton: A Study in Ideology and Form*, New York, 1986.
136. Knoppers, Laura Lunger, *Historicizing Milton: Spectacle, Power, and Poetry in Restoration England*, Athens, GA, 1994.
137. Lieb, Michael, *Milton and the Culture of Violence*, Ithaca, 1994.
138. Loewenstein, David, *Milton and the Drama of History: Historical Vision, Iconoclasm, and the Literary Imagination*, Cambridge, 1990.

139. Milner, Andrew, *John Milton and the English Revolution*, London, 1981.
140. Sauer, Elizabeth, *Barbarous Dissonance and Images of Voice in Milton's Epics*, Montreal, 1996.
141. Turner, James, *One Flesh: Paradisal Marriage and Sexual Relations in the Age of Milton*, Oxford, 1987.
142. Walker, Julia M. (ed.), *Milton and the Idea of Woman*, Urbana, 1988.
143. Wittreich, Joseph, *Feminist Milton*, Ithaca, 1987.
See also 138, 150, 151, 157, 199, 249–50, 260–1, 264–8, 280, 307, 314, 318, 321–2, and 324.

Other collections:
144. Arthos, John, *Dante, Michaelangelo, and Milton*, London, 1963; rptd. Westport, 1979.
145. Di Cesare, Mario (ed.), *Milton in Italy: Contexts, Images, Contradictions*, Binghamton, 1991.
146. Fallon, Stephen M., *Milton Among the Philosophers: Poetry and Materialism in Seventeenth-Century England*, Ithaca, 1991.
147. Haskin, Dayton, *Milton's Burden of Interpretation*, Philadelphia, 1994.
148. Martz, Louis, *Poet of Exile: A Study of Milton's Poetry*, New Haven, 1980.
149. Mulryan, John (ed.), *Milton and the Middle Ages*, Lewisburg, 1982.
150. Nyquist, Mary, and Margaret Ferguson (eds.), *Re-membering Milton: Essays on the Texts and Traditions*, London, 1988.
151. Rumrich, John Peter, *Milton Unbound: Controversy and Reinterpretation*, Cambridge, 1996.
152. Steadman, John, *Milton and the Paradoxes of Renaissance Heroism*, Baton Rouge, 1987.
153. Svendsen, Kester, *Milton and Science*, Cambridge, 1956; rptd. New York, 1969.
154. Tillyard, E. M. W., *Milton*, rev. edn, London, 1967.

Influence on others; early criticism and note:

155. Altizer, Thomas J., *History as Apocalypse*, Albany, 1985.
156. Anglen, Kevin P. van, *The New England Milton: Literary Reception and Cultural Authority in the Early Republic*, University Park, 1993.
157. Armstrong, Nancy, and Leonard Tennenhouse, *The Imaginary Puritan: Literature, Intellectual Labor, and the Origins of Personal Life*, Berkeley, 1992, [rptd.] 1994.

158. Brisman, Leslie, *Milton's Poetry of Choice and Its Romantic Heirs*, Ithaca, 1973.
159. Griffin, Dustin, *Regaining Paradise: Milton and the Eighteenth Century*, Cambridge, 1986.
160. Labriola, Albert C., and Edward Sichi (eds.), *Milton's Legacy in the Arts*, University Park, 1988.
161. Murray, Patrick, *Milton: The Modern Phase, A Study of Twentieth-Century Criticism*, New York, 1967.
162. Nelson, James G., *The Sublime Puritan: Milton and the Victorians*, Madison, 1963; rptd. Westport, 1974.
163. Parker, William Riley, *Milton's Contemporary Reputation*, Columbus, 1940; rptd. Norwood, 1979.
164. Sensabaugh, George F., *Milton in Early America*, Princeton, 1964; rptd. New York, 1979.
165. Shawcross, John, *John Milton and Influence*, Pittsburgh, 1991.
166. (ed.), *Milton: The Critical Heritage [1628–1731]*, London, 1970; rptd. London, 1995.
167. (ed.), *Milton, 1732–1801: The Critical Heritage*, London, 1970; rptd. London, 1995.
168. Wittreich, Joseph A., *The Romantics on Milton*, Cleveland, 1970.
169. (ed.), *Milton and the Line of Vision*, Madison, 1975.
See also 78, 85–6, 120, 122, 206, 233, 265, and 269.

Language, prosody, poetics, imagery, and style:

170. Banks, Theodore H., *Milton's Imagery*, New York, 1950, [rptd.] 1969.
171. Budick, Sanford, *The Dividing Muse: Images of Sacred Disjunction in Milton's Poetry*, New Haven, 1985.
172. Burnett, Archie, *Milton's Style: The Shorter Poems, 'Paradise Regained', and 'Samson Agonistes'*, London, 1981.
173. Cable, Lana, *Carnal Rhetoric: Milton's Iconoclasm and the Poetics of Desire*, Durham, 1995.
174. Corns, Thomas N., *Milton's Language*, Oxford, 1990.
175. Daniells, Roy, *Milton, Mannerism and Baroque*, Toronto, 1963.
176. Emma, Ronald, and John Shawcross (eds.), *Language and Style in Milton: A Symposium in Honor of the Tercentenary of 'Paradise Lost'*, New York, 1967.
177. Evans, Robert O., *Milton's Elisions*, Gainesville, 1966.
178. Frye, Roland, *Milton's Imagery and the Visual Arts: Iconographic Tradition in the Epic Poems*, Princeton, 1978.

179. Hale, John K., *Milton's Languages: The Impact of Multilingualism on Style*, Cambridge, 1997.
180. Lieb, Michael, *The Sinews of Ulysses: Form and Convention in Milton's Work*, Pittsburgh, 1989.
181. McColley, Diane K., *A Gust for Paradise: Milton's Eden and the Visual Arts*, Urbana, 1993.
182. Mustazza, Leonard, *'Such Prompt Eloquence': Language as Agency and Character in Milton's Epics*, Lewisburg, 1988.
183. Oras, Ants, *Blank Verse and Chronology in Milton*, Gainesville, 1966.
184. Ricks, Christopher, *Milton's Grand Style*, Oxford, 1963, [rptd.] 1983.
185. Shoaf, R. A., *Milton, Poet of Duality: A Study of Semiosis in the Poetry and the Prose*, New Haven, 1985; rptd. Gainesville, 1993.
186. Sprott, Samuel E., *Milton's Arts of Prosody*, Oxford, 1953; rptd. Norwood, 1978.
187. Steadman, John M., *The Wall of Paradise: Essays on Milton's Poetics*, Baton Rouge, 1985.
188. Tuve, Rosemond, *Images and Themes in Five Poems by Milton*, Cambridge, 1957.

See also 77, 92, 126, 130, 203, 224, 312, and 314.

Anthologies and collections:

189. Barker, Arthur E. (ed.), *Milton: Modern Essays in Criticism*, New York, 1965, [rptd.] 1968.
190. Benet, Diana Treviño, and Michael Lieb (eds.), *Literary Milton: Text, Pretext, Context*, Pittsburgh, 1994.
191. Bloom, Harold (ed.), *John Milton*, New York, 1986.
192. *Critical Essays on Milton from 'ELH'*, Baltimore, 1965.
193. Durham, Charles, and Kristin Pruitt McColgan (eds.), *Spokesperson Milton: Voices in Contemporary Criticism*, London, 1994.
194. Frye, Northrop, *The Return of Eden: Five Essays on Milton's Epics*, Toronto, 1965, [rptd.] 1975.
195. Kendrick, Christopher (ed.), *Critical Essays on John Milton*, New York, 1995.
196. Kermode, Frank (ed.), *The Living Milton*, London, 1960, [rptd.] 1967.
197. Le Comte, Edward, *Milton Re-Viewed*, New York, 1991.
198. Martz, Louis (ed.), *Milton: A Collection of Critical Essays*, Englewood Cliffs, 1966; rptd. 1986 as *Milton, 'Paradise Lost': A Collection of Critical Essays*.

199. McColgan, Kristin, and Charles Durham (eds.), *Arenas of Conflict: Milton and the Unfettered Mind*, Cranbury, 1997.
200. Patrides, C. A. (ed.), *Milton's Epic Poetry: Essays on 'Paradise Lost' and 'Paradise Regained'*, Harmondsworth, 1967.
201. Patterson, Annabel (ed.), *John Milton*, New York, 1992.
202. Rudrum, Alan (ed.), *Milton: Modern Judgements*, London, 1968.
203. Stanwood, P. G. (ed.), *Of Poetry and Politics: New Essays on Milton and His World*, Binghamton, 1995.
204. Stein, Arnold S. (ed.), *On Milton's Poetry: A Selection of Modern Studies*, Greenwich, 1970.
205. Summers, Joseph H. (ed.), *The Lyric and Dramatic Milton*, New York, 1965.
206. Thorpe, James E. (ed.), *Milton Criticism: Selections From Four Centuries*, New York, 1950; rptd. London, 1969.
207. Williamson, George (ed.), *Milton and Others*, Chicago, 1965, [rptd.] 1970.
208. Wittreich, Joseph (ed.), *Calm of Mind: Tercentenary Essays on 'Paradise Regained' and 'Samson Agonistes' in Honor of John S. Diekhoff*, Cleveland, 1971.

Studies with single-work emphasis

Paradise Lost – broad studies, introductions:

209. Blessington, Francis C., *'Paradise Lost': Ideal and Tragic Epic*, Boston, 1988.
210. Bush, Douglas, *'Paradise Lost' in Our Time*, Ithaca, 1945; rptd. Gloucester, 1957.
211. Corns, Thomas, *Regaining 'Paradise Lost'*, London, 1994.
212. Gardner, Helen, *A Reading of 'Paradise Lost'*, Oxford, 1965, [rptd.] 1971.
213. Kirkconnell, G. Watson, *The Celestial Cycle: The Theme of 'Paradise Lost' in World Literature with Translations of the Major Analogues*, Toronto, 1952; rptd. New York, 1967.
214. Lewis, C. S., *A Preface to 'Paradise Lost'*, Oxford, 1942, [rptd.] 1961, [rev.] 1974.
215. Loewenstein, David, *Milton – 'Paradise Lost'*, Cambridge, 1993.
216. Rumrich, John R., *Matter of Glory: A New Preface to 'Paradise Lost'*, Pittsburgh, 1987.
217. Stocker, Margarita, *Paradise Lost*, London, 1988.

218. Summers, Joseph H., *The Muse's Method: An Introduction to 'Paradise Lost'*, Cambridge, 1962; rptd. Binghamton, 1981.

Paradise Lost – theological context:

219. Berry, Boyd M., *Process of Speech: Puritan Religious Writing and 'Paradise Lost'*, Baltimore, 1976.
220. Corcoran, Mary I., *Milton's Paradise with Reference to the Hexameral Background*, Washington, 1945; rptd. Folcroft, 1970.
221. Danielson, Dennis, *Milton's Good God: A Study in Literary Theodicy*, Cambridge, 1982.
222. Empson, William, *Milton's God*, rev. edn, London, 1961, [rev.] 1965; rptd. Cambridge, 1981.
223. Evans, J. Martin, *'Paradise Lost' and the Genesis Tradition*, Oxford, 1968.
224. Hunter, William B., C. A. Patrides, and J. H. Adamson, *Bright Essence: Studies in Milton's Theology*, Salt Lake City, 1971.
225. Lieb, Michael, *Poetics of the Holy: A Reading of 'Paradise Lost'*, Chapel Hill, 1981.
226. MacCallum, Hugh, *Milton and the Sons of God: The Divine Image in Milton's Epic Poetry*, Toronto, 1986.
227. Patrides, C. A., *Milton and the Christian Tradition*, Oxford, 1966; rptd. Hamden, 1979.
228. Reichert, John, *Milton's Wisdom: Nature and Scripture in 'Paradise Lost'*, Ann Arbor, 1992.
See also 79, 90, 93, 96–8, 100, 102, 105–6, 109, 152, 232, 234, 257–8, 268, and 273.

Paradise Lost – narrator, reader, and argument:

229. Burden, Dennis, *The Logical Epic: A Study of the Argument of 'Paradise Lost'*, Cambridge, 1967.
230. Diekhoff, John. *Milton's 'Paradise Lost': A Commentary on the Argument*, New York, 1946; rptd. New York, 1958, 1963.
231. Ferry, Anne, *Milton's Epic Voice: The Narrator in 'Paradise Lost'*, Cambridge, 1963; rptd. and rev. Chicago, 1983.
232. Fish, Stanley, *Surprised By Sin: The Reader in 'Paradise Lost'*, London, 1967; rptd., 2nd edn, Cambridge, 1998.
233. Rajan, Balachandra, *'Paradise Lost' and the Seventeenth-Century Reader*, London, 1947, [rptd.] 1966.

234. Riggs, William G., *The Christian Poet in 'Paradise Lost'*, Berkeley, 1972.
235. Stein, Arnold S., *The Art of Presence: The Poet and 'Paradise Lost'*, Berkeley, 1977.
See also 140.

Paradise Lost – epic, and considerations of form:

236. Blessington, Francis C., *'Paradise Lost' and the Classical Epic*, Boston, 1979.
237. Crump, Galbraith M., *The Mystical Design of 'Paradise Lost'*, Lewisburg, 1975.
238. Demaray, John G., *Milton's Theatrical Epic*, Cambridge, 1980.
239. Gilbert, Allan H., *On the Composition of 'Paradise Lost'*, Chapel Hill, 1947; rptd. New York, 1966.
240. Grose, Christopher, *Milton's Epic Process*, New Haven, 1973.
241. Lewalski, Barbara, *'Paradise Lost' and the Rhetoric of Literary Forms*, Princeton, 1985.
242. Lieb, Michael, *The Dialectics of Creation: Patterns of Birth and Regeneration in 'Paradise Lost'*, Amherst, 1970.
243. Martindale, Charles, *John Milton and the Transformation of Ancient Epic*, Totowa, 1986.
244. Steadman, John M., *Epic and Tragic Structure in 'Paradise Lost'*, Chicago, 1976.
245. *Milton's Epic Characters*, Chapel Hill, 1964, [rptd.] 1968.
246. Treip, Mindele Anne, *Allegorical Poetics and the Epic: The Renaissance Tradition to 'Paradise Lost'*, Lexington, 1994.
247. Webber, Joan. *Milton and His Epic Tradition*, Seattle, 1979.
See also 97, 135, 194, and 271.

Paradise Lost – war in heaven:

248. Forsyth, Neil, *The Old Enemy: Satan and the Combat Myth*, Princeton, 1987, [rptd.] 1989.
249. Freeman, James A., *Milton and the Martial Muse: 'Paradise Lost' and European Traditions of War*, Princeton, 1980.
250. Murrin, Michael, *History and Warfare in Renaissance Epic*, Chicago, 1994, [rptd.] 1997.
251. Revard, Stella P., *The War in Heaven: 'Paradise Lost' and the Tradition of Satan's Rebellion*, Ithaca, 1980.
See also 109, 129, and 224.

Paradise Lost – Eden, Edenic life, and the Fall:

252. Duncan, Joseph E., *Milton's Earthly Paradise*, Minneapolis, 1972.
253. Knott, John R., *Milton's Pastoral Vision*, Chicago, 1971.
254. Marilla, Esmond L., *The Central Problem of 'Paradise Lost': The Fall of Man*, Cambridge, 1953; rptd. Philadelphia, 1979.
255. McColley, Diane, *Milton's Eve*, Urbana, 1983.
256. Ryken, Leland, *The Apocalyptic Vision in 'Paradise Lost'*, Ithaca, 1970.
257. Schwartz, Regina, *Remembering and Repeating: Biblical Creation in 'Paradise Lost'*, Cambridge, 1988.
258. Stein, Arnold S., *Answerable Style: Essays on 'Paradise Lost'*, Minneapolis, 1953; rptd. Seattle, 1967.
259. Swaim, K., *Before and After the Fall*, Amherst, 1986.
See also 127, 141, 181, 221, 271, and 318.

Paradise Lost – further considerations:

260. Babb, Lawrence, *The Moral Cosmos of 'Paradise Lost'*, East Lansing, 1970.
261. Evans, J. Martin, *Milton's Imperial Epic: 'Paradise Lost' and the Discourse of Colonialism*, Ithaca, 1996.
262. Hamlet, Desmond, *One Greater Man: Justice and Damnation in 'Paradise Lost'*, Lewisburg, 1976.
263. Leonard, John, *Naming in Paradise: Milton and the Language of Adam and Eve*, Oxford, 1990.
264. Marjara, Harinder Singh, *Contemplation of Created Things: Science in 'Paradise Lost'*, Toronto, 1992.
265. Miller, Timothy C., *The Critical Response to John Milton's 'Paradise Lost'*, Westport, 1997.
266. Porter, William M., *Reading the Classics and 'Paradise Lost'*, Lincoln, 1993.
267. Reid, David, *The Humanism of Milton's 'Paradise Lost'*, Edinburgh, 1993.
268. Stavely, Keith W. F., *Puritan Legacies: 'Paradise Lost' and the New England Tradition*, Ithaca, 1987, [rptd.] 1990.
269. Waldock, Arthur, *'Paradise Lost' and Its Critics*, Cambridge, 1947, [rptd.] 1966.
See also 110–11, 116–17, 119, 124, 130, 136, 140, 146, 149, 152, 155, 176, 178, 182, 184–5, and 194.

Paradise Lost – collections:

270. Dyson, A. E., and Julian Lovelock (eds.), *Milton: 'Paradise Lost'*, London, 1973.
271. Kranidas, Thomas, *New Essays on 'Paradise Lost'*, Berkeley, 1969, [rptd.] 1971.
272. Patrides, C. A., and John Arthos (eds.), *Approaches to 'Paradise Lost'*, London, 1968.
273. Rajan, Balachandra (ed.), *'Paradise Lost': A Tercentenary Tribute*, Toronto, 1969.

See also 120, 190–1, 193, 198, 201, and 203.

Paradise Regained:

274. Bloom, Harold (ed.), *John Milton's 'Paradise Regained', 'Samson Agonistes', and the Minor Poems*, New York, 1988.
275. Kirkconnell, G. Watson, *Awake the Courteous Echo: The Themes and Prosody of 'Comus', 'Lycidas', and 'Paradise Regained' in World Literature with Translations of the Major Analogues*, Toronto, 1973.
276. Lewalski, Barbara K., *Milton's Brief Epic: The Genre, Meaning, and Art of 'Paradise Regained'*, Providence, 1966.
277. Martz, Louis L., '*Paradise Regained*: The Interior Teacher' 169–201 in *The Paradise Within: Studies in Vaughan, Traherne, and Milton*, New Haven, 1964.
278. McAdams, James R., 'The Pattern of Temptation in *Paradise Regained*', *Milton Studies* 4 (1972), 177–93.
279. Pope, Elizabeth M., *'Paradise Regained': The Tradition and the Poem*, Baltimore, 1947; rptd. New York, 1962.
280. Rusdhy, Ashraf, *The Empty Garden: The Subject of Late Milton*, Pittsburgh, 1992.
281. Shawcross, John, *'Paradise Regain'd': Worthy T'Have Not Remain'd So Long Unsung*, Pittsburgh, 1988.
282. Stein, Arnold S., *Heroic Knowledge: An Interpretation of 'Paradise Regained' and 'Samson Agonistes'*, Hamden, 1957, [rptd.] 1965.
283. Sundell, Roger R., 'The Narrator as Interpreter in *Paradise Regained*', *Milton Studies* 2 (1970), 83–101.
284. Weber, Burton J., *Wedges and Wings: The Patterning of 'Paradise Regained'*, Carbondale, 1974, 1975.

See also 98, 102, 105–6, 109, 113, 127, 130, 136, 140, 152, 172, 178, 182, 193–5, 197, 201, 208, 245, 247, and 280.

Samson Agonistes:

285. Crump, Galbraith M. (ed.), *Twentieth Century Interpretations of 'Samson Agonistes'*, Englewood Cliffs, 1968.
286. Kirkconnell, G. Watson, *That Invincible Samson: The Theme of 'Samson Agonistes' in World Literature with Translations of the Major Analogues*, Toronto, 1964.
287. Krouse, F. Michael, *Milton's Samson and the Christian Tradition*, Princeton [for Cincinnati], 1949; rptd. New York, 1974.
288. Labriola, Albert C., and Michael Lieb (eds.), *The Miltonic Samson. Milton Studies* 33, Pittsburgh, 1997.
289. Low, Anthony, *The Blaze of Noon: A Reading of 'Samson Agonistes'*, New York, 1974.
290. Parker, William R., *Milton's Debt to Greek Tragedy in 'Samson Agonistes'*, Baltimore, 1937; rptd. New York, 1969.
291. Radzinowicz, Mary Ann, *Toward 'Samson Agonistes': The Growth of Milton's Mind*, Princeton, 1978.
292. Rudrum, Alan, *A Critical Commentary on Milton's 'Samson Agonistes'*, London, 1969.
293. Skulsky, Harold, *Justice in the Dock: Milton's Experimental Tragedy*, London, 1995.
294. Wittreich, Joseph A., *Interpreting 'Samson Agonistes'*, Princeton, 1986.

See also 76, 96, 98, 100, 113, 127, 129–30, 136, 138, 149, 152, 172–3, 180, 191, 193–5, 203, 208, 274, 280, and 282.

Shorter poems, *A Masque* [*Comus*], *Lycidas*:

295. Berkeley, D., *Inwrought with Figures Dim: A Reading of Milton's 'Lycidas'*, The Hague, 1974.
296. Brooks, Cleanth, and John Edward Hardy (eds.), *Poems of Mr. John Milton: The 1645 Edition with Essays in Analysis*, New York, 1951; rptd. New York, 1968.
297. Demaray, John G., *Milton and the Masque Tradition: The Early Poems,* Arcades, *and* Comus. Cambridge, 1968.
298. Evans, J. Martin, *The Miltonic Moment*, Lexington, 1998.
299. *The Road From Horton: Looking Backwards in 'Lycidas'*, Victoria, 1983.
300. Flannagan, Roy (ed.), *'Comus': Contexts* [special issue of *Milton Quarterly* 21 (1987); see 326], Binghamton, 1988.
301. Fletcher, Angus, *The Transcendental Masque: An Essay on Milton's 'Comus'*, Ithaca, 1971.

302. Honigmann, E.A. (ed.), *Milton's Sonnets*, London, 1966.
303. Hunt, Clay, *'Lycidas' and the Italian Critics*, New Haven, 1979.
304. Hunter, William B., *Milton's 'Comus': Family Piece*, Troy, 1983.
305. Jones, Edward, *Milton's Sonnets: An Annotated Bibliography, 1900–1992*, Binghamton, 1994.
306. Leishman, J. B., *Milton's Minor Poems*, edited by Geoffrey Tillotson, Pittsburgh, 1969.
307. McGuire, Maryann Cale, *Milton's Puritan Masque*, Athens, GA, 1983.
308. Miller, William S., *The Mythology of Milton's 'Comus'*, New York, 1988.
309. Nardo, Anna K., *Milton's Sonnets and the Ideal Community*, Lincoln, 1979.
310. Patrides, C. A. (ed.), *Milton's 'Lycidas': The Tradition and the Poem*, New York, 1961; rev. edn, Columbia, 1983.
311. Revard, Stella P., *Milton and the Tangles of Neaera's Hair: The Making of the 1645 'Poems'*, Columbia, 1997.

See also 106, 113, 120, 129, 172, 191, 193–5, 197, 203, 274–5, and 280.

Prose:

312. Corns, Thomas, *The Development of Milton's Prose Style*, Oxford, 1982.
313. *John Milton: The Prose Works*, New York, 1998.
314. Dowling, Paul M., *Polite Wisdom: Heathen Rhetoric in Milton's 'Areopagitica'*, Lanham, 1995.
315. Fish, Stanley, 'Reason in *The Reason of Church Government*', 265–302 in *Self-Consuming Artifacts: The Experience of Seventeenth-Century Literature*, Berkeley, 1972.
316. Fletcher, Harris F., *The Use of the Bible in Milton's Prose*, Urbana, 1929.
317. Gilman, Wilbur E., *Milton's Rhetoric: Studies in his Defense of Liberty*, Columbia, 1939; rptd. Norwood, 1977.
318. Halkett, John, *Milton and the Idea of Matrimony: A Study of the Divorce Tracts and 'Paradise Lost'*, New Haven, 1970.
319. Honeygosky, Stephen R., *Milton's House of God: The Invisible and Visible Church*, Columbia, 1993.
320. Lieb, Michael, and John Shawcross (eds.), *Achievements of the Left Hand: Essays on the Prose of John Milton*, Amherst, 1974.
321. Loewenstein, David, and James Grantham Turner (eds.), *Politics, Poetics, and Hermeneutics in Milton's Prose*, Cambridge, 1990.

322. Maltzahn, Nicholas von, *Milton's 'History of Britain': Republican Historiography in the English Revolution*, Oxford, 1991.
323. Mohl, Ruth, *John Milton and His Commonplace Book*, New York, 1969.
324. Stavely, Keith, *The Politics of Milton's Prose Style*, New Haven, 1975.
325. Weaver, Richard M., 'Milton's Heroic Prose.' In *The Ethics of Rhetoric*, South Bend, 1953; rptd. Davis, 1985.
See also 91, 125, 135, 138, 173, 176, 185, 190, and 193–5.

Periodicals, reviews, discussion group

326. *Milton Quarterly*, Roy Flannagan (ed.), Athens, OH, 1966–. Home page <URL: http://voyager.cns.ohiou.edu/~somalley/milton.html>. Electronic rpt. Baltimore. <URL: http://muse.jhu.edu/journals/milton_quarterly/>. [Formerly *Milton Newsletter*, vols. 1–3.]
327. *Milton Review*, Roy Flannagan and Kevin J. T. Creamer (eds.) <URL: http://www.richmond.edu/~creamer/review.html>.
328. *Milton Studies*, Albert C. Labriola (ed.), Pittsburgh, 1969–.
329. *Milton-L*, Kevin J. T. Creamer, moderator. <URL: http://www.richmond.edu/~creamer/milton/>; <E-mail: Milton-L@Richmond.edu>.
330. *Seventeenth-Century News*, Donald R. Dickson (ed.), College Station, 1942–. Home page <URL: http://www-english.tamu.edu/pubs/scn/>.

Other:

331. *Early Modern Literary Studies: A Journal of Sixteenth- and Seventeenth-Century English Literature*, R. G. Siemens (ed.). <URL: http://purl.oclc.org/emls/emlshome.html>. Electronic texts <URL: http://purl.oclc.org/emls/emlsetxt.html>; internet resources <URL: http://purl.oclc.org/emls/emlsweb.html>; articles, notes, and reviews <URL: http://purl.oclc.org/emls/emlsjour.html>; search engines <URL: http://purl.oclc.org/emls/emlswsrc.html>.
332. *Luminarium*, Anniina Jokinen (ed.). <URL: http://www.luminarium.org/lumina.htm>; Milton materials <URL: http://www.luminarium.org/sevenlit/milton/>.
333. *Milton Reading Room*, Thomas Luxon (ed.). <URL: http://www.dartmouth.edu/~milton/>.

334. *Renascence Editions: Works Printed in English, 1477–1799*, Richard Bear (gen. ed.). <URL: http://darkwing.uoregon.edu/~rbear/ren.htm>.

335. Smith, Alastair G., 'Testing the Surf: Criteria for Evaluating Internet Information Resources'. *The Public-Access Computer Systems Review* 8.3 (1997). <URL: http://info.lib.uh.edu/pr/v8/n3/smit8n3.html>.

Index